Holistic IoT Security, Privacy and Safety

Integrated, Approaches Protecting a Highly Connected World

Konstantinos Loupos
(Editor)

now
the essence of knowledge

Published, sold and distributed by:
now Publishers Inc.
PO Box 1024
Hanover, MA 02339
United States
Tel. +1-781-985-4510
www.nowpublishers.com
sales@nowpublishers.com

Outside North America:
now Publishers Inc.
PO Box 179
2600 AD Delft
The Netherlands
Tel. +31-6-51115274

ISBN: 978-1-63828-506-9
E-ISBN: 978-1-63828-507-6
DOI: 10.1561/9781638285076

Suggested citation: Konstantinos Loupos (ed.). (2025). *Holistic IoT Security, Privacy and Safety: Integrated Approaches Protecting A Highly Connected World.* Boston–Delft: Now Publishers

Table of Contents

Preface

The Internet of Things (IoT) has emerged as a transformative force, weaving a complex tapestry of interconnected devices that permeate every aspect of our lives. From the ordinary to the extraordinary, these devices collect, process, and exchange data, shaping our experiences and driving innovation across industries. However, this interconnectedness comes at a cost. As we increasingly rely on IoT devices for critical tasks and sensitive information, ensuring their security and trustworthiness becomes paramount.

This book delves into the intricate world of IoT security, exploring the challenges and opportunities presented by this rapidly evolving landscape. It is born from the collective efforts of the ERATOSTHENES project and several other complementary research initiatives, funded by the European Commission, dedicated to developing innovative solutions for securing the IoT.

Within these pages, we embark on a journey through the core concepts, technologies, and methodologies that underpin these cutting-edge research outcomes. We explore the challenges posed by the heterogeneity of IoT devices, the intricacies of identity management in a decentralized world, and the critical importance of user privacy. We delve into the technical architecture of various frameworks, examining key components such as verifiable data registries, intrusion detection systems, and secure software update mechanisms, and their role in establishing trust, securing communication, and protecting data.

We investigate the potential of blockchain technology and Self-Sovereign Identity (SSI) to enhance security in 6G networks, addressing vulnerabilities in APIs and distributed architectures. We analyze the role of tracing techniques in securing connected medical devices, ensuring data integrity and continuous monitoring for enhanced trust. Furthermore, we explore the development of AI-powered intrusion detection systems, utilizing deep learning and federated learning approaches for near real-time threat detection in complex IoT environments.

This book also considers the evolving regulatory landscape, with insights into the EU's Cyber Resilience Act and AI Act, and their implications for secure IoT development, particularly for AI-driven connected medical devices. We delve into risk management strategies and standards relevant to the secure development and deployment of these devices.

This book is not merely a technical exposition; it is a testament to the power of collaboration and knowledge sharing in addressing complex challenges. It brings together a diverse community of researchers, practitioners, and policymakers, each contributing their expertise and insights to advance the state of IoT security. This collaborative spirit is reflected throughout, drawing upon the collective wisdom and experience of numerous contributors.

As you navigate through the chapters, you will gain a deeper understanding of the challenges and opportunities presented by the IoT. You will learn about innovative solutions for securing IoT devices, managing their identities, and protecting user data. You will also gain insights into the broader implications of IoT security for individuals, organizations, and society as a whole. This book serves as a valuable resource for anyone invested in building a more secure and trustworthy future for the Internet of Things.

Chapter 1 [Introduction to IoT Security and Privacy]: Overall book introduction, setting the scene to IoT security and privacy and current situation. Includes perspectives on the overall Secure and Privacy-Preserving iot and A Holistic Vision, cyber-threat Information (CTI) Sharing, Incident response as a mentality changer, Device lifecycle identity management needs, solutions and challenges, Threat Modeling and Risk Assessment in the iot as well as Legal and Ethical Considerations in iot Security and Privacy, and Security By Design considerations.

Chapter 2 [Technologies and Opportunities Overview]: Summary and overview of existing technologies and opportunities in the domain of iot. Includes technologies for Holistic iot Security, privacy and Safety, Secure device design and production, protecting communication pathways, Privacy and data security, Identity and Access Management, Threat intelligence and security analytics. Also includes Dynamic Trust and Identity Management approaches on Behavioral analysis, dynamic trust management etc. Additionally, includes Lifecycle Management of iot Devices, and AI approaches for trust and identity management in IOT.

Chapter 3 [ERATOSTHENES Project Integrated Solution]: Introduction to the ERATOSTHENES project, a collaborative research initiative dedicated to developing innovative solutions for securing the IoT. It provides a roadmap for the book, inviting readers to explore the intricacies of IoT security, the technical architecture of the ERATOSTHENES framework, and the collaborative efforts driving advancements in this field.

Chapter 4 [An Architecture for Dynamic Trust Management in IoT security]: Delving into the architecture and implementation of dynamic trust management in IoT security. It examines the challenges of securing diverse and resource-constrained devices in untrusted environments. The chapter explores the ERATOSTHENES project's approach to establishing and re-assessing trust scores for devices based on their capabilities, context, prior knowledge, and security guarantees. It discusses key components like the Trust Manager & Broker, Threat Modeling & Risk Assessment module, and Trust Agent, highlighting their role in creating adaptive and resilient IoT systems.

Chapter 5 [Decentralized Identity Management]: Exploration of the innovative approach to decentralized identity management in IoT systems developed by the ERATOSTHENES project. It focuses on the implementation of Self-Sovereign Identity (SSI) principles, empowering IoT devices with control over their digital identities. The chapter delves into the Ledger uSelf SSI solution, a core innovation of the project, and its key components, including the PUF client, VDR-fabric, Advanced Data Protection (ADP) module, and Identity Recovery Mechanism. It also examines the integration of advanced cryptographic techniques, such as privacy-enhancing Attribute-Based Credentials (p-ABC), and the role of disposable identities in enhancing privacy and security.

Chapter 6 [Inter-ledger platform for Cyber-threat information sharing and Lifecycle Security]: Exploration in the crucial role of cyber threat intelligence (CTI) sharing and lifecycle security in IoT ecosystems. It examines how the ERATOSTHENES project leverages distributed ledger technology (DLT) and an inter-ledger approach to facilitate secure and privacy-preserving CTI exchange across different domains. The chapter also discusses the use of Manufacturer Usage Description (MUD) files, including the proposed Threat MUD extension, to manage security configurations and mitigation actions throughout the device lifecycle. Additionally, it highlights the integration of these components to achieve a system that dynamically responds to cybersecurity incidents, ensuring the ongoing protection of devices and domains.

Chapter 7 [Advanced/Efficient DLT/VDR for Identity and Trust Management]: Delving into the design and implementation of a verifiable data registry (VDR) for decentralized identity and trust management in IoT environments. The authors utilize HyperLedger Fabric as the underlying blockchain infrastructure and introduce a novel hybrid consensus algorithm tailored for IoT networks. The chapter also details the creation of an efficient and secure VDR using gRPC services, emphasizing both security and scalability for IoT applications.

Chapter 8 [Intrusion detection for IoT-based context and networks]: Exploring the implementation of a robust Monitoring and Intrusion Detection System (IDS) within the ERATOSTHENES project. It details the integration of machine learning techniques for enhanced threat detection in complex IoT environments. The chapter also discusses the development and implementation of FedLPy, a federated learning approach for collaborative threat detection on edge devices, enhancing network security through distributed intelligence

Chapter 9 [Digital Twins for Secure Software Updates to Maintain IoT Device Trustworthiness]: Comprehensive analysis to securing software updates for IoT devices, a critical aspect of maintaining trust and security in IoT ecosystems. It explores the challenges of managing updates in dynamic IoT environments and introduces a novel approach using Digital Twins to enhance the software update lifecycle. The chapter details the integration of Digital Twins with existing security frameworks, emphasizing the benefits of this approach in terms of timeliness, reliability, and scalability. It also presents a proof-of-concept implementation and discusses the practical implications for real-world IoT deployments.

Chapter 10 [Tracing Techniques for Connected Medical Devices]: Investigation of the crucial role of tracing techniques in securing Connected Medical Devices (CMDs) within the Internet of Things (IoT) ecosystem. It examines how these techniques help monitor device behavior and ensure data integrity across both high-end and low-end devices. The chapter introduces the ENTRUST framework, which integrates tracing technologies to assess the operational integrity of CMDs continuously. It also discusses the challenges and solutions associated with tracing in different device categories, emphasizing the importance of continuous monitoring for maintaining trust and security in healthcare IoT.

Chapter 11 [Securing the Software Supply Chain: Innovations and Approaches]: This chapter emphasizes the critical need for securing the software supply chain in modern development, where applications rely heavily on external components. It introduces RESCALE, a comprehensive framework that integrates advanced security testing with blockchain technology to create a Trusted Bill of Materials (TBOM). This TBOM provides transparency and trust by recording the security status of both hardware and software components, mitigating risks associated with vulnerabilities and supply chain attacks.

Chapter 12 [Cybersecurity challenges and pitfalls in 6G networks]: This chapter explores the intersection of 6G technology and cybersecurity, examining the unique vulnerabilities of this new era of connectivity and proposing solutions based on blockchain and Self-Sovereign Identity (SSI). It discusses the challenges of API vulnerabilities, the expanded attack surface of distributed architecture, data privacy risks, and the potential for user misconfigurations and insider threats. The chapter argues for a combined approach, utilizing blockchain's immutability and transparency alongside SSI's decentralized identity management to enhance security in 6G networks.

Chapter 13 [Towards a Framework and Methodology Adherent to the EU Cyber Resilience Act – The CERTIFY Project]: Comprehensive overview of the CERTIFY project, a research initiative focused on establishing a robust framework for IoT security throughout the entire device lifecycle. The chapter details CERTIFY's lifecycle methodology, encompassing secure design, bootstrapping, continuous monitoring, update management, and decommissioning, highlighting its alignment with the EU's Cyber Resilience Act (CRA). It also presents a use case of a connected cabin system to illustrate the practical application of the framework in a high-connectivity environment.

Chapter 14 [Developing A near-real Time AI-based Network Intrusion Detection System]: Delving into the development of an AI-powered Network Intrusion Detection System (NIDS) designed for near-real-time threat detection in IoT networks. It explores the challenges of using outdated datasets for training intrusion detection models and proposes the use of a modern, in-house dataset reflecting current network traffic patterns and vulnerabilities. The chapter details the architecture and implementation of a Deep Learning (DL) model based on Convolutional Neural Networks (CNNs), trained on this dataset to accurately classify network traffic as benign or malicious. The proposed NIDS is evaluated in a realistic network environment, demonstrating its effectiveness in detecting intrusions in near-real time.

Chapter 15 [Connected Medical Devices: The Cybersecurity Nexus of the AI Act and MDR]: Analysis of the interplay between the EU's Artificial Intelligence Act (AIA) and Medical Device Regulation (MDR) concerning cybersecurity in the context of AI-driven Connected Medical Devices (CMDs). It explores the convergence of these regulations, highlighting potential challenges and opportunities for harmonizing their cybersecurity provisions. The chapter also discusses risk management strategies and standards relevant to the secure development and deployment of AI-enabled CMDs.

The target audience of this book has identified and includes the following:

1. **Researchers in IoT Security:** Gain insights into the latest advancements in IoT security research, including novel approaches to trust and identity

management, secure communication protocols, and privacy-enhancing technologies. Discover practical applications of these technologies through real-world pilot projects and case studies. Access valuable resources and contribute to the ongoing development of open-source tools and technologies for IoT security.

2. **Practitioners in Cybersecurity:** Learn about practical solutions for securing IoT devices and networks in various industries and applications. Understand the challenges and opportunities associated with implementing security measures in diverse IoT environments. Gain familiarity with the ERATOSTHENES framework and its potential for enhancing the security posture of IoT deployments.
3. **Policymakers and Regulators:** Gain insights into the policy implications of IoT security and the need for regulatory frameworks that promote trust and innovation. Understand the role of technology in addressing security challenges and enabling responsible IoT adoption. Learn from the ERATOSTHENES project's approach to balancing security, privacy, and innovation in the IoT ecosystem.
4. **Students and Educators:** Access a comprehensive overview of IoT security concepts, technologies, and challenges. Learn about cutting-edge research and real-world applications of IoT security solutions. Gain inspiration and guidance for pursuing careers in the growing field of IoT security.
5. **Technology Enthusiasts and the General Public:** Gain a better understanding of the security implications of the growing IoT landscape. Learn about the importance of protecting personal data and privacy in a connected world. Become informed consumers of IoT technologies and make informed decisions about their use.

Epilogue

The ERATOSTHENES project has significantly advanced the field of IoT security by developing and implementing a holistic Trust and Identity Management Framework. This framework showcases the potential of innovative technologies to tackle the complex security challenges inherent in the IoT landscape. The project's emphasis on creating solutions that are distributed, automated, auditable, and privacy-respectful has established a foundation for a more secure and trustworthy IoT ecosystem.

Specifically, ERATOSTHENES focuses on addressing several critical challenges:

1. **Heterogeneity of Devices:** The project acknowledges the wide variety of devices and communication protocols within the IoT, which makes it difficult to establish uniform security standards. ERATOSTHENES tackles this challenge by developing a flexible and adaptable framework that can accommodate the diverse nature of IoT devices.
2. **Lack of Standardized Security Measures:** The absence of standardized security measures in the IoT landscape poses a significant challenge. ERATOSTHENES addresses this by proposing a comprehensive framework that incorporates various security mechanisms, including trust management, identity management, and intrusion detection, to enhance the overall security posture of IoT networks.
3. **Data Security and Privacy:** With the increasing amount of data generated and transmitted by IoT devices, ensuring data security and privacy is paramount. ERATOSTHENES prioritizes these aspects by incorporating privacy-preserving techniques, such as advanced cryptography

and decentralized data management, to protect sensitive information and empower users with control over their data.

4. **Scalability and Interoperability:** As the IoT continues to expand, scalability and interoperability are crucial considerations. The ERATOSTHENES framework is designed to be scalable and interoperable, enabling seamless integration of new devices and technologies into the ecosystem while maintaining a consistent security posture.

Through its three pilot projects, ERATOSTHENES has showcased the practical applications of its framework in diverse domains, including connected vehicles, remote patient monitoring, and industrial network security. These real-world demonstrations have validated the effectiveness of ERATOSTHENES's technologies in detecting and mitigating cyber threats, protecting sensitive data, and ensuring the reliability of critical IoT infrastructure. For instance, in the V2X pilot, the project successfully demonstrated the ability to detect and prevent malicious software updates in connected vehicles, ensuring the integrity and safety of critical vehicle systems. In the remote patient monitoring pilot, ERATOSTHENES showcased the secure and privacy-preserving management of sensitive health data, empowering patients to receive care from the comfort of their homes while maintaining control over their personal information.

As the pages of this book close, the journey through the details of IoT security and the innovative solutions offered by ERATOSTHENES and several other EC research projects comes to an end. But the story of securing the Internet of Things is far from over. The challenges we face in this ever-evolving technological landscape are dynamic and multifaceted, demanding continuous research, collaboration, and adaptation.

ERATOSTHENES, with its holistic approach to trust and identity management, has undoubtedly made significant contributions to the field. The project's emphasis on distributed, automated, and privacy-preserving solutions has laid a strong foundation for building a more secure and trustworthy IoT ecosystem. By demonstrating the practical applications of its framework in diverse domains, ERATOSTHENES has inspired further exploration and innovation in IoT security.

The lessons learned from ERATOSTHENES extend beyond the technical realm. The project has highlighted the importance of collaboration and knowledge sharing in addressing complex security challenges. By bringing together researchers, practitioners, and policymakers from different disciplines and backgrounds, ERATOSTHENES has fostered a vibrant community dedicated to advancing the state of IoT security.

As we move forward, it is crucial to build upon the foundation laid by ERATOSTHENES and continue to push the boundaries of IoT security research. This includes exploring new technologies, developing innovative solutions, and fostering collaboration across different sectors. The future of the IoT depends on our collective efforts to ensure its security and trustworthiness.

The journey towards a secure IoT is an ongoing one, but with projects like ERATOSTHENES leading the way, we can confidently embrace the transformative potential of this technology while safeguarding the security and privacy of individuals and organizations alike.

DOI: 10.1561/9781638285076.ch1

Chapter 1

Introduction to IoT Security and Privacy

By Konstantinos Loupos

In today's world of ever-increasing connectivity, countless devices—from personal gadgets and office equipment to industrial machinery—exchange information and communicate with each other, often carrying large amounts of personal data. These devices typically connect to private and public networks using advanced security protocols and secure transmissions. However, the complexity and diversity of these devices and networks raise concerns about the security and privacy of the data involved. This chapter provides an overview of the current state of the Internet of Things (IoT), serving as an introduction to the rest of the book. It summarizes existing challenges and high-level solutions and measures currently used to address these challenges. The chapter also includes background information on current technologies and future insights into both the technology and the challenges themselves. The IoT is rapidly transforming, moving from a futuristic concept to a real part of our daily lives. This network of connected devices includes everything from smart home appliances and wearable fitness trackers to complex sensors in industrial machines and systems for self-driving cars. The IoT has the potential to make our lives more efficient, convenient, and automated. However, this interconnected world also increases security and privacy risks. We will explore the basics of the IoT, focusing on its main parts and the vulnerabilities that come from how it is made. We will look at the challenges of device heterogeneity, where different devices have different hardware, software, and ways of communicating, which makes it difficult to implement standard security measures. We will also discuss the limitations of many IoT devices, such as not having enough processing power, memory, or battery life to support strong security measures. Additionally, we will examine the risks that come from insecure development practices, which often happen because of the rush to get products to market quickly. We will also look at the challenges of insecure communication channels, which are often found in IoT networks. These channels can allow eavesdropping, data manipulation, and denial-of-service attacks. The large amount of personal data created and sent by IoT devices raises concerns about who owns the data, how it is used, and whether it could be misused. Many users don't know about the security and privacy risks of IoT devices, which makes them easier targets for social engineering and phishing attacks. The changing nature of cyber threats means security measures need to be constantly monitored and updated. By understanding these basic challenges, we can start to create and use comprehensive security solutions. This book will help you understand the complicated world of IoT security, showing you the latest research and new ways to improve security. The goal is to give you the knowledge and tools to create an IoT world that is safer and more trustworthy.

1.1 Introduction

The Internet of Things (IoT) is currently undergoing a rapid transformation, starting from a concept confined to science fiction to an undeniable reality deeply interwoven into our daily lives. This interconnected network of devices, encompassing many components of our life, from smart refrigerators in our kitchens and fitness trackers on our wrists to the intricate sensors embedded in industrial machinery and the sophisticated systems guiding autonomous vehicles, holds the promise of a world characterized by unprecedented efficiency, convenience, and automation. However, this hyper-connected world, while brimming with potential, presents a double-edged sword. The very interconnectedness that drives its transformative power also significantly expands the attack surface, leading to a corresponding escalation in security and privacy risks.

This inherited opposition lies at the heart of the IoT revolution. On one hand, we are experiencing a large emergence of smart homes where lighting, security systems, and appliances seamlessly interact to optimize energy consumption and enhance comfort and leisure. Wearable technology empowers individuals to monitor their health and well-being with unprecedented precision, track sports etc. In the industrial spectrum, sensors and control systems orchestrate manufacturing processes, boosting productivity and minimizing costs. Smart cities leverage connected infrastructure to optimize traffic flow, manage parking systems, and monitor environmental conditions, ultimately enhancing urban living. Even the healthcare sector is undergoing a profound transformation, with remote patient monitoring, smart medical devices, and connected healthcare systems promising to revolutionize patient care. Still, this longer-term vision is shadowed by the awareness of the vulnerabilities inherent in this interconnected and hyper-connected world.

The spread of IoT devices has created an expansive network of potential entry points for malicious actors, leaving individuals and organizations exposed to a large threat landscapes. In later chapters, this book will provide a deep journey into IoT security, privacy, and safety, seeking to unravel the complex challenges that arise from this interconnectedness. It aims to provide a comprehensive understanding of the multifaceted risks while presenting integrated approaches and cutting-edge research aimed at safeguarding this increasingly interconnected world. Several research solutions will be presented and discussed as outcomes of recent research projects, efforts and initiatives.

Our exploration begins with a deep dive into the foundational aspects of the Internet of Things (IoT), focusing on its core components and the unique vulnerabilities that arise from its specific characteristics. We will investigate the complexities of device heterogeneity, where the wide variety of devices—each with distinct hardware, software, and communication protocols—poses significant challenges to implementing uniform security standards. Additionally, the resource limitations of many IoT devices, such as restricted processing power, memory, and battery life, further complicate efforts to secure them effectively. We will also delve into the risks stemming from insecure development practices, which often result from the rush to market, leaving devices vulnerable. Moreover, the challenges related to insecure communication channels—frequently present in IoT networks—will be explored, highlighting the risks of data interception, manipulation, and denial-of-service attacks. The massive amount of personal data generated and transmitted by IoT devices raises serious concerns about data ownership, consent, and the potential for misuse. Another critical issue we will address is the lack of user awareness, which amplifies security risks. Many users remain unaware of the threats associated with IoT devices, making them more vulnerable to social engineering and phishing attacks. Lastly, we will focus on the evolving nature of the threat landscape, which requires ongoing monitoring, adaptation, and innovation in security measures. By understanding these core challenges, we can begin to create and apply comprehensive security strategies. This book aims to guide readers through the complexities of IoT security, offering insights into the latest research and showcasing innovative solutions. Ultimately, the goal is to equip readers with the knowledge and tools needed to build a more secure, privacy-focused, and trustworthy IoT ecosystem.

1.1.1 Internet of Things as an Expanding Layer

The Internet of Things (IoT) is no longer a futuristic vision; it's the present, subtly and pervasively integrated into our modern lives. This network of interconnected devices extends far beyond the familiar examples of smart refrigerators and fitness trackers. It encompasses a vast and rapidly expanding ecosystem of objects embedded with sensors, software, and network connectivity, enabling them to collect and exchange data, and often, to act autonomously based on that data. These data stem from sensing, networking, data exchange, automation services as well as other day to day services like transportation etc.

At the very heart of the IoT lies the **ability to sense** and interpret the physical world. This is achieved through a diverse array of sensors embedded within IoT devices. These sensors act as the eyes and ears of the IoT, capturing a wide spectrum of data, including: Environmental data (Temperature, humidity, air quality, light intensity, and noise levels), Physical data (Pressure, motion, acceleration, location, and proximity), Biological data (Heart rate, blood pressure, sleep patterns, and activity levels) and Other Operational data (Machine performance, energy consumption, and equipment status). This constant stream of sensory data provides a real-time picture of the world around us, enabling informed decision-making and automated responses.

The true power of the IoT lies in its **ability to connect** these devices, enabling them to communicate and collaborate. This interconnectedness is facilitated by a variety of network technologies, each with its own strengths and limitations. Wi-Fi (used for short-range communication in homes and offices, offering high bandwidth and relatively low latency), Bluetooth (connecting personal devices like smartphones and wearables, low energy consumption), Cellular/GSM Networks (wide-area coverage, enabling connectivity for devices on the move, vehicles, etc.), Low-Power Wide-Area Networks (LPWAN) (Designed for long-range communication with low power consumption, particularly suitable for applications like smart agriculture and environmental monitoring), Zigbee and Z-Wave (home automation, offering low-power, mesh networking capabilities). The choice of network technology depends on the specific requirements of the IoT application, considering factors such as range, bandwidth, power consumption, and cost.

The vast amounts of data generated by IoT devices are not just raw numbers; they are the lifeblood of the IoT leveraging their **ability to scale and adapt**, holding valuable insights waiting to be unlocked. This is where data processing and analysis start to come into play, including Edge Computing (Processing data closer to the source, at the "edge" of the network, reduces latency and bandwidth requirements, enabling real-time decision-making), Cloud Computing (Leveraging the scalability and processing power of cloud platforms to store, process, and analyze massive datasets, facilitating complex analytics and machine learning), Data Analytics (Extracting meaningful patterns and insights from raw data, enabling informed decision-making, predictive modeling, and anomaly detection). By transforming raw data into actionable intelligence, the IoT unlocks the potential for optimization, automation, and innovation.

The ultimate goal of the IoT is not just to collect and analyze data but lies into its intelligence **ability to automate** tasks, optimize processes, and create personalized experiences. This is where intelligent automation comes into play into Smart Homes (e.g. Automated lighting systems that adjust based on occupancy and natural light, thermostats that learn user preferences, and security systems that detect and respond to potential threats), Industrial Automation (Predictive maintenance systems that anticipate equipment failures, optimizing production processes and minimizing downtime), Autonomous Vehicles (Self-driving cars that navigate complex environments, relying on sensor data and sophisticated algorithms to make real-time decisions), Personalized Healthcare (Wearable devices that monitor vital signs and alert healthcare providers to potential health issues, enabling proactive interventions). Intelligent automation is the driving force behind the transformative power of the IoT, promising to revolutionize various sectors and reshape the way we live and work.

As far as the **applications of the IoT** are concerned we can highlight that they are also as diverse as the devices themselves, spanning various sectors and impacting every aspect of modern life. Some key areas where the IoT is making a significant impact include: Smart Cities (Connected infrastructure, traffic management systems, smart streetlights, and environmental monitoring, enhancing the efficiency and sustainability of urban environments), Healthcare (Remote patient monitoring, smart medical devices, and connected healthcare systems, improving patient outcomes and transforming the delivery of healthcare services), Agriculture (Precision agriculture techniques leveraging sensors and data analytics to optimize irrigation, fertilization, and pest control, increasing crop yields and promoting sustainable farming practices), Retail (Personalized shopping experiences, inventory optimization, and supply chain management, enhancing customer satisfaction and improving operational efficiency), Transport and Logistics (Real-time tracking of goods, fleet management, and route optimization, improving efficiency and reducing costs in the transportation and logistics industry).

This is just a glimpse into the vast potential of the IoT. As technology continues to evolve, we can expect even more innovative applications to emerge, further blurring the lines between the physical and digital worlds. However, this rapid expansion of the IoT ecosystem also brings with it a complex set of challenges, particularly in the realm of security and privacy. The interconnected nature of the IoT creates an expansive attack surface, exposing individuals and organizations to a myriad of threats. In the next section, we will delve into these challenges, exploring the unique vulnerabilities that arise from the inherent characteristics of the IoT [1, 2].

1.2 Towards a Secure and Privacy-Preserving IoT: A Holistic Vision

The Internet of Things holds tremendous promise, but its inherent vulnerabilities demand a proactive and comprehensive approach to security and privacy. Building a truly secure and trustworthy IoT ecosystem requires a paradigm shift, moving beyond isolated solutions to embrace a holistic vision that encompasses every facet of this interconnected world. This long-term vision must begin with a fundamental understanding that security is not an afterthought, but rather an integral part of the design process itself as well as the network/devices lifecycle. When a new IoT device is conceived, security considerations must be woven into its very fabric, from the hardware components to the software that drives it. This means incorporating secure boot mechanisms to ensure that only trusted code is executed, utilizing Hardware Security Modules (HSMs) to protect sensitive cryptographic operations, and implementing robust memory management to prevent unauthorized access to data. Furthermore, devices should be designed with tamper detection capabilities, raising alarms or initiating protective measures if physical intrusion is detected. And crucially, a secure and reliable mechanism for firmware updates is essential to patch vulnerabilities and enhance security throughout the device's operational life.

However, securing the device itself is only the first line of defense. The communication channels, networks and devices that connect these devices are equally vital and require robust protection. Data traversing the IoT network must be shielded from intruder eyes, manipulation, and disruption. This necessitates the use of strong encryption protocols like Transport Layer Security (TLS) and Advanced Encryption Standard (AES) to ensure confidentiality and integrity. Authentication mechanisms are equally crucial, verifying the identity of devices and users before granting access to the network and preventing unauthorized entry. Granular access control policies should be enforced, restricting access to sensitive data and functionalities based on clearly defined roles and privileges. Furthermore, deploying Intrusion Detection and Prevention Systems (IDPS) can provide active defense, monitoring network traffic for suspicious activity and taking proactive measures to prevent or mitigate potential attacks.

The **exceptionally rising volume of personal data** generated by IoT devices raises profound concerns about privacy. Protecting this data is not merely a legal obligation but also an ethical imperative. A holistic approach to IoT security must therefore prioritize data protection and privacy. This begins with the principle of data minimization, collecting only the data that is absolutely necessary for the intended purpose. Where possible, anonymization and pseudonymization techniques should be employed to de-identify personal data, making it difficult to link back to individuals while preserving its utility for analysis. Strict access control policies are important, ensuring that only authorized individuals can access sensitive information. Clear data retention policies should be established, outlining how long data is stored and when it is deleted, minimizing the risk of data breaches and ensuring compliance with privacy regulations like GDPR (General Data Protection Regulation, EU) and CCPA (California Consumer Privacy Act, US). Furthermore, exploring and implementing privacy-preserving technologies like differential privacy and federated learning can enable data analysis while safeguarding individual privacy.

In the ever-evolving threat landscape of the IoT, a static approach to security is inadequate. Proactive security monitoring and incident response are essential to stay ahead of emerging threats in a dynamic approach. This involves deploying real-time monitoring systems that can detect anomalies, suspicious activities, and potential security breaches. Security Information and Event Management (SIEM) systems can play a crucial role in collecting and analyzing security logs from various sources, identifying patterns and trends that may indicate potential threats. Leveraging threat intelligence feeds can provide valuable insights into the latest vulnerabilities and attack vectors, enabling proactive mitigation measures. Developing and regularly testing incident response plans is crucial to ensure a swift and effective response to security incidents, minimizing damage and downtime.

However, technology alone cannot solve the security and privacy challenges of the IoT. The **human element** is a critical factor, and empowering users with knowledge and awareness is paramount. Security awareness training can equip users with the skills to identify phishing attacks, social engineering attempts, and other common threats. Clear and concise guidance on secure device configuration, including strong passwords and enabling security features, is essential. Users should also be educated about data privacy, consent, and how to manage their privacy settings on IoT devices. Promoting responsible usage encourages users to be mindful of the security and privacy implications of their actions in the interconnected world. However, individual efforts are not enough still. A truly secure and privacy-preserving IoT requires a collaborative ecosystem where stakeholders work together to establish a robust foundation. This is where regulatory frameworks and standards play a crucial role. Governments and industry bodies must develop and enforce security standards for IoT devices and systems, ensuring a minimum level of security and interoperability. Privacy regulations, such as the General Data Protection Regulation (GDPR) and the California Consumer Privacy Act (CCPA), provide a legal framework for protecting personal data collected by IoT devices. Establishing clear liability frameworks helps address security breaches and data privacy violations, promoting accountability and responsible innovation. International cooperation and harmonization of standards are also crucial to address the global nature of the IoT and its security challenges.

Beyond regulations, fostering and maintaining a **culture of collaboration and information sharing** is essential. Encouraging the exchange of threat intelligence and security best practices can enhance collective security. Promoting the development and adoption of open-source security tools and technologies can foster innovation and transparency. Public-private partnerships can facilitate collaboration between governments, industry, and academia to address the complex challenges of IoT security. Continuous investment in research and development is crucial to advance the state of the art in IoT security and privacy, developing innovative solutions to address emerging threats. This collaborative approach must extend to the users themselves. Empowering users with knowledge and tools to secure their own devices and data is essential. This can be achieved through user-friendly interfaces, clear security and privacy settings, and educational resources that explain potential risks and best practices. By fostering a sense of shared responsibility, we can create a more secure and resilient IoT ecosystem.

The rapid pace of technological innovation, the diversity of devices and protocols, and the evolving nature of cyber threats bring however **constant vigilance and adaptation**. But by embracing a holistic vision, fostering collaboration, and prioritizing security and privacy at every level, we can build a future where the transformative power of the IoT can be fully realized without compromising the security and privacy of individuals and organizations. This is not merely a technological challenge, but a societal one, requiring the collective effort of all stakeholders to build a future where the benefits of the IoT can be enjoyed by all [3].

1.2.1 Cyber Threat Information (CTI) Sharing

Cyber Threat Intelligence (CTI) sharing has become increasingly vital in the ongoing battle against evolving cyber threats. Organizations are recognizing the power of collective defense, understanding that sharing information about vulnerabilities, attack vectors, and malicious actors can significantly strengthen their overall security posture and allow for proactive risk mitigation. This collaborative approach is gaining traction, with more organizations realizing the value of pooling their knowledge and insights to combat the ever-changing threat landscape.The development of standardized frameworks, such as STIX and TAXII, has been instrumental in facilitating this exchange of information. These frameworks provide a common language for representing and sharing threat intelligence, enabling seamless communication and interoperability between different systems and organizations.

Furthermore, various platforms and initiatives have emerged to support CTI sharing, including Information Sharing and Analysis Centers (ISACs), industry consortia, and government-led programs. These platforms provide secure channels for exchanging information, fostering trust and collaboration among participants.

Automation is also playing an increasingly important role in CTI sharing. Automated tools and platforms can collect, analyze, and disseminate threat intelligence in real-time, enabling organizations to respond to threats more quickly and effectively. This reduces the burden on security analysts, allowing them to focus on more strategic tasks while automated systems handle the routine aspects of information sharing. Moreover, public-private partnerships are becoming more prevalent, with governments recognizing the importance of collaborating with the private sector to enhance national cybersecurity. Governments are providing threat intelligence feeds, encouraging information sharing between organizations, and facilitating collaboration through various initiatives.

Despite this progress, challenges remain. Sharing sensitive information requires a high degree of trust between organizations. Concerns about confidentiality, data ownership, and potential misuse can hinder information sharing, especially when clear guidelines and agreements are lacking. The quality and relevance of shared information is also paramount. Sharing inaccurate or incomplete information can lead to false alarms and wasted resources. Therefore, providing context and actionable insights is crucial for effective CTI sharing. Legal and regulatory barriers can also pose challenges. Concerns about liability, privacy regulations, and intellectual property rights can create obstacles to information sharing. Navigating these legal and regulatory complexities can be challenging for organizations, particularly those lacking dedicated legal expertise [4].

1.2.2 Incident Response as a Mentality Changer

The highly connected nature of the IoT introduces unique challenges for incident response. Traditional security incident response frameworks, which are typically designed for centralized networks with well-defined boundaries, struggle to cope with the distributed and dynamic nature of IoT environments. This calls for a new approach to incident response that accounts for the distinct features of this interconnected landscape. To effectively address these challenges, a comprehensive incident response strategy for the IoT must be developed, focusing on the following key components:

1. **Visibility and Monitoring**: It is essential to maintain comprehensive visibility across the IoT network by deploying monitoring tools and sensors that collect and analyze data from multiple sources. This real-time insight is critical for understanding the security status and overall health of the network.

Advanced technologies such as machine learning and artificial intelligence can help analyze this data, detect anomalies, and identify potential threats that might be missed by human analysts.

2. **Automated Response/Actions**: Developing automated playbooks and scripts that trigger predefined actions in response to specific security incidents is crucial. This automation allows for quicker and more efficient responses to emerging threats.
3. **Collaboration and Coordination**: Effective incident response requires seamless collaboration and coordination among all stakeholders. This includes establishing clear communication channels and protocols, as well as developing shared incident response plans that define roles and responsibilities. Information-sharing platforms can facilitate the exchange of threat intelligence and best practices, helping to ensure a coordinated response to new threats.
4. **Continuous and Dynamic Improvement**: Incident response should be seen as a continuous process of improvement. Regular reviews and updates to incident response plans, incorporating lessons from past incidents, and staying informed about new threats and vulnerabilities are essential. Ongoing training and exercises will help ensure that incident response teams are prepared to tackle a range of security scenarios.

1.2.3 Device Lifecycle Identity Management Needs, Solutions and Challenges

The need for effective device lifecycle identity management arises from several critical factors. First, the sheer scale and diversity of IoT devices make manual identity management impractical. With billions of devices, each featuring unique characteristics and communication protocols, automated solutions are essential for efficient and scalable identity management. Second, the dynamic nature of the IoT involves continuous changes, with devices being added, updated, or removed from networks. This necessitates a flexible identity management system capable of adapting to these changes while maintaining security. Third, compromised device identities pose serious security risks. A compromised device could be leveraged to attack other devices, steal sensitive information, or disrupt essential services. As a result, strong identity management is essential to prevent unauthorized access and safeguard the integrity of the IoT ecosystem. To address these challenges, various solutions have been developed for managing device identities throughout their lifecycle. Public Key Infrastructure (PKI) is a widely adopted approach, providing a framework for managing digital certificates that authenticate devices and secure communication through encryption.

For example, **Sectigo** offers a comprehensive IoT identity management platform that leverages PKI to issue and manage device certificates, ensuring secure communication and authentication. Device identity management platforms offer centralized solutions for managing device identities, providing functionalities such as registration, authentication, authorization, and credential management. **AWS IoT Device Defender** is a service that allows organizations to audit device fleets, monitor device behavior, and enforce security policies, helping to manage device identities and security postures at scale. **Google Cloud IoT Core** provides a similar suite of tools, with features like secure device provisioning and access control. Blockchain technology is also being explored as a potential solution for device identity management, offering decentralized and tamper-proof identity registries. For instance, **IoTeX** is a blockchain platform specifically designed for IoT, providing decentralized identity and access management for devices. Furthermore, lightweight authentication and authorization protocols have been developed specifically for resource-constrained IoT devices, enabling secure communication without compromising performance. The **Constrained Application Protocol (CoAP)** is an example of such a protocol, designed for use in resource-constrained environments like those found in many IoT deployments [5, 6].

1.2.4 Threat Modeling and Risk Assessment in the IoT

Threat modeling is a systematic approach used to identify potential threats and vulnerabilities in a system. By thoroughly analyzing the system's design, functionality, and environment, it helps uncover possible attack vectors and weaknesses that could be exploited by malicious actors. This process is essential for identifying security gaps and prioritizing mitigation efforts. There are various methodologies for threat modeling, each with its own advantages and areas of focus. In the context of the Internet of Things (IoT), threat modeling and risk assessment must take into account the unique characteristics of the IoT ecosystem. The large scale and diversity of IoT devices, communication protocols, and their distributed nature pose significant security challenges. Additionally, many IoT devices are resource-constrained, limiting their ability to implement advanced security measures. Therefore, threat modeling in the IoT context must be adapted to these constraints, factoring in device capabilities, network architecture, and the sensitivity of the data involved.

There are several established tools for threat modeling. For instance, STRIDE categorizes threats into Spoofing, Tampering, Repudiation, Information Disclosure, Denial of Service, and Elevation of Privilege, enabling organizations to identify vulnerabilities systematically. Another approach, DREAD, evaluates the Damage potential, Reproducibility, Exploitability, Affected users, and Discoverability of a threat, helping organizations prioritize threats based on potential impact and likelihood of exploitation. PASTA focuses on the business implications of threats, aligning security analysis with organizational goals. Meanwhile, the OCTAVE framework provides a broader risk assessment approach that considers both technical vulnerabilities and organizational factors. Once potential threats are identified, risk assessment frameworks can be used to assess their likelihood and potential impact. This evaluation includes analyzing the consequences of a successful attack, such as financial losses, reputational harm, or disruptions to critical services. The NIST Cybersecurity Framework offers widely recognized standards and guidelines for managing cybersecurity risks, emphasizing a risk-based approach tailored to an organization's specific risk profile. Similarly, the FAIR (Factor Analysis of Information Risk) framework quantifies risk in financial terms, aiding organizations in making informed decisions about their security investments. There are several tools and solutions to support threat modeling and risk assessment in the IoT. The OWASP IoT Threat Modeling Guide offers a comprehensive framework for identifying and mitigating threats specific to IoT systems. Microsoft's Threat Modeling Tool provides a visual interface for mapping out threats and identifying vulnerabilities. Additionally, the IoT Security Foundation's Security Compliance Framework offers best practices for securing IoT devices and systems. Various commercial vendors also provide specialized tools and services for IoT threat modeling.

Examples of threat modeling and risk assessment in the IoT are found across multiple sectors. In healthcare, threat modeling is used to identify vulnerabilities in connected medical devices, like insulin pumps and pacemakers, to prevent unauthorized access and manipulation. In industrial settings, risk assessments help gauge the impact of cyberattacks on critical infrastructure such as power grids or manufacturing plants, allowing for the implementation of necessary security measures. In smart homes, threat modeling helps protect connected devices like smart locks and security cameras, ensuring the privacy and safety of homeowners [7].

1.3 Legal and Ethical Considerations in IoT Security and Privacy

1.3.1 Data Protection and Privacy

One of the key legal and ethical challenges surrounding the Internet of Things (IoT) is safeguarding personal data. IoT devices gather vast amounts of information about users, such as their locations, behaviors, and preferences. While this data enhances personalized services and operational efficiency, it also raises significant privacy concerns and the risk of misuse. Laws like the General Data Protection Regulation (GDPR) in Europe and the California Consumer Privacy Act (CCPA) in the U.S.

establish guidelines for managing personal data. These regulations give individuals control over their data, including rights to access, correct, and delete their information. They also require organizations to protect data from unauthorized access or misuse. For companies in the IoT sector, complying with these rules is crucial. This involves implementing strong technical and organizational measures, such as encryption, access control, and data anonymization. Additionally, businesses must be transparent about their data practices, offering clear privacy notices and obtaining informed consent when necessary.

1.3.2 Liability and Accountability

The IoT ecosystem's distributed structure gives rise to intricate issues regarding liability and accountability. In the event of a security breach or privacy infringement, identifying the responsible party can prove challenging. The obligations may fall on the device manufacturer, software developer, network provider, or end-users. It is essential to create well-defined liability frameworks to ensure accountability and provide individuals with recourse for any harm suffered. Product liability laws can be extended to IoT devices, making manufacturers responsible for any defects that lead to damage. Nevertheless, the complexity of IoT systems—characterized by their interconnected components and frequent software updates—complicates the process of pinpointing the cause of any failures. Additionally, the absence of clear security standards and best practices contributes to uncertainty about what may qualify as a "defect" in these devices. Guidelines such as the Cybersecurity Act in Europe and the NIST Cybersecurity Framework in the United States offer direction on security practices and incident responses. These frameworks help establish a foundational level of security expectations and foster accountability within the IoT landscape. However, due to the constantly evolving nature of cyber threats and rapid technological advancements, continual adjustment and enhancement of these frameworks are necessary.

1.3.3 Ethical Considerations

Ethical considerations are essential for responsible IoT development and deployment, moving beyond mere legal compliance to address fairness, transparency, and respect for human values. This involves recognizing and mitigating potential biases embedded within IoT systems. Algorithms often inherit societal biases from their training data, leading to discriminatory outcomes. For instance, facial recognition systems have demonstrated lower accuracy for people of color, raising concerns about their use in law enforcement. Therefore, it's crucial to proactively address these biases and ensure equitable design and deployment of IoT systems.

Furthermore, the potential for IoT devices to enable surveillance and tracking raises ethical concerns about privacy and individual autonomy. These devices can gather extensive data on people's movements and activities. Organizations must be transparent about their data collection practices, obtain informed consent, and implement safeguards to prevent misuse for surveillance or other privacy-violating purposes. Transparency and accountability are paramount. Organizations should openly communicate their data collection, usage, and sharing practices. Individuals should have access to their data and the ability to correct or delete it. Additionally, organizations should establish mechanisms for individuals to seek redress if their rights are violated.

1.3.4 Ethics Committees and Review Boards

The increasing complexity of ethical considerations surrounding the Internet of Things (IoT) necessitates a greater reliance on oversight mechanisms such as ethics committees and review boards. These entities play a vital role in guiding the responsible development and utilization of IoT technologies, ensuring alignment with societal values. Ethics committees serve as valuable resources for organizations navigating the ethical landscape of IoT projects. They offer expertise on a range of issues, including data privacy, algorithmic bias, and other ethical challenges. By engaging with ethics committees, organizations can proactively identify and address potential concerns, ensuring that their IoT initiatives are ethically sound. Moreover, these committees can review research proposals and product development plans to ensure that ethical considerations are integrated from the outset. Review boards provide an additional layer of oversight, specifically evaluating the ethical implications of particular IoT applications. For instance, they may assess the ethical dimensions of using facial recognition technology in public spaces or deploying connected medical devices that collect sensitive patient data. Through their independent evaluation, review boards help ensure that IoT technologies are deployed in a manner that respects individual rights and promotes societal well-being. This collaborative approach, involving both internal ethics committees and external review boards, is essential for navigating the complex ethical landscape of the IoT. By engaging with these oversight mechanisms, organizations can demonstrate their commitment to responsible innovation and ensure that their IoT initiatives contribute to a more ethical and equitable technological future.

1.4 Security By Design

Security by Design is a philosophy that emphasizes building security into every stage of the IoT device lifecycle. It involves anticipating potential threats and vulnerabilities and implementing security controls to mitigate those risks. By embedding security into the DNA of IoT systems, we can create a more resilient and trustworthy foundation for the interconnected world. This means granting devices and users only the necessary privileges to perform their functions, minimizing the potential damage from unauthorized access. It also involves implementing multiple layers of security controls to provide redundancy and resilience in case one layer is compromised. Devices should be configured with secure settings out of the box, reducing the reliance on users to implement security measures. Systems should be designed to fail securely, minimizing the impact of failures and preventing cascading effects. It's crucial to ensure that all access to resources is authenticated and authorized, preventing unauthorized access and data breaches. Security should not rely on the secrecy of the design or implementation. Open standards and transparent security practices promote trust and accountability. The sharing of resources and mechanisms between different components should be minimized, reducing the impact of a single point of failure. Finally, security measures should be user-friendly and intuitive, encouraging adoption and compliance.

Implementing Security by Design in the IoT faces several challenges. Many IoT devices have limited processing power and memory, making it challenging to implement complex security mechanisms. The wide variety of devices and protocols makes standardization difficult. Integrating security into existing systems can be complex and costly. There's a shortage of skilled security professionals in IoT security. Keeping up with the latest security threats and vulnerabilities is also challenging. To address these challenges and promote Security by Design, several standards and reference architectures have been developed. The NIST Cybersecurity Framework provides standards, guidelines, and best practices for managing cybersecurity risk. The OWASP Internet of Things Project offers resources and guidance on securing IoT devices and systems. The Industrial Internet Consortium (IIC) Security Framework provides a security framework for industrial IoT systems. The ISO/SAE 21434 Road Vehicles – Cybersecurity Engineering is a standard for cybersecurity engineering in road vehicles. The ETSI EN 303 645 Cyber Security for Consumer Internet of Things specifies security requirements for consumer IoT products. These standards offer guidance on security best practices, risk assessment, and secure development lifecycles.

Acknowledgements

This project has received funding from the European Union's Horizon 2020 research and innovation programme under grant agreement no 101020416. The authors acknowledge the research outcomes of this publication belonging to the ERATOSTHENES (101020416) project consortium.

References

[1] K. Loupos, B. Caglayan, A. Papageorgiou, B. Starynkevitch, F. Vedrine, C. Skoufis, S. Christofi, B. Karakostas, A. Mygiakis, G. Theofilis, A. Chiappetta, H. Avgoustidis, George Boulougouris – COGNITION ENABLED IOT PLATFORM FOR INDUSTRIAL IOT SAFETY, SECURITY AND PRIVACY – THE CHARIOT PROJECT, IEEE International Workshop on Computer Aided Modeling and Design of Communication Links and Networks (CAMAD), IEEE XPLORE, 11-13 September 2019, Limassol, Cyprus, DOI: 10.1109/CAMAD.2019.8858488.

[2] K. Loupos, A. Papageorgiou, A. Mygiakis, B. Caglayan, B. Karakostas, T. Krousarlis, F. Vedrine, C. Skoufis, S. Christofi, G. Theofilis, H. Avgoustidis, G. Boulougouris, A. Battaglia, M. Villiani – COGNITIVE PLATFORM FOR INDUSTRIAL IOT SYSTEM SECURITY, SAFETY AND PRIVACY, Embedded World 2020 Conference and Exhibition, 25–27 Feb. 2020, Nuremberg, Germany.

[3] K. Loupos – INTEGRATED SOLUTION FOR PRIVACY AND SECURITY OF IOT DEVICES IN CRITICAL INFRASTRUCTURES, Critical Infrastructure Protection and Resilience Europe (CIPRE 2020), 6–8 Oct. 2020, Bucharest, Romania.

[4] K. Loupos, C. Kalogirou, H. Niavis, A. F. Skarmeta, E. Torroglosa-Garcia, A. Palomares, H. Song, P.E. Brun, F. Giampaolo, D. V. Landuyt, S. Michiels, B. Podgorelec, C. Xenakis, M. Bampatsikos, K. Krilakis – A HOLISTIC APPROACH FOR IOT NETWORKS' IDENTITY AND TRUST MANAGEMENT – THE ERATOSTHENES PROJECT, 4th Workshop on Internet of Things Security and Privacy (WISP), Global IoT Summit 2022, Dublin, June 2022.

[5] O. Vermesan, M. Coppola, M. Diaz Nava, A. Capra, G. Kornaros, R. Bahr, E. Darmois, M. Serrano, P. Guillemin, K. Loupos, L. Karagiannidis, S. McGrath – New Waves of IoT Technologies Research – TRANSCENDING INTELLIGENCE AND SENSES AT THE EDGE TO CREATE MULTI EXPERIENCE ENVIRONMENTS, Internet of Things – The Call of the Edge – Everything Intelligent Everywhere, River Publishers, DK, October 2020, ISBN: 9788770221962, e-ISBN – 9788770221962.

[6] K. Loupos, C. Kalogirou, H. Niavis, A. F. Skarmeta, E. Torroglosa-Garcia, A. Palomares, H. Song, P.E. Brun, F. Giampaolo, D. V. Landuyt, S. Michiels,

B. Podgorelec, C. Xenakis, M. Bampatsikos, K. Krilakis – A HOLISTIC APPROACH FOR IOT NETWORKS' IDENTITY AND TRUST MANAGEMENT – THE ERATOSTHENES PROJECT, Lecture Notes in Computer Science book series (LNCS,volume 13533), DOI: 10.1007/978-3-031-20936-9_27.

[7] A. M. Frutos, J. G. Rodríguez, A. Skarmeta, K. Loupos, S. Vavilis, F. Michalopoulos – IDENTITY AND TRUST ARCHITECTURE FOR DEVICE LIFECYCLE MANAGEMENT, Future Generation Computer Systems, Volume 162, January 2025, Science Direct, Elsevier.

DOI: 10.1561/9781638285076.ch2

Chapter 2

Technologies and Opportunities Overview

By Konstantinos Loupos

With billions of devices connected and massive volumes of data being generated, the Internet of Things (IoT) is drastically changing our world. Although this interconnection creates new security and privacy challenges, it also offers enormous opportunity for efficiency and innovation. We must make sure that IoT technologies are developed and used responsibly, with security and privacy as top priorities, as our reliance on IoT devices in our homes, workplaces, and public areas grows. Examining the particular technologies that power this networked world is crucial to understanding the IoT's implications for security and privacy. This covers not just the actual gadgets but also the data management programs, security features, and communication protocols that make them possible. An enormous variety of devices, each with unique capabilities and limits, are included in the Internet of Things. Sensors and actuators are examples of resource-constrained devices that are difficult to secure and maintain since they are frequently placed in inaccessible or remote areas. On the other side, more potent edge computing devices can enable stronger security measures and carry out more intricate calculations. Designing and putting into practice suitable security measures requires an understanding of the features of various device kinds.

This chapter explores the capabilities, constraints, and security and privacy concerns of the technologies that support the Internet of Things. From resource-constrained sensors to potent edge computing devices, we will look at the wide variety of gadgets that make up the Internet of Things ecosystem. Additionally, we will examine the several communication protocols that allow these devices to communicate and share information, pointing out both their advantages and disadvantages in terms of security. This chapter will also look at the ways that the Internet of Things might improve security and privacy. We'll look at how IoT technology can be used to enhance security across a range of areas, including data protection, cybersecurity, and physical security. We'll also talk about how the Internet of Things can enable people to take charge of their own privacy by giving them the resources and technology they need to handle their personal information and safeguard their online privacy.

But there are also a lot of security and privacy issues with the Internet of Things. Implementing standardized security measures is challenging due to the IoT ecosystem's extreme size and variability. Many IoT devices have limited resources, which makes it difficult for them to provide sophisticated security features. Managing device identities and security credentials is made more difficult by the IoT's dynamic nature, which involves devices being added, updated, and withdrawn from the network on a regular basis. Furthermore, privacy issues and possible misuse are brought up by the way IoT devices gather and use personal data. Adoption may be hampered by a lack of control and openness over data collection procedures. A multifaceted strategy including technology innovation, legal frameworks, and ethical considerations is needed to address these issues. An extensive review of the potential and technologies influencing IoT security and privacy will be given in this chapter. We may strive toward a future where the Internet of Things is utilized responsibly and ethically, optimizing its advantages while protecting security and privacy, by comprehending the potential and constraints of IoT technologies, as well as the opportunities and problems they provide. The work presented in this chapter is directly linked with the work done in the ERATOSTHENES EC research project.

2.1 Introduction

The Internet of Things (IoT) is rapidly transforming our world, connecting billions of devices and generating very larger amounts of data including personal or other data. This brings large prospects for innovation and efficiency, but it also raises new challenges for security and privacy that are constantly rising, further increasing the technology spectrum and requirements. It us true that we are becoming increasingly reliant on IoT devices in our homes, workplaces, and public spaces, while it is crucial to ensure that these technologies are developed and deployed responsibly and in a trusted manner, with security and privacy as paramount considerations.

This chapter describes some technologies underpinning the IoT, exploring their capabilities, limitations, and implications for trust, security and privacy. Later, in this chapter and the upcoming ones, we will examine the diverse range of devices that comprise the IoT ecosystem, from resource-constrained sensors to powerful edge computing devices. We will also explore the various communication protocols that enable these devices to interact and exchange data, highlighting their security strengths and weaknesses. Furthermore, this chapter will examine the opportunities that the IoT presents for enhancing security and privacy. We will explore how IoT technologies can be leveraged to improve security in various domains, such as physical security, cybersecurity, and data protection.

Getting back to the challenges discussion, we need to highlight that the IoT also presents significant challenges for security and privacy. The huge span, scale and heterogeneity of the IoT ecosystem make it difficult to implement standardized security measures. On top, the resource constraints of many IoT devices limit their ability to support complex security mechanisms. The dynamic nature of the IoT, with devices constantly being added, updated, and removed from the network, poses challenges for managing device identities and security credentials. On top, the collection and use of personal data by IoT devices raise concerns about privacy and potential misuse. The lack of transparency and control over data collection practices can erode trust and create barriers to adoption. Addressing these challenges requires a multiple and dynamic approaches, involving large technological innovation, regulatory frameworks, and ethical considerations.

To fully grasp the implications of the IoT for security and privacy, it is essential to examine the specific technologies that drive this interconnected world. This includes not only the devices themselves, but also the communication protocols, data management systems, and security mechanisms that enable them to function. The IoT encompasses a vast array of **devices**, each with its own capabilities and limitations. Resource-constrained devices, such as sensors and actuators, are often deployed in remote or inaccessible locations, making them challenging to secure and maintain. More powerful edge computing devices, on the other hand, can perform more complex computations and support more robust security mechanisms. Understanding the characteristics of different device types is crucial for designing and implementing appropriate security measures. IoT devices communicate with each other and with central servers using a variety of **Communication Protocols**, each with its own security strengths and weaknesses. Some protocols, like MQTT and CoAP, are designed for lightweight communication and may not offer strong security features. Others, like TLS and DTLS, provide robust encryption and authentication but may be too resource-intensive for some devices. Choosing the right communication protocol is essential for balancing security and performance. The vast amounts of data generated by IoT devices require efficient and secure **data management** systems. Cloud platforms offer scalability and flexibility for storing and processing data, but they also raise concerns about data privacy and security. Edge computing can address some of these concerns by processing data closer to the source, but it also introduces new challenges for managing and securing distributed data. A variety of **security mechanisms** can be employed to protect IoT devices and data, including encryption, authentication, access control, and intrusion detection. However, implementing these mechanisms in a resource-constrained environment can be challenging. Lightweight security protocols and efficient algorithms are needed to minimize the overhead on device resources.

Despite the challenges, the IoT also presents significant **opportunities** for enhancing security and privacy. IoT technologies can be leveraged to improve physical security, such as through surveillance cameras, smart locks, and intrusion detection systems. In the large realm of cybersecurity, the IoT can enable real-time threat detection and response, automated security patching, and improved network visibility. Further, the IoT can empower individuals to take control of their own privacy. Personal data management tools can help individuals track and manage their data, while privacy-enhancing technologies can provide anonymity and pseudonymity. By giving individuals more control over their data, we can foster trust and encourage the adoption of IoT technologies.

2.2 Technologies for Holistic IoT Security, Privacy and Safety

Secure device design and production are critical to meeting the IoT industry's security requirements. Beginning with the design and production of the devices themselves, security must be ingrained in the very fundamental processes and architecture of IoT systems. This entails adding security features to both software and hardware to make sure that gadgets can withstand attacks and safeguard private information. Hardware Security Modules (HSMs), like the OPTIGATM Trust series from Infineon Technologies, offer secure key storage, encryption, and authentication features in a hardware component. Only reliable software is loaded at launch thanks to secure boot features, such as those in the U-Boot bootloader, which stop malicious programs from compromising the device. Secure firmware is equally crucial.

Another crucial component of comprehensive IoT security is **protecting communication pathways**. This entails using strong authentication and encryption procedures to safeguard data both at rest and in transit, guarding against denial-of-service attacks, data tampering, and eavesdropping. A popular cryptographic technology called Transport Layer Security (TLS) encrypts data transferred between devices and cloud platforms to enable safe network communication. One well-known open-source TLS implementation is the OpenSSL library. For Internet of Things applications that demand real-time communication, Datagram Transport Layer Security (DTLS), a variation of TLS made for use with datagram-based protocols like UDP, is especially well-suited. A lightweight implementation created especially for limited IoT devices is provided by the TinyDTLS library. Secure tunnels are created by virtual private networks (VPNs), such the well-known open-source OpenVPN system, for sending data over open networks, protecting it from illegal access and eavesdropping. For more secure and adaptable networking in Internet of Things deployments, Software-Defined Networking (SDN), using platforms such as OpenDaylight, offers centralized management over network traffic, enabling dynamic security policies and enhanced network visibility.

Privacy and data security are also critical. Data availability, confidentiality, and integrity must all be protected. This entails putting data security techniques like data anonymization, access control, and encryption into practice. Data is shielded against unwanted access and alteration by encryption, both in transit and at rest, using methods like the popular Advanced Encryption Standard (AES). By limiting access to sensitive information and features, access control mechanisms—such as authorization frameworks like OAuth 2.0—make sure that only authorized parties are able to use particular resources. Differential privacy and other data anonymization and pseudonymization techniques de-identify personal data, making it challenging to trace it back to specific people while maintaining its analytical value.

An additional crucial element of comprehensive IoT security is **Identity and Access Management** (IAM). Preventing unwanted access and data breaches requires controlling the identities and access rights of individuals and devices. Digital certificates are used to encrypt communications and authenticate devices. Public Key Infrastructure (PKI) offers a framework for managing these certificates. Free TLS certificates are offered by Let's Encrypt, a non-profit certificate authority. As previously stated, OAuth 2.0 is an authorization framework that makes secure delegated access possible. JSON Web Tokens (JWTs) enable authentication and authorization in Internet of Things systems by providing a small and self-contained method of securely transmitting data between parties.

Threat intelligence and security analytics are essential for proactively detecting and reducing security threats. This entails putting threat intelligence platforms, intrusion detection and prevention systems, and security information and event management (SIEM) systems into place. A well-known SIEM platform, Splunk, can gather and examine security data from several sources to reveal possible dangers. An open-source IDPS called SNORT is capable of identifying and stopping harmful network activities. A threat intelligence platform called VirusTotal examines files and URLs to find malware and other dangers.

2.2.1 Dynamic Trust and Identity Management

A security model known as "**dynamic trust management**" continuously assesses and modifies the trust relationships between IoT devices and users in light of a number of variables, including device behavior, environmental conditions, and security policies. It makes it possible to take a more detailed and contextually aware approach to security, enabling systems to react instantly to new threats and adjust to shifting circumstances. Building confidence in the connected world requires a dynamic approach to trust that reduces the dangers of harmful behavior and illegal access while facilitating safe collaboration and data sharing. Dynamic trust management in the Internet of Things is made possible by a number of techniques and technologies. Reputation systems are one example of this type of technology, which uses the combined experiences of devices and users to determine how trustworthy other people are. Reputation systems can detect malicious or untrustworthy devices by combining input and observations from several sources. This enables the system to take the necessary action, like removing the device from the network or restricting its access rights. For instance, the European Union-funded CONFIDANT project created a distributed trust management system for the Internet of Things that is based on risk assessment and reputation.

Behavioral analysis is another important tool that tracks user and device activity to identify irregularities and possible security risks. Behavioral analysis can uncover unwanted activities, including malware infections or unauthorized access attempts, by establishing baseline behavior patterns and spotting variations from them. In behavioral analysis, machine learning algorithms are essential because they allow systems to recognize and adjust to changing threat patterns. The study by Sikorski et al. [1], which suggests a machine learning-based method for identifying irregularities in IoT networks, serves as an illustration of this. Decisions about trust can also be influenced by contextual data, such as the location of the device, the time of day, and the surrounding environment. For example, a device may be deemed suspicious and subject to additional scrutiny or security measures if it suddenly begins transmitting huge amounts of data at an odd time or location. Researchers have presented the idea of "**trustworthiness zones**" in which the location of the device and the security restrictions related to that zone dynamically modify the trust levels. Huang et al.'s (2019) study [2], which suggests an IoT trust management architecture based on trustworthiness zones, serves as an example of this. Moreover, security policies that specify trust relationships and access control guidelines can be enforced thanks to policy-based trust management. The system can adjust to new threats and vulnerabilities by dynamically updating these policies in response to evolving security requirements or risk assessments. For instance, the policy may be modified to limit access or demand extra authentication for specific device types if a new vulnerability is found in those devices.

In the Internet of Things, **dynamic trust management** has various advantages. By offering a more precise and context-aware method of access control, it improves security by allowing the system to react instantly to new threats and adjust to shifting circumstances. By automating trust choices and minimizing the need for manual involvement, it increases efficiency. By facilitating safe data exchange and communication between people and trustworthy devices, it encourages teamwork. By allowing the system to bounce back from security lapses and continue operating even while hacked devices are present, it also boosts resilience. But there are drawbacks to dynamic trust management as well. One difficulty is the intricacy of managing and putting dynamic trust models into practice, which call for real-time data processing and complex algorithms. The possibility of biasing trust judgments is another difficulty, since the information used to gauge trust could be biased by society. Additionally, protecting the privacy of sensitive data used in trust calculations is essential, necessitating careful consideration of privacy-preserving and data anonymization strategies. Dynamic trust management is a crucial instrument for IoT security in spite of these drawbacks. Systems can adjust to the changing threat landscape and foster confidence in the globalized world by offering a more flexible and adaptive approach to security. In order to build a more secure and reliable IoT environment, ongoing research and development in this area is concentrated on resolving the obstacles and constraints, creating increasingly complex trust models, and combining dynamic trust management with other security solutions.

2.2.2 Lifecycle Management of IoT Devices

A key component of lifecycle management for IoT devices is creating and maintaining distinct identities. This makes it possible to authenticate, authorize, and track devices across the course of their lives. A popular solution for controlling device IDs is Public Key Infrastructure (PKI), which offers a mechanism for creating and maintaining digital certificates. These certificates can be used to authorize access to resources, encrypt communications, and confirm the identification of devices. For instance, a cloud-based PKI solution for controlling device IDs and protecting communication in IoT installations is provided by the GlobalSign IoT Identity Platform. Blockchain technology, which provides decentralized and impenetrable identity registries, is also being investigated as a possible device identity management solution. Decentralized identification and access management for IoT devices is made possible by the IoTeX blockchain technology, guaranteeing safe and open communication.

Setting up devices with the required settings and credentials to function safely on the network is known as provisioning. This entails setting up secure communication channels, configuring network settings, and installing firmware. For devices to be correctly setup for security and to avoid unwanted access, secure provisioning is essential. A hardware-based security technique called the Trusted Platform Module (TPM) can be used to store cryptographic keys, enable secure boot, and authenticate devices.

Device performance and behavior must be continuously monitored in order to spot irregularities, spot any security risks, and guarantee peak performance. Platforms for device management offer resources for remote diagnostics, telemetry data collection, and device health monitoring. For instance, with services like device registration, firmware updates, and remote troubleshooting, AWS IoT Device Management helps businesses to keep an eye on and manage their IoT fleets.

Patching vulnerabilities, enhancing performance, and introducing new features to IoT devices all depend on firmware updates. However, if firmware updates are not adequately secured, they may likewise pose security threats. Updates are verified and authorized before being installed on devices thanks to secure firmware update procedures, like those outlined in the Firmware Over-the-Air (FOTA) standard by the Open Mobile Alliance.

To avoid data breaches and unwanted access, it is essential to safely decommission IoT devices when their useful lives are over or they are replaced. This entails deleting the device's data safely, removing it from the network, and rescinding its login credentials. Data is permanently erased from the device using secure erasure procedures, as those outlined in NIST Special Publication 800-88.

There are various advantages to IoT device lifecycle management done right. Organizations may greatly increase the security of their IoT installations by controlling device IDs, providing secure passwords, keeping an eye on device behavior, and updating secure firmware. Proactive maintenance and ongoing monitoring can help guarantee peak performance and avoid device breakdowns. Task automation and process simplification are two ways that effective lifecycle management can lower operating expenses. Organizations can adhere to security standards and data protection laws with the use of lifecycle management.

2.3 AI Approaches for Trust and Identity Management in IOT

With billions of devices connected and massive volumes of data being generated, the Internet of Things (IoT) has completely changed the way we interact with the outside world. Due to the possible vulnerabilities posed by each device, this interconnection creates new security and privacy challenges. The dynamic and changing nature of the Internet of Things makes it difficult for traditional security methods to keep up. More flexible, intelligent, and resilient security measures are made possible by artificial intelligence (AI), which provides a potent suite of tools for improving identity management and trust in the Internet of Things. AI systems are excellent at sifting through enormous volumes of data from many sources, finding trends, and forecasting outcomes, which makes security measures more proactive and successful. AI can identify risks and irregularities, evaluate risk, confirm identities, and manage trust in the context of identity and trust management including threat prediction.

There are a series of added values that can be offered by automated solutions of Artificial intelligence. These include: **Anomalies and Threats detection** (learn normal behavior patterns of devices and users, enabling them to detect anomalies that may indicate malicious activity. This can help prevent attacks before they cause significant damage), **Risk Assessment** (assess the risk level of devices and users based on various factors, such as their behavior, reputation, and context leading to dynamic allocation of security resources and prioritization of threats), **Identities Verification** (verify the identity of devices and users, using techniques such as facial recognition, voice recognition, and behavioral biometrics preventing unauthorized access and protect against identity theft), **Trust management** (dynamically manage trust relationships between devices and users, adapting to changing conditions and security policies towards more flexible and context-aware security mechanisms), **Future Threats Analysis and prediction** (analyze historical data and identify patterns that may indicate future threats, enabling proactive security measures and preventing attacks before they occur).

There are usual AI Approaches for Trust and Identity Management in the IoT including **Machine Learning** (ML) (algorithms that can learn from data without explicit programming, enabling them to adapt to changing conditions and identify patterns that may not be apparent to humans). Supervised learning, unsupervised learning, and reinforcement learning are all being used in the context of IoT security. **Deep Learning** (DL) (as a subset of ML uses artificial neural networks to learn complex patterns from data. DL has been shown to be particularly effective in tasks such as image recognition and natural language processing, which can be applied to identity verification and threat detection in the IoT, **Natural Language Processing (NLP)** (that enables computers to understand and process human language, which can be used to analyze security logs, identify threats, and communicate security information to users) and **Computer Vision** (to "see" and interpret images, which can be used for tasks such as facial recognition and object detection).

Examples of AI-Powered Solutions are already being used to enhance trust and identity management in the IoT such as FogHorn Lightning™ (edge AI platform provides real-time analytics and machine learning capabilities for IoT devices, enabling anomaly detection, predictive maintenance, and other security functions), Siemens MindSphere (cloud-based IoT operating system uses AI to analyze data from connected devices, providing insights into operations, performance, and security), Google Cloud IoT Core (AI-powered services for IoT device management, including anomaly detection and predictive maintenance).

Benefits of AI for Trust and Identity Management are numerous including Improved Accuracy, Increased Efficiency, Adaptability and Scalability. There are however serious **limitations and challenges**, despite the potential benefits including Data Requirements (require large amounts of data to train and function effectively. Obtaining and labeling this data can be challenging, especially in the context of security, where sensitive data may need to be protected), Bias (AI algorithms can inherit biases from the data they are trained on, which can lead to discriminatory outcomes. It is important to address these biases and ensure that AI systems are fair and equitable), Explainability (difficult to understand how some AI algorithms make decisions, which can make it challenging to identify and correct errors or biases), and Privacy (use of AI for security and identity management can raise privacy concerns, as it may involve collecting and analyzing sensitive data about individuals. It is important to implement privacy-preserving techniques and ensure that data is used responsibly and ethically).

Acknowledgements

This project has received funding from the European Union's Horizon 2020 research and innovation programme under grant agreement no 101020416. The authors acknowledge the research outcomes of this publication belonging to the ERATOSTHENES (101020416) project consortium.

References

[1] Sikorski, M., Choraś, M., & Kozik, R. (2018). Intrusion detection in IoT networks based on machine learning. In Proceedings of the 2018 IEEE 3rd International Conference on Collaboration and Internet Computing (CIC) (pp. 198–205). IEEE.

[2] Huang, X., Yu, F. R., Zhang, S., & Liu, L. (2019). A trustworthiness zone-based trust management framework for the internet of things. IEEE Internet of Things Journal, 6(3), 4637–4648.

DOI: 10.1561/9781638285076.ch3

Chapter 3

ERATOSTHENES Project Integrated Solution

By Sokratis Vavilis, Fotis Michalopoulos, Harris Niavis, George Misiakoulis, Konstantinos Loupos, Konstantinos Dafloukas, Jesús García-Rodríguez, Ekam Puri Nieto, Juan Francisco Martínez Gil, Agustín Marín Frutos and Antonio Skarmeta

The Internet of Things (IoT) is transforming our world, connecting countless devices and enabling new levels of automation and data sharing. But this connectivity also creates security risks, as each device becomes a potential target for attackers. Traditional security methods often fall short in protecting these diverse and widespread networks. Many IoT devices have limited resources, making it difficult to implement strong security measures like encryption or complex authentication protocols. The wide variety of devices and communication methods also makes it challenging to establish consistent security standards, as a one-size-fits-all approach simply doesn't work in such a fragmented landscape.

The ERATOSTHENES project aims to solve these problems by creating a new system for managing trust and identities in the IoT. This system is designed to work across an entire network without relying on any central control point, making it more resilient and less vulnerable to attacks that could compromise the whole system. It's automated for efficiency, meaning many tasks are handled automatically without human intervention. It's also transparent for accountability, allowing actions to be tracked and verified, which helps build trust among users and stakeholders. Importantly, it prioritizes user privacy, giving users control over their data and how it is used. By managing the entire lifespan of IoT devices, from initial setup to eventual decommissioning, this system strengthens trust and security within the network. It also complies with all relevant data protection and cybersecurity regulations, like GDPR and the Cybersecurity Act, ensuring it meets the highest standards for security and privacy.

One of the key challenges is the sheer variety of IoT devices, which makes it difficult to get a clear picture of their security status. Existing methods for establishing trust often lack proper upkeep, and outdated software can be exploited by attackers. This is further complicated by the fact that many IoT devices are "set it and forget it," meaning they are deployed in remote locations or inaccessible environments where regular updates and maintenance are difficult. Another challenge is managing the identities of devices and ensuring user privacy. A lack of security training and proper protocols for both users and devices creates further risks, as users may not be aware of the security implications of connecting their devices, and manufacturers may prioritize functionality over security.

Blockchain technology offers a promising solution for improving IoT security. Its decentralized and tamper-proof nature makes it well-suited for managing trust and identities. Because blockchain records every transaction across multiple computers, it's incredibly difficult to alter or tamper with the data, ensuring its integrity and reliability. The ERATOSTHENES solution includes several key components to address these challenges. The Trust Manager & Broker calculates trust scores for each device based on various factors and manages relationships between devices. The MQTT Broker filters security-related events and stores session data, acting as a central communication hub for security information. The Threat Modelling & Risk Assessment component creates a virtual model of the system to identify potential threats and vulnerabilities. The MUD Manager interprets device information and creates access control lists, determining which devices have access to which resources. The Trust Agent Deployer manages security software on devices, ensuring they are up-to-date and functioning correctly. The Trusted Execution Environment provides a secure area within the device for key services to run, protecting them from tampering. And the Self-Sovereign Identity system gives users control over their data and privacy, allowing them to manage their digital identities and decide how their information is used.

ERATOSTHENES uses privacy-preserving credentials to enhance security during authentication. This allows users to prove their identity without revealing unnecessary personal information. It leverages Physical Unclonable Functions to create unique keys for devices, exploiting tiny physical variations in their hardware. A Distributed Ledger Technology provides a secure infrastructure for storing and managing critical information, ensuring its integrity and availability. A Cyber Threat Intelligence Sharing Agent helps share security information across the network, allowing different parts of the system to learn from each other and respond to threats more effectively. And a Monitoring and Intrusion Detection System constantly monitors the network for potential threats, using machine learning to identify suspicious activity and anomalies.

The effectiveness of the ERATOSTHENES solution is being tested in three real-world pilot projects. One focuses on securing communication between vehicles and infrastructure, ensuring the safety and reliability of connected cars. Another secures a remote patient monitoring system, protecting sensitive patient data and ensuring the integrity of medical devices. And the third uses unique device IDs and secure data transfer methods to protect industrial networks, safeguarding critical infrastructure and preventing disruptions.

3.1 Introduction

With its ability to connect billions of objects and provide previously unheard-of levels of automation, data interchange, and ease, the Internet of Things (IoT) is drastically changing our world. IoT devices are influencing every part of our lives and industries, from industrial sensors and connected cars to smart homes and wearable fitness trackers. To guarantee the security and privacy of people and organizations, major security issues brought forth by this broad adoption must be resolved. The enormous growth of the attack surface is one of the main security issues with the Internet of Things. Every connected device is a possible point of entry for bad actors, and because there are so many of them, it is very challenging to properly secure them all. Because IoT systems are scattered and heterogeneous, traditional security solutions—which were created for centralized networks and personal computers—are frequently insufficient. In addition, a large number of IoT devices are built with constrained memory, computing power, and battery life. Because of this, it is difficult to put strong security measures in place without sacrificing functionality or efficiency, such as encryption and authentication procedures. Because of this, attackers looking to take advantage of weaknesses and obtain sensitive information without authorization can easily target these devices. Another major security concern is the heterogeneity of IoT devices. Numerous manufacturers produce these devices, and each has unique communication protocols, software, and hardware. It is challenging to create a single security posture and apply uniform security standards throughout the IoT ecosystem due to this lack of standardization.

The security of data created and sent by IoT devices is another significant worry. Large volumes of data, such as location data, behavioral patterns, and personal information, are gathered by these devices about users and their surroundings. This data may be intercepted, altered, or misused in the absence of appropriate security measures, which could result in identity theft, privacy violations, and other negative outcomes. These security issues are made worse by the intricacy of IoT ecosystems. Various devices, platforms, and networks are frequently integrated into these ecosystems, resulting in a complex web of relationships and interactions. Access control regulations, data exchange methods, and communication protocols must all be carefully considered in order to secure these interactions. To create uniform security standards and best practices, stakeholders must work together at the ecosystem level. Policymakers, network operators, software developers, and device manufacturers are all included in this. Together, they can build an IoT ecosystem that is more robust and safe. Another crucial component of IoT security is data governance. For the collection, storing, and processing of data produced by IoT devices, organizations must set up explicit policies and processes. This entails putting data anonymization and pseudonymization strategies into practice, getting user consent before collecting data, and adhering to pertinent data protection laws.

IoT security also depends on user awareness and education in addition to these technical precautions. Users must take precautions to protect themselves, such as using strong passwords, updating software, and exercising caution when disclosing personal information online, and be aware of the possible threats connected devices may pose. Although the IoT presents many difficulties, they are not insurmountable. We can maximize the advantages of modern technology while reducing the hazards by adopting a proactive and all-encompassing approach to security. All parties involved—device manufacturers, software developers, network operators, legislators, and users—must work together to accomplish this [1].

3.1.1 The ERATOSTHENES Project

Named after the famous Greek researcher, the ERATOSTHENES project seeks to address the complex security issues affecting the Internet of Things (IoT). It manages the full lifespan of IoT networks and focuses on a holistic approach to security. This ambitious project is part of the European Commission's intelligent security and privacy management program and was given 6 million in funding. ERATOSTHENES focuses on solutions for digital identification and distributed trust management in these intricate networks. Under the coordination of INLECOM INNOVATION in Greece, a broad group of 14 partners from 8 different countries work together on this project. The project begun in October 2021 and will be completed on March 2025. ERATOSTHENES recognizes a number of significant security obstacles impeding the development of an IoT environment that is truly secure.

First of all, it is very challenging to build trust and keep a clear image of the overall security position due to the vast diversity of devices and providers involved in the Internet of Things. The development of a cohesive and safe workplace is hampered by the frequently inadequate effectiveness of current trust-enforcement techniques and standards. Second, a lot of Internet of Things devices don't have frequent firmware updates or security patches installed. They become easy targets for attackers as a result of being exposed to known vulnerabilities and exploits. Thirdly, current procedures for safeguarding the privacy of user and device data frequently lack transparency. Users are frequently kept in the dark about the handling of their data.

Significant challenges are also created by a lack of proper security training and the adoption of security measures for both devices and people. Simply put, a lot of users are unaware of the security risks associated with using linked devices. Lastly, inadequate information exchange with cyberattack response teams, such Computer Emergency Response Teams (CERTs) and Computer Security Incident Response Teams (CSIRTs), impedes quick reaction and security threat mitigation. ERATOSTHENES is creating a unique Trust and Identity Management Framework especially for IoT devices in order to address these issues. This structure functions independently of a central authority and is dispersed throughout the network. It is more robust and less vulnerable to single points of failure because of its dispersed approach [2].

The following fundamental ideas guided the design of the framework:

- **Automation**: It reduces the human strain of security management by streamlining procedures for greater efficiency.
- **Auditability**: It facilitates security audits and ensures accountability by enabling transparent tracking and verification of actions.
- **Privacy**: It gives people more control over how their information is utilized and prioritizes their data privacy.

This framework seeks to strengthen trust, protect identities, and improve the overall resilience of the IoT ecosystem by efficiently managing the lifecycle of IoT devices, from initial deployment to decommissioning. Crucially, the framework will be constructed in accordance with pertinent laws, including the Cybersecurity Act, GDPR, and the NIS Directive, guaranteeing that it satisfies moral and legal requirements for data security and protection.

3.1.2 Challenges and Opportunities

Many IoT devices, such basic sensors or smart lightbulbs, are made with little memory and processing capability. Because of this, it is challenging to apply strong security measures, such as robust encryption, without compromising their efficiency or functionality. Similar to attempting to place a large security door on a tiny garden shed, it may not be feasible or even feasible. Additionally, some IoT devices have out-of-date software or no built-in security safeguards, leaving them vulnerable to manipulation, data breaches, and illegal access. Imagine someone accessing your security camera feed to snoop on you or breaking into your smart thermostat and turning up the heat.

Another level of complication is introduced by the IoT ecosystem's fragmented structure. Because of the wide variety of platforms, communication protocols, and devices, it is challenging to create uniform security requirements. The components may not fit together correctly, much like when you try to assemble a puzzle with pieces from various sets. It is difficult to guarantee security and compatibility throughout the IoT ecosystem due to this lack of standards. Lax restrictions don't always help, and some manufacturers regrettably put new features and usefulness ahead of security. Users' privacy is jeopardized and they become open to attacks.

In addition to these fundamental difficulties, there are a number of other important problems that must be resolved in order to secure IoT networks and devices. Numerous devices can be taken over by hackers, who can then use them to launch botnet attacks, which are large-scale attacks. These assaults have the potential to destroy vital infrastructure, steal data, and interfere with internet services. Concerns over the usage and security of the personal data collected by numerous IoT devices, including location data, browsing history, and health information, have been raised. This data may be intercepted, misused, or sold to third parties without your permission if appropriate security measures are not in place. For data transferred between devices to be protected, secure communication routes are necessary. Imagine your voice commands being sent over the internet by your smart speaker, unencrypted, so that anyone might listen in. To maintain confidentiality and stop unwanted access to private data, strong encryption is essential. To confirm the identification of users and devices, authentication procedures are required. This guarantees that only authorized individuals may operate your devices and stops unwanted access. Imagine someone breaking into your house without your knowing by using your smart lock.

It is essential to manage who can access and use IoT devices. To guarantee that users have control over their data and devices, this involves putting user consent procedures and access control policies into place. Security may also be jeopardized by flaws in the production and delivery procedures. Consider a malevolent actor tampering with devices before they are delivered to customers, introducing malware or backdoors that could be used later. Hackers can easily crack the weak encryption used by some devices. In addition to endangering your data, this enables hackers to intercept and alter device-to-device connections. It can be exceedingly difficult to maintain security over a wide network of different devices. To efficiently monitor and regulate access, identify threats, and handle incidents, centralized security management technologies and procedures are needed. The low resources of many IoT devices limit their capacity to identify intrusions. Because of this, they are susceptible to complex attacks that get beyond established defenses. Customers find it challenging to select secure equipment due to the absence of defined security testing and certification procedures. Customers are now responsible for researching and comprehending the security features of any device they buy, which can be a difficult undertaking. Most concerning of all is the possibility that compromised IoT devices may be exploited as entry points to assault entire networks, endangering everything. When it comes to vital infrastructure, such as power grids or healthcare systems, this is particularly troubling. Strong security measures are vitally necessary in these locations to avoid possibly devastating outcomes [3].

3.1.2.1 The Heterogeneous Landscape of IoT Security Challenges

The way we live, work, and engage with the world is being revolutionized by the Internet of Things (IoT), which is creating a complex web of interconnected devices. However, the cost of this interconnection is a complicated security environment that is always growing and changing. Securing this digital frontier is extremely difficult because to the wide variety of devices, specs, and suppliers that make up the IoT ecosystem. Consider a busy metropolis with a wide variety of structures, each with its own distinct architecture, security measures, and occupants. This is akin to the IoT landscape, where billions of devices with varying functionalities and security postures coexist. Because of this heterogeneity, it is quite challenging to fully comprehend the security threats that exist in an IoT network. It's similar to attempting to judge a city's level of security based on a few isolated buildings. The IoT ecosystem's wide range of devices are produced by numerous manufacturers and sellers, each with unique design principles, security procedures, and update schedules. This lack of standardization and coordination creates a fragmented security landscape where establishing trust becomes a significant hurdle. How can you be certain that a linked car from one manufacturer complies with the same security regulations as a smart refrigerator from another? The quick development of the Internet of Things frequently outpaces the capabilities of current trust protocols and standards. Many devices are installed with out-of-date firmware or software, which leaves them vulnerable to attacks. It's similar to having a city full of structures with antiquated security, which makes them prime targets for burglars.

Furthermore, the security threats are increased when these devices are not properly maintained and controlled. Many IoT devices are placed in remote areas or in settings where it is not feasible to perform routine security audits and updates. This exposes them to possible threats and compromises, such as leaving a building's doors open and unattended. These security problems may have far-reaching effects. IoT devices that have been compromised may be used as springboards for assaults on other networks or devices, the theft of private information, or even the disruption of vital infrastructure. Consider a hacker gaining access to a hospital's network via a weak medical equipment or taking over a traffic light network to wreak havoc. A multi-layered strategy is essential to navigating this dangerous terrain. Manufacturers of devices must put security first while designing and developing their products, adding strong security features and patching vulnerabilities on a regular basis. To safeguard their infrastructure and keep an eye out for questionable activities, network operators must put robust security measures in place. Additionally, users must be aware of the security threats connected to IoT devices and take precautions to keep themselves safe, like creating strong passwords, updating software, and sharing data with others.

3.1.2.2 Identity Management and Training Gaps

When it comes to identity management, the Internet of Things (IoT) poses a special difficulty. The Internet of Things is a huge network of devices, each with its own distinct identity and potential security flaws, in contrast to traditional computer networks where users are the main focus. This brings up important issues regarding the management and security of these identities as well as the protection of user and device privacy. Transparency is frequently lacking in current IoT identity management procedures. Users might not be aware of how their connected devices are gathering, storing, and using their data. In a similar vein, a network's authorization and authentication procedures could be inadequately thought out or executed. This lack of openness damages confidence and makes it challenging to hold people accountable in the event of security breaches.

Imagine living in a smart house with numerous linked devices that are all gathering information about your daily activities and habits. Are you aware of who has access to this data, where it is going, and how it is being used? Users are unaware of the security and privacy implications of their connected devices if identity management procedures are unclear and opaque. The absence of proper security procedures and training for both users and devices exacerbates this problem. Many consumers might not take the required safety precautions because they are ignorant of the security threats connected to IoT devices. Similar to this, a lot of devices are deployed with default settings or lack fundamental security protections, making them open to assaults. Furthermore, a lack of defined protocols and communication channels frequently hinders the efficacy of information sharing with incident response teams, such as Computer Emergency Response Teams (CERTs) and Computer Security Incident Response Teams (CSIRTs). This makes it more difficult for everyone to work together to quickly resolve security threats and vulnerabilities. It is comparable to a neighborhood watch in which nobody is aware of how to call the police in an emergency. Reacting to security events and lessening their effects require efficient information exchange.

A thorough strategy to identity management and security training is required to address these issues. This entails creating transparent and unambiguous identity management procedures that inform users about the collection and use of their data and enable safe, transparent authentication and authorization of devices. In order to educate consumers about the security threats connected with IoT devices and how to protect themselves, it is also necessary to provide them with thorough security training. It is crucial to put strong security standards in place for devices, making sure they have solid security features and are updated frequently to fix vulnerabilities. Lastly, timely information exchange regarding security risks and vulnerabilities would be made possible by the establishment of efficient communication channels with incident response teams. By addressing these challenges, we can create a more secure and trustworthy IoT ecosystem where users can confidently embrace the benefits of connected devices without compromising their privacy or security [4].

3.1.2.3 Blockchain

Blockchain technology provides a glimmer of light within the complicated security environment that the Internet of Things (IoT) presents. Think of blockchain as a digital ledger that is spread over several computers and records and verifies each transaction. Blockchain is a potent tool for boosting security in the IoT ecosystem because of its decentralized and impenetrable nature, which makes it extremely impossible for anyone to change or manipulate the data.

The capacity of blockchain to handle identities and build trust in the Internet of Things is one of its main advantages. On the blockchain, each device and user may have a distinct, verified identity, making authorization and authentication considerably simpler. This stops harmful activity and unauthorized access by limiting network and data access to trustworthy devices and people. Consider it your IoT devices' digital passport system. Every device has a distinct "passport" that is kept on the blockchain, confirming its identification and enabling safe communication with other users and devices. This lowers the possibility of single points of failure and does away with the requirement for a central authority to control IDs. Blockchain can also make it easier for devices to communicate securely with one another. It guarantees that only authorized parties can access and decode data by encrypting and verifying it within the blockchain itself. In the Internet of Things, where sensitive data is continuously transferred between devices, this is essential. Consider a factory with a network of sensors that communicate with one another to keep an eye on and manage the production process. By prohibiting hostile interference and data modification, blockchain technology can guarantee that this connection is safe and impenetrable.

Additionally, blockchain can provide firmware update integrity. Attackers are unable to alter or install harmful software because these changes are recorded and validated on the blockchain. Given that many IoT devices are placed in remote areas and might not be readily accessible for manual upgrades, this is especially crucial. Blockchain has the potential to offer decentralized governance, data integrity, and user privacy in the Internet of Things in addition to security. Blockchain can provide people more control over their data and how it is used by facilitating safe and transparent data management.

3.2 The ERATOSTHENES Project Technical Scope

3.2.1 Summary of Outcomes

ERATOSTHENES is creating a new system for managing trust and identities in the Internet of Things. This system is designed to work across an entire network of devices without relying on any central control point. This makes it more resilient and less vulnerable to attacks. The system is automated, which means it can handle many tasks automatically, making it more efficient. It's also designed to be transparent, allowing actions to be tracked and verified. This ensures accountability and helps build trust. Most importantly, the system prioritizes user privacy. It gives users control over their data and ensures their privacy is protected. By effectively managing the entire lifespan of IoT devices, from when they are first connected to when they are retired, this system strengthens trust and security within the network. It also makes the entire system more resilient to attacks and disruptions. Finally, the system is designed to comply with all relevant data protection and cybersecurity regulations, ensuring it meets the highest standards for security and privacy [5–7].

3.2.2 Technical Description of Components

3.2.2.1 Dynamic Trust Management

To build trust within the IoT network, the ERATOSTHENES solution uses a special **"Trust Broker" mechanism.** This mechanism has several components that work together to ensure security. Initially, a "trust score" is determined for every device. Similar to a credit score, this number indicates a device's level of reliability. The "trust manager," which also maintains track of device relationships and communicates trust data to the network, performs this computation. It securely stores and distributes this data using a technique known as Hyperledger Fabric. Consider the trust manager as a central repository that collects data about every device and establishes its level of trustworthiness. Other components of the system are then informed of this information. The "**MQTT Broker**," which serves as a filter for all events pertaining to trust, comes next. It also records the devices that are currently in use and any messages that they may have overlooked.

Think of this broker as a receptionist who manages all trust-related correspondence, both inbound and outbound. It ensures that no crucial signals are missed and that only pertinent information is conveyed. The "**Threat Modelling & Risk Assessment (TMRA)**" module is another crucial component of this process. To find possible risks and determine a risk score for every device, this module builds a virtual model of the system. Additionally, it has the ability to dynamically modify these scores in response to fresh data or system modifications. Consider this module as a security guard that continuously checks the system for possible threats and evaluates each device's risk level.

Last but not least is the "**MUD manager**," which decodes data regarding the device's access requirements from the manufacturer. After that, it generates access control lists (ACLs), which function similarly to digital "permission slips" and specify what each network device is allowed to access. Consider the MUD manager as a permissions administrator who controls which network resources are accessible to which devices. The Trust Broker mechanism offers a thorough method of controlling security and trust in the Internet of Things network by integrating these elements. It guarantees secure communication between trusted devices and restricts access to the network.

The **Trust Agent Deployer** (TAD) is a unique tool used by the **Trust Manager & Broker** (TMB). Consider the TAD as a manager for "trust agents"—small software components that aid in maintaining network device security. The TAD oversees these agents' whole lifecycle, not just their installation. This entails updating them, repairing them in the event that they malfunction, and even swapping them out for more recent, secure models. The TAD continuously collects data from the devices it oversees in order to accomplish this efficiently. It uses this data to make informed decisions about how to control the software on every device. It is comparable to a gardener who continuously checks on their plants to ensure they are receiving enough nutrients, sunlight, and water. The TAD simultaneously maintains a list of every trust agent that is available. This enables it to select the appropriate agent for every device according to its unique requirements and attributes. Each item is paired with the ideal trust agent to ensure its safety, much like a dating service. When trust agents malfunction or are compromised, the TAD is also essential in repairing them. It can either replace them completely with a new, updated version or return them to a safe state. It's like a mechanic who can repair a damaged car part or replace it with a brand new one. To put it briefly, the TAD acts as a committed protector for the trust agents, making sure they are always operating properly and safeguarding the devices in the network. This helps maintain the overall security and trustworthiness of the IoT ecosystem.

Consider certain IoT devices to have an integrated, safe vault. This "vault," known as a **Trusted Execution Environment** (TEE), guards against unauthorized parties accessing or altering crucial software components. This safe vault is used by several components of the ERATOSTHENES system. This secured environment, for instance, is where the "Advanced Data Protector," which protects sensitive data, operates. This vault is also where components of the system that handle trust and digital identities function. The TEE improves the system's overall security by offering this safe area. It serves as a fortress, preventing attacks on vital operations and guaranteeing their secure operation. Although trust, identities, and data protection are not directly managed by the TEE, these tasks are indirectly supported by it by offering a safe environment in which its essential components operate. It ensures the stability and security of the entire building, acting as a foundation.

3.2.2.2 Advanced Identity Management

ERATOSTHENES puts users in control of their own digital identities and data. It does this through a system called "**Self-Sovereign Identity**" (SSI), which you can think of as a digital ID card that you own and control. This SSI system has two main parts:

1. **SSI Management:** This part lives on a central server and helps create and manage user identities. It works with a special tool called the "Ledger uSelf Broker" to do this. Imagine this as the office where you would go to get your ID card issued.
2. **SSI Agent:** This part lives directly on your IoT device. It allows your device to use its digital ID card to interact with the system securely. Think of this as the card reader that checks your ID card.

The **Trusted Execution Environment** (TEE), a secure section of your device, is where the SSI Agent operates to further increase security. This guarantees that all of your personal data is safe and available only in this restricted area. Keeping your ID card kept in a safe is analogous to that. Additionally, the TEE employs cutting-edge data protection mechanisms to provide an additional degree of security, guaranteeing that your private data is only accessible within the safe hardware environment. It is comparable to having a security guard guard your safe.

ERATOSTHENES employs cutting-edge technologies to safeguard your identity and private data. One of these devices functions similarly to a unique ID card, revealing only the information that is strictly required and concealing the rest. A method known as "**privacy-preserving Attribute-Based Credentials**" (p-ABC) is used to do this. Consider having to provide proof of age in order to attend a movie theater. You can use this unique ID card to merely demonstrate that you are of legal age without disclosing your name, address, or other personal information, as opposed to presenting your full driver's license with all of your personal information. Additionally, the system makes use of a technology known as "**Distributed Ledger Technology**" (DLT), which functions similarly to an open public record book. Important data, including as public keys and credential types, are kept in this record book, but your personal information is not. ERATOSTHENES employs a unique module that enables safe authentication without disclosing extraneous information in order to further improve privacy. It functions similarly to a secret code that verifies your identification without disclosing any personal information.

Privacy is safeguarded during the identity management process thanks to the cooperation of this module with other system components. Another important function is played by the public record book (DLT), which offers transparent and safe means of exchanging information without jeopardizing your privacy. ERATOSTHENES also employs other instruments to bolster security. It's similar to having several levels of security, such as a distinct fingerprint for every device and a unique system to safeguard private data. Combining these cutting-edge methods, ERATOSTHENES develops an identity management system that protects your personal information in the Internet of Things and provides you control over your data. Identity information security is a top priority for ERATOSTHENES, particularly when it comes to retrieving such data from your Internet of Things devices. To protect this data, it makes use of a unique part known as the **Advanced Data Protector** (ADP).

Think of the ADP as a secure storage container on your device, specifically designed to protect your identity data. This container utilizes your device's built-in security features to ensure your information is encrypted and stored safely. This secure storage is important for backing up your identity data to a separate server. However, because the ADP is so focused on security, it makes it a bit tricky to simply export your information. To make backup and recovery easier, ERATOSTHENES is enhancing the ADP. The goal is to find a balance between keeping your data secure and making it accessible when you need to recover it.

Unique and unpredictable keys are essential for strong security, and ERATOSTHENES employs a new method known as PUFs (Physical Unclonable Functions) to accomplish this. PUFs provide unique and unclonable keys by exploiting small, random physical variances within each device, such as variations in the material it is built of. It's similar to how every device has a distinct fingerprint. The IoT devices themselves are referred to as "low-level" entities in the ERATOSTHENES system, while the central components that oversee the system are referred to as "high-level" entities. Imagine it like employees and managers in a business.

The clients (devices) can only interact with specific managers (system components) after they've been registered and authorized. This registration process happens during manufacturing to ensure the devices are secure from the start. Each device uses special applications to connect securely with the system. These applications are like secure communication channels that ensure only authorized devices can connect. They are also tailored to each specific device, preventing counterfeits and duplicates. For highly sensitive devices, these applications can even self-destruct if they detect any tampering, adding an extra layer of protection. It's like a secret agent destroying their communication device if it falls into the wrong hands. The system can also be combined with other security measures to protect against various attacks, like someone trying to inject malicious code or manipulate the device's software. The flexible design of ERATOSTHENES allows for customized security applications for each device. It can even be fully automated, making it work like a security service that constantly protects the system. In essence, ERATOSTHENES leverages PUFs and other security measures to create a robust and adaptable security ecosystem for the IoT. This ensures that devices are authenticated, communication is secure, and sensitive data is protected from unauthorized access and tampering.

3.2.2.3 Lifecycle Consideration of IoT Devices

"**Distributed Ledger Technology**" (DLT), a unique technology used by ERATOSTHENES, functions similarly to a shared and secure digital ledger. This blockchain-based technology facilitates the seamless operation of many system components. Consider this digital record book as a primary repository for sharing and storing vital information. This includes details regarding cyberthreats, trust scores, and device IDs. This shared record book is used by various system components, such as the Trust Manager and Identity Manager, to access and maintain their data. Because Hyperledger Fabric provides the necessary security, flexibility, and storage capacity, ERATOSTHENES employs it expressly for this purpose.

Different portions, referred to as "channels," within this shared record book correspond to various system components. Additionally, there is a dedicated channel that facilitates information exchange between various regions. It's similar to having safe communication and information sharing amongst various departments inside a business. Additionally, ERATOSTHENES makes use of special agents who exchange data regarding cyberthreats. By gathering information from many sources and disseminating it to other areas of the system, these agents serve as messengers.

Consider these agents as interconnected security personnel who work together to maintain the system's security. To enable other guards to respond, they collect information about possible threats and disseminate it to them. These agents operate in two ways: they gather data from external sources and from within the system, such as an intrusion detection system. Other components of the system are then given access to this data in order to enhance their security protocols.

3.2.2.4 Intrusion Detection for IoT

Additionally, this security system employs a method known as "federated learning" to detect attacks on network edge devices. Consider a system of security cameras that communicate with one another to provide a comprehensive view of the situation. As a result, the system is better equipped to learn and adjust to emerging threats. In order to keep the entire community secure, everyone shares their observations, just as in a neighborhood watch.

These elements work together to form a potent threat analysis and detection system. They make it simple to monitor and react to security occurrences by offering unified warnings via a common interface. Security staff can swiftly evaluate and react to any situation thanks to a central security hub that gets notifications from all of the network's cameras and sensors.

Through a communication link, the system also exchanges data with other components of the ERATOSTHENES security system. This makes it possible to react to any risks that are identified in a coordinated manner. It functions similarly to a direct channel of communication between the security cameras, the central hub, and the ground-based security staff, guaranteeing that everyone is aware of any security breaches and can cooperate to resolve them.

3.3 Results Validation and Use Cases

The deployment of all technological components (as previously mentioned) into three industrial use cases is part of the robust integration and deployment stage that the various technologies of the ERATOSTHENES security stack are presently undergoing. These pilots operate as hands-on tests to confirm the ERATOSTHENES solution's operational and technical efficacy. Below is a discussion of the three pilots:

V2X Communication Security: Vehicle-to-Everything (V2X) communication in a regulated setting is the main focus of the first pilot. It looks at two important use cases: standardized software update procedures for connected cars and cybersecurity protocols. The pilot will illustrate the difficulties in establishing confidence in V2X communication, especially while software updates are being implemented. Next, it will demonstrate how ERATOSTHENES technology can identify malevolent actors, detect network anomalies, and keep systems resilient to cyberattacks. The project's capacity to resolve security issues and guarantee the dependability of V2X communication infrastructure is highlighted by this trial.

Remote Patient Monitoring: A remote patient monitoring system for long-term conditions like COPD or diabetes is the focus of the second trial. By enabling patients to control their diseases and get care from home, this method encourages self-care and lowers the number of hospital visits. The Personal Health Gateway, which is situated in each patient's home, is a crucial part of this study. Data from a variety of medical sensors is gathered by this gateway and safely sent to cloud-based services for monitoring and analysis.

Disposable IDs for Industrial Network Security: The third pilot, which aims to secure connected devices, data transfer, and analytics in dynamic and heterogeneous industrial networks, is focused on Industry 4.0 applications. This project, called "Industry 4.0 (disposable IDs)," uses PUFs and DLT in tandem to create secure, one-of-a-kind disposable IDs for every device. By serving as unique device fingerprints, these IDs allow for safe network identification. By guaranteeing strong device identification and improving data security and reliability, this novel method fortifies the industrial network's overall security architecture.

Acknowledgements

This project has received funding from the European Union's Horizon 2020 research and innovation programme under grant agreement no 101020416. The authors acknowledge the research outcomes of this publication belonging to the ERATOSTHENES (101020416) project consortium.

References

[1] K. Loupos, B. Caglayan, A. Papageorgiou, B. Starynkevitch, F. Vedrine, C. Skoufis, S. Christofi, B. Karakostas, A. Mygiakis, G. Theofilis, A. Chiappetta, H. Avgoustidis, George Boulougouris – COGNITION ENABLED IOT PLATFORM FOR INDUSTRIAL IOT SAFETY, SECURITY AND PRIVACY – THE CHARIOT PROJECT, IEEE International Workshop on Computer Aided Modeling and Design of Communication Links and Networks (CAMAD), IEEE XPLORE, 11–13 September 2019, Limassol, Cyprus, DOI: 10.1109/CAMAD.2019.8858488.

[2] K. Loupos, A. Papageorgiou, A. Mygiakis, B. Caglayan, B. Karakostas, T. Krousarlis, F. Vedrine, C. Skoufis, S. Christofi, G. Theofilis, H. Avgoustidis, G. Boulougouris, A. Battaglia, M. Villiani – COGNITIVE PLATFORM FOR INDUSTRIAL IOT SYSTEM SECURITY, SAFETY AND PRIVACY,

Embedded World 2020 Conference and Exhibition, 25–27 Feb. 2020, Nuremberg, Germany.

[3] K. Loupos – INTEGRATED SOLUTION FOR PRIVACY AND SECURITY OF IOT DEVICES IN CRITICAL INFRASTRUCTURES, Critical Infrastructure Protection and Resilience Europe (CIPRE 2020), 6–8 Oct. 2020, Bucharest, Romania.

[4] K. Loupos, C. Kalogirou, H. Niavis, A. F. Skarmeta, E. Torroglosa-Garcia, A. Palomares, H. Song, P.E. Brun, F. Giampaolo, D. V. Landuyt, S. Michiels, B. Podgorelec, C. Xenakis, M. Bampatsikos, K. Krilakis – A HOLISTIC APPROACH FOR IOT NETWORKS' IDENTITY AND TRUST MANAGEMENT – THE ERATOSTHENES PROJECT, 4th Workshop on Internet of Things Security and Privacy (WISP), Global IoT Summit 2022, Dublin, June 2022.

[5] O. Vermesan, M. Coppola, M. Diaz Nava, A. Capra, G. Kornaros, R. Bahr, E. Darmois, M. Serrano, P. Guillemin, K. Loupos, L. Karagiannidis, S. McGrath – New Waves of IoT Technologies Research – TRANSCENDING INTELLIGENCE AND SENSES AT THE EDGE TO CREATE MULTI EXPERIENCE ENVIRONMENTS, Internet of Things – The Call of the Edge – Everything Intelligent Everywhere, River Publishers, DK, October 2020, ISBN: 9788770221962, e-ISBN – 9788770221962.

[6] K. Loupos, C. Kalogirou, H. Niavis, A. F. Skarmeta, E. Torroglosa-Garcia, A. Palomares, H. Song, P.E. Brun, F. Giampaolo, D. V. Landuyt, S. Michiels, B. Podgorelec, C. Xenakis, M. Bampatsikos, K. Krilakis – A HOLISTIC APPROACH FOR IOT NETWORKS' IDENTITY AND TRUST MANAGEMENT – THE ERATOSTHENES PROJECT, Lecture Notes in Computer Science book series (LNCS,volume 13533), DOI: 10.1007/978-3-031-20936-9_27.

[7] A. M. Frutos, J. G. Rodríguez, A. Skarmeta, K. Loupos, S. Vavilis, F. Michalopoulos – IDENTITY AND TRUST ARCHITECTURE FOR DEVICE LIFECYCLE MANAGEMENT, Future Generation Computer Systems, Volume 162, January 2025, Science Direct, Elsevier

DOI: 10.1561/9781638285076.ch4

Chapter 4

An Architecture for Dynamic Trust Management in IoT Security

By Stef Verreydt, Dimitri Van Landuyt, Michail Bampatsikos, Rustem Dautov, Hui Song, Shukun Tokas, Tom Van Eyck, Sam Michiels, Apostolis Zarras, Thodoris Ioannidis, Christos Xenakis, Danny Hughes and Wouter Joosen

Contemporary IoT applications are faced with unprecedented security challenges: they often operate in untrusted or adversarial environments, and the large number of devices creates management complexity and amplifies attack surfaces that are easily beyond manual control. These challenges are exacerbated by limited computational capabilities of some devices and the sheer heterogeneity in terms of technology and capability across device classes.

As traditional security by design approaches focus on introducing and imposing specific countermeasures, these solutions are rigid and static by nature. They are unfit for dealing with the highly dynamic and changing reality in which new technologies continuously emerge, devices migrate, and new attacks and vulnerabilities are discovered at high frequency. In this chapter, we present our joint work on dynamic trust, more specifically, we present a set of mutually reinforcing and integrated technologies that contribute to the run-time assessment of device trust. This notion of trust is highly-context specific, and takes into account (i) device capabilities, (ii) application context, (iii) prior knowledge of devices, and (iv) existing security guarantees.

The establishment and the continuous re-assessment of trust scores is a key enabler for building adaptive systems that change their behavior and expectations in function of these trust scores, and this risk-adaptive capability in the end leads to more resilient and secure IoT systems.

Glossary of Terms and Abbreviations Used

Abbreviation	Definition
ADP	Advanced Data Protector (or Data Protector)
API	Application Programming Interface
CPS	Cyber Physical System
CPU	Central Processing Unit
CTI	Cyber Threat Intelligence
DFD	Data Flow Diagram
DID	Decentralized Identifier
DLT	Distributed Ledger Technologies
DoS	Denial-of-Service
DT	Digital Twin
DTA	Deployer of Trust Agents (or Trust Agent Deployer)
FAIR	Factor Analysis of Information Risk
gRPC	Google Remote Procedure Call
ID	Identifier
IDS	Intrusion Detection System
IoT	Internet of Things
MADM	Multi-Attribute Decision Making
MQTT	Message Queuing Telemetry Transport, a publish-subscribe messaging protocol
MQTTS	Secure variant of MQTT
MUD	Manufacturer Usage Description
OP-TEE	Open-source operating system for Arm-TrustZone TEEs
OS	Operating System
PDP	Policy Decision Point
PoSE	Proof of Secure Erasure
PUF	Physical Unclonable Function
QEMU	Quick Emulator
RA	Remote Attestation
REST	Representational State Transfer, an architectural style for APIs
RPC	Remote Procedure Call
SC	Smart Contract

SP	Service Provider
SPARTA	Threat modeling tool developed at DistriNet
SR	Service Requester
SSH	Secure Shell, a protocol for secure communication
SSI	Self-Sovereign Identity
SSL	Secure Sockets Layer, a standard for encrypted communication
STRIDE	A threat modeling acronym for Spoofing, Tampering, Repudiation, Information disclosure, Denial of service, and Elevation of privilege.
TA	Trust Agent
TCG	Trusted Computing Group
TEE	Trusted Execution Environment
TLS	Transport Layer Security
TMB	Trust Manager and Broker
TMRA	Threat Modeling and Risk Assessment
TOPSIS	Technique for Order of Preference by Similarity to Ideal Solution
URL	Uniform Resource Locator
UUID	Universally Unique Identifier
VC	Verifiable Credentials
VP	Verifiable Presentations
W3C	World Wide Web Consortium
ZKP	Zero-Knowledge Proof

4.1 Introduction

Contemporary Internet of Things (IoT) applications rely on diverse IoT devices embedded typically in an untrusted environment such as public spaces or within the physical control of users that may be incentivized to attack or game the overall system. For example, smart vehicles can be tampered with by their owners or other malicious actors, which may negatively impact the behavior of a smart traffic application. In other words, the trustworthiness of an IoT application depends on the trustworthiness of the individual IoT devices. In this context, 'trustworthiness' of an IoT device encompasses several aspects, including trust in the device's identity, trust in its behavior, and trust in the accuracy of the data produced by it. Therefore, measures should be taken to detect devices which are not who they claim to be, behave in unexpected ways, or produce inaccurate data, and to tackle such issues. Furthermore, communications with IoT devices in untrusted environments should also be secured to prevent tampering and information disclosure threats. Finally, as IoT devices are usually heterogeneous in nature, and some may employ legacy

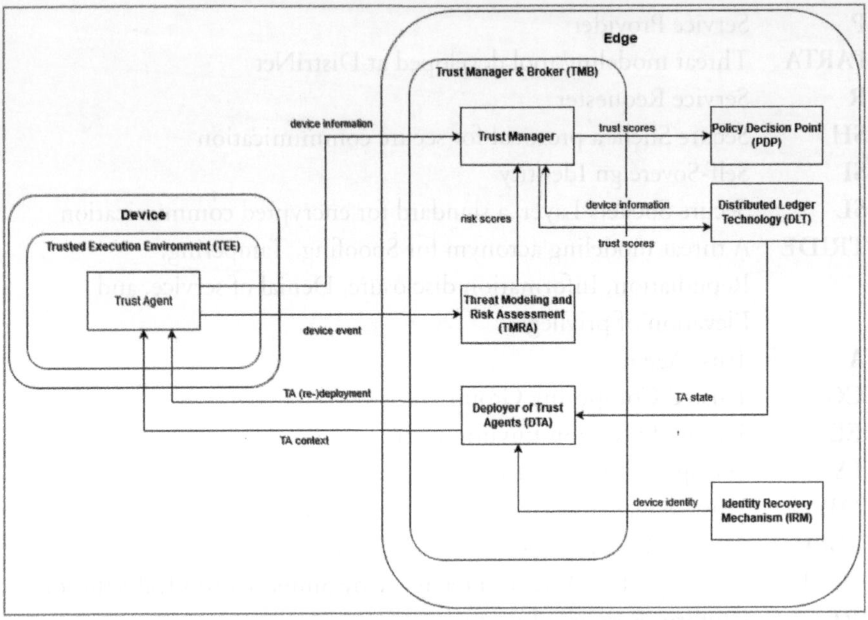

Figure 4.1. High-level overview of the trust components and their interaction.

technologies, managing device trust and secure communications becomes even more challenging. This chapter describes the efforts taken during the ERATOSTHENES project (Horizon 2020 research and innovation program under grant agreement No 101020416) to foster trust management throughout the device life cycle.

From the architectural perspective, a trust layer is created in the Edge that hinges upon the interplay between a central Trust Manager and Broker (TMB) that interacts with a Trust Agent (TA) installed on the IoT device. This is shown in Figure 4.1.

The TA (depicted on the left) runs on the IoT device and locally collects information such as contextual parameters (e.g., CPU/memory/storage usage, services available and their version numbers, etc.) and relays them to the TMB, either on demand (via a 'pull' interface), or proactively/recurrently (via a 'push' interface).

The TMB is a subsystem residing on the computational layer near the device – the Edge – and subscribes to and aggregates this information coming from the devices. It also subscribes to other external sources of information related to individual devices. For example, when a device has migrated from a different domain, prior device information such as trust scores are fetched through the Distributed Ledger (DLT), which is a blockchain-driven information sharing system. Based on all these inputs, trust calculation is performed by the Trust Manager, leading to a score that expresses the extent to which the device can be trusted, and this device trust information is made accessible to trust consumers. For example, when the user or the application wants to perform a certain action in the system, the access control system, and more specifically the Policy Decision Point (PDP) may take into account traditional elements such as user attributes but also can base specific access decisions on the trust score of the device.

In the presented solution, these information exchanges between the TA and the TMB are performed using the MQTT protocol. The fetching of local device context is highly dependent on the nature of the device and the implementation of the TA. The TMB itself shares trust calculation outcomes via MQTT events, but also stores these trust scores in the aforementioned shared ledger (DLT).

The interplay between the device and the TMB is the main point of focus of this chapter. The TMB itself groups a number of technologies and the trust calculation algorithms take into account different types of security mechanisms that may or may not be at play in the specific context of a device.

Several trust-related services and tools have been incepted, implemented, and integrated in this broader architecture:

- The Threat Modeling and Risk Assessment (TMRA) module performs threat modeling to evaluate specific threat scenarios—specific cases that may involve security issues—in an application-specific manner. The TMRA creates and maintains a digital twin model of the operational systems and performs the automated generation of STRIDE threat scenarios and FAIR-based risk quantification. Risk scores and outcomes are then shared with the TMB.
- The core mechanism described above hinges upon the availability and reliability of Trust Agents on the IoT devices. Technology for the automated (re)deployment of Trust Agents (DTA) on heterogenous devices has been created with specific attention for practical feasibility and scalability of the mechanism towards larger collections of devices (fleets) while dealing with the spurious availability of the devices. Furthermore, to foster the availability and integrity of the Trust Agents, specific support has been created for remote, automatic and secure recovery/roll-back of the TA itself. In specific scenarios where the integrity of the TA cannot be fully guaranteed, or when bootstrapping new devices (e.g. upon initial enrolment), this mechanism provides a key secure stepping stone.
- The capability of some device classes to support Trusted Execution Environments (TEE) is an enabler for trust. Trusted execution refers to the ability to perform remote attestation, i.e. to remotely verify and ensure the correctness of a computational outcome. Evidently, when such technology is available on devices, it can be used and should be taken into account in trust calculation, as the stronger guarantees of the correct execution on the devices

greatly increase the trust in these devices. Specific middleware support has been created to enable secure, remote communication to services running in the TEE, which is crucial to attain the desired level of guarantee.

- The trust mechanism complicates the overall enrollment and bootstrapping process of new devices. Indeed, it may occur that the overall system becomes overly restrictive, i.e. that a new device has not yet provided any enabler for trust, and thus is simply not allowed to perform any action, thus further prohibiting any meaningful use. To alleviate this, and make the overall bootstrapping process practically viable, the entire enrolment process or workflow of a new device has been incepted, designed and implemented for a diverse set of devices, heterogeneous in capability and level of support. The predominant focus in these developments has been to come up with viable strategies to deal with differences in device capability.

Together, these technologies contribute to a new approach of dealing with IoT security, with dynamism and adaptiveness at the core of the trust mechanism.

The remainder of this Chapter provides a more in-depth and technological overview of each of these technical contributions.

4.2 Trust Broker

4.2.1 Introduction to the Trust Manager and Broker

Trust is fundamental to IoT security since establishing trust between devices, networks, and users is essential for secure and reliable interoperability in IoT ecosystems. More specifically, trust in IoT networks refers to the belief that one IoT device, the Service Provider (SP), will behave correctly and as expected by prospective Service Requester (SR) IoT devices. The enforcement of trust in an artificial society such as IoT is far more difficult, as things do not have an inherent judgmental ability to assess risks and other influencing factors to evaluate trust as humans do. Hence, it is important to quantify "trust" in a manner that can be understood by artificial entities such as IoT devices.

One way to quantify trust is the trust score, a value that reflects a relationship between trustor and trustee, measured by trust metrics, and evaluated by a trust assessment mechanism. Several trust management and evaluation mechanisms focus mainly on security and privacy issues instead of considering the universal meaning of trust and its inherently dynamic nature.

A trust algorithm must calculate a device's trust score, considering various scenarios and trustworthiness-related parameters. To this end, the trust algorithm must be able to collect this information. Due to the high complexity and dynamic of

IoT networks with a constantly increasing and changing number of devices, it became apparent that the trust algorithm had to be run on several nodes with high computational resources known as the TMB nodes. This design decision enabled IoT devices to perform their duties without unnecessarily occupying their limited resources by offloading the computation burden to computationally powerful nodes.

With these considerations in mind, the ERATOSTHENES project deemed it necessary to charge the TMB with the following duties:

- To evaluate an IoT device's trustworthiness and compute its trust score.
- To facilitate the exchange of trust-related information among IoT devices and domain services.

To evaluate a device's trustworthiness, the TMB aggregates trust-related information from multiple sources, including the ERATOSTHENES Intrusion Detection System (IDS), the TMRA (discussed in Section 4.3), and the IoT devices. This results in a comprehensive trust evaluation approach encompassing device-specific characteristics, network threats, and security incidents. Communication between the devices, modules, and the TMB is facilitated through the MQTT protocol, enabling the TMB to calculate a device's trust score.

The MQTT protocol is a lightweight messaging protocol specifically engineered for small sensors and mobile devices. It is optimized for operation over high-latency or unreliable networks, common characteristics of IoT environments.

The MQTT protocol functions through two primary components: the **MQTT Broker** and the **MQTT Clients**. The **MQTT Broker** serves as the server that receives and directs client messages to the relevant destination clients. On the other hand, **MQTT clients** are devices or applications that connect to the broker to publish messages, subscribe to specific topics, or engage in both activities.

To guarantee secure communication, the MQTT protocol supports client authentication through usernames and passwords. It also encrypts the data exchanged between clients and the broker using SSL/TLS and implements topic-based access control to manage the permissions related to publishing and subscribing.

An important consideration in the design and implementation of the TMB, particularly the trust score calculation algorithm, is the diversity of application contexts in which IoT devices operate. The ERATOSTHENES project identifies three main IoT network application contexts: (a) Connected Vehicles, (b) Industry 4.0, and (c) Smart Health. Accordingly, different trust metrics are prioritized within each context, with certain metrics carrying more weight than others in determining a device's overall trust score.

4.2.2 Device Trustworthiness Evaluation

The evaluation of a device's trustworthiness, as discussed earlier, is influenced by various device-specific parameters (e.g., the device's CPU utilization) as well as assessments derived from ERATOSTHENES services, such as the TMRA and IDS. As a result, assessing a device's trustworthiness becomes a complex multi-attribute problem. Additionally, an SR may need to determine which SP to approach for a specific service. Thus, evaluating device trustworthiness is formulated as a Multi-Attribute Decision Making (MADM) [1] problem.

To address this issue, the TMB offers two key functionalities: (a) the computation of a device's trust score and (b) the ranking of devices within the network based on their trustworthiness. The first functionality quantifies a device's trustworthiness, while the second aids prospective SRs in selecting the appropriate SP for the desired service.

Both functionalities rely on a set of device-related parameters (e.g., root of trust, associated cyber risks), along with corresponding weights that reflect the significance of each parameter in determining the device's trustworthiness. The trust score is calculated using a weighted sum function, while the ranking of devices is carried out via the Technique for Order of Preference by Similarity to Ideal Solution (TOPSIS) [2], a widely adopted ranking method.

Whenever a significant event occurs for a device (e.g., a software update), the TMB triggers the trust score calculation and TOPSIS functions to reassess the device's trustworthiness. The specific weights used in the weighted sum function and TOPSIS are context-dependent, varying according to the particular application domain in which the IoT device operates. The concept "application context" refers to the type of IoT ecosystem the device is part of, such as Connected Vehicles, Industry 4.0-enabled factories, or Smart Medical Devices. Even if certain trust-related parameters remain consistent across different contexts, the weighting of those parameters differs according to the specific ecosystem.

The TMB works as follows. Initially, an IoT device's TA establishes an MQTT connection to the TMB, and then the former publishes the device's data on an MQTT topic. The broker component of the TMB collects this data. It forwards them to the TMB's internal modules, namely the TMRA, Manufacturer Usage Description (MUD) manager, IDS, and the Cyber Threat Intelligence (CTI) manager, which are also MQTT clients. These modules process the device data and send their outputs to the MQTT broker, who forwards them to the Trust Manager functionality of the TMB or other MQTT clients. Then, the Trust Manager invokes the trust score calculation function and the TOPSIS implementations to conduct the device trust assessment. Once the trust score is calculated, the TMB invokes a gRPC Remote Procedure Call through its gRPC client to the DLT's gRPC server.

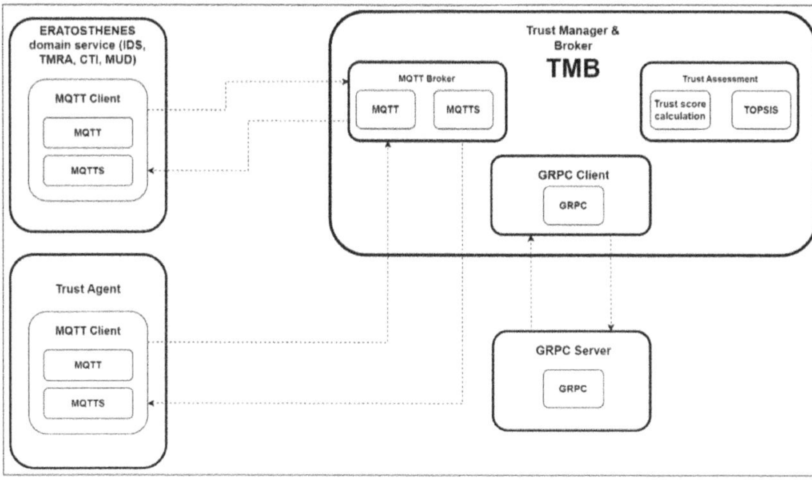

Figure 4.2. High-level overview of the protocols facilitating the interaction between the TMB, IoT Devices and ERATOSTHENES services.

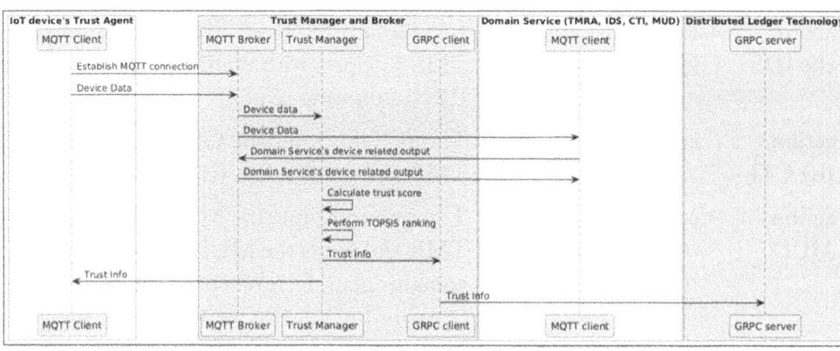

Figure 4.3. Trust score calculation sequence diagram.

Through this call, it writes the trust score to the DLT while it informs the device via an MQTT message about its corresponding trust score [3]. Figure 4.2 provides a high-level overview of the interactions between the TMB, the devices, and the other services of the ERATOSTHENES architecture. Furthermore, it depicts the components that make up the TMB. The operational flow of a device's trust score calculation is shown in the sequence diagram depicted in Figure 4.3.

The trust evaluation is event-triggered; these events are messages transmitted over MQTT topics. Table 4.1 describes these events and their corresponding topics.

4.2.3 Summary

In summary, the TMB plays a vital role in the ERATOSTHENES ecosystem's architecture since it acts as the enabler of communication between the TMRA, the IoT devices, the MUD manager, the CTI agent and the IDS. Moreover, it facilitates

Table 4.1. MQTT events that trigger trust evaluation.

Event	Topic	Payload/description
New device	entity/entityID/new	Device (entity) type and parameters (A new device sends its trust related information).
Device removed	entity/entityID/remove	An announcement to remove a device from the network.
Device data	device/entityID/data	Device Data (Through this topic, the TA sends the Device Data to the TMB.)
Trust Score Calculation	entity/entityID/agent/calculate	Initial or updated trust score for a device (the TMB calculates the trust score of a device with a specific ID and forwards it to the subscribers of that topic.)
Risk score calculation	entity/entityID/tmra/riskscore	A risk score computed by the TMRA module. (Through this topic, the TMB will receive the risk score from the TMRA module for the device with the specified ID.)
Interaction with the IDS	entity/entityID/ids	IDS monitoring score. (Through this topic, the TMB interacts with the IDS module to obtain an IDS monitoring score.)
Interaction with the CTI	entity/entityID/cti	Through this topic the CTI interacts with the TMB and sends threat related information.
Interaction with MUD	entity/entityID/mud/MUDfilejson	Through this topic the MUD interacts with the TMB and sends the MUDfile, a json file which contains manufacturer specification and expected behavior for a device with a specific ID.

the formation of trust relationships between entities in the IoT network as well as evaluates the trustworthiness of IoT devices and manages trust records for every IoT device. The most prominent feature of the TMB is that it considers multiple aspects related to an IoT device before evaluating its trustworthiness. Finally, by facilitating the transmission of trust information through the DLT the TMB plays a crucial role in forming trust relationships among different domains.

4.3 Threat Modeling and Risk Assessment

Trust in an IoT system entails multiple aspects: trust in the identity of a device, trust in it behaving according to expectations, trust in the validity of the messages it sends, and so on. Assessing these aspects requires considering potential security threats and their associated risk. For example, an IoT device that implements outdated authentication mechanisms is more likely to be spoofed, and unencrypted

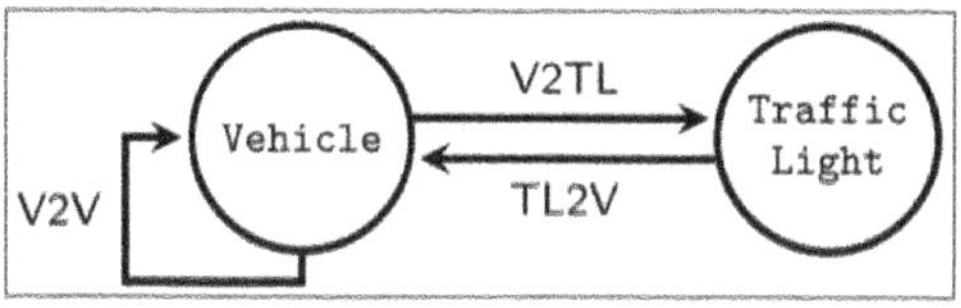

Figure 4.4. Example DFD for a connected vehicles application.

data flows are easily tampered with, which should be taken into account when calculating trust scores.

One way to identify security threats and estimate their risk is threat modeling, which involves the up-front investigation of common security threats in a system's design or architecture, both in terms of whether they would be feasible (likelihood) and the consequential harm (impact). Systematic, system-centric approaches act upon an abstraction of the system under design. This abstraction usually takes the form of a Data Flow Diagram (DFD), which defines the envisioned or anticipated data flows between processes, (external) entities and data stores. An example DFD for a connected vehicles system is depicted in Figure 4.4. Based on this DFD, potential security and privacy threats can be identified by iterating over all elements, for example that vehicles can be spoofed, and data flows can be tampered with.

Numerous threat modeling methodologies and tools [4] exist to automate (parts of) this workflow, for example through automated threat elicitation or risk calculation. All of these, however, consider risk at the design level, without considering that the risk for specific entities or instances of design-level entities may differ considerably based on certain parameters or the specific context. For example, spoofing a priority vehicle is potentially more severe compared to spoofing a non-priority one, and different vehicles may implement different authentication methods, some of which may be stronger than others. The lack of expressivity in existing threat modeling approaches has shown to be especially problematic in architectural styles such as peer-to-peer or decentralized systems in which the modeled system elements are not singular nor centrally governed. For example, an earlier study has identified this particular issue hindering the threat analysis of distributed ledger applications [5]. While such approaches allow to assess risk at the basis of class-level elements, they fail to consider and address risk factors that emerge at instance level. This, in turn, hinders device-specific trust calculation taking into account security risk factors, for example for the specific vehicles depicted in Figure 4.5.

4.3.1 Instance-centric Threat Modeling

To tackle this issue, and allow risk assessments for specific IoT devices, the TMRA module implements a novel threat modeling framework called 'instance-centric threat modeling' [6] which enables specifying and analyzing both the high-level

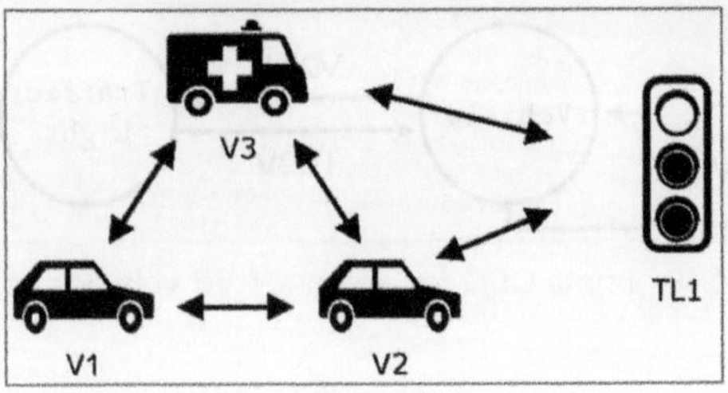

Figure 4.5. Example of a specific connected vehicles scenario [6].

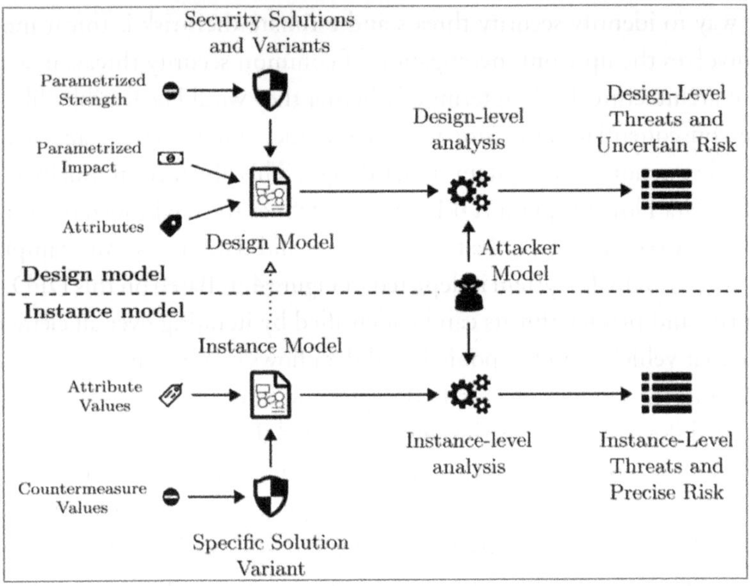

Figure 4.6. High-level overview of instance-centric threat modeling. The design model (e.g. Figure 4.4) specifies the high-level structure of a system and can be analyzed to reveal major flaws in the design, but the resulting risk values will be inherently uncertain as the design model covers all potential configurations and scenarios. One or more instance models (e.g. Figure 4.5) can be created to model specific instances of the entities in the design model, with concrete parameters, which allows for more precise risk calculation [7].

design of a system (e.g., Figure 4.4) as well as specific instances of entities specified in the design (e.g., Figure 4.5). Specifically, the main goals of the framework are to enable structured modeling of instance-level situations and configurations, and in turn to support more precise risk calculation based on the additional, instance-level information. A high-level overview of the proposed threat modeling approach is shown in Figure 4.6.

In short, the instance-centric threat modeling framework enables threat modelers to capture the general structure and context of the system by creating the design model, and manually explore different (potential) instance-level scenarios by modeling one or more instance models. For example, if a design-level analysis reveals that spoofing vehicles remains a high-risk threat even though vehicles are authenticated, threat modelers might try to identify in which situations spoofing threats are more likely and/or impactful by systematically modeling and analyzing scenarios. We refer to the original paper [6] for additional details.

4.3.2 Digital Twin Threat Modeling

The TMRA leverages the proposed instance-centric threat modeling approach in a more automated manner by capturing and maintaining an instance model which represents the digital twin of an operational system [7]. Specifically, the design model captures types of entities (i.e., IoT devices), for example smart vehicles and traffic lights, and the digital twin captures instances of these devices, for example several specific vehicles with unique parameters. This digital twin can be updated continuously based on real-world events, allowing for accurate and real-time re-evaluation of threats and risk. The outcome of such threat analysis is then be leveraged during operations by the Trust Manager (Figure 4.1) to calculate trust metrics taking into account the likelihood of devices being spoofed. Figure 4.7 illustrates this approach which involves synchronizing the digital twin model at the basis of real-world events and then leveraging the risk calculation outcomes in a risk-adaptive security context.

The TMRA consists of three components: the digital twin model is an abstract representation of the real-world system, the engine re-analyses the digital twin when it is updated, and the controller interprets real-world events and updates the digital twin model accordingly. Events and analysis results are relayed through a message broker. We shortly summarize each of these components in what follows.

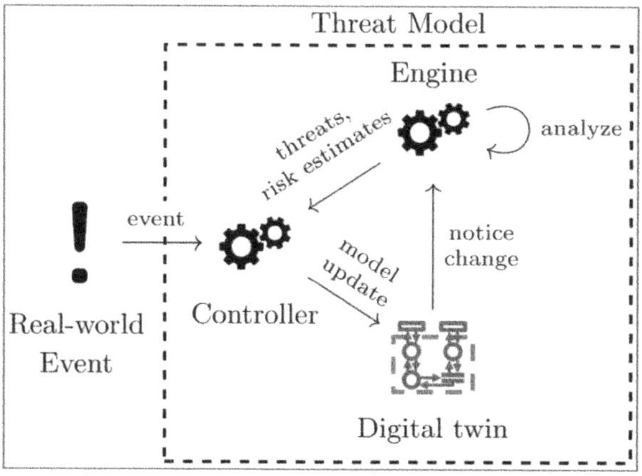

Figure 4.7. Conceptual overview of the digital twin threat model as implemented by the TMRA [7].

Table 4.2. Real-world events relevant to the TMRA, and the corresponding MQTT topics.

Event	Topic	Payload
New device	entity/entityID/new	Entity type (e.g. 'Vehicle') and parameters
Device removed	entity/entityID/remove	
New communication	dataflow/entityID/new	SenderID;RecipientID
Parameter changed	entity/entityID/atr/atr name	New parameter value

Table 4.3. MQTT topics for output risk values.

Output	Topic	Payload
Overall risk	entity/entityID/riskscore	Risk value
Specific threat type	entity/entityID/threatType/riskscore	Risk value

Real world events are relayed to the TMRA via MQTT. This could either be done by the devices themselves (e.g., vehicles announcing that they approach a traffic light), or by some observer which detects devices and sends corresponding events to the message broker. Relevant events for the threat model include (i) entities entering a system (e.g., a vehicle approaching a traffic light), (ii) entities being removed from a system (a vehicle driving away from a traffic light), (iii) entities interacting with one another (vehicles communicating with one another), and (iv) entities being updated (vehicles re-authenticating). A generic, context-agnostic MQTT topic is defined for each of the above-mentioned events, as shown in Table 4.2. Updates to the threat model are also published to the message broker, allowing other components to subscribe to threat or risk updates. The specific output topics are shown in Table 4.3. Interested parties (for example, the Trust Manager in Figure 4.1) can subscribe to all risk updates or to fine-grained events, for example the risk of spoofing for a specific vehicle.

The **digital twin model** is a modeled abstraction of a real-world system and corresponds to an instance model. For example, for the smart traffic case, this would be the collection of specific traffic lights and vehicles, and instances of data flows occurring between them. The digital twin model also captures attribute values (e.g., whether or not the vehicle is a priority vehicle) and security solutions (e.g., which authentication protocol is used by each vehicle, and the elapsed time since they last authenticated).

The **engine** is an extended version of SPARTA[1] which runs as a service listening for changes to the digital twin and automatically re-analyses the model if any

1. https://sparta.distrinet-research.be/.

changes are detected. It elicits threats and calculates risk estimates for each threat, taking into account security solutions (e.g., authentication) and attributes (priority, time since last authentication). Furthermore, it keeps track of all identified threats and their risk scores and can be queried to request the latest updates.

The **controller** parses MQTT messages, updates the digital twin model accordingly, and publishes the updated threats and risk estimates to the message broker. During initialization, the controller subscribes to the topics in Table 4.2. This is done through wildcards to allow subscribing to multiple topics at once. For example, the topic 'entity/ + /new' matches with any topic where the wildcard ('+') is replaced with an arbitrary string, so the controller is notified when any new entity enters the system. As described, the MQTT topics are generic, and need to be translated to application-specific model updates. For example, if the controller receives a message with topic 'entity/V1/new' and payload 'Vehicle', then a new vehicle should be created and added to the digital twin. Updates to the digital twin may induce new threats or change risk scores, as identified by the engine. The controller tracks the threats and risk scores in the engine to be notified of any updates to the threat landscape. Furthermore, the controller publishes such updates to the MQTT broker.

Figure 4.8 illustrates the workflow for a smart traffic system where vehicles announce their presence as they approach a traffic light. Such system could be used to dynamically regulate traffic lights and minimize the amount of time vehicles are waiting at an intersection. Furthermore, priority vehicles such as ambulances approaching a traffic light may request immediate actions from a traffic light in case of emergency. In this context, dynamically managing trust is critical to avoid actors from maliciously influencing the system such that they can move along traffic as fast as possible, potentially at the expense of other vehicles. Specific threats include attackers claiming to be priority vehicles, sending messages from non-existent vehicles to make the queue appear longer, and intercepting or tampering with messages sent from other vehicles.

To illustrate how threats and risk scores support dynamic decision making in an IoT system, consider the scenario where a vehicle claims to be a priority vehicle, and requests immediate right of way at an intersection. When such vehicle announces its presence, the threat model is updated by adding an entity to the system model, and the new model is analysed, resulting in new threats (e.g., the vehicle being spoofed), as well as risk scores for each threat. Depending on the specific situation, different actions could be taken by the system:

- If the vehicle implements state-of-the-art authentication protocols, and can thus provide strong evidence for its identity, the likelihood of that vehicle being spoofed is low, resulting in a lower risk score and, in turn, a higher

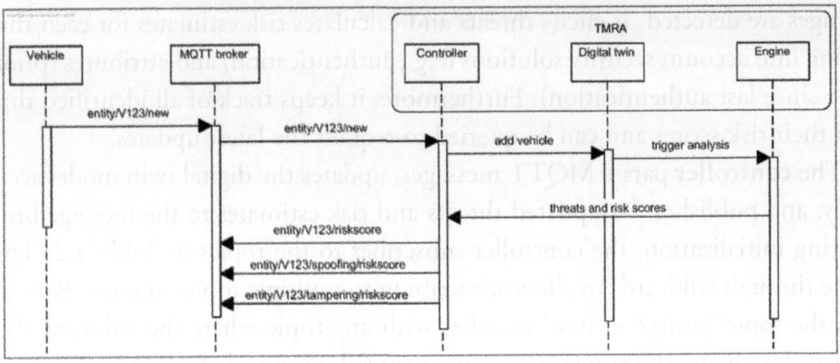

Figure 4.8. Sequence diagram for vehicles announcing their presence to a traffic light.

trust score, which will most likely result in immediate actions from the traffic light.

– If the vehicle cannot provide strong evidence for its identity, the likelihood of spoofing is higher, which may lead to the system ignoring the request, or to the system requesting the vehicle to re-authenticate. In the latter case, re-authentication induces changes to the digital twin model and updates to the threats and risk scores calculated by the TMRA, and thus also updates to the trust scores calculated by the TMB, which in turn may lead to a different decision by the system.

4.3.3 Summary

In summary, by continuously updating a digital twin threat model, the TMRA dynamically identifies new threats and updates risk scores based on the specific situation. In the ERATOSTHENES project, these outputs are leveraged by the Trust Manager to calculate trust scores for IoT devices, which requires taking into account the likelihood and potential impact of certain security threats such as devices being spoofed, or messages being tampered with. More in general, the TMRA enables self-adaptive security controls, for example by enforcing stronger countermeasures when the overall risk of spoofing exceeds a certain threshold, fine-grained and informed access control based on specific device parameters, and other run-time policy enforcements.

4.4 Automated Deployment and Recovery of Trust Agents

A TA is a software component deployed on IoT devices within the ERATOSTHENES ecosystem to collect run-time information used for assessing the trustworthiness of the device. It collects trust-related data, such as hardware resource usage, installed software, and security metrics. This information is then used by the TMB to ensure that the device's behavior aligns with predefined trust parameters. The TA plays an important role in maintaining the security, integrity, and reliability of IoT devices, and TA lifecycle management is an important challenge in this context. Throughout its lifecycle, a TA may undergo multiple updates triggered by various factors, such as security vulnerabilities, software bugs, or performance enhancements. By aligning the TA lifecycle with secure software update practices, the ERATOSTHENES project ensures that the IoT devices in its ecosystem remain secure, reliable, and trustworthy.

Please note that this section focuses only on managing the TA lifecycle as part of the TMB functionality. From a broader perspective, a TA can essentially be seen as a software component, which itself can decrease or increase the level of device trustworthiness depending on the presence of vulnerabilities, applied security patches, execution traces, etc. From this perspective, supporting the lifecycle of any software deployed and running on IoT devices is another important instrument for IoT trust management in ERATOSTHENES, which we discuss separately in more detail in Chapter 4.

4.4.1 Trust Agent Lifecycle

The lifecycle of a TA in the ERATOSTHENES ecosystem follows the Trusted Computing Group's (TCG) 'Guidance for Secure Update of Software and Firmware on Embedded Systems'[2] and includes five main steps: secure development, secure signing, robust distribution, secure installation, and post-installation verification. This lifecycle, depicted in Figure 4.9, is closely tied to the lifecycle of the IoT device itself, merging when the device is initially enrolled into the trusted ecosystem. At this point, the IoT device receives its initial TA, marking the start of its trusted operations. From this moment, the TA lifecycle becomes intertwined with the IoT device lifecycle, as the device will continually receive updates to its TA during its operational lifespan.

1. **Secure Development:** The secure development of TAs is expected to be implemented by IoT device manufacturers or trusted third-party developers following strict security standards. TAs are designed with security in mind, ensuring they do not introduce any additional threats themselves. This includes securing the software from the ground up, considering the potential

2. https://trustedcomputinggroup.org/resource/tcg-guidance-for-secure-update-of-software-and-firmware-on-embedded-systems/.

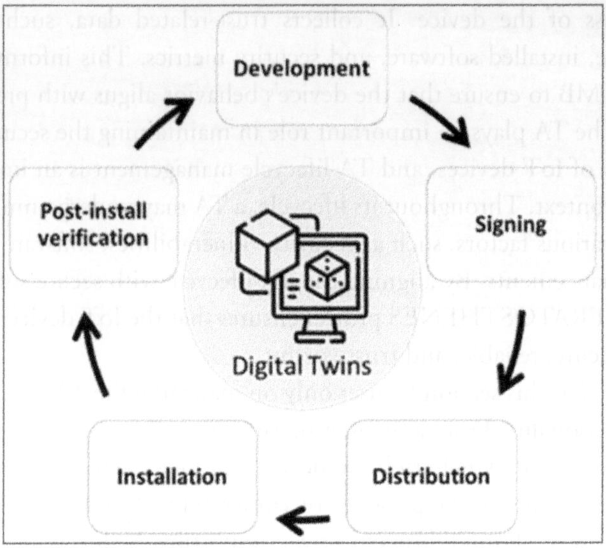

Figure 4.9. Trust Agent lifecycle supported by the Digital Twin platform.

attack vectors in the IoT environment. It is also envisioned by ERATOSTHENES that the newly released TA versions will contain patches to certain vulnerabilities identified as a result of continuous trust monitoring and assessment. The development process also ensures that the TA can function across various hardware and software configurations typical in IoT systems, like edge gateways and personal health monitoring devices used in the Smart Healthcare pilot.

2. **Secure Signing:** Once developed, the TA is cryptographically signed, ensuring its integrity and authenticity. In ERATOSTHENES, we assume that device manufacturers generate and manage a pair of cryptographic keys: a private key for signing TA updates and a corresponding public key for verifying them. The private key is stored securely to prevent unauthorized access and potential misuse. On the other hand, the public key is embedded within the IoT devices during the manufacturing process, enabling these devices to verify the authenticity of received updates at a later stage. The signing mechanism guarantees that any TA received by an IoT device can be trusted as originating from an authorized source and has not been tampered with. This step ensures that only verified TAs are allowed to be distributed and installed within the managed IoT ecosystem.
3. **Robust Distribution:** In ERATOSTHENES, the robust distribution phase is one of the key innovations, ensuring that TAs are deployed across a distributed network of IoT devices securely and efficiently. Inspired by the model-driven engineering techniques [8, 9], this process is facilitated by the

use of **Digital Twins** (DTs), which represent each IoT device in the virtual space, reflecting the real-time status and context of each device [10]. The DT platform listens for new updated contextual information collected by device-side monitoring agents, and then uses this cyber-physical-social context of each device to ensure that the correct TA is assigned. This means that various factors such as hardware capabilities, network conditions, and the operational context of the IoT device are considered during the assignment of TAs, making sure that the right TA is deployed for each device. A key part of this phase is the asynchronous installation, enabled by the **Desired-Reported Property** pattern of DTs. The system first applies updates to the DT, where the desired state of the TA is written to the corresponding property. This desired state is then continuously communicated to the real physical device. Noteworthy, the device might be temporarily offline, but as soon as it gets back online it eventually receives its desired state. This pattern supports a scalable approach, allowing updates to occur even across large fleets of devices, potentially numbering in the hundreds or thousands. This way, DTs also help in scalability, as they allow ERATOSTHENES to manage updates across large fleets of devices in parallel. The use of publish-subscribe communication via MQTT ensures efficient and timely distribution of updates, while the DTs enable real-time tracking and coordination, making the system robust enough to handle a large number of devices in varying states of readiness for updates.

4. **Secure Installation:** After robust distribution, the secure installation of TAs ensures that the update is applied safely to the IoT device. This is implemented using device- and platform-specific adapters instantiated for each device (or a group of functionally identical devices) [11]. Mostly, at this step ERATOSTHENES relies on the existing tools for software installation over the network. Some common examples include adapters for interacting with the Docker Engine API, over SSH, or using a RESTful API. The IoT device then reports back with its reported state after installation, creating a smooth update process that does not require synchronous communication.
5. **Post-installation Verification:** The final phase of the TA lifecycle involves verifying that the newly installed TA is functioning as expected. In ERATOSTHENES, this step involves confirming that the TA is successfully running on the IoT device and is providing accurate trust metrics. This is verified through the DT, which compares the desired state (the expected TA version) with the reported state (the actual state of the device post-installation). If the reported state matches the desired state, the TA is considered successfully installed. If discrepancies are detected, the system can initiate recovery or roll-back procedures.

4.4.2 Trust Agent Updates, Roll-back and Recovery

TA lifecycle management in the ERATOSTHENES ecosystem is a threefold process, encompassing actual updates, roll-back, and recovery. Each of these processes is designed to maintain the security, stability, and functionality of TAs, and thus – of the host IoT devices, ensuring that they remain trustworthy throughout their lifecycle.

- **Actual updates** are the primary type of TA lifecycle activities and are typically triggered in response to identified security vulnerabilities, threats or risks. These updates are released either by the device manufacturer or a trusted third-party software developer to patch known security flaws or improve the performance and functionality of the TA. Such updates are critical for proactively maintaining the trustworthiness of IoT devices, especially as new threats or weaknesses are discovered in the broader ecosystem. The update process follows the principles of secure distribution and installation to ensure that the IoT device receives and applies the update in a secure and reliable manner.
- **Roll-backs** occur when the system needs to revert to a previous stable version of the TA, or even the very initial default version. Roll-backs are usually triggered in response to malfunctioning or operational issues rather than cybersecurity incidents. For instance, if a recently installed TA version causes performance problems or system instability, the system can perform a roll-back to restore the device to a previously stable state. This process ensures that devices continue to function smoothly without being affected by faulty or incompatible updates. Roll-backs are different from recovery in that they generally address software issues rather than failures caused by attacks or significant disruptions. In relation to this, ERATOSTHENES employs a **blue-green deployment strategy**, where two environments (blue and green) are maintained on each IoT device. The new TA version is first deployed to the green environment for testing and validation. If everything functions as expected, traffic is switched from the blue (previous version) to the green (new version) environment. This seamless transition reduces downtime and ensures a fallback option is available. If any issues arise during installation, the system can roll back to the blue environment, effectively reverting to the previous TA version without causing disruptions.
- **Recovery** involves the re-installation of the TA along with the recovery of its state from a stored backup, typically in the DLT system. Unlike roll-backs, recoveries are often triggered by more severe incidents, such as device failures or cyberattacks, where the TA has been compromised or rendered inoperable. In these cases, the system not only reinstalls the TA but also restores its state,

including key contextual information and trust metrics, to ensure continuity of service and the integrity of the device. Recoveries are designed to restore the trustworthiness of the device after significant disruptions, which is an important aspect of maintaining IoT security and reliability.

4.4.3 State Preservation

State preservation is crucial when updating, recovering, or rolling back TAs because it maintains the continuity and integrity of operations within IoT devices. A stateful approach, as implemented in the ERATOSTHENES project, allows the system to maintain important contextual information and trust metrics across these processes. This is essential for IoT ecosystems where the history of device actions, configurations, and security settings play a significant role in determining the trustworthiness and proper functioning of devices.

In contrast to stateless methods, which only focus on reinstating functionality without keeping track of the device's operational history, a stateful approach allows for a more accurate recovery and update process [12]. Stateless updates or recovery would simply re-apply the software without regard for the previously held configuration or operational data, potentially leading to gaps in trust, security, and performance continuity. For instance, critical settings such as device identity, security logs, or resource usage would be lost during a stateless recovery, potentially making the device vulnerable to security threats or operational inefficiencies. A stateful recovery or update preserves these critical parameters, so that the device resumes operations as they were before the interruption.

In ERATOSTHENES, stateful transitions of TAs are made possible by storing the device and TA states in a DLT system, specifically Hyperledger Fabric. The DLT serves as a tamper-proof, decentralized repository where key contextual information and operational data about each IoT device and its TA are stored as assets. This includes data such as the installed software packages, hardware usage metrics, trust scores, etc. By storing this information in the DLT, it is possible to retrieve it later in a secure and non-mutable manner whenever necessary. During updates, rollbacks, or recoveries, the stored state information is fetched from the DLT and 're-applied' to the newly deployed or restored TA. For instance, in the Smart Healthcare context, this could include retrieving the list of critical software packages installed on a healthcare gateway or past resource usage readings to assess the device's health. Without this stateful transition, devices might return to a default state, losing key operational data and compromising the continuity of service. In this context, the stateful recovery process ensures that devices can not only restore functionality but also regain their previous level of trust and reliability without losing important historical data.

The use of DTs in ERATOSTHENES further facilitates the stateful transition by acting as a **recovery checkpoint** representing the last-known status and context of each device before. When an update or recovery is triggered, the DT helps compare the desired state (what the TA or device should be) with the reported state (what it currently is), ensuring that any state differences are identified and corrected. This state preservation and comparison process serves to bring the IoT device back to a fully operational and trustworthy state after an update or recovery, with its critical operational history intact.

4.4.4 Summary

TAs are deployed on the IoT devices and collect run-time information which is used by the TMB to assess the overall trustworthiness of a device. To safeguard the correctness of this run-time information, and thus of the calculated trust scores associated with devices, it is crucial to protect the TA itself from tampering and other security threats. The ERATOSTHENES project therefore defines a secure lifecycle for the TA, as well as strategies for secure roll-backs and recovery, with a particular focus on state preservation to ensure continuity as the TA are updated or recovered.

4.5 Trusted Execution Environments and Remote Communication

The ERATOSTHENES architecture includes several components deployed on the IoT devices themselves, such as the TA described in the previous section or an SSI Agent, which are required to assess the trustworthiness of the device. However, IoT devices may be deployed in untrusted environments, and malicious applications may be running on them, so additional protections are needed to guarantee the integrity components on the IoT devices, and the confidentiality of the data they process. The ERATOSTHENES architecture therefore leverages Trusted Execution Environments (TEEs).

A TEE is a set of hardware and software components that realizes a secure area of memory on the main processor (the Secure World) and guarantees that the code and data loaded in the Secure World is protected from untrusted software running in the Normal World. Additionally, a root of trust[3] ensures that authenticity and integrity hold for the code that is loaded during boot. The TEE can run arbitrary code that can be loaded at boot or at runtime. As such, a TEE offers an isolated computational

3. https://csrc.nist.gov/glossary/term/roots_of_trust.

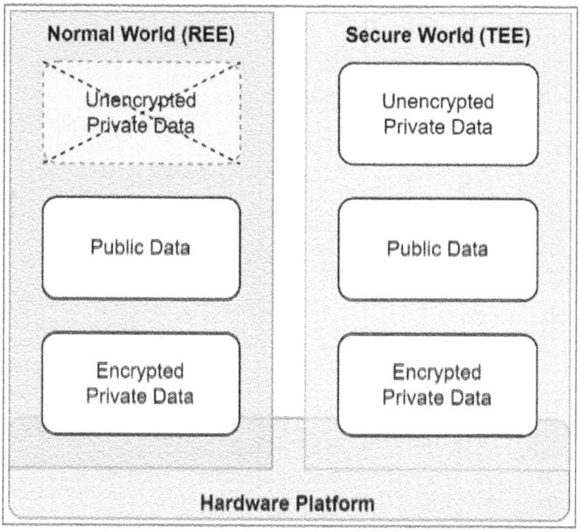

Figure 4.10. Overview of multiple types of data and their allowed processing on IoT devices.

environment that provides authenticity, integrity and confidentiality of all code running in it as well as data and runtime state of the environment stored inside. An overview is shown in Figure 4.10.

The ERATOSTHENES project provides a generic TEE and supporting services for IoT devices, building upon state-of-the-art technologies such as i.MX6,[4] the QEMU[5] emulator, Arm TrustZone,[6] OP-TEE[7] operating system, the GlobalPlatform Sockets[8] API, and Mbed TLS 3.6.0. The TEE acts as a root of trust on IoT devices that can deliver security features throughout an IoT device's software lifecycle, even in the presence of untrusted applications. Two enhancements to existing TEE technologies were made as part of the ERATOSTHENES project, which will be summarized in this section.

4.5.1 Secure Scheduling and Sharing of Peripherals

While existing TEE technologies provide confidentiality and integrity for resources in the Secure World, they do not protect critical tasks running in the Secure World

4. i.MX6 platform: https://boundarydevices.com/product/bd-sl-i-mx6/

5. QEMU: https://optee.readthedocs.io/en/latest/building/gits/build.html#get-and-build-the-solution.

6. ARM Trustzone: https://www.arm.com/technologies/trustzone-for-cortex-a.

7. OP-TEE: https://www.trustedfirmware.org/projects/op-tee/.

8. GlobalPlatform Sockets API: https://globalplatform.org/specs-library/tee-client-api-specification/.

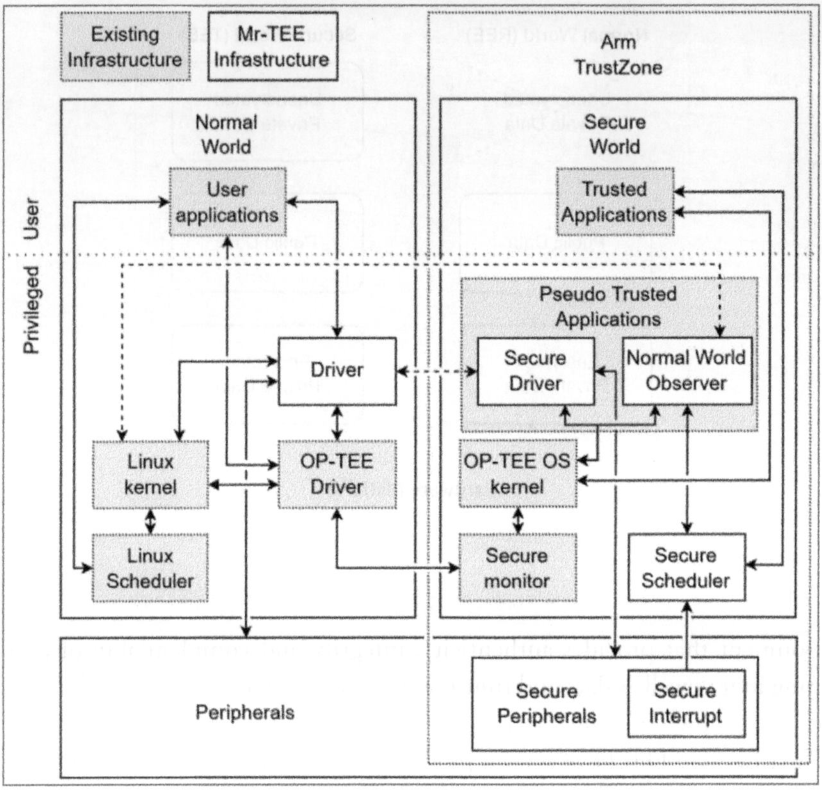

Figure 4.11. Architecture of Mr-TEE.

from Denial of Service (DoS) attacks. Especially in Cyber Physical Systems (CPSs), which interact continuously with the physical world and are hence bound by stringent timing and safety requirements, this can cause serious security and safety hazards, for example by delaying sensor readings. This problem is exacerbated by the fact that CPSs are increasingly connected to the internet, for example with Industry 4.0, where industrial assets such as machines, robots and production lines are connected with real-time analytics and control systems. In practice, CPSs are connected to the internet by using reputable commodity OS components and applications because of their ease of implementation and well-tested nature. Unfortunately, these significantly increase the attack surface due to their large code base, exposing vulnerabilities which range from nuisances to life-threatening malfunctions.

To prevent attackers from tampering with the schedule of real-time tasks or overloading resources, Mr-TEE [13], a novel, hardware-enabled TEE to host and schedule safety-critical code, was developed as part of the ERATOSTHENES project. Concretely, Mr-TEE protects against remote adversaries which may exploit software vulnerabilities to launch DoS attacks on system resources or critical peripherals by executing arbitrary code in the Normal World. An overview of the Mr-TEE architecture is shown in Figure 4.11. A short summary of the main components is provided below.

- **Secure Scheduler.** Most existing TEE implementations lack a full-featured scheduler, depending instead on the Normal World scheduler. To provide availability guarantees, we integrate a minimal yet sound real-time scheduler in the Secure World, which makes it possible to schedule critical tasks in real-time independently from the Normal World. This provides a mechanism through which developers can partition computational resources between critical and non-critical functionality.
- **Secure Peripherals.** To protect peripherals against bugs or attacks from the (compromised) Normal World, Mr-TEE provides the ability to map certain peripherals to the Secure World. This mapping disables direct access to these peripherals by any Normal World process, forcing all interactions through the Secure World. Naturally, because of the trusted state of the Secure World, applications running in the Secure World can still access peripherals mapped to the Normal World. As the criticality of each peripheral is application-dependent, Mr-TEE gives the designer of the system the choice as to which peripherals are mapped to which world. This ensures the best response time for peripherals that will be exclusively used in only one of the worlds, while minimizing code base size and developer effort by avoiding the need to manage all peripherals in the Secure World.
- **Shared Peripherals.** Not all peripherals can be mapped to a single world, as software in both worlds may require access to the same peripheral for normal operation. In this case, Mr-TEE provides a novel mechanism called Shared Secure Peripherals, shown in Figure 4.2, wherein the Secure World provides a Secure Driver that is responsible not only for providing access to these peripherals for Trusted Applications, but also for providing interfaces via which the Normal World can access the functionality of these same peripherals. The Secure Driver is thus able to control the access of the Normal World to the peripheral, preventing any untrusted applications from blocking peripheral access for critical software running in the TEE.
- **Normal World Observer.** Building upon the presence of a real-time scheduler in the Secure World and a notification system to the Normal World, Mr-TEE offers a Normal World Observer, which is capable of periodically checking the running state of the Normal World OS. Whenever scheduled, the Normal World Observer challenges the Normal World kernel to respond in a certain time frame. The fulfilment of the challenge implies that the Normal World is still actively running and is neither frozen nor crashed. Additionally,

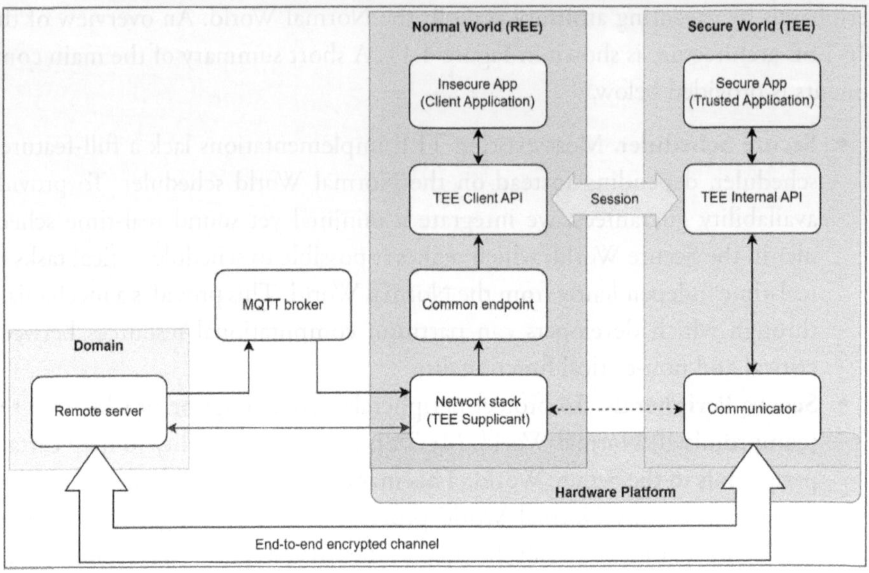

Figure 4.12. Overview of the end-to-end encrypted communication channel.

if the Normal World has crashed, a status report can be obtained through a snapshot of the Normal World registers and memory. In this way, the Secure World can trigger positive actions in the case of unexpected behaviour.

In summary, Mr-TEE provides a sound yet minimal real-time scheduler in the Secure World to guarantee safe execution of critical tasks, as well as the means to securely share critical peripherals between the Secure World and the Normal World to guarantee availability yet enable Normal World applications to execute as normal.

4.5.2 Secure Communication

Next to the TEE itself, which secures resources on IoT devices, the ERATOSTHENES project also provides a generic, end-to-end encrypted communication channel to move private data in or out of the TEE, allowing outside devices and remote servers to initiate connections with those applications. A high-level overview of this communication channel is shown in Figure 4.12. The main components are the following.

- The **Communicator** library in the TEE provides a generic interface for trusted applications to initiate end-to-end encrypted communications channels for connections to remote devices or servers.
- Because applications inside the TEE can only be called by applications running in the Normal World, remote devices or servers cannot directly initiate

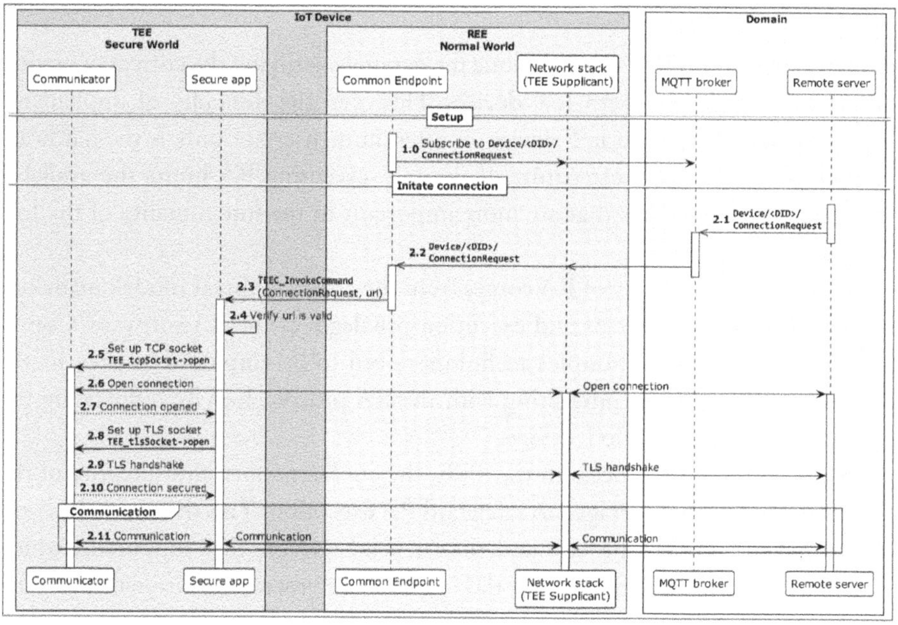

Figure 4.13. Message flow for a connection request to an IoT device.

connections. The **Common endpoint** in the Normal world is therefore responsible for listening for connection requests coming from outside the device and forwarding these requests to the trusted applications in the TEE.

- Connection requests are delivered through an **MQTT broker** to facilitate communications between multiple devices and servers, and should specify the UUID of the trusted application that is addressed by the requester, the URL the trusted application should connect to, and an optional port to make this connection to.

When receiving a connection request, the trusted application is solely responsible for opening the connection, so that certain (application-specific) security conditions can be verified before connecting. For example, if the trusted application decides that the timing of the request is suspicious, or if the parameters of the request do not align with the expected values, the trusted application can refuse this connection attempt. An overview of the message flow is shown in Figure 4.13.

4.5.3 Use Cases

The next sections describe how the enhanced TEE can be used to more easily extend the ERATOSTHENES architecture with two applications, remote attestation and proof of secure erasure, which are classically difficult to design and implement well.

4.5.3.1 Remote Attestation

Remote Attestation (RA) is a technique for remotely verifying the correct operation of a device, often used with IoT devices. However, the difficulty of implementing many RA schemes on IoT devices is often immense; not only is the hardware limited due to the low-cost nature of the IoT, executing RA limits the available time and energy for tasks that are more important to the functionality of the IoT devices.

Most of the complexity of RA comes from the assumed threat model: malicious software has the same access and execution privileges as the RA software. Consequently, a multitude of complex techniques need to be employed to prevent the malicious software from interfering with the RA process, heavily influencing the total performance of the IoT device.

By moving the RA process to the TEE, the confidentiality and integrity of the TEE can instantly be leveraged to safeguard RA execution. This decreases the complexity of both the RA process and the backend services that support it, which only need to trust the TEE to trust the result of the process. Additionally, because the TEE has full access to and control over the device, more complex attestation can be performed with only limited impact on the overall performance of the device.

4.5.3.2 Proof of Secure Erasure

Proof of Secure Erasure (PoSE) is a process wherein a piece of memory is erased by the IoT device and a proof is generated for the verifying party that the memory actually was erased. PoSE can be used to ensure secret data is securely removed or malicious software is completely erased from the device.

As with RA, the process of PoSE is difficult to complete securely on a device where malicious code has the same privileges as the PoSE process. Classic approaches to these problems have relied on the generation of random data, which is used to overwrite the secret data or malicious software, and a time limit to ensure malicious code cannot generate similar data before the completion of the process is expected. As a result, the overhead on both the network between the verifier and the IoT device and the computational effort for the verifier is non-negligible, making the system less scalable.

Similar to the RA example, by moving the PoSE process inside the TEE, the security properties of that TEE are gained, with little to no cost. Additionally, because the environment in which the PoSE process is now running can be trusted, there is no need to employ techniques like explained in the previous paragraph, and a simple algorithm can be used to execute PoSE of which the result can inherently be trusted by the verifier.

4.5.4 Summary

The enhanced TEE capabilities offered by the ERATOSTHENES project are a key enabler for trust management in IoT systems. For example, correctly calculating the risk associated to IoT devices in the TMRA (Section 4.3) requires integrity of the data provided by the Trust Manager, which can be safeguarded by running the Trust Manager in a TEE and securing communications as described above. Furthermore, the TEE and secure communication channel enable securely deploying updates to the Trust Manager itself (Section 4). More in general, the provided TEE capabilities provide the necessary building blocks for confidentiality and integrity for multiple ERATOSTHENES components, namely the TA, SSI agent, and Data Protector.

4.6 Device Network Enrolment

In the context of the ERATOSTHENES project, the device enrolment process enables devices to obtain identities with limited lifetimes based on various technologies such as PUF, TEE, and Decentralized Identifiers (DIDs). To enroll in a domain, a device must first produce encryption and authentication material using its root of trust (PUF or TEE). This material includes identity proofs such as Verifiable Credentials (VCs) and DID ownership claims, as well as owner information. The domain can check through this identity-related information trust values through the DLT deployed in the domain and the multi-domain DLT. If there is prior information related to the device from any domain, it can be used for the enrolment process and the initial trust computations. Another important aspect of device enrolment is that it binds the device's owner identity with the device's identity for accountability and nonrepudiation of actions.

Device network enrolment plays a crucial role in recovering an IoT device's identity and software components in case a device is compromised during an attack or fails. That is because the IoT device's identity is associated with a certain configuration and a user during enrolment. Recovery examines the list of applications and software installed in the enrolled device and attempts to recover the IoT device to its most genuine status possible. There are two types of enrolment: domain enrolment and cross-domain enrolment.

4.6.1 Components Involved in the Device Network Enrolment Process

To facilitate the device network enrolment process, a set of components from the ERATOSTHENES architecture [14, 15] must collaborate. These components reside on the device side and the ERATOSTHENES domain side.

The following entities from the infrastructure's side participate in the enrolment process:

The **TMB** [3] is responsible for evaluating the trustworthiness of IoT devices and acts as an MQTT broker to enable the communication between its various submodules: the TMRA module, MUD Management module, CTI Sharing Agent, Monitoring IDS, and the Trust Manager. It is the entry point for device enrolment and continuous usage of the ERATOSTHENES trust framework.

The **Self-Sovereign Identity (SSI) Management** module is a crucial component for the enrolment of devices, issuing the VCs used by devices to show their identity attributes during the authentication and authorization processes.

The **SC/DLT** enables different components and features in the ERATOSTHENES architecture to share and verify public information needed for their proper functioning, such as registering and retrieving DIDs, CTI data, trust scores, and identity verification-related information. Therefore, it makes the process of sharing information secure, reliable, verifiable, and transparent.

The **Management and Recovery** module manages devices in the ERATOSTHENES ecosystem, particularly regarding monitoring and recovery processes. During enrolment, it participates in the linkage of the device's identity to its introducer or owner.

The **device introducer/owner**, though not per se a component of the architecture, plays a key role in the device's enrolment process. Specifically, the introducer is a human user who associates themselves with the device they install in the IoT ecosystem for accountability. They are the IoT ecosystem's security manager.

The **Inter-DLT** is a platform that enables the interactions between DLTs from different ERATOSTHENES domains.

The following entities from the device's side participate in the enrolment process:

- The **Data Protector (ADP)** supports other components or subcomponents with features for handling data encryption that must be securely stored employing device hardware or software security features (e.g., TEE). Moreover, the ADP provides features of secure data (e.g., private key) exchange for fine-grained, confidential information sharing.
- The **TEE** (Section 4.5) is an area on a device's main processor separated from the system's main OS, creating a secure world for executing trustworthy code. It ensures that data is stored, processed, and protected in a secure and isolated environment. It can generate cryptographic material (e.g., keys and credentials) that serves as a basis for authentication in ERATOSTHENES. It cooperates with the ADP to enable other components to use said credentials.
- The **PUF client** handles the interconnection/interaction with the PUF Auth Server securely, acting as a root of trust for the identification/authentication

of the device. It can generate cryptographic material that serves as a basis for authentication in ERATOSTHENES, cooperating with the ADP to enable the usage of said credentials by other components (e.g., SSI Agent).

- The **SSI Agent** is responsible for supporting the flows for collecting and manipulating identity data, including cryptographic operations like the generation of Zero-Knowledge Proofs (ZKP). It will manipulate VCs and generate Verifiable Presentations (VPs) for a given access policy following a SSI approach using DIDs and VCs, both published by the World Wide Web Consortium (W3C). Additionally, it will take advantage of the TEE and the ADP module for the secure storage and retrieval of the necessary private cryptographic material.
- The **TA** handles multiple activities related to Trust Management on the device's side, such as software boot and monitoring. Mainly, it handles interactions with the TMB to calculate trust and reputation during interactions, including the initial enrolment of the device in the system that results in the initial trust score evaluation and the culmination of the enrolment process.

4.6.2 IoT Device Network Enrolment Background

Enrolling an IoT device is a key process within its lifecycle, serving as an enabler for all functionalities that will occur during the operational time. Before enrolment occurs, it is assumed that the initial bootstrapping of devices during the manufacturing process is carried out, and right after the device is deployed, the initial bootstrapping is finished. The ERATOSTHENES enrolment covers three cases depending on the device's root of trust (PUF, TEE, or none), demonstrating the flexibility of the ERATOSTHENES architecture to deal with heterogeneous devices and network settings.

To achieve the above objectives, the enrolment process deals with identity and trustworthiness. Regarding identity, the ERATOSTHENES enrolment process follows the SSI paradigm, where each device manages its own credentials that comprise its identity in the IoT ecosystem. This facilitates fine-grained, attribute-based control when devices access services in the IoT ecosystem. To obtain the aforementioned credentials, the device has to undergo an onboarding process, where it registers its DID document, which contains the public keys that enable the device's identification and the VCs that contain its identity attributes through an issuance process against the SSI Management component in the domain's infrastructure. During this process, the device is subjected to a proof of identity process, where the root of trust for identifying the device plays a key role. Ideally, PUF-based authentication is used, but alternatives are possible and are considered. Consequently, in this process, the device's PUF authentication module facilitates device authentication and identification, while the SSI agent deployed on the device manages the interactions and processes relevant to the DIDs and VCs, supported by the ADP as a secure environment for storing and managing cryptographic material. On the ecosystem's infrastructure side, the SSI management module plays the role of the credential issuer, providing devices with the identity material as a result of the enrolment. A DLT supports the enrolment as a verifiable data registry, while manufacturer services such as PUF authentication servers facilitate the initial identity proof.

The device's enrolment process includes an additional step for the inclusion of the device in the ecosystem's trust framework. The device, through its TA, will connect to the domain's TMB and be given an initial evaluation of its trustworthiness that depends on parameters including but not limited to its identity, the endorsement of the introducer (e.g., a security domain manager), or threat modeling and risk assessment (with the TMB's subcomponents collaborating). As indicated before, a crucial source for this evaluation is the trustworthiness of the identification mechanism of the device through the identity's root of trust. Once the evaluation process is completed, an initial trust score is assigned to the device. It will be updated throughout its operation in the domain depending on events related to its behavior or the discovery of new threats.

Only when both processes are completed, and a device has the corresponding identity and trust information, is it fully enrolled and can interact with other elements in the domain as part of its operational phase.

4.6.3 IoT Devices Single Domain Network Enrollment Operation Flow

The IoT Devices Network Enrollment mechanism has three phases of operations: Phase 1 – Onboarding and Creation of Public DID, Phase 2 – Introducer-device pairing, and Phase 3 – Device enrolment and initial calculation of trust. Enrolling IoT devices within the ERATOSTHENES framework is accompanied by the completion of formal registration as a recognized ERATOSTHENES ecosystem member.

During the first phase, two suboperations occur: generating a public DID and registering it in the SSI Management. Creating a public DID involves generating a unique DID for the device and crafting a DID document that complies with the specifications outlined in the DID W3C standard. In this sub-process, the SSI Agent (ID client) component must utilize the associated cryptographic keys within the system to generate the DID Document. The cryptographic material is generated, stored, and obtained through three distinct sources: Hyperledger Aries (legacy), TEE, and PUF cryptographic material generation. The source can be selected by configuring an environmental variable.

The value of this variable is established based on the specific requirements and needs of the ERATOSTHENES ecosystem. This flexibility in configuration allows the SSI Agent component to adapt to the unique requirements of the ERATOSTHENES ecosystem.

When the variable is set to 'ADP + PUF', the SSI Agent utilizes the PUF client library through the ADP component to acquire physically unclonable cryptographic material. However, when the value is set to 'ADP+TEE', the SSI Agent utilizes the TEE through the ADP. Conversely, when the value is set to 'default', the SSI Agent component generates its own cryptographic material by utilizing the SSI standard by the W3C.[9]

Once the SSI Agent possesses the cryptographic keys, it generates the DID Document. However, before generating the DID Document, the DID itself is created, offering two distinct methods for publishing the public DID:

- did:web: adhering to the did:web standard[9]
- did:erat: a customized method developed for the ERATOSTHENES project that enables the publication of the DID into a permissioned blockchain implemented with Hyperledger Fabric.

Upon successfully publishing a new DID linked to its identity, the next step involves registering the IoT device in the SSI Management module. Afterward, the device generates a VC that includes its unique footprint. It then requests the SSI Management module to issue the credential.

The second phase is the Introducer-Device pairing, during which the device's certificate generated during Phase 1 is associated with the introducer for accountability purposes. A typical envisioned association between the introducer and the device occurs as follows. Initially, the device requests from the Management and Recovery service to be linked to the introducer. Upon receiving that request, the Management and Recovery service requests the introducer to authenticate. The introducer authenticates to the Management and Recovery Service and then receives a request to approve the device's DID from the latter. The introducer approves the device, resulting in a signed DID, which the Management and Recovery Service sends to the device.

9. https://www.w3.org/TR/did-core/.

Finally, in the third phase, the device enrolment and initial calculation of trust commences, during which the device sends its trust data along with its, signed by the introducer, DID, to the TMB. The TMB calculates the device's initial trust score and, via its gRPC client, sends it along with the device's DID to the gRPC server of the DLT. The gRPC server invokes the chaincode that writes the trust score to the DLT. Once the trust score is recorded in the DLT, the chaincode will send an acknowledgment to the TMB. Afterward, the TMB forwards the trust score to the IoT device.

4.6.4 IoT Devices Cross-domain Network Enrollment Operation Flow

The cross-domain network enrolment focuses on the enrolment of a device from domain A to domain B. The process starts with the SSI Agent generating a VP from a VC obtained from domain A. Then, the information related to the enrolment of the device to domain A, along with the VP, is sent to the SSI Management module of domain B, which in turn validates the identity proofs and retrieves the issuer's DID from the Inter-DLT service. Once the SSI Management module retrieves the DID of the issuer from domain A, the respective VP is validated. Upon successful validation, the SSI Management module sends the device enrolment response to the SSI Agent. Afterward, domain B's Management & Recovery service links the device's identity with its owner's. Once the linking is done, the TA sends the trust-related data to the TMB, which checks in the Inter-DLT for prior trust evaluation-related data and retrieves them through smart contracts. Then, it computes the device's initial trust score for domain B by considering its context and the trust data from domain A. The calculated trust score is stored on the DLT of domain B, and then the TMB sends the enrollment result to the device.

4.6.5 Summary

In summary, enrolment is pivotal in enhancing accountability within IoT ecosystems, fostering traceability, and reinforcing security auditing procedures. This is achieved by linking the device owner's identity to that of their IoT device, thereby ensuring accountability and non-repudiation of actions. Additionally, all outcomes stemming from the three phases of the enrolment process are logged onto the DLT, serving as an immutable ledger. Thus, regardless of how much malicious actors endeavor to disassociate themselves from the connected IoT device, the process remains resilient, making it arduous to complete disassociation. Furthermore, the enrolment process provides valuable insight into a device's trustworthiness once it joins the IoT ecosystem, enabling prospective IoT service consumers to make informed decisions when choosing an IoT service provider.

4.7 Conclusion

IoT-based applications involve devices that are deployed typically in uncontrolled and uncontrollable environments. For example, in a smart traffic system, IoT devices are installed in the public domain as part of the infrastructure (e.g., a traffic light) or within vehicles, in a remote patient monitoring service, devices are handed out to patients who use them at home, and in a smart manufacturing case, devices are deployed at large scale in complex factory settings.

Distributed trust – the ability to evaluate trust from an externalized perspective – therefore is the only viable approach in such environments. Yet, there is no single-size-fits-all solution to establish trust in heterogeneous devices and dynamic environments, and careful application-specific trade-offs must be made by application engineers and operators, taking into account many factors such as device capabilities (e.g. hardware provisions for trusted execution, computational cost, battery cost, bandwidth), level of security and assurance, and residual risk.

This chapter presented an architecture – and the integration of diverse architectural enablers therein – to accomplish exactly this. This solution is customizable, as this toolkit of diverse technologies can be selected and composed in a mix-and-match manner to accomplish trust in a way that is tailored to the specific use case at hand. A dynamic calculation of trust is performed by the TMB, which considers these enablers in terms of their trust contributions and residual risks. This trust qualification is then used to inform run-time systems (for example to inform acccss control decisions), and even to drive proactive or reactive actions (e.g., dynamic re-deployment or rollback of software state on a specific device).

While the ensuing tool kit by no real means can be considered complete, it does yield a diverse and versatile set of technological enablers, which have been successfully technically integrated within the scope and intent of the ERATOSTHENES project.

Acknowledgements

This work is partially funded by Research Fund KU Leuven, and the European Union's Horizon 2020 research and innovation program under grant agreement No 101020416.

References

[1] G.-H. Tzeng and J.-J. Huang, Multiple Attribute Decision Making: Methods and Applications (1st ed.), Chapman and Hall/CRC, 2011.

[2] S. Chakraborty, "TOPSIS and Modified TOPSIS: A comparative analysis," *Decision Analytics Journal*, vol. 2, 2022.

[3] M. Bampatsikos, T. Ioannidis, A. Sideris and I. Politis, "D2. 1 Trust Broker Mechanism," 2020.

[4] Z. Shi, K. Graffi, D. Starobinski and N. Matyunin, "Threat modeling tools: A Taxonomy," *IEEE Security and Privacy*, vol. 20, no. 4, 2022.

[5] D. Van Landuyt, L. Sion, E. Vandeloo and W. Joosen, "On the applicability of security and privacy threat modeling for blockchain applications," in *Computer Security: ESORICS 2019 International Workshops, CyberICPS, SECPRE, SPOSE, and ADIoT, Luxembourg City, Luxembourg, September 26–27, 2019 Revised Selected Papers*, Springer-Verlag, 2019, pp. 195–203.

[6] S. Verreydt, D. Van Landuyt and W. Joosen, "Expressive and Systematic Risk Assessments with Instance-Centric Threat Models," in *Proceedings of the 38th ACM/SIGAPP Symposium on Applied Computing*, Tallinn, Estonia, 2023.

[7] S. Verreydt, D. Van Landuyt and W. Joosen, "Run-time Threat Models for Systematic and Continuous Risk Assessment [accepted, to be published]," *Software and Systems Modeling.*

[8] H. Song, R. Dautov, N. Ferry, A. Solberg and F. Fleurey, "Model-based fleet deployment in the IoT–edge–cloud continuum," *Software and Systems Modeling*, vol. 21, no. 5, pp. 1931–1956, 2022.

[9] H. Song, D. Dautov, N. Ferry, A. Solberg and F. Fleurey, "Model-based fleet deployment of edge computing applications," in *Proceedings of the 23rd ACM/IEEE International Conference on Model Driven Engineering Languages and Systems*, 2020.

[10] R. Dautov and H. Song, "Context-Aware Digital Twins to Support Software Management at the Edge," in *International Conference on Research Challenges in Information Science*, Switzerland, 2023.

[11] R. Dautov, H. Song and N. Ferry, "Towards a sustainable IoT with last-mile software deployment," in *IEEE Symposium on Computers and Communications (ISCC)*, 2021.

[12] R. Dautov and E. J. Husom, "Raft Protocol for Fault Tolerance and Self-Recovery in Federated Learning," in *Proceedings of the 19th International Symposium on Software Engineering for Adaptive and Self-Managing Systems*, 2024.

[13] T. Van Eyck, H. Trimech, S. Michiels, D. Hughes, M. Salehi, H. Janjuaa and T.-L. Ta, "Mr-TEE: Practical Trusted Execution of Mixed-Criticality

Code," in *Proceedings of the 24th International Middleware Conference: Industrial Track*, Bologna, Italy, 2023.

[14] J. G. Rodríguez, A. Skarmeta and A. M. Frutos, "D1.4 ERATOSTHENES Blueprint – Final Architecture," 2021.

[15] A. Skarmeta, G. R. Torres-Moreno, J. García-Rodríguez, A. Marín-Frutos, E. Torroglosa-García, B. Danczul, S. More and B. Podgorelec, "D1.3 Preliminary ERATOSTHENES Architecture," 2021.

DOI: 10.1561/9781638285076.ch5

Chapter 5

Decentralized Identity Management

By Angel Palomares Perez and Laura Esbri Vidal

The ERATOSTHENES project aims to revolutionize identity management in IoT systems by leveraging Self-Sovereign Identity (SSI) principles, which allow IoT devices to maintain control over their digital identities throughout their lifecycle. Traditional centralized identity management systems often face scalability and security issues when applied to IoT environments, which contain a vast number of interconnected devices. By contrast, SSI offers a decentralized approach that not only enhances security and privacy but also simplifies identity management processes.

The Ledger uSelf SSI solution, a core innovation of the ERATOSTHENES project, plays a pivotal role in this decentralized framework. This solution integrates key components such as the PUF client, VDR-fabric, Advanced Data Protection (ADP) module, and the Identity Recovery Mechanism to provide a holistic identity management system. Through the creation of Decentralized Identifiers (DIDs) and Verifiable Credentials (VC), IoT devices are empowered with unique, cryptographically secure identities that can be used for authentication and authorization. These identities are self-managed, allowing devices to independently prove their identity while maintaining privacy, reducing the risks of tracking, profiling, or identity theft.

The importance of SSI in IoT environments lies in its ability to address the specific challenges that come with managing billions of devices, each with different hardware and software requirements. Ledger uSelf has been designed to accommodate these constraints, offering flexibility through environmental configurations that support the deployment across various devices. Furthermore, the system's integration with advanced cryptographic techniques, such as privacy-enhancing Attribute-Based Credentials (p-ABC), ensures minimal data disclosure and enhances security through zero-knowledge proofs.

By applying SSI principles, the ERATOSTHENES project not only ensures secure device onboarding, identity verification, and authorization processes but also builds a zero-trust framework that aligns with modern privacy regulations. The use of disposable identities further bolsters privacy by creating unique identifiers for specific interactions, minimizing the risk of tracking.

In conclusion, the ERATOSTHENES project demonstrates the potential of SSI in transforming identity management for IoT devices, offering a scalable, privacy-centric, and secure solution that addresses the challenges of the increasingly interconnected digital landscape. The Ledger uSelf solution exemplifies the project's commitment to advancing secure, decentralized identity management in the IoT domain.

5.1 Introduction

Decentralized Identity represents a paradigm shift in how individuals, machines and IoT devices manage and control their digital identities. Traditional identity systems are typically centralized or federated, where a central authority, such as a government or large tech company, is responsible for verifying and controlling an individual's identity. This centralized approach is vulnerable to data breaches, privacy violations, and the concentration of power in single entities, leading to concerns about trust, security, and privacy.

Since IoT environments are typically distributed and highly dynamic, decentralized identity management has emerged as a transformative solution for addressing the challenges posed by centralized identity systems. Key principles such as self-sovereignty, verifiable credentials, trustless networks, and data minimization enable IoT devices to authenticate and interact securely, without over-exposing sensitive data. In contrast to traditional systems, decentralized identity reduces the risks of data breaches, enhances user control, and scales better with the exponential growth of IoT devices, making it a vital innovation in securing the future of IoT networks.

One of the primary objectives of the ERATOSTHENES project is to implement a Decentralized Identity Management system based on the Self-Sovereign Identity (SSI) paradigm throughout the entire lifecycle of IoT devices.

5.2 Overview of Decentralized Identity Frameworks and Standards

The Self-Sovereign Identity (SSI) community is still in an early stage of definition and implementation, and as a result, many of its main standards are continuously evolving, adapting, and being refined. Despite these changes, there is consensus within the community regarding the core building blocks needed to design and implement solutions following the SSI paradigm. These standards are essential for ensuring interoperability and security in decentralized identity systems. This chapter outlines the main findings related to these standards and how they will be applied in the solution developed for the ERATOSTHENES project.

The building blocks for SSI can be classified into tree main groups: standards that define the format of identity information, standards that define how identity information is transmitted between different actors, stakeholders and credential standard formats.

5.2.1 Identity Information Format Standard

In this category, two key standards from the **World Wide Web Consortium (W3C)**[1] play a crucial role:

- **W3C – Decentralized Identifiers (DID)**[2]: This standard defines a method for generating unique identifiers in a decentralized environment. DIDs are Uniform Resource Identifiers (URIs) that link a DID subject (such as a person, organization, or IoT device) with a DID Document. This DID Document contains cryptographic information, including public keys, which enable trusted interactions with the subject. The cryptographic proofs facilitate services like verification and authentication, essential for securing digital identities.

  The DID specification also introduces DID methods, which define how the DIDs are created, resolved, updated, and deactivated across various decentralized registries. The ERATOSTHENES project will implement two DID methods:

  - did:web[3]: This DID method, defined by W3C, uses standard web infrastructure to host DID Documents. It is particularly useful when

1. https://www.w3.org/standards/.
2. https://www.w3.org/TR/did-core/.
3. https://github.com/w3c-ccg/did-method-web.

decentralized registries are not needed, allowing DIDs to be hosted on trusted websites.

- did:erat: This is an ad-hoc DID method developed specifically for the ERATOSTHENES project. It stores DID Documents within Hyperledger Fabric, a permissioned blockchain framework developed for the project. This approach ensures that identities are managed securely within a controlled, permissioned environment.

A Decentralized Identifier (DID) follows a structured format, as illustrated in the image below. It is a simple text string consisting of three main components: the DID URI scheme identifier, the identifier for the specific DID method, and the method-specific unique identifier.

Figure 5.1. Example of a decentralized identifier (DID).

As mentioned before, the DID resolves to a DID Document that contains the DID and the associated cryptographic information such us public keys or verification methods, which are essential for authentication and verification processes. In the figure below shows an example of a DID Document that uses the "did:erat" method.


```
{
  "didDoc": {
    "@context": [
      "https://www.w3.org/ns/did/v1"
    ],
    "id": "did:erat:d56c97d236e93337dd3ec896d5185358595d57edd91d63da4fd2715eb0abd45d:9545a4009f8a8723402035f455879f6b0962167722d9f9e9d56fc
    "verificationMethod": [
      {
        "controller": "did:erat:d56c97d236e93337dd3ec896d5185358595d57edd91d63da4fd2715eb0abd45d:9545a4009f8a8723402035f455879f6b096216772
        "id": "did:erat:d56c97d236e93337dd3ec896d5185358595d57edd91d63da4fd2715eb0abd45d:9545a4009f8a8723402035f455879f6b0962167722d9f9e9d
        "publicKeyBase58": "4daZTzDC2VuWuYECFH549eJrGTVdZ4rv2BBChadAY8YERRXtdhNWzkWCpLX",
        "type": "Ed25519VerificationKey2018"
      },
      {
        "controller": "did:erat:d56c97d236e93337dd3ec896d5185358595d57edd91d63da4fd2715eb0abd45d:9545a4009f8a8723402035f455879f6b096216772
        "id": "did:erat:d56c97d236e93337dd3ec896d5185358595d57edd91d63da4fd2715eb0abd45d:9545a4009f8a8723402035f455879f6b0962167722d9f9e9d
        "publicKeyBase58": "3VZp2yNASMhXdLEeUwCoGQvSt3NvWRmbUm1WVFwzYNiQb99WJBxJy9JLwmBWCHm2nBiovFzaeuosaxJ5fvwB1GLhxuopGE4o32oKFc5nQjJKok
        "type": "X25519KeyAgreementKey2019"
      }
    ],
    "authentication": [
      "did:erat:d56c97d236e93337dd3ec896d5185358595d57edd91d63da4fd2715eb0abd45d:9545a4009f8a8723402035f455879f6b0962167722d9f9e9d56fc130e
    ],
    "assertionMethod": [
      "did:erat:d56c97d236e93337dd3ec896d5185358595d57edd91d63da4fd2715eb0abd45d:9545a4009f8a8723402035f455879f6b0962167722d9f9e9d56fc130e
    ],
    "keyAgreement": [
      "did:erat:d56c97d236e93337dd3ec896d5185358595d57edd91d63da4fd2715eb0abd45d:9545a4009f8a8723402035f455879f6b0962167722d9f9e9d56fc130e
    ],
    "created": "2023-10-05T08:41:08.104246721Z",
    "updated": "2023-10-05T08:41:08.104246721Z"
  }
}
```


Figure 5.2. Example of a DID Document, did:erat method.

- **W3C – Verifiable Credentials (VC)[4]:** VC offer a cryptographic mechanism to express and verify claims about an entity (such as an IoT device or individual) in a privacy-preserving and machine-verifiable manner. These credentials are essential for ensuring that sensitive data, like identity or device attributes, can be shared securely across decentralized networks. VCs are structured into three main roles:
  - o *Holder*: The entity possessing one or more verifiable credentials and generating verifiable presentations from them. For instance, in an IoT context, the holder could be a device carrying a certificate of authenticity. Holders include students, employees, and customers.
  - o *Issuer:* The entity responsible for creating a verifiable credential by asserting claims about a subject. Examples include corporations, governments, nonprofit organizations, trade associations and individuals issuing credentials that confirm device provenance or user identity.
  - o *Verifier:* The entity responsible for receiving and validating verifiable credentials, often in the context of access control or authentication. Examples include services that validate the credentials of devices before allowing them onto a secure network that might include employers, security personnel, and websites.
  - o *Verifiable Data Registry*: a system that mediates the creation, verification, and revocation of credentials. It maintains public keys, credential schemas, and revocation registries to ensure that credentials are valid and trustworthy.

The following figure shows the different roles in action and how they interact with each other.

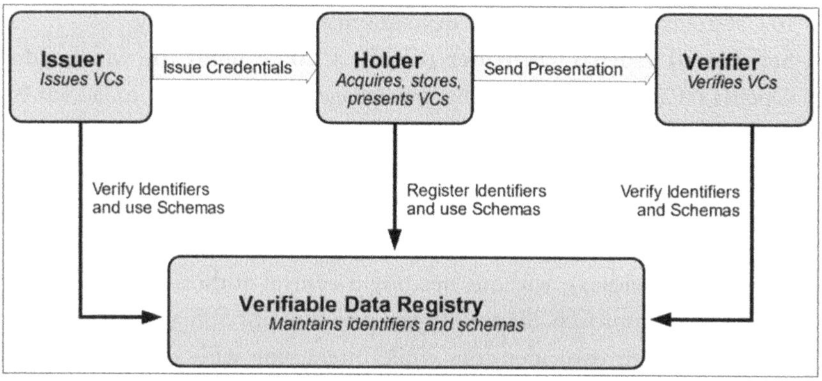

Figure 5.3. W3C Verifiable Credentials description.

4. https://www.w3.org/TR/vc-data-model/.

5.2.2 Communication Protocols for Decentralized Identity

In addition to defining the format of identity information, the Self-Sovereign Identity (SSI) community has proposed several standards to address how identity information that is transmitted between different roles and stakeholders. Two prominent standards in this area are:

- **DID Communication Messaging (DID Comm) v2.0**[5] is a communication protocol that facilitates secure and confidential messaging between stakeholders when interchanging identity information. It is designed to enable verifiable data exchange between SSI actors while maintaining privacy and security. This standard provides a robust mechanism for transmitting identity information across decentralized networks. DIDComm v2.0 defines protocols and workflows that specify how different SSI operations are executed, such as issuing credentials or presenting proof of a verifiable credential. These workflows enable the seamless exchange of identity-related information between holders, issuers, and verifiers. DIDComm also supports encryption, digital signatures, and message integrity checks, ensuring that identity information cannot be tampered with during transmission.

  Importantly, DIDComm v2.0 was specifically designed for Self-Sovereign Identity solutions, making it tailor-made for decentralized identity use cases. Major projects within the SSI community, such as Hyperledger Indy and Hyperledger Aries, utilize DIDComm to enable trusted communication between decentralized entities. By using DIDComm, decentralized identities can securely interact in a privacy-preserving way without needing intermediaries or central authorities. This communication framework allows for flexible and scalable identity management, which is essential for large-scale IoT systems, where billions of devices must interact securely.
- **Self-Issued OpenID Provider (SIOP) v2.0**[6] extends the widely adopted OpenID Connect protocol by introducing the concept of a Self-Issued OpenID Provider (Self-Issued OP). Unlike traditional OpenID Providers (OPs), which are controlled by third parties, a Self-Issued OP is fully controlled by the end-user. This means that individuals or entities can self-issue ID Tokens and present self-attested claims directly to Relying Parties (such as service providers), without needing a central authority to validate those claims. This approach aligns with the principles of SSI, as it empowers users to manage their own identities while interacting with services that rely on

5. https://identity.foundation/didcomm-messaging/spec/v2.0/.

6. https://openid.net/specs/openid-connect-self-issued-v2-1_0.html.

identity verification. SIOP v2.0 provides a way to bridge SSI solutions with existing identity management systems, making it possible to integrate modern, decentralized identities into traditional federated systems.

5.2.3 Credentials Format Standards

JSON Web Token (JWT)

As previously mentioned, the Self-Sovereign Identity (SSI) community is still in the early stages of defining and implementing its core concepts. Consequently, the primary standards are continuously evolving and adapting. During the ERATOSTHENES project, the W3C Verifiable Credential[7] standard was updated to support the JSON Web Token (JWT) format, which is a significant advancement.

JWT is an open standard that provides a compact and self-contained way of securely transmitting information between parties in the form of a JSON object. The data it carries can be verified and trusted because the tokens are cryptographically signed.

By incorporating support for JWT, the W3C Verifiable Credential standard simplifies the integration of verifiable credentials with existing Identity Management systems that already utilize the JWT format. This is particularly beneficial for systems based on OpenID Connect, making it easier to incorporate SSI principles without a complete overhaul of legacy infrastructure.

The following figures illustrate an example of how to apply the JWT format to verifiable credentials. The first Figure 5.4 displays a credential in JSON format, which includes the "*credentialSubject*" field that is used to hold the claims associated with the subject.

```
{
  "@context": [
    "https://www.w3.org/ns/credentials/v2",
    "https://www.w3.org/ns/credentials/examples/v2"
  ],
  "id": "http://university.example/credentials/3732",
  "type": ["VerifiableCredential", "ExampleDegreeCredential"],
  "issuer": "https://university.example/issuers/565049",
  "validFrom": "2010-01-01T00:00:00Z",
  "credentialSubject": {
    "id": "did:example:ebfeb1f712ebc6f1c276e12ec21",
    "degree": {
      "type": "ExampleBachelorDegree",
      "name": "Bachelor of Science and Arts"
    }
  }
}
```

Figure 5.4. Example of Verifiable Credential in JSON format.

7. https://www.w3.org/TR/vc-data-model-2.0.

Figure 5.5 illustrates the same verifiable credential as before, but this version includes the "*proof*" field, which contains the cryptographic data required to verify the integrity of the credential. The proof field ensures that the claims made within the credential can be trusted by allowing verifiers to check the credential's digital signature or other cryptographic elements. This feature has been present in earlier versions of the standard and remains a critical component for establishing trustworthiness in verifiable credentials.

```
{
  "@context": [
    "https://www.w3.org/ns/credentials/v2",
    "https://www.w3.org/ns/credentials/examples/v2",
    "https://w3id.org/security/suites/ed25519-2020/v1"
  ],
  "id": "http://university.example/credentials/3732",
  "type": [
    "VerifiableCredential",
    "ExampleDegreeCredential"
  ],
  "issuer": "https://university.example/issuers/565049",
  "validFrom": "2010-01-01T00:00:00Z",
  "credentialSubject": {
    "id": "did:example:ebfeb1f712ebc6f1c276e12ec21",
    "degree": {
      "type": "ExampleBachelorDegree",
      "name": "Bachelor of Science and Arts"
    }
  },
  "proof": {
    "type": "Ed25519Signature2020",
    "created": "2023-10-16T13:19:58Z",
    "verificationMethod": "https://university.example/issuers/565049#key-1"
,
    "proofPurpose": "assertionMethod",
    "proofValue": "zbEMsP6vpEKvwVvgv3uEe6u99hTUMm2MLhKPnZSsB9iy9KeXExUarCKr
95DrqCWpBqE8KDSSp3uJNXEk8Nhb2TLJ"
  }
}
```

Figure 5.5. Example of Verifiable Credential in JSON format with secured data integrity.

Figure 5.6 presents the same credential, this time shown in its decoded JSON Web Token (JWT) format. Readers familiar with tokens used in OpenID Connect will notice significant similarities between this format and the structure used in traditional Identity Management protocols. This resemblance allows for easier integration between modern Self-Sovereign Identity systems and legacy identity frameworks.

```
--------------- JWT header ---------------
{
  "alg": "ES256",
  "typ": "JWT"
}
--------------- JWT payload ---------------
// NOTE: The example below uses a valid VC-JWT serialization
//       that duplicates the iss, nbf, jti, and sub fields in the
//       Verifiable Credential (vc) field.
{
  "vc": {
    "@context": [
      "https://www.w3.org/ns/credentials/v2",
      "https://www.w3.org/ns/credentials/examples/v2"
    ],
    "id": "http://university.example/credentials/3732",
    "type": [
      "VerifiableCredential",
      "ExampleDegreeCredential"
    ],
    "issuer": "https://university.example/issuers/565049",
    "validFrom": "2010-01-01T00:00:00Z",
    "credentialSubject": {
      "id": "did:example:ebfeb1f712ebc6f1c276e12ec21",
      "degree": {
        "type": "ExampleBachelorDegree",
        "name": "Bachelor of Science and Arts"
      }
    }
  },
  "iss": "https://university.example/issuers/565049",
  "jti": "http://university.example/credentials/3732",
  "sub": "did:example:ebfeb1f712ebc6f1c276e12ec21"
}
```

Figure 5.6. Example of Verifiable Credential in decoded JSON Web Token format with secured data integrity.

Lastly, Figure 5.7 illustrates a verifiable credential encoded in JSON Web Token (JWT) format.


```
--------------- JWT ---------------
eyJhbGciOiJFUzI1NiIsInR5cCI6IkpXVCJ9.eyJ2YyI6eyJAY29udGV4dCI6WyJodHRwczovL3
d3dy53My5vcmcvbnMvY3JlZGVudGlhbHMvdjIiLCJodHRwczovL3d3dy53My5vcmcvbnMvY3JlZ
GVudGlhbHMvZXhhbXBsZXMvdjIiXSwiaWQiOiJodHRwOi8vdW5pdmVyc2l0eS5leGFtcGxlL2Ny
ZWRlbnRpYWxzLzM3MzIiLCJ0eXBlIjpbIlZlcmlmaWFibGVDcmVkZW50aWFsIiwiRXhhbXBsZUR
lZ3JlZUNyZWRlbnRpYWwiXSwiaXNzdWVyIjoiaHR0cHM6Ly91bml2ZXJzaXR5LmV4YW1wbGUvaX
NzdWVycy81NjUwNDkiLCJ2YWxpZEZyb20iOiIyMDEwLTAxLTAxVDAwOjAwOjAwWiIsImNyZWRlb
nRpYWxTdWJqZWN0Ijp7ImlkIjoiZGlkOmV4YW1wbGU6ZWJmZWIxZjcxMmViYzZmMWMyNzZlMTJl
YzIxIiwiZGVncmVlIjp7InR5cGUiOiJFeGFtcGxlQmFjaGVsb3JEZWdyZWUiLCJuYW1lIjoiQmF
jaGVsb3Igb2YgU2NpZW5jZSBhbmQgQXJ0cyJ9fX0sImlzcyI6Imh0dHBzOi8vdW5pdmVyc2l0eS
5leGFtcGxlL2lzc3VlcnMvNTY1MDQ5IiwianRpIjoiaHR0cDovL3VuaXZlcnNpdHkuZXhhbXBsZ
S9jcmVkZW50aWFscy8zNzMyIiwic3ViIjoiZGlkOmV4YW1wbGU6ZWJmZWIxZjcxMmViYzZmMWMy
NzZlMTJlYzIxIn0.QO_3_VhkpQC_nwgcSjXpG1PQHjilNtqPp0-3ylmM3exVGT9HbnoDXysGTWq
mCqXszgz9MFcT7Y6Vfedio7QuqQ
```


Figure 5.7. Example of Verifiable Credential in encoded JSON Web Token format with secured data integrity.

The addition of JSON Web Token (JWT) support to verifiable credentials simplifies their integration with legacy Identity Management systems by allowing credentials to be included in request headers, similar to OpenID and OAuth. The ERATOSTHENES consortium has adopted these changes to enhance their Self-Sovereign Identity solution for managing the entire lifecycle of IoT devices, from onboarding to decommissioning.

Selective Disclosure for JWT's (SD-JWT)

Selective Disclosure JWT (SD-JWT)[8] is an extension of the standard JWT that introduces the capability for selective disclosure of information. In SSI contexts, selective disclosure is a critical privacy feature because it allows users to share only specific pieces of their credentials with verifiers, rather than the full set of claims.

The process of issuing a Verifiable Credential with selectively hidden claims is outlined as follows. First, the Verifiable Credential (VC) is created. Then, the issuer designates specific claims as selectively disclosable by generating disclosures. These hidden claims are incorporated into the credential, producing an SD-JWT that conforms to a data model compatible with a Verifiable Credential containing concealed claims.

The process of issuing a Verifiable Credential with hidden claims is illustrated in Figure 5.8. First, a Verifiable Credential (VC) is created. After that, the issuer marks specific claims as selectively hidden, generating disclosures. These hidden claims are then embedded into the credential. The final result, known as SD-JWT, follows a data structure that ensures it is compatible with a Verifiable Credential containing concealed claims.

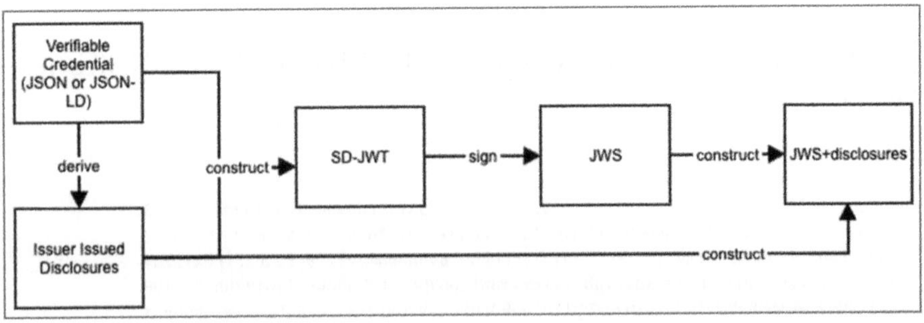

Figure 5.8. Issuing process following SD-JWT standard.

8. https://datatracker.ietf.org/doc/draft-ietf-oauth-selective-disclosure-jwt/.

The following section outlines the process of issuing a credential using real data. The first step involves collecting the necessary information and formatting it in accordance with the W3C Verifiable Credentials Data Model v1.1[9] standard. The figure below shows an example of a verifiable credential that is prepared for issuance.

```
{
  "@context": ["https://www.w3.org/ns/credentials/v2"],
  "id": "9bcc9aaa-3bdc-4414-9450-739c295c752c",
  "type": ["VerifiableCredential", "StudentID"],
  "issuer": "did:ebsi:zvHWX359A3CvfJnCYaAiAde",
  "validFrom": "2023-01-01T00:00:00Z",
  "validUntil": "2033-01-01T00:00:00Z",
  "credentialSubject": {
    "id": "did:key:z2dmzD81cgPx8Vki7JbuuMmFYrWPgYoytykUZ3eyqht1j9KbsDbVZXdb3jzCagESyY4EE2x7Y
    "familyName": "Carroll",
    "givenName": "Lewis",
    "birthDate": "1832-01-27",
    "student": true
  },
  "credentialSchema": {
    "id": "https://api-pilot.ebsi.eu/trusted-schemas-registry/v2/schemas/0x23039e6356ea6b703
    "type": "FullJsonSchemaValidator2021"
  }
}
```

Figure 5.9. Original Verifiable Credential before issuing process.

The next step involves calculating the disclosure values by applying the SHA-256 hashing method.

```
Content: '["2GLC42sKQveCfGfryNRN9w", "familyName", "Carroll"]'
calculated Disclosure: WyIyR0xDNDJzS1F2ZUNmR2ZyeU5STjl3IiwgImZhbWlseU5hbWUiLCAiQ2Fycm9sbCJd
calculated Digest: zSmImWHPJzQ7Rx8ZG0IYhUF1Ozj8f17wDKJGhxUkrdU


Content: '["eluV5Og3gSNII8EYnsxA_A", "givenName", "Lewis"]'
calculated Disclosure: WyJlbHVWNU9nM2dTTklJOEVZbnN4QV9BIiwgImdpdmVuTmFtZSIsICJMZXdpcyJd
calculated Digest: T4RnDm1clVLCav2Mrsel6sNMz8pqGCeMrrp__YrV_-w

Content: '["6Ij7tM-a5iVPGboS5tmvVA", "birthDate", "1832-01-27"]'
calculated Disclosure: WyI2SWo3dE0tYTVpVlBHYm9TNXRtdlZBIiwgImJpcnRoRGF0ZSIsICIxODMyLTAxLTI3Il0
calculated Digest: SFQTjr91IkPi6betQ0EYs5rdJ2TbMesJGftF6h7hjTA
```

Figure 5.10. Calculating disclose values.

9. https://www.w3.org/TR/vc-data-model/.

With the disclosed values, the Verifiable Credential is formed.


```
{
  "@context": ["https://www.w3.org/ns/credentials/v2"],
  "id": "9bcc9aaa-3bdc-4414-9450-739c295c752c",
  "type": ["VerifiableCredential", "StudentID"],
  "issuer": "did:ebsi:zvHWX359A3CvfJnCYaAiAde",
  "validFrom": "2023-01-01T00:00:00Z",
  "validUntil": "2033-01-01T00:00:00Z",
  "credentialSubject": {
    "id": "did:key:z2dmzD81cgPx8Vki7JbuuMmFYrWPgYoytykUZ3eyqht1j9KbsDbVZXdb3jzCagESyY4EE2x7Y
    "_sd": [
      "zSmImWHPJzQ7Rx8ZG0IYhUF1Ozj8f17wDKJGhxUkrdU",
      "T4RnDm1clVLCav2Mrsel6sNMz8pqGCeMrrp__YrV_-w",
      "SFQTjr91IkPi6betQ0EYs5rdJ2TbMesJGftF6h7hjTA"
    ],
    "student": true
  },
  "credentialSchema": {
    "id": "https://api-pilot.ebsi.eu/trusted-schemas-registry/v2/schemas/0x23039e6356ea6b703
    "type": "FullJsonSchemaValidator2021"
  },
  "_sd_alg": "sha-256"
}
```


Figure 5.11. Verifiable credential woth the disclosed calculated values.

For issuing the credential, it must be in JWT format. The process is illustrated in the image below.


```
eyJ0eXAiOiJKV1QiLCJhbGciOiJFUzI1NiIsImtpZCI6ImRpZDplYnNpOnp2SFdYMzU5QTNDdm-
ZKbkNZYUFpQWRlI0YwcjVPeXRfbGFodnZ6Nk1XbFlzM21jWU5LWmlpUWRVZnF2OHRzaEh-
OOXcifQ.eyJpc3MiOiJkaWQ6ZWJzaTp6dkhXWDM1OUEzQ3ZmSm5DWWFBaUFkZSIsInN1Yi-
I6ImRpZDprZXk6ejJkbXpEODFjZ1B4OFZraTdKYnV1TW1GWXJXUGdZb3l0eWtVWjNleXFodD-
FqOUtic0RiVlpYZGIzanpDYWdFU3lZNEVFMng3WWp4M2dOd2N0b0V1UkNLS0RyZE5QM0h-
QRnRHOFJUdkJpWVN0VDVnaEJlaEhpekgyRHk2eFF0VzNQZDJTZWNpekw5YjJqekRDTX-
I3S2E1Y1JBV1pGd3Zxd0F0d1RUN3hldDc2OXk5RVJoNiIsIm5iZiI6IjIwMjMtMDEtMDFUMDA6M-
DA6MDBaIiwiZXhwIjoiMjAzMy0wMS0wMVQwMDowMDowMFoiLCJqdGkiOiI5YmNjOWFhYS0z-
YmRjLTQ0MTQtOTQ1MC03MzljMjk1Yzc1MmMiLCJ2YyI6eyJAY29udGV4dCI6WyJodHRwczov-
L3d3dy53My5vcmcvbnMvY3JlZGVudGlhbHMvdjIiXSwiaWQiOiI5YmNjOWFhYS0zYmRj-
LTQ0MTQtOTQ1MC03MzljMjk1Yzc1MmMiLCJ0eXBlIjpbIlZlcmlmaWFibGVBdHRlc3RhdGlvbiIsIl-
ZlcmlmaWFibGVDcmVkZW50aWFsIiwiU3R1ZGVudElEIl0sImlzc3VlciI6ImRpZDplYnNpOnp2SFd-
YMzU5QTNDdmZKbkNZYUFpQWRlIiwidmFsaWRGcm9tIjoiMjAyMy0wMS0wMVQwMDowM-
DowMFoiLCJ2YWxpZFVudGlsIjoiMjAzMy0wMS0wMVQwMDowMDowMFoiLCJjcmVkZW50aW-
FsU3ViamVjdCI6eyJpZCI6ImRpZDprZXk6ejJkbXpEODFjZ1B4OFZraTdKYnV1TW1GWXJXUGd-
Zb3l0eWtVWjNleXFodDFqOUtic0RiVlpYZGIzanpDYWdFU3lZNEVFMng3WWp4M2d-
Od2N0b0V1UkNLS0RyZE5QM0hQRnRHOFJUdkJpWVN0VDVnaEJlaEhpekgyRHk2eFF0VzN-
QZDJTZWNpekw5YjJqekRDTXI3S2E1Y1JBV1pGd3Zxd0F0d1RUN3hldDc2OXk5RVJoNiIsIl9z-
ZCI6WyJ6U21JbVdIUEp6UTdSeDhaRzBJWWhVRjFPemo4ZjE3d0RLSkdoeFVrcmRVIiwiVDRSb-
kRtMWNsVkxDYXYyTXJzZWw2c05Nejhwcnd6c05Nejhwc05DZU1ycnBfX1lyVl8tdyIsIlNGUVRqcjkxSWtQaTZi-
ZXRRMEVZczVyZEoyVGJNZXNKR2Z0RjZoN2hqVEEiXSwic3R1ZGVudCI6dHJ1ZX0sImNy-
ZWRlbnRpYWxTY2hlbWEiOnsiaWQiOiJodHRwczovL2FwaS1waWxvdC5lYnNpLmV1L3Ryd-
XN0ZWQtc2NoZW1hcy1yZWdpc3RyeS92Mi9zY2hlbWFzL zB4MjMwMzllNjM1NmVhNmI3MDNj-
ZTY3MmU3Y2ZhYzBiNDI3NjViMTUwZjYzZGY3OGUyYmQxOGFlNzg1Nzg3ZjZhMiIsInR5cGUiOi-
JGdWxsSnNvblNjaGVtYVZhbGlkYXRvcjIwMjEifSwiX3NkX2FsZyI6InNoYS0yNTYifX0.wC1jmeb-
WUSVQYO18DluQhYUbTXDpvWuBSQv3apiiP3OdHlyPMRmFjX7jWPshjaWQkasuL_DBJ-
lQufgDzT8z7Q~WylyR0xDNDJzS1F2ZUNmR2ZyeU5STjl3IiwgImZhbWlseU5hbWUiLCAi-
Q2Fycm9sbCJd~WyJlbHVWNU9nM2dTTklJOEVZbnN4QV9BIiwgImdpdmVuTmFtZSIs-
ICJMZXdpcyJd~WyI2SWo3dE0tYTVpVlBHYm9TNXRtdlZBIiwgImJpcnRoRGF0ZSIsICIxODMy-
LTAxLTI3Il0
```


Figure 5.12. Issued verifiable credential following SD-JWT standard.

Figure 5.12 shows an example that includes both the signed SD-JWT and the disclosure information, which are separated by a "~" character.

The following Figure 5.13 provides a detailed view of the format used.

```
<SD-JWT>~<Disclosure 1>~<Disclosure 2>~...~<Disclosure N>
```

Figure 5.13. Combined format for issuance.

SD-JWT-based Verifiable Credentials (SD-JWT VC)

This standard builds upon the SD-JWT approach by incorporating specific updates from the latest W3C Verifiable Credentials Data Model 2.0, which introduces several changes from previous versions. Among these updates is the addition of new parameters, such as the "vct" parameter, which defines the type of content in a Verifiable Credential (VC). The "vct" parameter dictates rules regarding which claims can or must be included in the Unsecured Payload of the SD-JWT VC,[10] and whether these claims can be selectively disclosed. While the standard does not specify preset "vct" values, it expects individual ecosystems to define them, including the corresponding semantics and rules for issuing and validating credentials.

The "vct" parameter is represented by a unique URI, such as "https://credentials.example.com/identity_credential". For instance, this credential type specifies that certain claims, like given_name, family_name, birthdate, and address, are mandatory in the Unsecured Payload. Additionally, other claims such as email, phone_number, and private claims like is_over_18 or is_over_21 may be included. The standard also allows selective disclosure of these claims when needed.

5.3 Ledger uSelf: Decentralized Identity Solution for IoT Devices

5.3.1 Architectural Positioning within the ERATOSTHENES Framework

The diagram in Figure 5.14 illustrates the ERATOSTHENES architecture, highlighting the main components and services developed by the project. The lower section of the diagram (in purple) represents the elements embedded in IoT devices, while the upper section shows the servers that host the various ERATOSTHENES framework services.

Focusing specifically on the components responsible for the project's Self-Sovereign Identity (SSI) solution, the architecture includes two key elements: the SSI Management service on the server side and the SSI Agent within the IoT

10. https://datatracker.ietf.org/doc/draft-ietf-oauth-sd-jwt-vc/

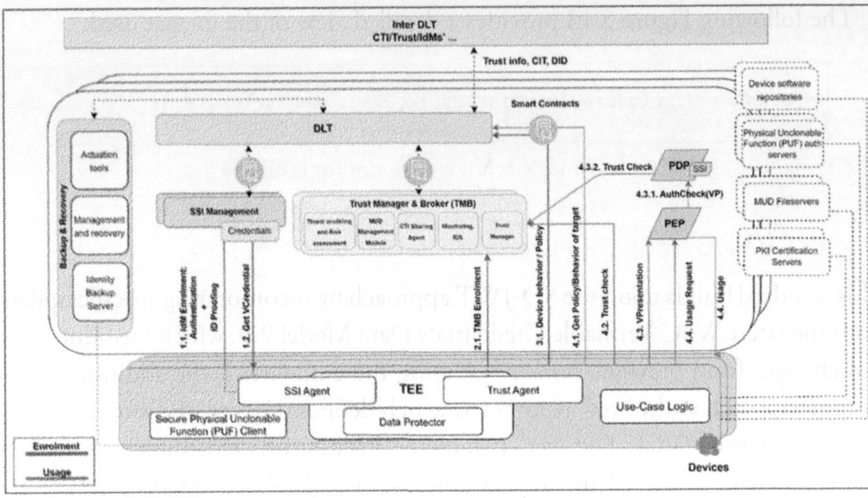

Figure 5.14. ERATOSTHENES general architecture diagram.

devices. The SSI Management service, known as the Ledger uSelf IdM component, operates on the server, while the SSI Agent, referred to as the Ledger uSelf IoT component, is deployed directly on the IoT devices. Although not explicitly shown in the diagram, the Context-aware component has been fully integrated within the Ledger uSelf IoT, ensuring seamless functionality across the SSI solution.

5.3.2 Integration of SSI in IoT Devices: Components Overview

The Ledger uSelf solution plays a pivotal role within the IoT device architecture, integrating several essential components that enhance both security and functionality:

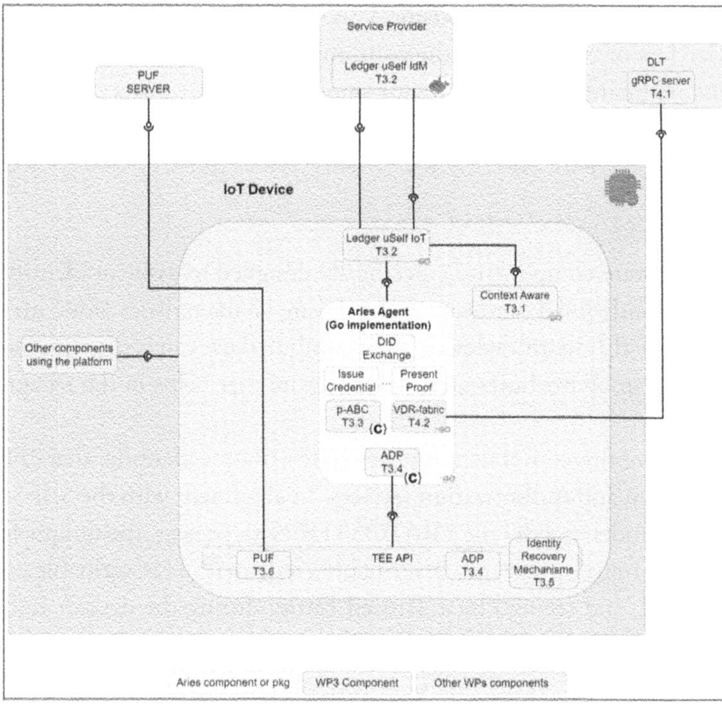

Figure 5.15. IoT components final integration for SSI solution.

- **Context-Aware Component:** This module enables the collection of crucial hardware and software information necessary to create a verifiable credential, which includes a unique device footprint for enhanced identification and authentication.
- **PUF Client and PUF Library:** These components utilize Physical Unclonable Functions (PUF), a form of hardware-based cryptography, to generate the public DID (Decentralized Identifier) associated with the device. This ensures robust device identification.
- **p-ABC Module:** This module provides advanced cryptographic capabilities that enable the generation of verifiable presentations and zero-knowledge proofs. This ensures that only necessary data is disclosed, protecting the privacy of the device's credentials.
- **Verifiable Data Registry Fabric (VDR-Fabric):** This module is responsible for generating public DIDs by leveraging a Hyperledger Fabric network. It stores DID documents, playing a crucial role in establishing the public DID for the device during the onboarding process.
- **Advanced Data Protection (ADP) Module:** The ADP module is designed to securely store identity information within the device. It also acts as a bridge to the Trusted Execution Environment (TEE), ensuring that sensitive identity data is protected.

- **Identity Recovery Mechanism:** This feature ensures that even in cases of device loss or replacement, the continuity and security of IoT data management are maintained, allowing for smooth identity recovery.

5.3.3 Key features of Ledger uSelf

5.3.3.1 Ledger uSelf Context Aware

The Context Aware component is specifically designed to assist in identifying IoT devices. While individual hardware and software characteristics alone may not be enough to distinctly identify a device, their combined use can form a unique profile. This combination of attributes creates a signature that helps in the recognition of each IoT device.

The key goal of this component is to generate a unique identifier that can be used in Authentication and Authorization services. In alignment with the Self-Sovereign Identity (SSI) model used by the ERATOSTHENES project, the unique footprint of the device is transformed into a verifiable credential. This verifiable credential is issued, signed, and secured by a Trusted Entity during the device's onboarding process. Once issued, this credential can be used within any SSI-compliant authentication framework.

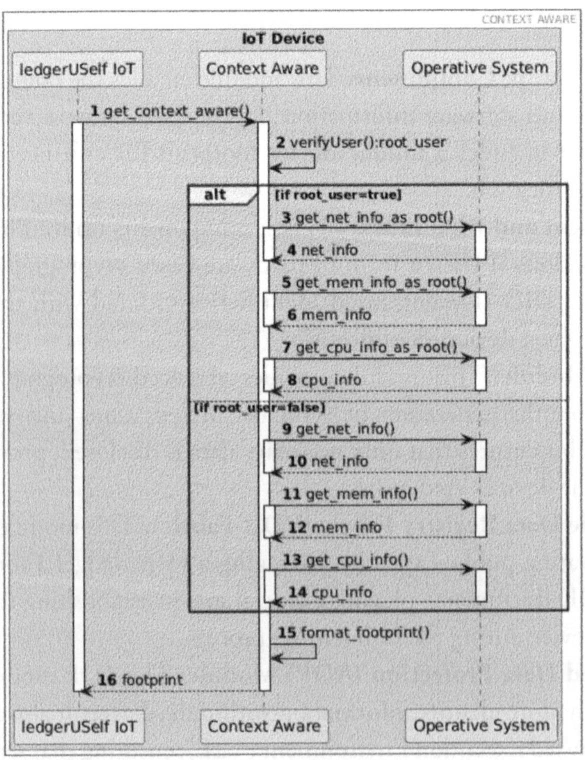

Figure 5.16. Context Aware sequence diagram.

Figure 5.16 illustrates the step-by-step process of gathering unique information from an IoT device, with access to this data dependent on the user's permission level. Superuser or root permissions allow for broader access to device information, while users with lesser permissions have more restricted access. This feature enables the service to generate distinct device profiles for each case. In the ERATOSTHENES project, it is expected that the process will typically run with superuser permissions. However, the component is also capable of generating a device footprint even when root access is not available, ensuring a flexible approach that strengthens the security of the overall process.

5.3.3.2 Ledger uSelf IoT Device

The primary purpose of the Ledger uSelf IoT component is to provide identity management for IoT devices within the ERATOSTHENES project, adhering to the principles of Self-Sovereign Identity (SSI). To meet the project's specific needs, this component has been designed as a single executable, integrating all necessary functions. This design choice simplifies the installation, management, and execution of the identity solution for IoT devices.

The final architecture of the SSI solution for the ERATOSTHENES project has been optimized to meet the project's unique requirements. Built on the Hyperledger Aries framework, the Ledger uSelf component acts as the core of the system, integrating with other essential project modules. Enhancements have been made to boost performance, add new features, and ensure smoother integrations. The solution is initially deployed in a containerized environment, which not only enhances operational efficiency but also facilitates better performance and scalability as new features are introduced.

The key features of the Ledger uSelf solution will be outlined in the following sections.

5.3.3.2.1 Create Public DID

The process of creating a Public Decentralized Identifier (DID) involves generating a unique identifier for the IoT device and developing a corresponding DID Document that adheres to the W3C DID specifications. This step is crucial for the onboarding process, as it establishes the device as a recognized participant within the system. The Identity Management component of the project plays a significant role in this functionality.

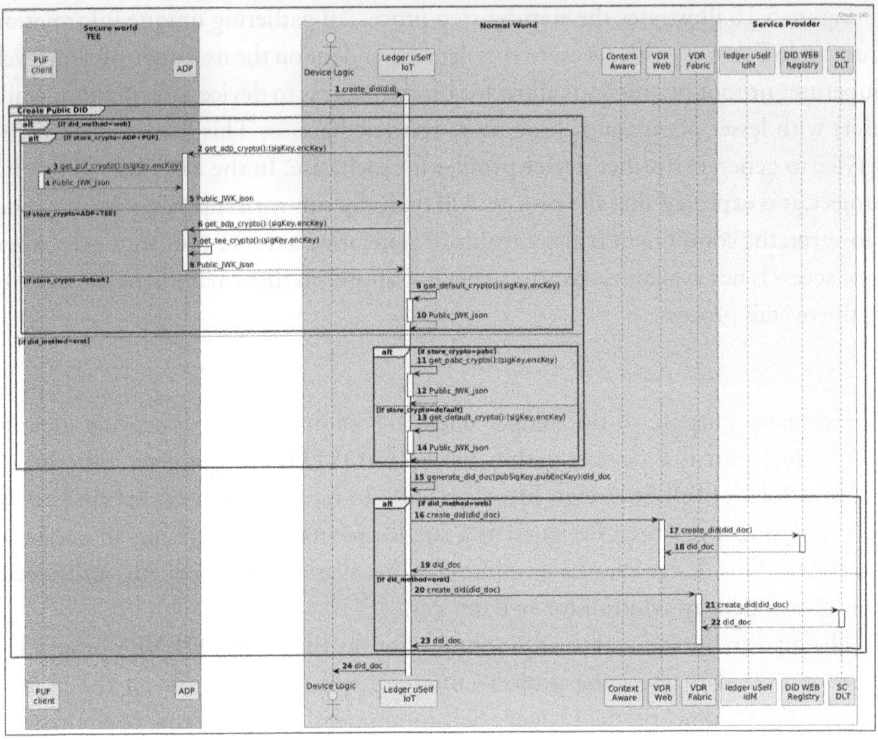

Figure 5.17. Create DID sequence diagram.

To accommodate the diverse needs of the ERATOSTHENES project, the system offers two methods for publishing the public DID:

- **did:web** This method follows established DID standards.
- **did:erat** A custom method specifically developed for the ERATOSTHENES project, this approach enables the DID to be published on a permissioned blockchain using Hyperledger Fabric. This ensures secure storage of decentralized identifiers while leveraging blockchain technology. The system incorporates the vdr-erat component, which includes a gRPC server and a Verifiable Data Registry (VDR), as illustrated previously in Figure 5.15.

The generation of cryptographic materials within the Ledger uSelf IoT is dynamic and involves three main sources:

1. PUF Client Library: This source produces physically unclonable cryptographic keys.
2. dP-ABC Module: This module offers cryptographic functionalities for generating derived verifiable presentations.
3. Hyperledger Aries: The framework manages its own cryptographic material generation.

5.3.3.2.2 Establish Connection

This method facilitates connections with other entities using the DID Exchange Protocol 1.0 and the Out-Of-Band Protocol (OOB) 1.1, as specified by Aries. Establishing a connection is essential for implementing any of the DID Communication standards.

To initiate a connection, each participant must generate a unique DID peer, followed by the exchange of these DIDs. This exchange enables secure communication between participants, utilizing the cryptographic methods linked to their respective DIDs.

From the device's perspective, the connection setup process is straightforward. The agent can simply invoke the connection functionality via the server-side URL, streamlining the establishment of the connection (see Figure 5.18 below).

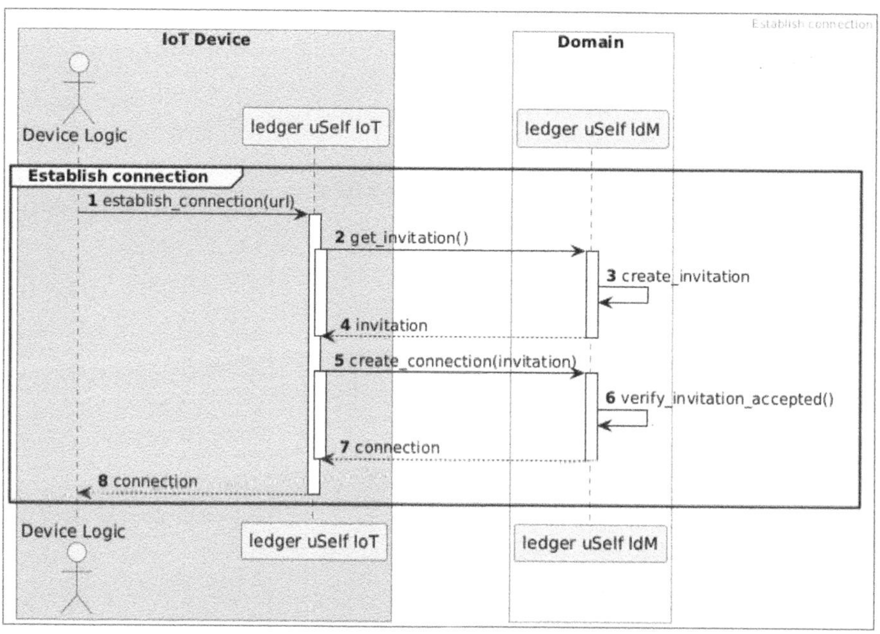

Figure 5.18. Establish Connection sequence diagram.

5.3.3.2.3 Device Onboarding

The management of Self-Sovereign Identity (SSI) is vital for the enrollment of IoT devices, as it involves issuing verifiable credentials that authenticate and authorize device identity attributes. Enrolling devices in the ERATOSTHENES framework formally registers them as members of its ecosystem, marking the second phase of the onboarding process, which begins with creating a Decentralized Identifier (DID).

The onboarding starts when the Ledger uSelf IoT component receives an onboarding request. Two primary tasks are performed: generating a public DID and registering it in the Identity Manager (IdM). The creation of a public DID includes generating a unique identifier for the device and constructing a corresponding DID Document that complies with the W3C DID standards. This process relies on cryptographic keys generated from three distinct sources, which are specified through environmental variables during installation.

The Ledger uSelf IoT component operates with a Hyperledger Aries agent, allowing flexibility to adapt to the specific requirements of the ERATOSTHENES project. After obtaining the necessary cryptographic keys, the system generates the DID Document using one of two methods: did:web or did:erat. Once the new DID is published, the device registers with the Ledger uSelf IdM agent and generates a verifiable credential that encapsulates its unique identity attributes, requesting the trusted entity to issue this credential (see Figure 5.19 below).

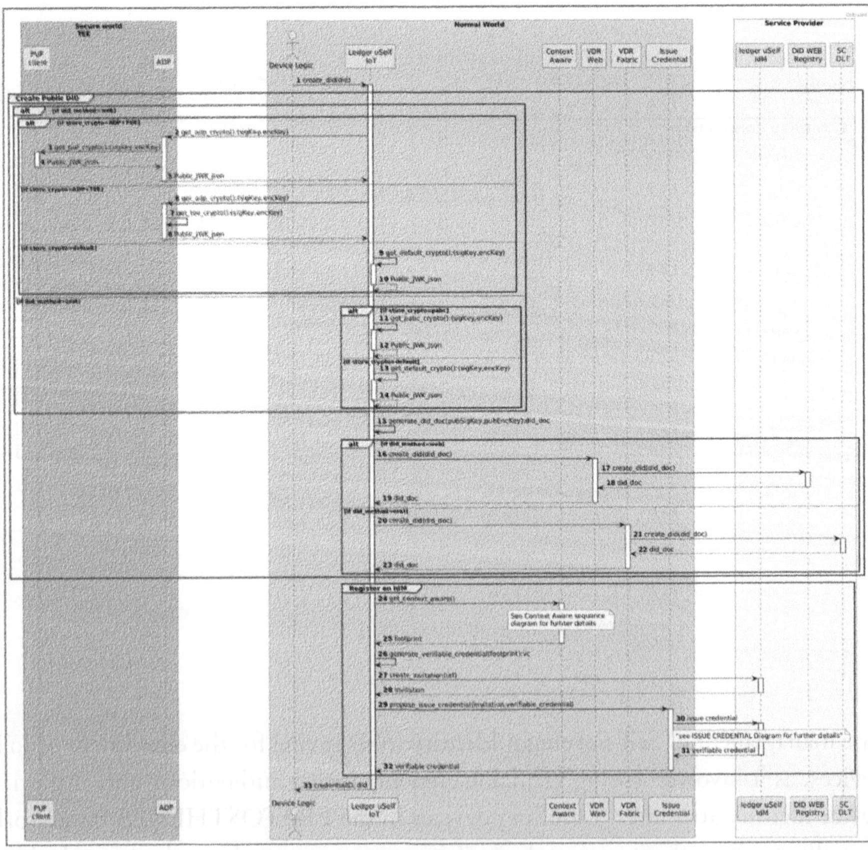

Figure 5.19. Onboarding sequence diagram.

5.3.3.2.4 Issue Credential

The implementation of this feature adheres to the guidelines established in the Issue Credential Protocol 2.0[11] from Hyperledger Aries and aligns with the DID Comm Messaging[12] standards set by the Identity Foundation. This protocol recognizes that communication between the Issuer and the Holder can be asynchronous, accounting for potential delays when the end user interacts with the system through a mobile or web wallet. However, adaptations have been made for situations requiring synchronous communication with IoT devices.

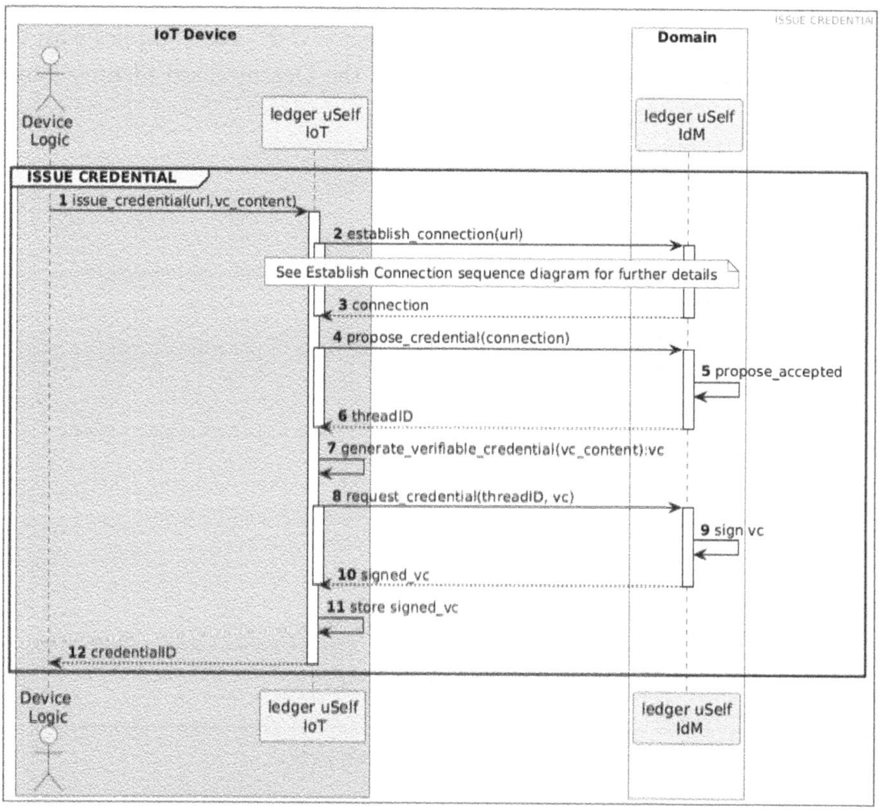

Figure 5.20. Issue Credential sequence diagram.

The process, illustrated in Figure 5.20, begins with the IoT device establishing a secure connection with the domain agent. Once the connection is in place, the Ledger uSelf IoT agent proposes to initiate the issuance process to the Ledger uSelf

11. https://github.com/hyperledger/aries-rfcs/tree/main/features/0453-issue-credential-v2.

12. https://identity.foundation/didcomm-messaging/spec/v2.0/.

IdM component, pending the issuer's agreement. This proposal includes a unique thread ID to track the process.

With the thread ID secured, the device then requests the Ledger uSelf IdM to issue the credential, providing the necessary verifiable credential content as a parameter. Upon receiving the signed verifiable credential from the issuer, the device stores it for future use.

5.3.3.2.5 Present Proof

The Present Proof feature enables IoT devices to prove ownership of a verifiable credential by presenting it to a verifier. This functionality is implemented in accordance with Hyperledger Aries' *Present Proof Protocol 2.0*[13] and complies with the DID Communication standards established by the Decentralized Identity Foundation (DIF).

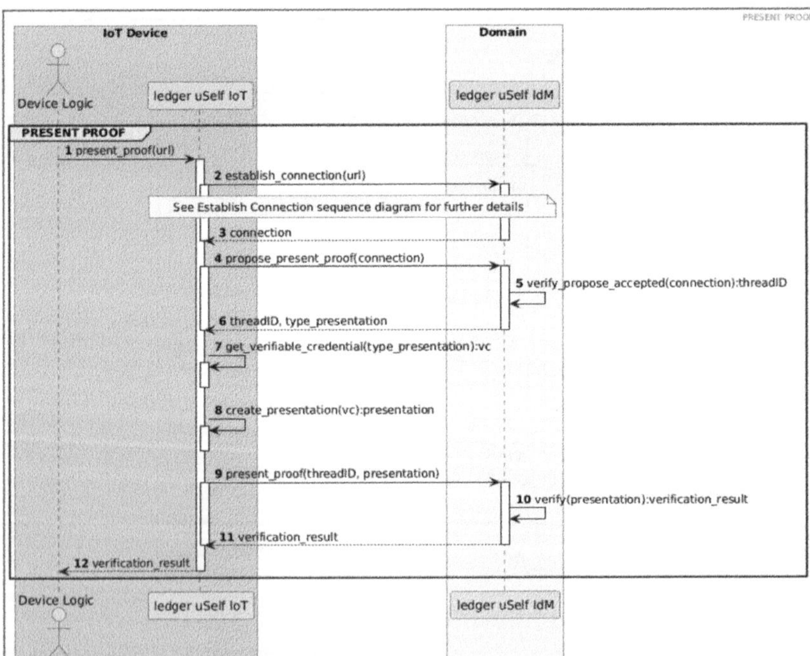

Figure 5.21. Present Proof sequence diagram.

The process typically begins with the device establishing a secure connection with the verifier. Once connected, the verifier provides a thread ID and defines the criteria for the proof. The device then searches its stored credentials to find one that matches the verifier's requirements. After identifying the appropriate credential, the

13. https://github.com/hyperledger/aries-rfcs/tree/main/features/0454-present-proof-v2.

device generates a verifiable presentation, demonstrating ownership of the credential. The presentation is then sent to the verifier for validation. If successful, the proof is accepted, allowing further steps in the process to proceed.

5.3.3.2.6 Get Verifiable Presentation

This feature allows IoT devices to create a verifiable presentation that proves their ownership and confirms their successful onboarding into the system. The process begins by retrieving the verifiable credential issued during onboarding. The device then uses this credential to generate a new verifiable presentation, which is re-signed for added security. Finally, the signed presentation is sent back to the device, confirming its authenticity and integration into the system.

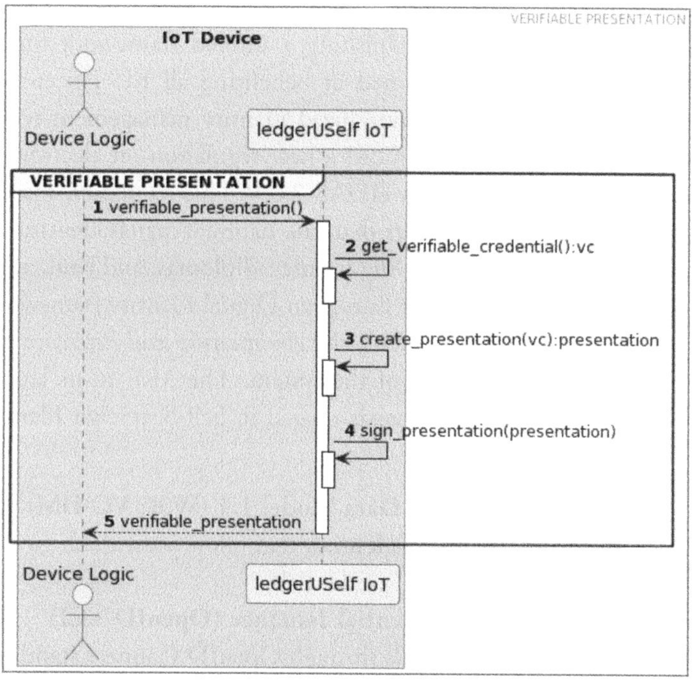

Figure 5.22. Get Verifiable Presentation sequence diagram.

5.3.3.2.7 Disposable ID

Disposable identities are temporary and limited-use identifiers, making them ideal for IoT devices in Self-Sovereign Identity (SSI) systems. Their short lifespan enhances privacy by preventing tracking and reducing the risk of identity theft, as a unique identifier is created for each interaction. This approach ensures that devices retain control over their data while complying with privacy standards.

In ERATOSTHENES, the disposable identity feature can be tailored to specific project needs through the configurable variable "USELF_EXPIRATION_TIME," which defines the identity's validity period in minutes. Once the IoT device is onboarded, its identity is created with a set expiration time. The "present proof" function is used to confirm if the identity remains valid. If expired, the system signals that the "verifiable presentation" is no longer valid. Additionally, the verifiable credential includes an "expirationDate" field, indicating when the credential will expire in a standard UTC format, ensuring clear timing for all parties involved.

5.4 Research and Scientific Innovation

In recent times, significant advancements have occurred in the realm of Self-Sovereign Identity (SSI), particularly within the European Union (EU). The EU has taken major steps towards establishing a unified framework for European Digital Identity. This initiative, aimed at benefiting all EU citizens, residents, and businesses, is grounded in decentralized identity management technologies. To support this, the EU has introduced a new regulation on electronic identification and trust services, known as eIDAS 2.0.[14] This regulation mandates that Member States provide digital wallets that link national digital identities with various personal attributes (such as driving licenses, diplomas, and bank accounts).

While the technical details of the European Digital Identity framework are still being refined, an important document, the *Architecture and Reference Framework (ARF)*,[15] outlines the key elements of the system. The ARF, in its latest version, defines the use of several core standards related to Self-Sovereign Identity. These include:

- **W3C Verifiable Credentials Data Model 1.1 (W3C VC-DM)**[16]: A framework for creating verifiable credentials that allow individuals to share trustworthy, tamper-evident digital credentials.
- **OpenID for Verifiable Credential Issuance (OpenID VCI)**[17]: A protocol for issuing verifiable credentials through OpenID Connect standards.
- **OpenID Connect for Verifiable Presentations (OpenID VP)**[18]: Facilitates the presentation of verifiable credentials using OpenID Connect.

---

14. https://digital-strategy.ec.europa.eu/en/policies/eidas-regulation.
15. https://github.com/eu-digital-identity-wallet/eudi-doc-architecture-and-reference-framework/blob/main/docs/arf.md.
16. https://www.w3.org/TR/vc-data-model/.
17. https://openid.net/specs/openid-4-verifiable-credential-issuance-1_0.html.
18. https://openid.net/specs/openid-4-verifiable-presentations-1_0.html.

- **Selective Disclosure for JWTs (SD-JWT)**[19]: Enables users to selectively disclose information from JSON Web Tokens (JWTs), ensuring greater privacy control.
- **SD-JWT-based Verifiable Credentials (SD-JWT VC)**[20]: Extends SD-JWT for verifiable credentials, allowing users to selectively disclose specific claims from their identity information.

The Ledger uSelf solution for the ERATOSTHENES project adheres to all relevant standards and integrates cutting-edge advancements in identity management technology. Its implementation includes innovations such as p-ABC (privacy-Attribute-Based Credentials) cryptography.

The solution holistically addresses the challenges of IoT identity management, starting from the creation of a root of trust for device identities, followed by enrollment, identification, and ongoing participation in a zero-trust and privacy-preserving framework for authorization. It supports Self-Sovereign Identity (SSI) principles for direct authentication and enables delegation of the authorization process to a Policy Decision Point (PDP) and Policy Enforcement Point (PEP) infrastructure. Furthermore, Distributed Ledger Technologies (DLTs) are employed to securely manage data, such as policies and trust scores, while preserving privacy using SSI methodologies.

An important innovation is the integration of p-ABCs with the W3C Verifiable Credentials (VC) specification. This combination allows for minimal disclosure and unlinkability, offering better privacy protection compared to other implementations like JWT-SD. This breakthrough addresses one of the previous limitations of p-ABCs, which lacked interoperability with other identity solutions, enhancing both scalability and efficiency.

Ultimately, the Ledger uSelf solution provides a flexible application of technologies, balancing security, privacy, and computational costs to cater to the diverse nature of IoT scenarios.

5.5 Conclusions

The ERATOSTHENES project has successfully achieved one of its core objectives: developing a decentralized identity management system grounded in Self-Sovereign Identity (SSI) principles for IoT devices throughout their lifecycle. This

19. https://datatracker.ietf.org/doc/draft-ietf-oauth-selective-disclosure-jwt/.

20. https://datatracker.ietf.org/doc/draft-ietf-oauth-sd-jwt-vc/.

SSI approach represents a significant leap forward, offering a decentralized, user-controlled identity management framework that contrasts with traditional centralized systems. By empowering IoT devices with autonomy over their identities, the solution greatly simplifies the complexities of device management while ensuring greater security and privacy.

In terms of technological development, the project concentrated on the integration and deployment of key components within IoT devices. The Ledger uSelf solution, in particular, serves as the central identity management component, seamlessly incorporating other essential features such as the PUF client, p-ABC cryptography, VDR-fabric, Advanced Data Protection (ADP) module, and the Identity Recovery Mechanism. These components were developed across multiple work packages, ensuring the solution meets the security, scalability, and performance needs of IoT environments.

A significant achievement in this project was the successful adaptation of these components to the specific hardware and software constraints of IoT devices, ensuring compatibility and ease of deployment. The modularity of the Ledger uSelf framework not only supports the devices used within ERATOSTHENES but also demonstrates the potential for broader application across various IoT systems. This adaptability allows for straightforward installation, execution, and management on different types of devices, offering a flexible, scalable solution that can be ported to other IoT contexts beyond the project.

In conclusion, the ERATOSTHENES project has created an innovative decentralized identity management framework that simplifies IoT device management while providing strong privacy, security, and scalability benefits, positioning it as a pioneering solution for the future of IoT identity systems.

DOI: 10.1561/9781638285076.ch6

Chapter 6

Inter-Ledger Platform for Cyber-Threat Information Sharing and Lifecycle Security

By Jesús García-Rodríguez, Ekam Puri Nieto, Juan Francisco Martínez Gil and Agustín Marín Frutos

The security configuration of devices within their deployment context is a key challenge for the secure management of IoT ecosystems in scientific and industrial environments. The challenge is not limited to the initial deployment of the device but branches out to the whole lifecycle of the device where it can be affected by dynamic environments and the arrival of new threats. The cybersecurity of the solution, particularly regarding the latter, hinges on an effective Cyber-Threat Intelligence (CTI) exchange, as pointed out by the NIS2 directive. However, the process of sharing CTI data must be itself secure, privacy-respecting and far-reaching to ensure meaningful participation and results. This chapter describes the solution developed within the ERATOSTHENES project for achieving privacy-preserving CTI sharing in IoT scenarios. It consists of dedicated components within security domains to share and receive this information, backed by an inter-ledger approach as trustworthy backbone for the inter-domain data exchange. Additionally, the chapter introduces the application and extension of Manufacturer Usage Description (MUD) files for applying security configurations and mitigation actions related to devices or threats within a domain. These components help achieve a system that reacts to cyber-security incidents across the whole lifecycle of devices and security domains.

6.1 Introduction

IoT devices are intended to improve people's daily life and business environments. However, several aspects, such as their generally low capabilities, long lifetimes, or ubiquitous access, make them an attractive attack vector, becoming a risk in any deployment. Thus, it is necessary to establish mechanisms for managing security aspects comprehensively throughout their lifecycle, including not only an initial secure deployment but also the protection and reaction to events during their operational phase. Because of the dynamic nature of threats and attacks, it is important to share up to date Cyber-Threat Intelligence (CTI), as highlighted by EU's Network and Information Security (NIS2) Directive. However, there are barriers to the adoption of such measures, such as the potential security and privacy risks that come from data sharing. In this chapter, we delve into the topics and techniques for privacy-preserving CTI sharing, and showcase how, in conjunction with the Manufacturer Usage Description (MUD) initiative for IoT devices and threats, it eases tackling aspects of lifecycle security in IoT ecosystems.

6.2 Privacy-Preserving CTI Sharing

Security-related events incur in many direct and indirect loses for business and industries. Thus, a key challenge in the IoT sector is the need for increased cybersecurity. To achieve meaningful results in terms of detection and mitigation of cyberthreats, it is imperative that information on cyber-threats is exchanged, as pointed out by the NIS2 directive [1]. This is not a trivial matter, with many of the associated challenges already pointed out in said document. This chapter describes a series of components that together provide a platform for inter-domain CTI sharing. Before going into the detailed description of the solution, we give a quick overview highlighting its relationship with the NIS2 directives. The solution applies Distributed Ledger Technology (DLT) as a supporting tool for sharing of CTI and threat data across domains and with the whole ecosystem, including CSIRTs, as specified in multiple directives (e.g., directive such as 18 or directive 26). Immutable DLTs enable the auditability of cyberthreat sharing and actions, taking into account the sentiment of the directive, e.g., established in article 19. For the sharing of information, we consider privacy means like anonymisation and pseudonymisation, as suggested, e.g., in directive 121. Lastly, the solution makes heavy use of open-source security tools and open standards that, as argued in directive 52, can contribute to improved security through transparency, diversification, and interoperability.

6.2.1 Cyber-Threat Intelligence

IDSs, IPSs, SIEMs, Firewalls, among many others, are elements provided for securing networks. This aims to protect the system both proactively and reactively against possible intrusions. The operation of these security elements traditionally consists of analysing traffic and matching it with a database containing signatures and patterns of known attacks, to detect and block possible intrusions. However, since protecting a system depends on many different factors, even with a robust active security plan in place, the security of a system is not guaranteed. When presented with novel attack vectors, it is possible for these devices to trigger false negatives and allow an attacker to intrude. This is why additional methods must be incorporated to secure the systems, complementing the active security they already have.

Cyber intelligence is an information gathering and analysis activity aimed at identifying, tracking and predicting capabilities, intentions and activities of hostile actors in the cybersecurity domain. CTI can be defined as evidence-based knowledge, including context, mechanisms, indicators, implications and actionable advice, about an existing or emerging threat that can be used to make decisions regarding similar threats. CTI is comprised of attributes that give overall meaning to such a report - malicious IP addresses or hashes alone are not considered CTI, but grouped in context along with other information they can form part of a CTI report. One of the crucial elements of Cyber Threat Intelligence are Indicators of Compromise (IoCs). They are the most easily actionable attributes and the ones that most tools working with this information focus on. IoCs are widely used in applications such as Intrusion Detection Systems, web blockers, identification of compromised hosts or malware. These indicators can be easily related to other indicators that have occurred previously, taking advantage of big data analysis techniques on stored indicators.

To facilitate and accelerate the intelligence sharing process between organizations, it is necessary to structure the information so that an automated exchange can take place. Therefore, there are different standards for sharing threat intelligence and different platforms that favour automation through the exchange of this type of information. Survey [2] explains the development paths of the cyber-intelligence domain, its usefulness and use cases, the main standards that have been adopted in the industry, the most widespread platforms, and a comparison between them. The study describes standards like STIX (Structured Threat Information Expression) and TAXII (Trusted Automated Exchange of Indicator Information), as well as OpenTPX, MAEC, IODEF or VERIS. Among these, STIX is currently considered the de facto standard for describing Threat-Intelligence related data and the most widely used in Threat Intelligence Sharing Platforms (TIPs). As for the most widespread platforms for exchanging Cyber Intelligence Information,

```
{
  "Event": {
    "date": "2020-03-12",
    "threat_level_id": "1",
    "info": "testevent",
    "published": "false",
    "analysis": "0",
    "distribution": "0",
    "Attribute": [
      {
        "type": "domain",
        "category": "Network activity",
        "to_ids": false,
        "distribution": "0",
        "comment": "",
        "value": "test.com"
      }
    ]
  }
}
```

Figure 6.1. Example MISP event [4].

the survey highlights MISP, NC4 CTX, ThreatConnect, AlienVault, IBM X-Force Exchange, Anomali, and CrowdStrike among others. In particular, MISP (Malware Information Sharing Platform) [3] is a TIP for collecting, sharing, storing and correlating indicators of compromise (IOCs), targeted attacks, cyber intelligence, financial fraud, vulnerability information, and even counter-terrorism information. MISP is open-source software, and its objective is to foster the exchange of structured information between the computer security community, to support the daily work of incident and malware analysts. and malware analysts. MISP utilizes the MISP Core Format, a subset of JSON, to represent threat information, and events can be published in the platform using the STIX 1.1.1 and STIX 2.0 specifications.

However, CTI in many cases can contain information that should only be transmitted to trusted stakeholders or not transmitted at all, such as Personally Identifiable Information (PII) which is irrelevant to create situation awareness. In wrong hands, this information can lead to a successful attack that could severely damage the reputation of the stakeholder. Therefore, a trust mechanism and a way to protect sensitive data before sharing must be implemented in almost any CTI environment. In recent years, the importance of this mitigation measures has been reflected in various research works. For instance, [5] presented a privacy-preserving protocol for threat intelligence sharing, based on the collaborative training of a decision tree classifier, and exchanging training data between organizations in a private way using homomorphic encryption. Another approach is shown in [6], where authors propose a framework that allows different providers to share their information according to privacy requirements contained in a Data Sharing Agreement (DSA) and apply data mining techniques to extract additional knowledge from it.

In order to increase the privacy level of the raw CTI data itself shared through a platform such as MISP, we focus on applying Privacy Preserving Techniques (PPTs) on the events. These events will thus have masked sensitive data with the main objective of maintaining a satisfactory level of meaning while simultaneously increasing privacy and avoiding risks related to identity disclosure, attribute disclosure or membership disclosure. More specifically, non-perturbative masking techniques such as generalization and suppression, perturbative masking techniques such as noise addition through Differential Privacy (DP), and finally PPTs such as k-anonymity and l-diversity are described and considered.

6.2.2 Data Anonymisation Techniques

There are some risks involved in CTI Sharing that make organizations often reluctant to share information on such platforms. This is partly because they feel that revealing information about intrusions could damage their reputation. Furthermore, this information can also carry IP addresses, email accounts, names, and other PII which can be used against the sharing organization if it falls into the possession of an attacker and the organization has not addressed security issues in their system yet. Particularly relevant with PII is the fact that this information can potentially fall into the hands of a dishonest partner, who can then make fraudulent use of this information. Data anonymisation/pseudonymisation techniques aim to solve these issues by transforming sensitive data in such a way that the new data cannot be used by an attacker to extract sensitive information about the organization, or alternatively the extent of the sensitive information conveyed by the data is reduced enough to render it useless to the attacker. Data pseudonymisation applies a reversible process and allows authorized parties to retrieve the hidden information by using identifiers or pseudonyms, while data anonymisation is used to irreversibly modify the data to guarantee the loss of sensitive information.

For the anonymisation of these identifiers' values, there are privacy preserving and data transformation techniques such as suppression, generalization, sampling, k-anonymity, l-diversity, t-closeness, d-presence, etc. These techniques attempt to minimize data risks related to identity disclosure (the ability of an adversary to correctly associate an individual within a dataset), attribute disclosure (the ability of an attacker to infer the value of an attribute due to the distribution of attribute values in the table), and membership disclosure (the ability of an attacker to be able to determine, with very high confidence, whether or not a particular individual is present in the dataset). They are derived from Statistical Disclosure Control (SDC) [7]. SDC, also known as Disclosure Avoidance, is the discipline that manages the balance between the privacy of respondent data and the usefulness of this data for research purposes. In the following, we give a brief description of some of

	ZIP Code	Age	Disease
1	47677	29	Heart Disease
2	47602	22	Heart Disease
3	47678	27	Heart Disease
4	47905	43	Flu
5	47909	52	Heart Disease
6	47906	47	Cancer
7	47605	30	Heart Disease
8	47673	36	Cancer
9	47607	32	Cancer

Table 1. Original Patients Table

	ZIP Code	Age	Disease
1	476**	2*	Heart Disease
2	476**	2*	Heart Disease
3	476**	2*	Heart Disease
4	4790*	≥ 40	Flu
5	4790*	≥ 40	Heart Disease
6	4790*	≥ 40	Cancer
7	476**	3*	Heart Disease
8	476**	3*	Cancer
9	476**	3*	Cancer

Table 2. A 3-Anonymous Version of Table 1

Figure 6.2. Example of k-anonimity applied to a table of patients[1].

the most widespread mechanisms, which have been implemented in the solution described in this chapter.

K-anonymity is a data protection model/dataset property proposed by Latanya Sweeney in [8]. Its objective is to minimize the risks of re-identification of individuals within anonymised datasets, stating that for a data publication to meet the k-anonymity condition, the information about any one individual in the dataset must be indistinguishable from at least k-1 other individuals in the same dataset. k-anonymity focuses on identity-disclosure by guaranteeing that k records hold the same values in a set of attributes, so that if an attacker had another external database containing data of individuals from the dataset, he would not be able to relate one of them within the privatized dataset to a degree of accuracy of no more than k individuals.

L-diversity [9] improves the k-anonymity proposition by aiming to decrease the attribute-disclosure risks that k-anonymity is susceptible to. To achieve this, it defines a new type of attribute, called sensitive, which contains sensitive data about an individual that is less identifiable than quasi-identifier data but whose distribution in the dataset can reveal information about it. An equivalence class is said to achieve l-diversity if there are at least l well represented values for a sensitive attribute. A dataset has l-diversity when all its equivalence classes satisfy l-diversity. l-diversity defines the concept "well-represented" in three separate ways, resulting in three alternative conditions. The first one defines "distinct l-diversity", where a well-represented element is one that appears at least once. The second one defines "entropy l-diversity", which places a lower bound on the entropy level of the element frequency. Finally, the "recursive (c, l)-diversity" variant seeks to guarantee that the most frequent value within an equivalence class appears less, and the least frequent value does not appear so little.

1. Source: https://blog.csdn.net/scuLVLV/article/details/71077689.

Despite improving the weaknesses of k-anonymity, l-diversity continues to present vulnerabilities related to attribute disclosure to a lesser extent. This is why T-closeness [10] is introduced, to overcome these risks and to introduce a model in which semantic meaning of values is considered. The way t-closeness works focuses on calculating the distance between the distributions of each equivalence class with respect to the rest of the dataset, to avoid problems arising from an uneven or skewed distribution of sensitive values.

Differential privacy [11] establishes a rigorous mathematical definition of the concept of privacy that guarantees the probability that the result of an anonymisation process applied on a dataset is virtually unchanged if any individual in the dataset is removed or added. This model attempts to provide privacy by perturbing the data through the addition of small amounts of noise.

6.2.3 Inter-Ledger Approach for Verifiable Data Sharing

The integration of Distributed Ledger Technologies (DLTs) has been a catalyst for significant advancements in the secure and verifiable exchange of data across various domains. However, in the context of sharing security data, it is usually necessary to connect many different security domains, and particularly make most of the data as available as possible. Thus, it is necessary to adopt DLT solutions that ensure interoperability of various instances and that enable global outreach for data sharing mechanisms. While there exist multiple approaches to this challenge, we in this chapter, we focus on the conceptualised concept of "Blockchain of blockchains," so that it is possible to facilitate smooth and secure transitions through smart contracts (instantiated as chaincodes) among different domains, tailored to the needs of the CTI sharing ecosystem.

The approach is based on the the creation of an inter-domain DLT instantiated as an inter-domain channel within Hyperledger Fabric.[2] This channel serves as the foundation for inter-domain communication. Essential elements include participants from various domains, their respective permissions, and endorsement policies. For example, each domain contributes at least one peer to this channel, and it ensures a majority endorsement policy. This strategy provides robustness and allows for a decentralized governance structure where domains participate in the sharing process as equals. Additionally, this enables the direct use of smart contracts across different channels within the same ecosystem. This approach boosts transaction efficiency and enhances security, interoperability, and scalability.

The inter-ledger approach is designed to address each domain's specific needs for data exchange. Using Hyperledger Fabric, each domain maintains private ledgers

2. https://github.com/hyperledger/fabric.

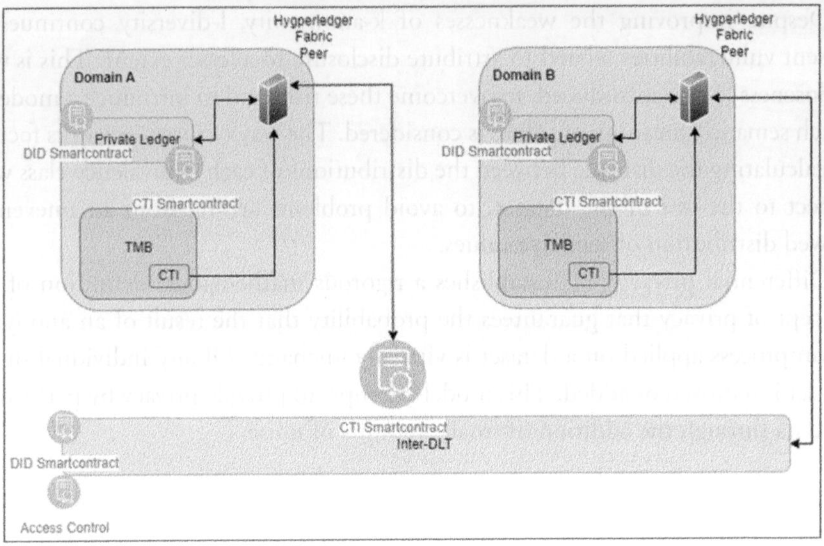

Figure 6.3. Inter-DLT deployment and functional interaction overview.

while also participating in an inter-domain channel. In this way, domains can take advantage of the adequate DLT capabilities according to the characteristics of the data sharing process in mind. For instance, the CTI sharing solution described in this chapter may create private records for auditability while also producing data sharing events that reach the whole ecosystem and relevant stakeholders through the inter-DLT. Smart contract invocations across channels facilitate communication, with data traceability linked to genesis hashes. A gRPC server supports efficient data management by directing it to appropriate channels, ensuring transparent and configurable operations for components handling data in the domain.

The diagram in Figure 6.3 provides a visual representation showcasing the deployment and interaction between different security domains using the inter-DLT framework. The diagram features Domain A and Domain B, each with their private ledgers within Hyperledger Fabric. Within these domains, various smart contracts provide functionality related to the DLT, such as the management of Decentralized Identifiers. Particularly, the CTI smart contracts handle Cyber Threat Intelligence data as part of the security information sharing process. As detailed in the following, this enables an auditable, secure and widespread solution for sharing CTI data across different security domains.

6.2.4 The CTI Sharing Agent

Figure 6.4 shows the detailed description of the CTI Sharing Agent as part of a Trust Manager and Broker, as well as the main communication flows involving the subcomponents.

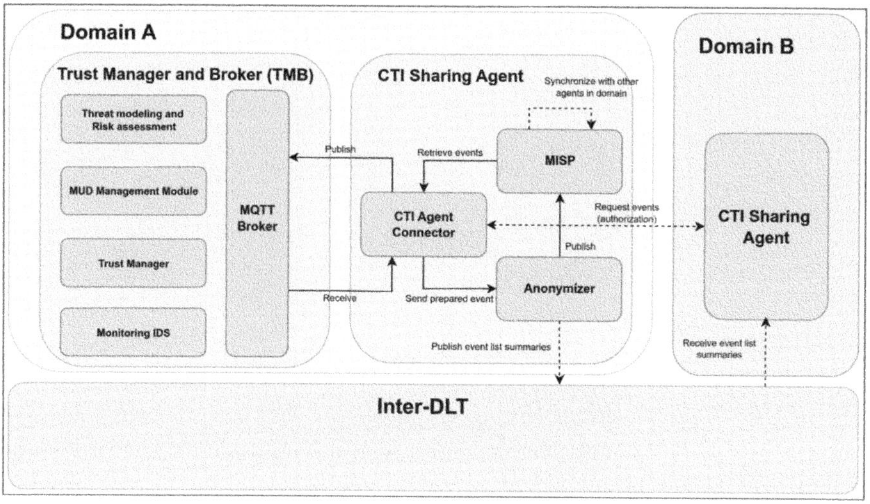

Figure 6.4. CTI sharing agent.

The CTI Sharing Agent consists of:

CTI Agent Connector: This component is in charge of communication to other components of the security and trust framework in the domain. Particularly, our instantiation includes communication through the Trust Manager and Broker using a publish/subscribe MQTT approach. The connector will be the intermediary that receives threat alerts coming from the Monitoring components. It also retrieves events from the CTI sharing platform for later forwarding them to relevant components through the broker. Lastly, it governs the authorization of sharing processes with CTI Sharing Agents from other domains.

Anonymizer: Receives a threat-related event coming from the CTI Agent Connector and applies anonymisation techniques that are specified in the privacy policy file related to that type of event. After the anonymisation process the resultant event is published on the domain's instance of the CTI sharing tool, e.g. MISP. Additionally, the DLT is used for auditability and signalling of this publication process. The techniques implemented in this component are generalization, suppression, k-anonymity, l-diversity, and noise addition by differential privacy.

MISP: An instance of the MISP platform for publication and sharing of security events. It acts as the repository of threat events received. Its synchronization capabilities are useful to keep instances within a security domain synchronized (i.e., for distributed instantiations of the security framework to provide resilience and scalability). What is more, it can be synchronized with external MISP instances, such as those of manufacturers or public CSIRTs/CERTs, so that the database of threats

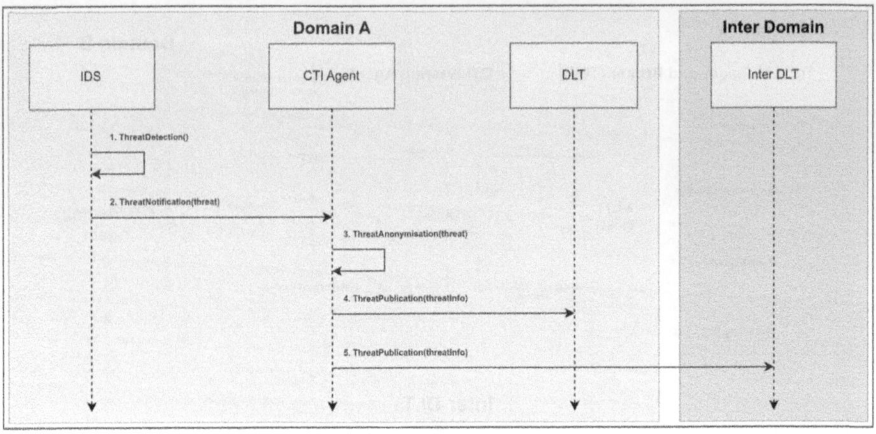

Figure 6.5. Threat detection and sharing.

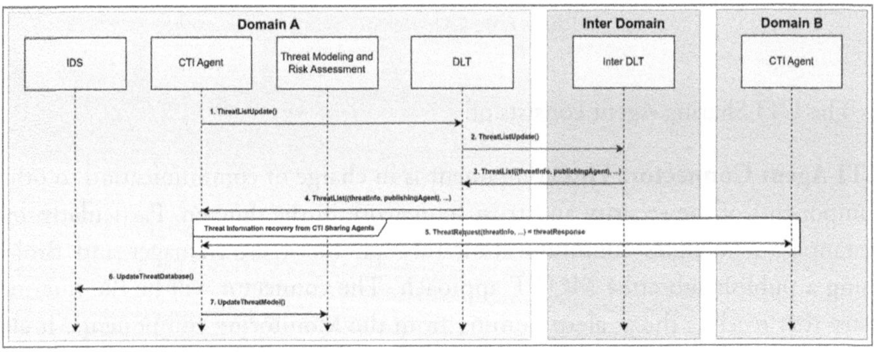

Figure 6.6. Threat list update from CTI sharing.

reaches relevant people in the security sector and improves the security of the overall ecosystem.

Figures 6.5 and 6.6 show diagrams for the threat detection, sharing and threat list update processes. The first flow starts when the monitoring tools detect a threat, at which point they notify the domain's CTI Sharing Agent with detailed information about the threat. The sharing agent then transforms the event data using the Anonymizer to obfuscate sensitive information. The anonymized event is then made available, and the DLT infrastructure is used to register this event. Particularly, the domain's DLT is used for registering the publication of the threat so as to allow for auditability of the process. Additionally, the inter-DLT is used as a means to register and make available summaries of the published information to other domains, so that relevant stakeholders are notified of the event.

Later, a different security domain may desire to update its threat information database to improve its security. Then, its CTI Sharing Agent queries the inter-domain DLT (through a smart contract) for recorded relevant threat information.

From this query, the agent receives threat event records, which include both threat information as well as contact information for the sharing agent that originally reported the threat. The domain's sharing agent then initiates a process of threat evaluation where, based on the specific domain properties, it selects those threat events which are pertinent to the domain and queries the external sharing agent for additional information. This threat exchange is subject to an authorisation process overviewed by the publisher CTI agent, according to information relevant in the application scenario. For instance, this may include checks of the requestor's identity or its inclusion on trusted entity lists maintained in the own DLT infrastructure. This process is repeated for every relevant threat event. Finally, once all the threat information is gathered, the domain's sharing agent forwards the updated information to both the IDS and the risk assessment module in order to update the relevant databases.

6.3 Manufacturer Usage Description Files

The large-scale nature of IoT deployments, the heterogeneity of device characteristics, the distributed and replicated nature of deployments, or the involvement of people with low or no technical background result in important needs for certification and security configuration for automatized lifecycle management. On the one hand, this topic includes the challenge of easing and automatizing the deployment of devices in a secure way. On the other hand, it is necessary to go beyond those initial steps, covering the whole lifecycle of the device including the necessary adaptations as security contexts change, because of configuration changes, addition of new devices, or the arrival of new threats.

Our proposed solution leverages Manufacturer Usage Description (MUD) files to address these challenges, integrating their use with other components in a domain's security and trust framework. This integration enables the discovery and parsing of behavioural information for devices enrolling in the framework, which is instrumental in enhancing analytical models, trust evaluations, and domain-specific monitoring. Furthermore, we account for the dynamic nature of security requirements by allowing updates to MUD files and incorporating new security information through threat-specific MUDs. In a holistic solution, by incorporating monitoring and cyber-threat intelligence sharing tools, our approach facilitates the exchange of security measures and mitigation strategies among relevant stakeholders, in alignment with guidelines such as those outlined in the NIS2 directive [1]. Overall, the outcomes of our research provide a crucial mechanism for ensuring secure lifecycle management of IoT devices, from their initial security configuration, during deployment and registration, to their eventual decommissioning, thereby addressing a significant business and technical challenge in the IoT domain.

6.3.1 MUD Standard

The heterogeneity of IoT environments, spanning from dynamic home settings to industrial IoT (IIoT), and the wide variety of devices using different technologies and communication protocols, introduces several challenges. These include ensuring compatibility across devices, managing diverse communication patterns, and addressing security vulnerabilities that vary depending on the specific environment and device capabilities. Furthermore, the restrictions inherent to certain IoT devices (e.g., the lack of user interface) make management of IoT devices cumbersome for non-expert users. Despite these complexities, it remains important to understand or predict the expected behaviour of these devices in order to effectively detect and mitigate security threats. Given these challenges, standardization in identifying and managing device behaviour is essential for tackling the unique demands of these varied IoT ecosystems.

In this direction, Manufacturer Usage Description (MUD) standard was published in 2019 by the Internet Engineering Task Force (IETF) [12]. The MUD specification's major goal is to limit the threat and attack surface of a certain IoT device by allowing manufacturers to establish network behaviour profiles for their devices. Each profile is specified through Access Control Lists (ACLs), which establish policies for communication endpoints. They are defined using Yet Another Next Generation (YANG) [13] to model network restrictions, and JavaScript Object Notation (JSON) [14] as the serialization format. Figure 6.2 shows an example of a MUD file, where we can appreciate the two core containers of the specification. The first "ietf-mud:mud" container provides information about the MUD file itself, such as its URL, how long it should be cached and information about the device. Additionally, the MUD model is extended with the "ietf-access-control-list:acls" container based on [15], including network communication restrictions to configure the forwarding behaviour in the device, e.g., representing communications with certain hosts, ports or protocols. An example of a MUD file showing these characteristics can be found in Figure 6.7.

Additionally, the standard introduces a comprehensive architecture designed to manage MUDs, and mechanisms for its implementations. Also, it defines several extensions for the transmission mechanism of the MUD such as an DHCP option, an LLDP extension, a X.509 extension that links device's identity and MUD profile together, signature verification and extensibility considerations.

Figure 6.8 shows said architecture, where the device emits the MUD URL (through one of the capable protocols) to router or switch, which forwards the

```
{
    "ietf-mud:mud":{
        "mud-version":1,
        "mud-url":"https://localhost:9443/examples/lightbulb2000.json",
        "cache-validity":48,
        "systeminfo":"The BMS Example Light Bulb",
        ...
        "from-device-policy":{
            "access-lists":{"access-list":[{"name":"mud-76100-v6fr"}]}
        }
    },
    "ietf-access-control-list:acls":{
        "acl":[
            {
                "name":"mud-76100-v6to",
                "type":"ipv6-acl-type",
                "aces":{
                    "ace":[
                        {
                            "name":"cl0-todev",
                            "matches":{
                                "ipv6":{
                                    "ietf-acldns:src-dnsname":"test.example.com",
                                    "protocol":6
                                },
                                "tcp":{
                                    "ietf-mud:direction-initiated":"from-device",
                                    "source-port":{
                                        "operator":"eq",
                                        "port":443
                                    }
                                }
                            },
                            "actions":{
                                "forwarding":"accept"
                            }
                        }
                    ]
                }
            }
        ]
    }
}
```

Figure 6.7. Example of a MUD file [12].

URL to the MUD Manager and then retrieve the MUD file from the MUD File Server on the manufacturer's premises.

Since its adoption, MUD has been object of interest both from researchers and standardization bodies. In particular, the National Institute of Standards and Technology (NIST), and the European Union Agency for Cybersecurity (ENISA) consider the use of MUD as part of future IoT security good practices to increase security against cyberattacks in IoT domains [1, 16].

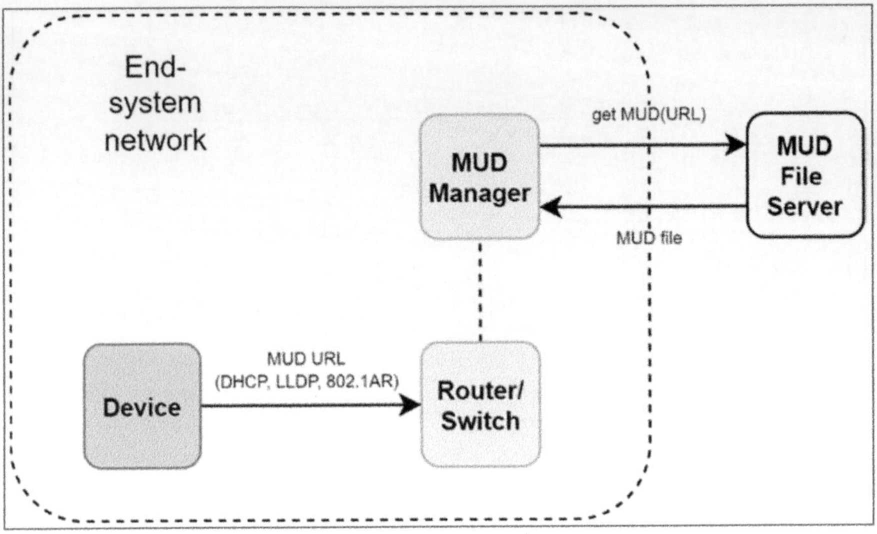

Figure 6.8. MUD Standard Architecture [12].

6.3.2 Threat MUD Proposal

The task of securing environments that incorporate IoT devices extends far beyond the initial installation. Numerous vulnerabilities and potential attacks often emerge during the operational lifecycle of these devices, making continuous monitoring and protection essential. For example, in 2022 alone, over 25,000 vulnerabilities were identified [17]. Manufacturers often face challenges in addressing these vulnerabilities promptly, as updates require navigating a complex process. Additionally, the involvement of third-party services can further complicate timely resolutions. Although MUD files can be updated, this method fails to address the majority of vulnerable scenarios. In these circumstances, security-information sharing systems play a crucial role by enabling the rapid, collaborative exchange, analysis, and mitigation of vulnerabilities or attacks, even before a patch becomes available. In fact, the importance of cyber-threat information sharing to strengthen cybersecurity capabilities has been a significant focus of ENISA's NIS2 Directive [1].

In this context, the NIST introduced the concept of Threat Manufacturer Usage Description (Threat MUD) [16], aimed at facilitating the sharing of vulnerability information and corresponding mitigations. Threat MUD builds upon the MUD standard maintaining a similar structural foundation. Despite this close connection, Threat MUD stands as an independent concept focused on mitigation strategies. However, NIST provides only partial guidance on the Threat MUD model, leaving some aspects undefined but still framed within broader guidelines.

In the following section, we examine the Threat MUD model as described in [18]. The NIST guidelines and this work serve as a foundation for our approach,

```
{
    "ietf-threatmud:mud": {
        "threat-mud-version": 1,
        "threat-mud-url": "https://ThreatMudServer/afcf19e3-750b-45ab-adce-b535afe1200d",
        "threat-mud-signature": "Nd8NVgPOpdRjhnbZ+WjREq/DVdZSWdIHXeOx77ean8hr6nT2Uf8cS52bl2gbGk7CmG34xhDVXaq4B0JtAqZ359+dxB
        "threat-id": "afcf19e3-750b-45ab-adce-b535afe1200d",
        "last-update": "2024-02-16T11:35:25+01:00",
        "cache-validity": 48,
        "is-supported": true,
        "threat-intelligence-provider": "CyberSecurity Insights",
        "cvss-vector": "CVSS:3.1/AV:N/AC:L/PR:N/UI:N/S:C/C:H/I:H/A:H",
        "documentation": "Apache Log4j2 2.0-beta9 through 2.15.0 (excluding security releases 2.12.2, 2.12.3, and 2.3.1) JND
        "from-device-policy": {
            "access-lists": {
                "access-list": [
                    {
                        "name": "threatmud-75129-v6fr"
                    }
                ]
            }
        },
        "to-device-policy": {
            "access-lists": {
                "access-list": [
                    {
                        "name": "threatmud-75129-v6to"
                    }
                ]
            }
        }
    },
    "ietf-access-control-list:acls": {
```


Figure 6.9. Extract of a Threat MUD file.

though we adapt certain elements, such as differences in the way the flows are implemented in the solution's architecture.

A key aspect to highlight about Threat MUD is the contrast in purpose with respect to the original MUD standard. Unlike regular MUDs, which describe the expected behaviour of a device, Threat MUD shifts its focus from the device to the threat itself, specifying network communication rules for sites linked to the identified threat. As a result, Threat MUD does not need to be tied to a particular device. Furthermore, instead of being developed by the manufacturer, the creation of Threat MUD files may fall under the responsibility of different threat intelligence providers and stakeholders, emphasizing its role in threat-centric rather than device-centric mitigation strategies.

As with the standard MUD, the Threat MUD model is structured into two key modules (c.f. Figure 6.9 for an example). The first module provides information about the Threat MUD itself, maintaining fields similar to those in the original MUD standard, such as version, URL, cache-validity, and signature. However, several fields are adapted to align with the threat-centric focus. For instance, the "manufacturer name" is replaced by "intelligence provider," and "device model name" is substituted with "threat name." Also, fields that are no longer relevant, such as those related to the specific device (e.g., system or firmware information), are removed. Additionally, new fields are introduced, such as cvss-vector, related to the CVSS (Common Vulnerability Scoring System) and documentation related, to offer detailed information about the threat and its mitigation strategies.

The second module is related to Access Control Lists (ACLs) that define the conditions and restrictions for network communication. Unlike the traditional MUD, where these ACLs are tailored to a specific device, Threat MUD applies these configurations more generically, given its focus on threat mitigation rather than device behaviour.

6.3.3 Shortcomings and Extensions

A notable limitation of the standard is the inability to implement security constraints beyond the network layer. This limitation is significant in this scope because it restricts the expressiveness of the MUD files, thereby hindering their potential to address a broader spectrum of security concerns. The definition of rules or conditions that extend beyond this layer could help to add substantial expressive capabilities that enhance the identification and mitigation of a wide range of attacks, including those targeting the application layer such as slow DDoS attacks.

In the following, we describe several potential extensions to enhance the expressiveness of MUD files. These extensions may cover characteristics known at design time or during updates, which the original MUD standard does not address. Additionally, they could be useful for defining mitigation actions through Threat MUDs, particularly in the context of this work.

- Application layer protocols significantly influence how devices should communicate within a network. In the context of the MUD standard, this selection directly relates to the application role of the devices, affecting the device's network behaviour. Allowing the specification of protocol restrictions at the application layer not only influences network layer functionality but also enables more granular control over the device within any given infrastructure.
- Exposed resources offered by the device, like HTTP/CoAP endpoints to retrieve information, which could be used both for discoverability of devices and to consider the expected behaviour for threat and risk models.
- Cryptographic algorithms, specify the supported algorithms of the device and its preferences or add restrictions to the communications. This could be useful for both communications (establishing secure channels) and higher-level needs of the infrastructure, like determining which cryptographic algorithms are preferred or supported, and the appropriate security level for managing identities, e.g. digital signatures that either or not support zero-knowledge proofs depending on the capabilities of the device.
- Known vulnerabilities associated with the device, through continuous MUD file updates, following the CVE entry format and additional details like CVSS scores, which could be associated with mitigations measures or restrictions to reduce the threat risk.
- Software and firmware restrictions designed to support and enhance automatic software update and deployment processes, such as defining a

minimum software version for optimal operation or establishing an update as part of a mitigation action.

Additionally, as identified in [19], the application of the MUD standard confronts several operational challenges, and extension points are being researched in many works on the topic.

Firstly, the standard does not address the dynamic nature of MUD files nor protocol for updates during deployment lifecycle. Another challenge is the necessary authentication during MUD acquisition so that the infrastructure may know that the MUD URL corresponds to the device sending it, and not to some other entity. Moreover, the described method in the standard for obtaining MUD files, typically via requests to switches or routers, may not be suitable for all operational environments. Lastly, the standard currently lacks detailed guidelines for applying MUD in specific sectors such as the Industrial Internet of Things (IIoT), where advanced functionalities and extended MUD models are crucial. This work aligns specifically with these areas of concern, in addition with the extension of the MUD file expressivity.

6.3.4 The Adapted MUD Solution

Within the proposed security and trust framework, the MUD approach is integrated as a key source of behavioral information for devices that enroll a domain. As in the standard, MUD file servers are located outside the framework domains, typically hosted by the device manufacturers. MUD components within each domain can communicate with these external servers to retrieve the relevant MUD files, for instance through a simple REST API. However, different approaches of retrieval could be used such as periodic requests or publish/subscribe models, enabling additional interactions such as MUD file updates. Similarly, threat MUD files will be controlled by external entities, such as cybersecurity agencies. On the other hand, the main functional components of the MUD standard and Threat MUD proposal will be active in each security domain, as part of the security and trust framework (e.g., the Trust Manager and Broker—TMB—component in the ERATOSTHENES solution).

Figure 6.4 shows the detailed instantiation of the MUD components and an overview on their interfaces. Note that the MUD management module is an aggregation of subcomponents, incorporating both the standard MUD and Threat MUD manager functionalities, alongside a Translation module.

- **MUD Manager:** the component is in charge of receiving MUD file resolution requests according to the URL associated to a device, e.g. through an MQTT broker. It then utilizes the URL to retrieve the MUD File from the

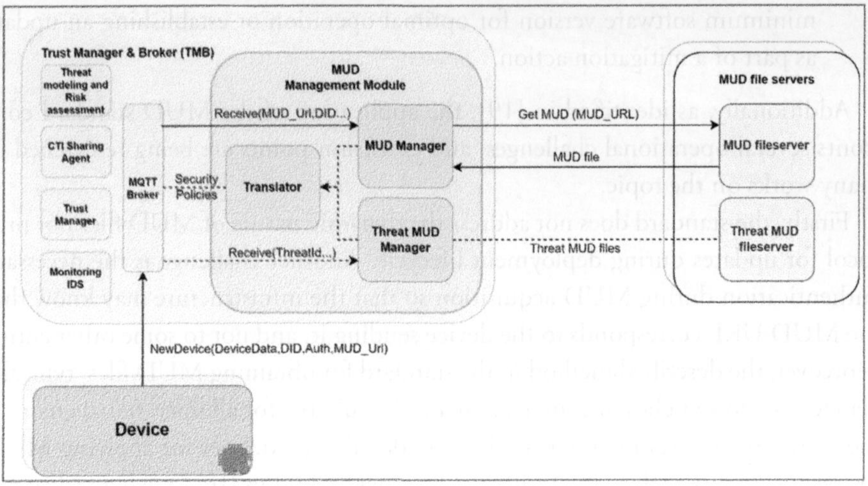

Figure 6.10. Instantiation of the MUD management module.

MUD File Server. Once done it returns the MUD File to the Translator module.

- **Translator:** transforms MUD and Threat MUD files into applicable security policies, ensuring seamless integration with the broader domain management processes. Receives the MUD & Threat MUD File related to a device and converts its conditions and restrictions into corresponding actions in MSPL format. Once translated it adds to the MSPL the information of the device or threat to which it's addressed and sends it to the rest of the infrastructure through the corresponding topic.
- **Threat MUD Manager:** similar to the MUD Manager, collects the Threat MUD File tied to the specific threat identifier received after a trigger from security components. After retrieving the file from the MUD File Server, it forwards it to the Translator module for its translation and sharing.
- **MUD File Server:** this service belongs to the manufacturer premises and contains the MUD files associated to the manufacturer devices. It's a single server for each manufacturer, leading to several servers[3] according to the number of manufacturers in the ecosystem.
- **Threat MUD File Server:** stores Threat MUD files associated to threat identifiers. Unlike the MUD File Servers, in this case the server does not belong to the manufacturers but acts as a common access point for entities within the framework serving mitigation strategies related to the threats present in

3. From a practical point of view this server may instead be distributed to improve scalability and resilience of the solution.

the ecosystem. Various security actors may control Threat MUD servers to create and share policies.

The main contrast with the standard MUD architecture in Figure 6.10 is the abstraction of the network layer. Indeed, one of the key advances over the MUD obtaining process in the standard comes from the integration of the MUD processing into a full-fledged trust framework. Now, we take advantage of the domain enrolment phase to get the MUD URL from the device. The integration in such flow, and within the complete ecosystem, also allows the exploration of further improvements for the MUD flow.

For instance, while the server-side communication can be simply secured with standard mechanisms (e.g., HTTPS), there is a security risk in the standard specification regarding the potential spoofing of a MUD URL by the device. In the application-level integration proposed, the authentication of the URL during MUD file obtention can be tackled through the domain's identity framework. Specifically, the manufacturer will associate the URL to the root of trust for identification of the device, for instance through the use of Physical Unclonable Functions as a root identity. When receiving the URL and retrieving the file, it is then possible to check that the device possesses the proper root identity, otherwise rejecting its claim. Furthermore, the extension of the MUD model and language with higher level concepts, like software updates or cryptographic parameters restrictions, is even more relevant through this layer abstraction. Nonetheless, the MUD solution will not ignore networking elements by working at the application level. As MUD files will be associated to devices that are relevant to an application domain, the networking rules will also be relevant to the specific deployment and must simply be translated to the appropriate enforcement measures.

Additionally, in the specific instantiation within ERATOSTHENES, the inclusion of the MUD elements in the TMB allows simple interactions with other domain components relevant to the application of its functionality and the management of the lifecycle of devices. For instance, as previously mentioned, the information provided in the MUD file can be leveraged by the Threat Modelling and Risk Assessment (TMRA) component to influence the trust level assigned to a device. Additionally, monitoring systems such as Intrusion Detection Systems (IDS) can utilize MUD data to understand the expected traffic patterns for each device. This allows IDS to more effectively identify deviations from expected behaviour and respond swiftly to potential threats. These interactions open various enforcement possibilities, not only at the network level through direct policy application, but also through indirect control by continuously evaluating device behaviour and adjusting its trust level based on its interactions within the domain. This approach strengthens the overall security posture and response capability within the network.

```
module: mspl
  +--rw name                string
  +--rw configuration
     +--rw capability                string
     +--rw rule_set_configuration
        +--rw name                   string
        +--rw default_action?        enumeration
        +--rw configuration_rule* [name]
           +--rw external_data
           |  +--rw priority    int32
           +--rw configuration_action
           |  +--rw software_protection_action
           |  |  +--rw software_protection_type    enumeration
           |  |  +--rw software_fixed_version*     string
           |  |  +--rw software_fix_url*           string
           |  +--rw filtering_action
           |  |  +--rw filtering_action_type    enumeration
           |  +--rw parental_control_action
           |  |  +--rw enable    string
           |  +--rw data_protection_action
           |     +--rw technology                                  string
           |     +--rw technology_action_security_property
           |        |  +--rw confidenciality
           |        |  |  +--rw encryption_algorithm    string
           |        |  |  +--rw key_size                string
           |        |  |  +--rw mode                    string
           |        |  +--rw integrity
           |        |  |  +--rw integrity_algorithm    string
           |        |  |  +--rw integrity_header       string
```

Figure 6.11. Extract of the MSPL YANG model tree.

To facilitate these communications, we rely on the Translator component, which converts MUD files into intermediate security policies. The policies provide a set of actions suitable to the most common applicable security settings. For this medium level of abstraction, we work with the Medium-level Security Policy Language (MSPL) [20]. The MSPL language specification is based on a YANG model, allowing it to be encoded in XML or JSON formats, providing flexibility in how MUD information is utilized (c.f. Figure 6.11).

This flexibility ensures that the data contained in MUD & Threat MUD files can be efficiently applied across different components. Assets in the security domain will have access to the medium-level policies and take advantage of them for improving their performance in their tasks, possibly with another translation into their own structures. For instance, the TMRA may use the policy directly to increase its knowledge base for building models, while the IDS may translate policies into rules that detect related events, and further authorization enforcement policies may be derived by PDPs.

6.4 Lifecycle Security Through Information Sharing

One of the main aspects of the cybersecurity world is the ever-changing nature of security contexts and threats. Thus, there is a need to dynamically change the security assessment and measures, especially in the heterogeneous and changeful world of IoT, with different phases along lifecycles. At the device level, while MUD files are especially relevant during bootstrapping and enrolment, they can be updated with new information (e.g., known vulnerabilities, recommended software updates) by the manufacturers, and uploaded to file servers. Those updates can then be used to improve the security protocols around the device and avoid obsolete information. Another tool for dynamic assessment, in this case mostly focused on threats and potential malicious actors themselves, is the sharing and analysis of threats through threat MUD files, which is carried out during the operation of a security domain. This knowledge can be taken advantage of in security domains with tools that can take into account and apply the threat information and mitigation actions defined in these files.

On this note, a key topic of the NIS2 directive by ENISA [1] is the importance of providing mechanisms for privacy-preserving and secure CTI sharing. As described above, the sharing processes should include relevant entities such as manufacturers, vulnerability databases, or cyber-response teams. With such solution, it is possible to improve detection, monitoring and assessment of threats and security domains. What is more, it enables widespread awareness of threats, resulting in a more secure ecosystem, for instance through the creation of mitigation policies. With this in mind, the tools and processes introduced in this chapter can be used to enhance security along the lifecycle of devices and IoT ecosystems, as we discuss in the following.

6.4.1 Secure Deployment of IoT Devices

A critical security event during the lifecycle of devices is their deployment within the domain of operation. During this process, several checks must be made to ensure the safety of the domain, from the identification of the device to the initial evaluation of its characteristics in a zero-trust approach. These processes are further explored in other chapters in the book. Here, we focus on how the security information coming from the MUD solution can be used to enhance the initial bootstrapping and enrolment process, acting within the context of a holistic solution. In this sense, we part from the MUD management solution based on an application-level interaction with the trust services of a security domain.

Figure 6.12 shows an extract of an enrolment process in such an integrated ecosystem, highlighting the interactions related to MUD files. The process takes

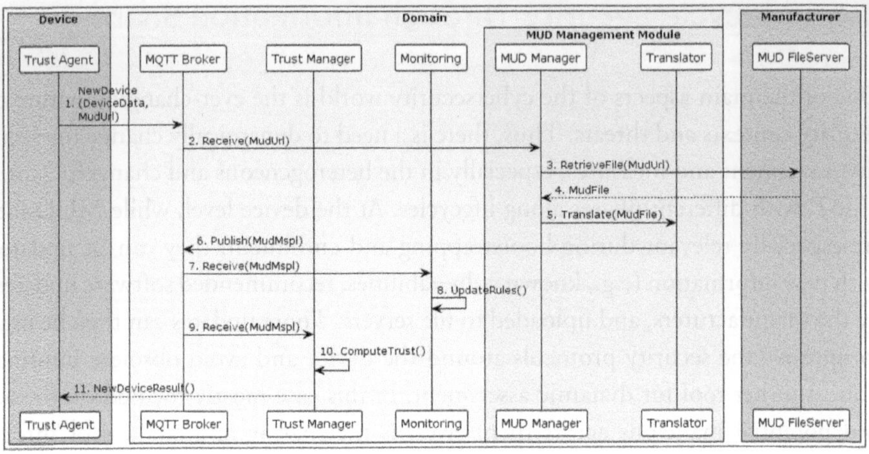

Figure 6.12. MUD Management during bootstrapping and enrolment.

advantage of the enrolment of a device within the trust framework of a domain to kickstart the MUD retrieval process. This MUD file contains information about expected behaviour, known vulnerabilities and general security data about the device. The MUD Management Module then translates the file into security policies in the MSPL language, which are shared throughout the security and trust framework of the domain. Thus, actions adapted to the security context can be taken to ensure a safe onboarding process. As related in the figure, it is possible, for instance, to take advantage of other tools described in this book, improving the monitoring capabilities of the detection systems and adapting the evaluation of the trustworthiness of the device according to the gathered information.

During the deployment of the device, its identification and the provisioning of identity in the domain are important steps for the security of the process and later operation of the device. Of course, this also affects the application of security measures according to device information, as it is necessary to ensure that the retrieved MUD file is adequate for the device. To do so, the MUD URL associated to a device can be linked to the root of trust for its identification process, which is set up by the manufacturer during the initial provisioning of the device. For instance, the MUD URL can be bound to a Physical Unclonable Function output, achieving strong unforgeability guarantees.

A simple extension of this secure deployment process can be done to account for the changing nature of security aspects throughout device lifecycles. MUD files are stored within the MUD Manager during their lifetime, and once expired they are retrieved again, checking for changes and if necessary, updating the MSPL policy associated with the device so that the other tools can take advantage of the new information. In some deployments, the fileserver may instead allow a

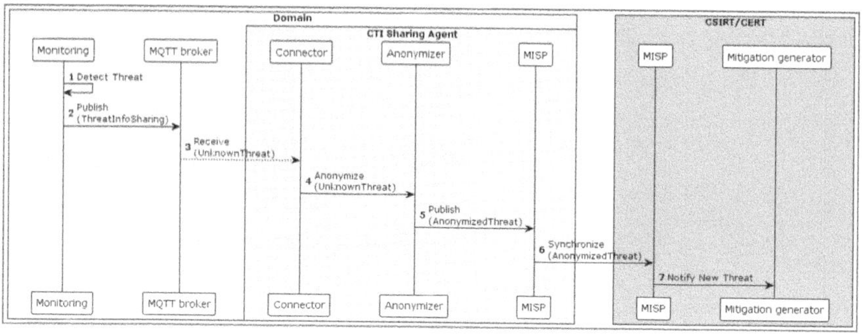

Figure 6.13. Threat detection and sharing.

subscribe-publish approach, so that immediately after a new version of a MUD file is generated, it will reach the relevant MUD managers.

6.4.2 Threat Sharing and Mitigation

While the previous section focuses on the aspects related to adopting initial and updated security configurations of a device within a domain, in the following the focus within the lifecycle security is on the functionalities achieved through the sharing of CTI information. As previously discussed, this is a critical process for ensuring the security of both the devices and the domain throughout their entire lifecycle, as well as enabling appropriate responses to information received in order to implement necessary mitigation measures.

Figure 6.13 gives a general overview of a threat sharing process that involves a new threat for which mitigation actions will be generated. First, a threat or attack is detected through the monitoring tools within a security domain, and the CTI information reaches the CTI Sharing Agent. The agent parses the data and applies anonymization techniques to protect sensitive data. The anonymized information about the threat is then shared outside the security domain, through sharing tools like MISP. The data will reach relevant cybersecurity actors, such as CSIRT or CERT teams, for instance of a device manufacturer The identified threat may include new information that can be analyzed by the appropriate tools or personnel, initiating the process of generating a suitable mitigation response. In some cases, the threat may already be known, including mitigation actions related to it, so that the mitigation process automatically starts from the domain tools.

In case the new mitigation is generated, it can be published as a Threat MUD file. A notification of the creation of the new file is sent through the CTI sharing network, so that it can reach any security domain where the threat is relevant. Particularly, following the previous example, the CTI Sharing Agent of the security domain receives the information and notifies through the broker about the existence of the new Threat MUD file associated to the previously detected threat.

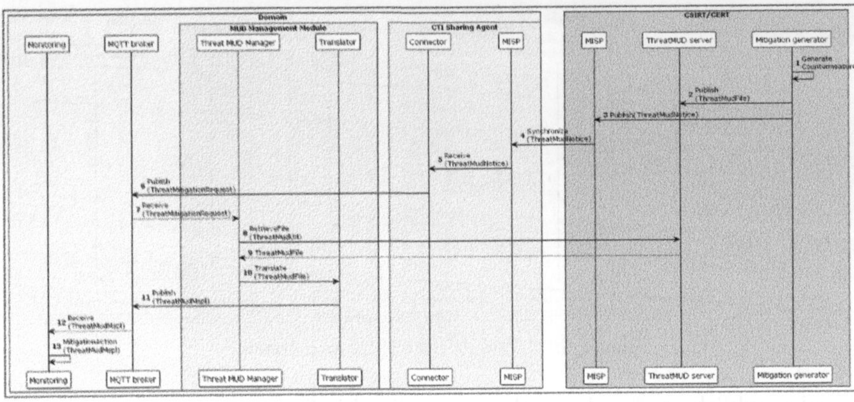

Figure 6.14. Threat mitigation sharing and enforcement.

The Threat MUD Manager receives the notification and retrieves the file, then forwards it to the Translator. The Translator generates an MSPL language policy based on the file's contents, tailoring the mitigation to the specific domain (e.g., adjusting IP addresses to those relevant within the domain). This MSPL policy contains mitigation actions for the specified threat. The policy is then published on the MQTT broker, so that its enforcement can take place according to the necessary actions. For instance, the flow in the image includes a mitigation action at the network level, so that the monitoring and protection tools can execute the policy by adding rules for detecting and stopping specific traffic. Other mitigation actions may be used depending on the context of the threat and the domain, such as having the digital twin fleet management tools issue a software update after a compromise.

These procedures are fully automated, except for specialized personnel who may be needed to develop appropriate mitigation actions. This automation enables the ecosystem to respond to cybersecurity incidents throughout the entire lifecycle of the devices and security domains. The approach is flexible, allowing various components to address different situations, including known threats and their mitigations. Moreover, these processes enhance the overall security ecosystem by ensuring that relevant CTI information—covering existing threats and their mitigations—reaches all stakeholders. Additionally, the tools facilitate the adaptation of measures to specific domain scenarios by considering the security context during information parsing and utilizing generic policies that can be modified by various tools for different enforcement procedures, such as traffic management and automated software upgrades. For instance, threat modelling and risk assessment tools can dynamically incorporate both the existence of a threat and the implementation of a mitigation action, allowing models to evolve in response to changing conditions. This adaptability can influence the perceived trustworthiness of participants and inform decisions on whether to authorize their actions.

Acknowledgements

The research leading to this work has been co-funded by the European Union's Horizon 2020 research and innovation program under Grant Agreement No 883335 ERATOSTHENES, the European Union's Horizon CL3 Increased Cybersecurity 2021 under grant number agreement 101069471, and Spanish Ministry of Economy and Digital Transformation, under the project CERBERUS-HERMES (Grant No. TSI-063000-2021-44). Views and opinions expressed are however those of the authors only and do not necessarily reflect those of the Spanish Ministry, European Union or the European Commission. Neither the European Union nor the granting authority can be held responsible for them.

References

[1] Directive (EU) 2022/2555 of the European Parliament and of the Council of 14 December 2022 on measures for a high common level of cybersecurity across the Union, amending Regulation (EU) No 910/2014 and Directive (EU) 2018/1972, and repealing Directive (EU) 2016/1148 (NIS 2 Directive) (Text with EEA relevance). ELI: http://data.europa.eu/eli/dir/2022/2555/oj.

[2] Wagner, Thomas; Mahbub, Khaled; Palomar, Esther and Abdallah, Ali. Cyber Threat Intelligence Sharing: Survey and Research Directions. Computers & Security. 87, 101589. 2019. DOI: 10.1016/j.cose.2019.101589.

[3] Wagner, Cynthia; Dulaunoy, Alexandre; Wagener, Gérard and Iklody, Andras. MISP: The Design and Implementation of a Collaborative Threat Intelligence Sharing Platform. Proceedings of the 2016 ACM on Workshop on Information Sharing and Collaborative Security 49–56. 2016. URL: https://www.misp-project.org/.

[4] Preuveneers, Davy; Joosen, Wouter; Bernal Bernabe, Jorge and Skarmeta, Antonio. Distributed Security Framework for Reliable Threat Intelligence Sharing. Security and Communication Networks. 2020. 1–15. https://doi.org/10.1155/2020/8833765.

[5] Badsha, S.; Vakilinia, I.; and Sengupta, S. Privacy Preserving Cyber Threat Information Sharing and Learning for Cyber Defense, 2019 IEEE 9th Annual Computing and Communication Workshop and Conference (CCWC), Las Vegas, NV, USA, pp. 0708–0714, 2019 DOI: 10.1109/CCWC.2019.8666477.

[6] Alishahi, Mina; Saracino, Andrea; Martinelli, Fabio and Marra, Antonio. Privacy preserving data sharing and analysis for edge-based architectures. International Journal of Information Security. 21. 1–23. 2022. 10.1007/s10207-021-00542-x.

[7] Elliot, M., and Domingo-Ferrer, J. The future of statistical disclosure control. arXiv preprint arXiv:1812.09204. 2018.

[8] Sweeney, Latanya. K-anonymity: a model for protecting privacy. Int. J. Uncertain. Fuzziness Knowl. Based Syst. 10, 5 557–570. 2002. https://doi.org/10.1142/S0218488502001648.

[9] Machanavajjhala, A.; Kifer, D.; Gehrke, J., and Venkitasubramaniam, M. l-diversity: Privacy beyond k-anonymity. Acm Transactions on Knowledge Discovery from Data (Tkdd), 1(1), 3. 2007. https://doi.org/10.1145/1217299.1217302.

[10] Li, N., Li, T. and Venkatasubramanian, S. t-Closeness: Privacy Beyond k-Anonymity and l-Diversity. 2007 IEEE 23rd International Conference on Data Engineering, Istanbul, Turkey, pp. 106–115. 2007. https://doi.org/10.1109/ICDE.2007.367856.

[11] Harvard University Privacy Tools Project. Differencial Privacy. https://privacytools.seas.harvard.edu/differential-privacy.

[12] Lear, E.; Droms, R.; and Romascanu, D. Manufacturer Usage Description Specification. RFC Editor. 2019. https://doi.org/10.17487/RFC8520.

[13] Björklund, M. The YANG 1.1 Data Modeling Language. RFC Editor. 2016. https://doi.org/10.17487/RFC7950.

[14] Bray, T. The JavaScript Object Notation (JSON) Data Interchange Format. RFC Editor. 2017. https://doi.org/10.17487/RFC8259.

[15] Jethanandani, M., Agarwal, S., Huang, L., and Blair, D. YANG Data Model for Network Access Control Lists (ACLs). RFC Editor. 2019. https://doi.org/10.17487/RFC8519.

[16] Securing Small-Business and Home Internet of Things Devices: NIST SP 1800-15, NIST, Gaithersburg, MD, USA. 2019. https://doi.org/10.6028/NIST.SP.1800-15.

[17] "CVE vulnerabilities by date," May 2022, [Online]. Available: https://www.cvedetails.com/browse-by-date.php.

[18] Matheu-García, S. N. and Skarmeta, A. Defining the threat manufacturer usage description model for sharing mitigation actions. In 2022 1st International Conference on 6G Networking (6GNet) (pp. 1–4). IEEE. 2002. DOI: 10.1109/6GNet54646.2022.9830415.

[19] Hernández-Ramos, J. L., Matheu, S. N., Feraudo, A., Baldini, G., Bernabe, J. B., Yadav, P., … and Bellavista, P. Defining the behavior of IoT devices through

the MUD standard: Review, challenges, and research directions. *IEEE Access*, *9*, 126265–126285. 2021. DOI: 10.1109/ACCESS.2021.3111477.

[20] García, S. N. M., Molina Zarca, A., Hernández-Ramos, J. L., Bernabé, J. B., & Gómez, A. S. (2019). Enforcing behavioral profiles through software-defined networks in the industrial internet of things. *Applied Sciences*, *9*(21), 4576. 2019. DOI: 10.3390/app9214576.

DOI: 10.1561/9781638285076.ch7

Chapter 7

An Efficient Verifiable Data Registry for Identity and Trust Management in IoT

By Sokratis Vavilis, Fotis Michalopoulos, Harris Niavis, George Misiakoulis and Konstantinos Loupos

In today's world, IoT devices play an integral role in various aspects of our daily lives, ranging from smart home appliances to healthcare systems and industrial applications, offering innovative services. However, the inherent diversity and heterogeneity of IoT networks introduce new challenges, particularly in managing devices. This diversity also opens vulnerabilities that malicious actors may exploit, compromising the security of IoT ecosystems. In this chapter, we present a verifiable data registry (VDR) solution designed for decentralized identity and trust management in IoT environments. Our approach leverages Blockchain and gRPC technologies, utilizing HyperLedger Fabric as the underlying blockchain infrastructure. We extend this with a novel hybrid consensus algorithm tailored to the specific needs of IoT networks. Additionally, we expose the VDR's identity and trust management capabilities through gRPC services. The proposed solution emphasizes both security and scalability, enhancing its relevance and effectiveness in IoT applications.

7.1 Introduction

Modern IoT networks consist of a wide range of heterogeneous devices that vary in nature, technical specifications, and are designed to fulfil different objectives across diverse domains [1, 2]. This heterogeneity introduces challenges in terms of management, deployment, maintenance, commissioning, inter-communication, and overall lifecycle management. Additionally, the subtle differences among IoT devices make security concerns more evident [3]. For example, the absence of common trust mechanisms and standardized security frameworks makes IoT devices particularly attractive targets for attackers. Unfortunately, there are currently no comprehensive solutions that can securely manage IoT devices while simultaneously addressing decentralization and privacy concerns. As noted in [4, 5], most existing IoT trust management frameworks focus only on specific aspects, such as security, flexibility, or privacy, while others are limited to particular domains, like smart mobility [6] and healthcare [8], where the heterogeneity of IoT devices is more controlled.

To address these challenges, the ERATOSTHENES research project proposes an innovative decentralized solution for the holistic lifecycle management of IoT devices. Specifically, ERATOSTHENES aims to achieve this through: (a) secure and privacy-preserving identity management for IoT devices, enabling decentralized enrolment, discovery, and overall management across various domains, (b) reliable communication and network operation via a trust mechanism that assesses the trustworthiness of nodes, and (c) sharing cyber-threat intelligence (CTI) information to strengthen the network and its devices against ongoing attacks. The ERATOSTHENES Trust Framework is designed to be versatile and applicable across multiple domains, such as smart mobility, remote healthcare, and Industry 4.0. Thus, the proposed solutions are intended to be flexible and efficient, accommodating heterogeneous and resource-constrained devices (e.g., IoT) without compromising security. Further details on the requirements are discussed in [9].

In this context, the current chapter introduces a new solution to enable the secure storage, retrieval, management, and sharing of identity data (i.e., DID Docs) alongside additional information, such as trust scores linked to IoT devices and CTI data. This solution enhances the resilience of the entire ERATOSTHENES IoT ecosystem, where various architectural components leverage the services provided by this approach. The solution is built upon the W3C Decentralized Identifiers (DIDs) standard,[1] implementing the concept of Self-Sovereign Identities (SSIs) for verifiable and decentralized identity management. In particular, we propose a secure and efficient Verifiable Document Registry (VDR) for decentralized identity and trust management. To achieve this, we utilize the Hyperledger Fabric (HLF) blockchain framework for storing information and create scalable and secure gRPC services

1. Decentralized Identifiers (DIDs) v1.0, https://www.w3.org/TR/did-core.

to expose its functionality. Additionally, we extend HLF with a novel, fair, and lightweight consensus algorithm to meet the specific needs of the IoT ecosystem and the ERATOSTHENES project.

The remainder of this chapter is structured as follows: The next section introduces the preliminary knowledge required to understand the contributions of this work. Section 7.3 presents the proposed VDR solution and its design. Section 7.4 details the creation of an efficient and secure VDR using gRPC services and a hybrid consensus algorithm. Lastly, Section 7.5 provides an experimental evaluation of the proposed innovations, and Section 7.6 concludes the chapter.

7.2 Preliminaries

In this section we introduce the fundamental concepts necessary for understanding the work presented in this chapter.

7.2.1 Self-Sovereign Identity

Self-Sovereign Identity (SSI) is a digital identity model that empowers individuals to control their personal data.[2] Unlike traditional systems where third parties manage and store identity information, SSI allows users to own, manage, and securely share their credentials through decentralized technologies like blockchain. This reduces dependency on centralized authorities, enhances privacy, and gives users the ability to decide what information to share and with whom, promoting greater autonomy and data security.

To support this, the World Wide Web Consortium (W3C) has standardized Decentralized Identifiers (DIDs), which enable verifiable and decentralized identity management.[3] As illustrated in Figure 7.1, DIDs refer to a subject and are managed by a DID controller (i.e., identity controller). Each DID is associated with a DID document that specifies the verification methods required to prove the authority of the DID controller over the DID, along with available interactions with the subject. This functionality is facilitated by a Verifiable Data Registry (VDR), which can be implemented as a blockchain network to store and manage information such as DIDs and DID documents. The VDR is a key component of SSI infrastructure, and its design and implementation significantly impact the achievement

2. The Path to Self-Sovereigh Identity, https://www.lifewithalacrity.com/article/the-path-to-self-sovereign-identity/.

3. Decentralized Identifiers (DIDs) v1.0, https://www.w3.org/TR/did-core.

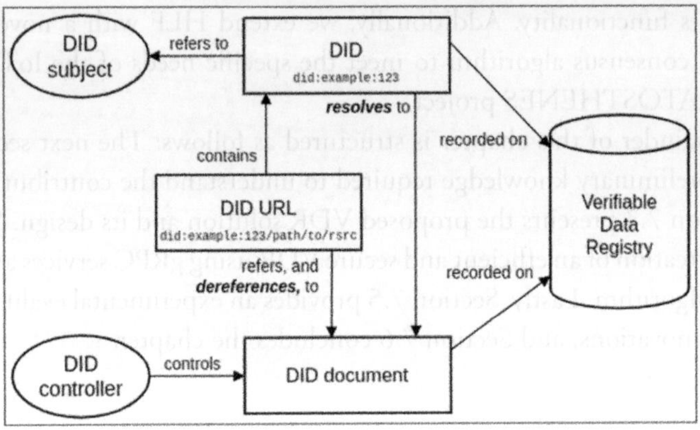

Figure 7.1. DID architecture.

of SSI objectives. In particular, implementing a secure, and scalable VDR for identity management is an open challenge, especially in resource-constrained environments like IoT [9]. To this end, in this work we present an efficient VDR aimed to facilitate the management of identity and trust information.

7.2.2 Blockchain

In today's interconnected world of IoT devices, security challenges in decentralized environments can be addressed using distributed ledger technology (DLT), which ensures secure and trustworthy access to records and data storage. The most widely recognized and mature DLT is blockchain. Originally developed to support Bitcoin in 2008 [10] as a verifiable append-only database for recording financial transactions, blockchain has since evolved into a powerful tool for decentralized data management.

A blockchain is essentially a chain of data blocks, each containing specific information and linked to the previous block through a cryptographic hash function. This structure guarantees the integrity and proper sequencing of data. Blockchain networks are designed for read-only traversal or the addition of new blocks, ensuring that data cannot be altered once recorded.

What sets blockchain apart from other distributed storage technologies is its decentralized and peer-to-peer nature. Each node in the blockchain network stores a local copy of the entire blockchain and collaborates with other nodes to add new blocks through consensus algorithms. These algorithms define the process for nodes to agree on the inclusion of new blocks, ensuring that all participants in the network maintain a shared and consistent view of the blockchain, even in a decentralized setup.

Blockchain networks can vary based on membership criteria. Public blockchains allow any node to join and access the chain, while private blockchains restrict participation to authorized nodes. Furthermore, blockchains can be permissioned, where only selected nodes can add new blocks, or permissionless, where any network participant can propose new blocks.

Another key feature of blockchain technology is the introduction of smart contracts, which debuted with Ethereum [11]. Smart contracts are immutable pieces of code executed on the blockchain, allowing for automated processes while maintaining transparency and auditability. This high level of programmability enables the automation of complex tasks with minimal human intervention.

Blockchain has a wide range of applications, including secure supply chain management, healthcare data management, and smart energy services. It is also seen as a foundational technology for Web 3.0, which aims to decentralize and democratize the internet. One significant example of this trend is Self-Sovereign Identity (SSI), which is discussed in this work.

7.2.2.1 HyperLedger Fabric

HyperLedger Fabric (HLF) is one of the leading frameworks for building permissioned blockchain networks. In HLF, each network is structured into channels, which represent well-defined groups of nodes (i.e., consortium) that may belong to different organizations. The nodes in an HLF network serve distinct functions and are classified as either **Peers** or **Orderers**. Peer nodes are responsible for hosting the ledger, executing chaincode (i.e., smart contracts), and providing services like the Fabric Gateway [12]. They play a key role in the smooth operation of the network by **endorsing** and **validating** transactions for inclusion in the blockchain. Transactions are submitted to the blockchain through the Fabric Gateway. Orderer nodes, on the other hand, are tasked with ordering these endorsed transactions into blocks and distributing them to Peer nodes. The collection of Orderer nodes across various organizations, all connected to the same channel, forms the network's Ordering service.

Most blockchain networks follow an **order-execute** architecture, where the consensus protocol first validates and organizes transactions into blocks, which are then propagated to all peer nodes for sequential execution. HLF, however, introduces an innovative **execute-order-validate architecture**. In this model, transactions are first executed and endorsed by Peer nodes, then ordered into blocks by the Ordering service. Afterward, the Peers validate the transactions within the block based on the network's endorsement policy before committing them to the ledger.

The transaction lifecycle in HLF begins with a client from one of the network's organizations. The client application connects to the Fabric Gateway in a Peer node, and the transaction goes through three key phases before being added to the blockchain:

- Proposal phase: The client sends a transaction proposal to the network's participating organizations. Each Peer executes the proposed transaction and signs it according to the network's endorsement policy.
- Ordering phase: The Fabric Gateway submits the endorsed transaction to an Orderer node, based on the consensus mechanism in place. For example, in Raft consensus algorithm, the signed transaction is sent to a specific Orderer, whereas in SmartBFT, it is broadcast to all members of the Ordering service. The Ordering service organizes the transaction into a block and forwards it back to the Fabric Gateway.
- Validation phase: Each Peer validates the transactions within the block. Valid transactions are committed to the ledger, and the client receives a confirmation from each Peer, signalling that the transaction has been successfully appended to the blockchain.

In this work we leverage HLF advanced functionalities to create the basis of the proposed VDR. To this end, on the one hand we incorporate a new consensus algorithm to it. On the other hand we expose the implemented identity and trust management functionalities via a gRPC interface to boost efficiency and security. We elaborate on this in Section 7.3.

7.2.2.2 Consensus Algorithms

Consensus algorithms are fundamental to blockchain technology, ensuring the secure storage and integrity of data on the blockchain. These mechanisms provide the core process by which nodes in a decentralized network agree on adding new blocks to the chain. Consensus algorithms can be broadly categorized into two types [13–15]. The first category consists of voting-based or leader-based approaches, which originate from distributed systems and rely on agreement protocols that mimic human decision-making processes. In these algorithms, nodes use a voting system to elect a leader, who is then responsible for adding a block to the chain. These approaches are typically used in permissioned blockchains, and the algorithms supported by HyperLedger Fabric (HLF), such as Raft and smartBFT, fall into this category.

The second category includes modern consensus algorithms, commonly found in public blockchains, which use randomness and competition. For example, in Proof-of-Work (PoW) algorithms [10], nodes compete to solve a cryptographic puzzle, with the winner adding the next block. In Proof-of-Stake (PoS) algorithms [16], nodes are selected based on the amount of stake they hold in the network, with higher stakes increasing the likelihood of selection. As already mentioned, in this work we integrate a novel hybrid consensus algorithm to HLF. This algorithm draws inspiration from modern approaches consensus while incorporating elements of voting mechanisms.

7.3 VDR Design

In this section we present the design of the proposed VDR solution. First we discuss the overall architecture of our VDR and its components. Then we move forward presenting the W3C compliant DID method we defined to manage identities through our VDR.

7.3.1 Architecture

Our goal is to create an efficient VDR to manage identities and trust information in a decentralized manner. The overall architecture of the proposed approach is depicted in Figure 7.2. At the core of the proposed VDR component lies the blockchain module, implemented using HLF, which is responsible for storing and managing DID documents and Trust information (i.e., trust scores). To facilitate the coordination of different nodes, the blockchain module utilizes different consensus algorithms, such as Raft, smartBFT and a novel hybrid consensus algorithm (see Section 4.2). Next to that, we create smart contracts, in the form of HLF chaincode, to manage the information stored in the blockchain infrastructure. In particular, we have implemented smart contracts to cover all the necessary CRUD (Create, Read, Update, Delete/Deactivate) operations for both DID Docs and Trust scores, and also share these data across multiple IoT networks (i.e., domains).

Despite their usefulness, interacting with the blockchain using smart contract in an IoT network can be challenging. That would require different services, such as the IdM and the TMB service, to implement their respective blockchain infrastructure and call the related smart contracts when needed to perform a particular operation. This can be proven to be a challenging task, both in terms of implementation and efficiency. Therefore, to facilitate the interaction with the VDR's smart contracts, we have built and external facing interface utilizing the gRPC protocol.

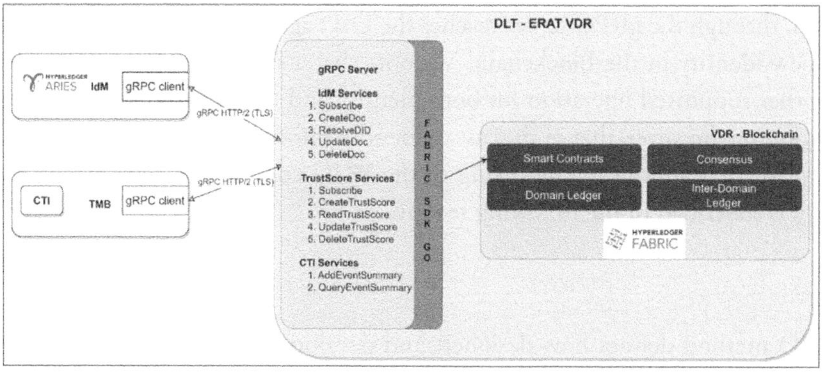

Figure 7.2. ERAT VDR architecture.

gRPC is an open source, cross-platform Remote Procedure Call protocol, initially developed by Google, which aims at providing high performance. This interface is exposed by a gRPC server, which implements services for the subscription of a DID agent or Trust agent, and the CRUD of DID Documents and Trust Scores. Internally, the gRPC server employs the Fabric SDK Go for the management and communication with the HLF network, translating the received request to smart contract calls. Compared to existing approaches [9, 17–19], which typically employ other protocols like REST and, the integration of gRPC enhances both security and scalability. We further discuss this aspect in Section 4.1. We note that our VDR also supports the management and sharing of Cyber Threat Intelligence (CTI) information, and to this end implements the related smart contracts and gRPC calls. A more comprehensive discussion on this matter can be found in Chapter 6.

To interact with our VDR solutions, the identity and trust agents need to implement gRPC clients that consume the functionality exposed by the VDR. Such communication requires a valid subscription to the respective service, by each component. Upon successful subscription, a DID or TMB agent can request the creation, resolution, update of deletion of a particular DID Doc or Trust Score. We note that such DID and TMB agents, are responsible for the logic behind managing identity and trust information, while the proposed VDR is only responsible for providing an efficient infrastructure for their management. In the case of the IdM, the Hyperledger Aries Framework Go [17] was used as a baseline and was extended with the gRPC client.

Example: We assume that a particular IdM agent is already subscribed to the gRPC service and wants to create a new DID document for an IoT device. The IdM agent constructs the DID Document using the public key related to the IoT device and sends it to the gRPC Server by calling the createDoc() gRPC service. The request is validated and authenticated by the gRPC server which then forwards it to the corresponding smart contract function that handles the storage of the DID Document in the Blockchain. This action triggers the emission of the docResolution event which, through the gRPC server reaches the DID agent and verifies the creation of the new identity in the Blockchain. We note that a similar process is followed for the other supported operation for both identity and trust information. It is worth mentioning, however, that in the case of identity information the agent must follow a standardized approach, complying to the W3C conformant erat DID method, which is described in the following section.

7.3.2 Erat DID Method

A DID method defines how designers and developers should materialise the features described by the W3C DID method specification [20] in association with a

Table 7.1. erat DID method syntax.

The erat DID Method Syntax ABNF Rules	
did	= "did:erat:" genesishash ":" identifier
genesishash	= 64(hexdigit)
identifier	= 64(hexdigit)
hexdigit	= "0" / "1" / "2" / "3" / "4" / "5" / "6" / "7" / "8" / "9" / "a" / "b" / "c" / "d" / "e" / "f"

particular VDR. In this work, we have created the **erat DID method**, to define the DID scheme used in the context of the ERATOSTHENES project. The erat DID method has been published as an official DID method in the list of known DID Methods by W3C https://www.w3.org/TR/did-extensions-methods/#did-methods.

As the DID method specification suggests, each DID is described by a unique DID URI that is conformant with the Uniform Resource Identifier (URI) generic syntax. In our system we have defined the erat DID method to describe DIDs. The rules and decisions to produce DID URIs that belong to the erat method and the DID Syntax ABNF Rules are presented in Table 7.1.

An **erat DID URI** consists of four key components. It starts with the prefix "did:", which is a universal identifier required by all DID URIs to conform to the official DID standard. According to RFC 3986[RFC] this "did:" prefix is followed by the method name—in this case, **erat**—which defines the ERATOSTHENES namespace. The remaining segments are specific to the method and must be globally unique within the ecosystem. The third segment is a globally unique identifier, which is the SHA-256 hash of the genesis block of the VDR ledger that the DID is associated with. Since each ledger has a unique genesis block, this hash allows a DID agent to identify a specific VDR. The final segment is an identifier linking to a specific entity. It is calculated as the SHA-256 hash of a combination of a random nonce, the genesis block hash, and the public key of the DID controller. The inclusion of a random nonce enhances privacy and prevents linkability, adding extra randomness to the identifier. This design prevents malicious actors from tracking a DID controller across networks by using its public key, ensuring that the identifier remains globally unique due to the nonce.

For the **erat DID method** specification, we have also defined key operations, including authorization mechanisms (e.g., cryptographic keys) and standard CRUD operations. The creation process is initiated by the DID agent via a service provided by the gRPC server, where the agent sends the controller's public key, the ledger's genesis hash, and the cryptographic details necessary for verification (as per W3C standards) to request the creation of a DID by the VDR. To resolve (i.e., read) a DID, the agent submits the DID URI to the VDR, which then returns the corresponding DID Document. For updates, the agent must provide the DID URI along with the requested changes, such as adding a new verification method. Finally, for deletion, the agent sends a deactivation request to the VDR using the DID and the associated public key. For both update and deactivation operations, the VDR ensures that the requester is the controller of the DID in question. The authentication method defined in the DID Document is used to verify the controller's identity before performing these operations.

7.4 Towards an Efficient Solution

The most defining property of the proposed VDR solution is its focus on efficiency. Towards this direction our contribution is twofold; on the one hand we increase the communication efficiency and scalability of blockchain-based VDR by integrating gRPC technology and on the other hand we integrate a novel hybrid consensus algorithm to HLF. In the remainder of this section, we elaborate on our key contributions.

7.4.1 gRPC Integration

As already mentioned, creating efficient and scalable VDR solutions is an open challenge. To expose their services in a user-friendly manner, most of the existing solutions [9, 17–19] rely on different protocols such as REST and WebSockets. However, compared to these approaches, research shows that gRPC technology can provide increased throughput and security [21]. This performance gain is largely attributed to its use of the HTTP/2.0 protocol, which allows for faster and more efficient bidirectional data transmission compared to the older HTTP/1.1.

In our solution the gRPC protocol was chosen to facilitate the interaction with the VDR due to its superior performance and robust security features (e.g., TLS for data confidentiality and authenticity). We note that such a choice is further justified by gRPC widespread adoption in various other platforms and frameworks, such as HyperLedger Fabric,[4] Dropbox,[5] and Uber.[6] As outlined in Section 7.3, we developed a bidirectional gRPC server to expose the VDR's functionalities. This server can manage multiple secure channels, with each channel corresponding to a distinct gRPC client, such as DID agents within an IoT network. This design significantly improves the scalability of the system. The gRPC

4. https://hyperledger-fabric.readthedocs.io/en/release-2.5/network/network.html.

5. https://dropbox.tech/infrastructure/how-we-migrated-dropbox-from-nginx-to-envoy

6. https://www.uber.com/en-GR/blog/architecture-api-gateway.

server implements various essential methods, including Subscribe, CreateDoc, and CreateTrustScore, to effectively manage identity and trust information stored in the VDR. To minimize the overhead associated with multiple TLS handshakes and enhance performance, both the gRPC server and clients make use of "Keepalive Settings." This configuration ensures that only a single TLS handshake occurs at the beginning of the connection, allowing the secure channel to remain open and available for event transmission with the blockchain without repeated handshakes.

Next to the above, gRPC protocol performance is closely tied to the serialization method employed for data transmission, particularly the codec used for encoding messages between the server and clients. Several serialization protocols are available for use over a gRPC channel, each offering specific advantages based on the use case. Among the most prominent are Protocol Buffers,[7] Gob,[8] and JSON. Gob is a serialization format unique to the Go programming language, optimized for encoding Go data types but lacking cross-language support. Protocol Buffers (protobufs), developed by Google, provide efficient serialization of structured data and support a variety of programming languages. JSON, a well-established and standardized format, remains a popular choice for structured data representation due to its broad compatibility. To select which encoding method is more suitable for our VDR implementation, we performed benchmarks to assess the performance of various codec implementations. We present our experiments and discuss their results in Section 7.5.

7.4.2 Fair and Lightweight Consensus

The second major novelty of our efficient VDR solution is the integration of a novel hybrid consensus algorithm in HLF [27]. Below we discuss its fundamental design principles and we proceed with presenting it implementation in HLF.

7.4.2.1 Algorithm Design Principles

As already discussed, consensus algorithms are one of the most critical components of blockchain technology, defining its key properties. Traditional leader-based approaches, such as the ones found in HLF, rely solely on voting and leader elections. Although quite efficient, these approaches lack flexibility and are not designed to cope with networks with fluid membership, such as dynamic IoT networks where nodes (e.g., devices) are frequently introduced or disbanded. Next to that, simpler algorithms like Raft cannot handle malicious entities, while more sophisticated approaches (e.g. smartBFT) introduce significant communication complexity.

---

7. https://protobuf.dev/overview/

8. https://pkg.go.dev/encoding/gob

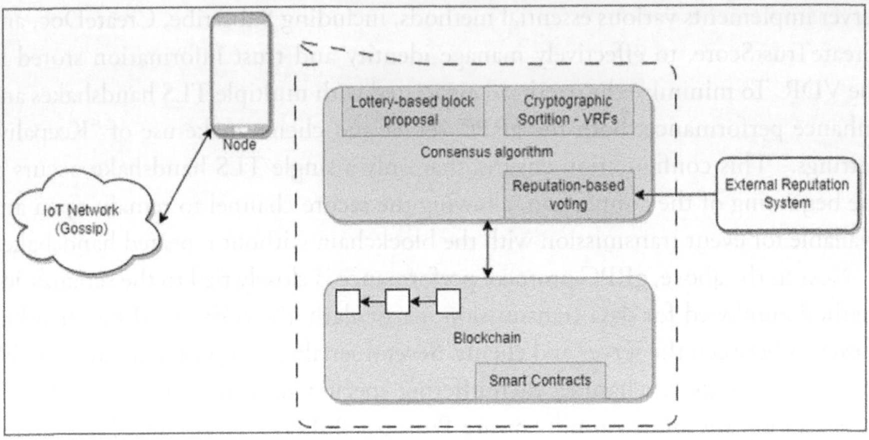

Figure 7.3. Consensus algorithm structure overview.

On the other hand, modern blockchain consensus algorithms address the limitations of traditional approaches, effectively cope with variable membership in the network (e.g., public networks) while showcasing increased tolerance to malicious nodes. Due to their design however, the most prominent algorithms of these category cannot be applied to an IoT context. In particular, algorithms such as Proof-of-Work require considerable resources (e.g., computational power, space, TEEs etc.) which are not available in the resource-constrained IoT ecosystem. Next to that, less heavy-weight approaches such as Proof-of-Stake (PoS) or Proof-of-Importance (PoI) [28] may give an unfair advantage to particular nodes of the network (e.g., favouring nodes with high monetary investments in the network) related to the block proposal, effectively demotivating newcomers or nodes with less involvement in the network.

To mitigate these challenges, we propose an innovative hybrid consensus algorithm designed specifically for IoT systems, with a focus on being lightweight and fair. As shown in Figure 7.3, the algorithm is structured into two main components: a decentralized lottery-based mechanism for block proposal and a reputation-driven voting process for block finalization. The lottery mechanism leverages Verifiable Random Functions (VRFs), which enable nodes to independently and securely generate a random lot in a decentralized and verifiable manner. In particular, a VRF [22] operates by taking a public/private key pair and a seed as inputs, and then generating a hash as its output. While only the holder of the private key can compute the VRF hash, anyone with access to the corresponding public key can independently verify its correctness. The VRF output is uniquely determined by the combination of the private key and seed, resulting in a uniformly distributed outcome that enhances the element of randomness and fairness in the block proposal phase [23]. Therefore, using VRFs nodes are able to compute a unique verifiable lot (i.e., hash) for a particular round defined by the corresponding seed. We note that VRFs have been widely adopted in various consensus algorithms, including Algorand's Pure Proof of Stake (PoS) model [24].

In the voting phase, a consortium of trusted nodes votes on the best seen block proposal (i.e., with highest lotter number) for the given round. The trustworthiness of each node is evaluated through an external reputation system. It is important to note that our proposed approach is flexible and not limited to any [29] specific reputation model, however, in the context of ERATOSTHENES we leverage the Trust Score information produced by the TMB component. In this work, we refer to trusted Orderer nodes (i.e., nodes with high reputation) as **reputable** and we allow them to participate in the voting phase. On the other hand, non-trusted nodes are called **non-reputable**.

Summarizing, the proposed algorithm deviates from traditional leader-based consensus models in Hyperledger Fabric (HLF) by eliminating the need for a designated leader to propose blocks. Instead, block proposals can originate from any network node through a randomized lottery process, with the final decision being made through a voting mechanism among trusted nodes. This lightweight, hybrid design is particularly suited for resource-constrained environments, such as those found in IoT networks, as it avoids the need for energy-intensive operations. Next, we delve into the implementation details of our solution.

7.4.2.2 HLF Implementation Details

We implemented the proposed consensus algorithm using Go programming language and integrated in HLF. The consensus process consists of three distinct phases: Proposal, Voting, and Commit, which we present below.

The **Proposal phase** begins when an Orderer node within the HLF network receives and organizes a batch of transactions into a block. During this process, the transactions included in the block are removed from the Orderer's transaction pool to prevent duplication. Each Orderer then proposes its block to be appended to the shared ledger. To ensure fairness and randomness, each Orderer computes a Verifiable Random Function (VRF) using its private key and a seed derived from the previous block's header.

The seed for the VRF is extracted from the header of the last confirmed block in the ledger, allowing any network node to verify the VRF hash using the seed and the corresponding public key of the Orderer. For consistency, the first block added to the ledger uses a VRF generated from a "genesis seed," which is randomly generated for each system to serve as the initialization point for the consensus mechanism.

Once the blocks are prepared, each Orderer broadcasts its proposed block to other Orderers while simultaneously listening for block proposals from others. In parallel, each Orderer continues to listen for incoming transactions from Peers,

```
Algorithm 1: Proposal Phase
calculate self hash;
bestVRF = self hash; // The bestVRF initialized with self hash and will
  hold the best VRF received from the Orderers
broadcast self hash to other Orderers;
while Proposal Phase timer NOT expired do
    receive a vrf request;
    if vrfReceived verified against Orderer's public key then
        if vrfReceived > bestVRF then
            bestVRF = vrfReceived
        blockProposals ++;
        if blockProposals == majorityOfOrderers then
            break;
```

Figure 7.4. Proposal phase algorithm.

```
Algorithm 2: Voting Phase
if reputable node then
    send the bestVRF to every other Orderer;
    quorum votes = quorum votes - 1;  // Not to count itself in the number
      of votes required
while Voting Phase timer NOT expired AND NOT quorum votes received do
    receive vote;
    votes ++;                          // Counter for number of votes received
    if votes == quorum votes then
        quorum votes received = true;  // Received the required number of
          votes
Check if a proposed block has the majority of votes;  // Find the winning block
```

Figure 7.5. Voting phase algorithm.

which are stored in the transaction pool for future proposals. The steps of this process are outlined in Figure 7.4.

This approach ensures decentralization by enabling any node to participate in block proposals, reducing potential bottlenecks caused by leader-based models, while maintaining security and randomness through the use of VRFs.

Followingly, the **Voting Phase** (see Figure 7.5) is responsible for determining which block will be appended to the shared ledger. A key requirement for participation in this phase is the reputation of the Orderer. Specifically, only nodes with established reputations are allowed to take part in the voting process. The steps involved in this phase are detailed in the algorithm provided below. By the end of the **Voting Phase**, each Orderer should have reached a consensus on the winning block to be committed to the ledger.

Lastly, in **the Commit phase** each Orderer commits the winning block to the shared ledger. Once the block is successfully validated, indicating that consensus has been reached across all Orderers, each node updates its state in preparation for the next round of consensus.

There are two scenarios that an Orderer must account for: (a) if the accepted block was self-proposed, and (b) if the accepted block was proposed by another Orderer. In the first case, the Orderer takes no further action. If there are any remaining transactions in the transaction pool, the Orderer moves on to the next round and proposes a new block. In the second case, where the block was proposed by another Orderer, the node must update its transaction pool by removing any transactions that were processed in the accepted block.For this, the Orderer cleans its self-proposed block, eliminating from its pool any transactions that overlap with those in the accepted block. The remaining transactions from the self-proposed block are returned to the pool. The Orderer also removes any transactions that appear in the accepted block from the transaction pool.

An important aspect of this phase is handling transactions that are not yet known to an Orderer but appear in the accepted block, which could result in duplicates in future blocks. To mitigate this risk, any unknown transaction from the accepted block is temporarily stored and later crosschecked to ensure it is not reprocessed in subsequent rounds. The Commit Phase process is shown in Figure 7.6.

7.5 Experimental Evaluation

In this section we present the experimental evaluation of the proposed VDR solution. First, we discuss the assessment of the different serialization methods for the gRPC service of the VDR. Then we present the experimental evaluation of our integrated consensus algorithm in HLF.

7.5.1 gRPC Benchmarks

As discussed in Section 7.4, different serialization methods have significant impact on the performance of the gRPC service (in terms of communication overhead). This evaluation will allow us to select a suitable serialization method for identity and trust information.

Existing benchmarks[9] typically evaluate codecs based on their performance and correctness. However, many of these assessments include redundant initialization phases, which can negatively impact the performance of certain codecs. In our evaluation we followed a similar approach, however, to improve accuracy, we optimized the approach by eliminating unnecessary encoding and decoding steps and

9. https://github.com/alecthomas/go_serialization_benchmarks.

Algorithm 3: Commit Phase

```
transactionPool;                         // The received - non processed- txns
proposedTxns;                       // The proposedTxns from the winning block
selfBlockTxns;                             // The txns of self proposed block
// removing duplicate txns
for txn in selfBlockTxns do
    if txn in proposedTxns then
        remove txn from the transactionPool;
        remove txn from the proposedTxns;
    else
        append txn to the transactionPool;

for txn in proposedTxns do
    if txn in transactionPool then
        remove txn from the transactionPool;
    else
        store txn in txnsMinted ;

txnsExtracted = 0;            // Counter of txns extracted from the txn pool
txnsMinted;   // The minted txns but not yet received from the Orderer
// check if there are any pending txns
for txn in transactionPool do
    if txn in txnsMinted then
        remove txn from txnsMinted;
        remove txn from transactionPool;
    else
        txnsExtracted ++;
        send transaction to the function responsible for cutting the next block;
        if txnsExtracted == batch size of block then
            break;
```

Figure 7.6. Commit phase algorithm.

enhancing the overall implementation. This allowed for a more reliable evaluation of each codec's performance, focusing on time efficiency and memory usage during the serialization and deserialization processes. Furthermore, in our benchmark we extended the test to assess various serialization methods using different data structures (e.g., DID Documents) specific to our use case.

In more detail, we evaluated three codecs: Protocol Buffers, Gob, and JSON, as outlined in These were tested by sending a range of data structures—such as a basic struct, a DID Document, and an x509 Certificate—over the gRPC channel. The selection of these data structures reflected different levels of complexity, providing a comprehensive evaluation of each codec's performance under diverse conditions. The experiments were conducted on a Linux system equipped with an Intel Core i7-9750H @2.6GHz and 16GB of RAM, ensuring a robust environment for testing.

To evaluate the performance of serialization (encoding) and deserialization (decoding), we conducted experiments using the aforementioned data structures.

Table 7.2. Benchmarking different codecs with gRPC for encoding operation.

	struct			didDoc			X509 cert		
Benchmarks	**proto**	**json**	**gob**	**proto**	**json**	**gob**	**proto**	**json**	**gob**
time/iter	56	95	280	1096	9110	3656	2682	27537	11352
bytes/op	8	27	39	1280	2571	4869	2304	8213	6484
alloc/op	1	1	0	1	33	3	1	25	35

Table 7.3. Benchmark different codecs with gRPC for decoding operation.

	struct			didDoc			X509 cert		
Benchmarks	**proto**	**json**	**gob**	**proto**	**json**	**gob**	**proto**	**json**	**gob**
time/iter	156	1659	1173	1292	255725	3095	5621	30808	19993
bytes/op	72	224	24	1976	134858	1584	5096	5452	8389
alloc/op	2	5	1	29	1539	25	80	90	177

We followed a similar approach to the existing benchmarks, and we evaluated the performance utilizing Go's default benchmarking metrics such as the time per iteration, bytes allocated per operation, and the number of distinct memory allocations per iteration. The time per iteration captures overall performance and CPU usage, while the memory-related metrics focus on memory consumption during the operations. For each case 500 iterations were performed.

The serialization benchmark results are displayed in Table 7.2 while the deserialization results are presented in Table 7.3. Our findings reveal that Protocol Buffers (protobufs) consistently provide the fastest serialization times, outperforming the other codecs. In two exceptional instances, however, Gob surpasses Protocol Buffers in both memory consumption and CPU utilization. In particular, the better performance of Gob was shown when decoding simple structures and DID Document structures. The relatively poor performance of JSON when decoding DID Documents can be attributed to the nested nature of these structures, which requires JSON to handle multiple layers during the deserialization process, thereby increasing its complexity and processing time. Further information about the data structures, experimental setup, results, and the associated source code is available in our open-source repository.[10] This repository provides additional insights into the performance of different codecs in serialization and deserialization operations.

10. https://gitlab.com/eratosthenes-h2020/grpc-benchmarks.

7.5.2 Consensus Evaluation

The aim of this experiments is to evaluate the performance of our consensus algorithm implementation in HLF and determine how it compares with the existing algorithms in HLF, namely Raft and smartBFT. The primary objective of this evaluation was not only to assess the throughput and resource utilization of the new algorithm but also to observe its overall behaviour and stability under various workloads and network conditions. We designed the experiments to provide a robust comparison by employing a range of configurations and scenarios.

The experiments were conducted in a controlled virtual machine environment with the following hardware specifications:

- 24-core AMD EPYC 7452 x86-64 CPU
- 64GB of RAM
- SSD storage for improved data access speeds

To ensure the benchmarking process was standardized and the results were reproducible, we employed Hyperledger Caliper, a dedicated benchmarking tool developed by the Hyperledger Foundation to evaluate the performance of blockchain frameworks [25]. Caliper provides a comprehensive suite of metrics that allows users to measure various performance aspects, such as throughput, latency, and resource consumption, across different blockchain configurations.

In the experiments, Caliper was configured to generate a pool of 15,000 transactions, which were transmitted by a client application at a fixed rate of 1,500 transactions per second. This transaction rate was chosen to simulate realistic conditions, effectively stress-testing the consensus mechanisms. The transactions were distributed to each Orderer node by 24 concurrent worker processes. This setup provided a reliable framework to observe how the newly implemented consensus algorithm behaves under heavy workloads and how it compares to Raft and smartBFT in terms of performance.

We followed the benchmarking approach outlined in the smartBFT study [26], designing test scenarios with varying configurations of Orderers. These scenarios were structured to include clusters of different sizes and multiple transaction batch sizes. Specifically, for smartBFT, we used clusters composed of 4, 7, and 10 Orderers. In contrast, for the Raft and hybrid consensus algorithms, clusters of 5, 7, and 11 Orderers were employed. In each cluster configuration, transaction batch sizes of 250, 500, and 1000 transactions per block were tested to evaluate performance under differing workloads.

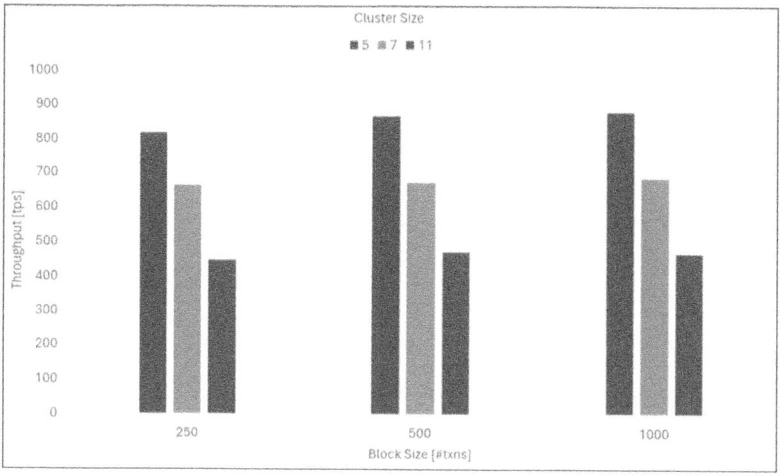

Figure 7.7. Hybrid consensus results.

7.5.2.1 Results and Discussion

In our testing process, each configuration described above was subjected to six repetitions to ensure robust and consistent results. The performance metrics for the hybrid consensus algorithm, Raft, and smartBFT are presented in Figures 7.7, 7.8, and 7.9 respectively. Each figure presents the average value derived from the six iterations, providing a comprehensive overview of the system's behaviour under different conditions.

By looking at the results, we see that Raft consistently demonstrated greater throughput compared to both smartBFT and the hybrid consensus approach. This performance advantage can largely be explained by Raft's lower communication overhead. As a leader-based mechanism, Raft operates by electing a leader responsible for making decisions regarding which blocks to append to the ledger. Once this decision is made, the leader broadcasts the block to the other nodes (Orderers), thus significantly streamlining the block addition process. This results in a reduced transaction lifecycle, as it requires only a single phase of communication between nodes, minimizing the amount of inter-node messaging required. In contrast, smartBFT, despite being leader-based, incurs additional communication overhead due to its multi-phase message validation process. Specifically, smartBFT required additional message exchanges during the Pre-prepare, Prepare, and Commit phases, adding complexity and slowing down the overall throughput. The hybrid consensus algorithm diverges from the leader-based paradigm, and although fairer in nature, it requires additional message exchanges between the nodes for proposing blocks and voting. In particular, in the hybrid consensus approach every node is expected to create a block proposal, while information dissemination is done using a gossip protocol.

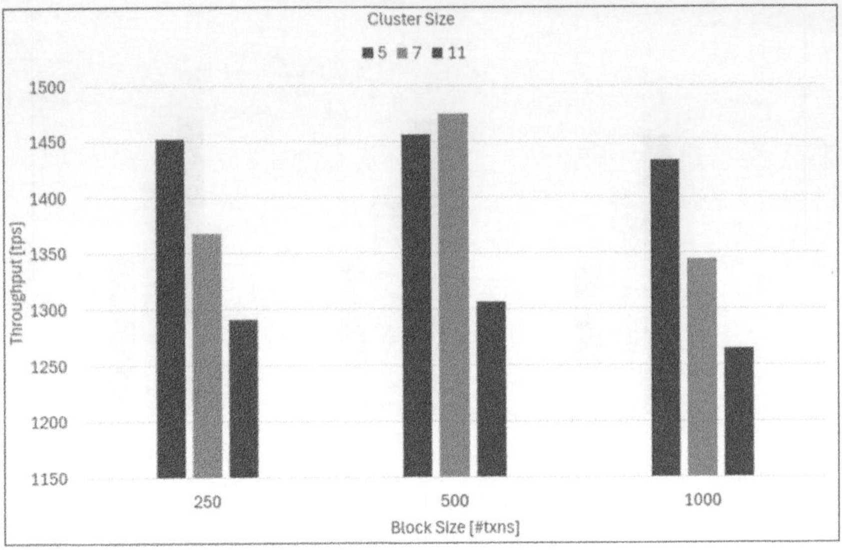

Figure 7.8. RAFT consensus results.

Interestingly, despite smartBFT better performance compared to our implementation, a deeper analysis of the results revealed several critical insights:

- **Reliability Concerns:** One of the most significant findings was the issue of transaction failures observed with smartBFT, particularly as the number of Orderers increased. For instance, in the 7-Orderer configuration, transaction failures ranged from 0 to 17, while in the 11-Orderer setup, failures increased and varied between 0 and 226, representing approximately 1.5% of total transactions. In extreme cases, transaction failures exceeded 2000, accounting for roughly 13% of all transactions. We, however, excluded such edge cases in our final analysis as we did not consider them representative of smartBFT average behavior. In contrast, both Raft and the hybrid consensus demonstrated strong reliability, with no reported transaction failures.
- **Duplicate Transactions:** Another observation was the significantly higher number of duplicate transactions generated by smartBFT when compared to Raft and the hybrid consensus. In scenarios involving 11 Orderers, smartBFT recorded over 200 duplicate transactions, indicating inefficiencies in transaction handling and network synchronization, which could further complicate system performance under heavy loads.
- **Handling of Batch Sizes:** While the batch size (the number of transactions per block) was explicitly configured to specific values (e.g., 1000 transactions per block), smartBFT frequently committed blocks containing far fewer transactions than the specified batch size limit. This suggests that smartBFT

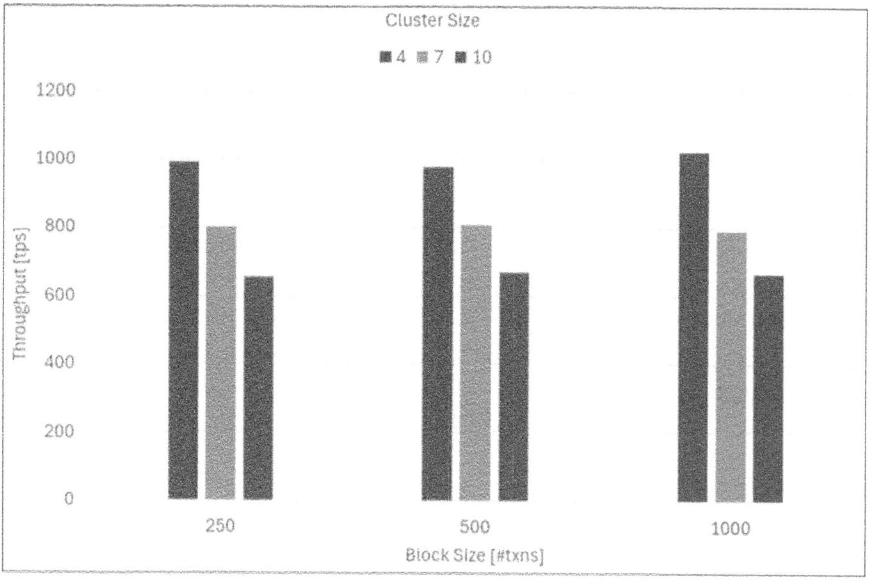

Figure 7.9. smartBFT consensus results.

treats the batch size as a theoretical maximum, rather than a strict guideline, likely optimizing for other factors, such as network latency or node synchronization. This practice potentially gives smartBFT a throughput advantage, but it complicates direct comparisons with Raft and the hybrid consensus, both of which adhere strictly to the configured batch size. The lack of such optimizations in the hybrid consensus implementation means that while smartBFT may appear to outperform in some scenarios, the comparison is not entirely fair, as the two systems are optimized differently.

The impact of batch size on algorithm throughput was another key area of investigation. Increasing the block size from 250 to 500 transactions generally resulted in improved performance across all the tested configurations. However, the hybrid consensus displayed a unique pattern: its throughput continued to increase even with batch sizes of 1000 transactions, whereas smartBFT exhibited a slight decline, and Raft experienced a more severe drop in performance. This suggests that the hybrid consensus can better handle larger batch sizes without sacrificing throughput, while Raft and smartBFT might encounter bottlenecks or inefficiencies as the batch size grows. Moreover, our analysis revealed that increasing the number of Orderers (i.e., cluster size) generally had a negative impact on throughput across all algorithms. This decline in performance is primarily attributed to the additional communication overhead that comes with managing larger networks, as more nodes need to be coordinated, increasing the time and resources required to achieve consensus. However, one notable exception was Raft, which showed improved performance with a batch size of 500 transactions and 7 Orderers, suggesting that under certain conditions, Raft can manage increased network size more efficiently than the other algorithms.

In conclusion, while our implementation demonstrated promising results, particularly in terms of its ability to scale without transaction failures, further optimization is needed. Our current implementation, although functional, is still in the proof-of-concept stage and is not yet ready for production deployment. Future work will focus on reducing communication costs by optimizing message sizes and streamlining inter-node interactions. Additionally, we plan to enhance the robustness of the algorithm by incorporating features to handle node failures and dynamic network changes post-initialization.

7.6 Conclusion

In this chapter, we introduced a secure and efficient solution for managing identities and trust information in decentralized IoT environments. Unlike existing methods, our approach capitalizes on the robust security features of Blockchain technology while enhancing scalability through a fine-tuned gRPC implementation. To meet the increased decentralization demands of IoT networks, we integrated a novel hybrid consensus algorithm into the chosen blockchain infrastructure, specifically HyperLedger Fabric (HLF). We provided a detailed explanation of our design and presented evaluation results of the proposed Verifiable Data Registry (VDR) within the scope of the ERATOSTHENES project. As part of our ongoing efforts, we are currently working on validating these solutions in the project's pilot implementations to further support and refine their functionality.

Acknowledgements

This work has received funding from the European Union's Horizon 2020 research and innovation programme under grant agreement no 101020416. The authors acknowledge the research outcomes of this publication belonging to the ERATOSTHENES (101020416) project consortium.

References

[1] Kollolu, R. "A Review on Wide Variety and Heterogeneity of IoT Platforms." The International journal of analytical and experimental modal analysis, 12, 2020.

[2] Choudhary, D. "Security challenges and countermeasures for the heterogeneity of IoT applications," Journal of Autonomous Intelligence, vol. 1, no. 2, 2018.

[3] Yousefnezhad, N., et. al., "Security in product lifecycle of IoT devices: A survey," Journal of Network and Computer Applications, vol. 171, 2020.

[4] Wei, L., et al., "Trust management for Internet of Things: A comprehensive study," IEEE Internet of Things Journal, vol. 10, no. 9, 2022.

[5] Kumar, L., et al., "Leveraging blockchain for ensuring trust in IoT: A survey," Journal of King Saud University-Computer and Information Sciences, vol. 10, no. 34, 2022.

[6] Ali, A., et al., "VABLOCK: A blockchain-based secure communication in V2V network using icn network support technology," Microprocessors and Microsystems, 2022.

[7] Abou-Nassar, E. M., et al., " DITrust chain: towards blockchain-based trust models for sustainable healthcare IoT systems.," IEEE access, 2020.

[8] Torroglosa-Garcia, E., et al. "A Holistic Approach for IoT Networks' Identity and Trust Management–The ERATOSTHENES Project." Internet of Things: 5th The Global IoT Summit, GIoTS 2022, 2022.

[9] Hosseini, S. M., et al., "Blockchain-Based Decentralized Identification in IoT: An Overview of Existing Frameworks and Their Limitations.", Electronics, 12(6), (2023).

[10] Bitcoin, Nakamoto S. Bitcoin: A peer-to-peer electronic cash system, 2008. 517.

[11] Wood, G., "ETHEREUM: A secure decentralized generalized transaction ledger." 2023.

[12] Hyperledger Foundation: HyperLedger Fabric (HLF) v2.5 Documentation (2024), https://hyperledger-fabric.readthedocs.io/en/release-2.5/network/network.html#what-is-a-blockchain-network, Last accessed 8 August 2024.

[13] Azbeg, K., Ouchetto, O., Jai Andaloussi, S., Fetjah, L.: An overview of blockchain consensus algorithms: comparison, challenges and future directions. Advances on Smart and Soft Computing: Proceedings of ICACIn 2020 pp. 357–369 (2021).

[14] Stefanescu, D., Montalvillo, L., Galán-García, P., Unzilla, J., Urbieta, A.: A systematic literature review of lightweight blockchain for iot. IEEE Access 10, 123138–123159 (2022).

[15] Lashkari, B., Musilek, P.: A comprehensive review of blockchain consensus mechanisms. IEEE access 9, 43620–43652 (2021).

[16] Nguyen, C.T., Hoang, D.T., Nguyen, D.N., Niyato, D., Nguyen, H.T., Dutkiewicz, E.: Proof-of-stake consensus mechanisms for future blockchain

networks: fundamentals, applications and opportunities. IEEE access 7, 85727–85745 (2019).

[17] HyperLedger Aries Framework Go, https://github.com/hyperledger/aries-framework-go. Last accessed March 2024.

[18] Ferdous, S., et al. "SSI4Web: a self-sovereign identity (SSI) framework for the web." International Congress on Blockchain and Applications, 2022.

[19] Satybaldy, A., et al. "A Taxonomy of Challenges for Self-Sovereign Identity Systems," in IEEE Access, vol. 12, 2024.

[20] Decentralized Identifiers (DIDs) v1.0, https://www.w3.org/TR/did-core. Last accessed March 2024.

[21] Weerasinghe, L., et al. "Evaluating the inter-service communication on microservice architecture." Proceedings of the 7th International Conference on Information Technology Research (ICITR). IEEE, 2022.

[22] Micali, S., Rabin, M., Vadhan, S.: Verifiable random functions. In: Proceedings of the 40th Annual Symposium on the Foundations of Computer Science (FOCS '99). pp. 120–130. IEEE (1999).

[23] Chainlink: Verifiable Random Functions (VRF) in simple terms (2023), https://chain.link/education-hub/verifiable-random-function-vrf, Last accessed 8 August 2024.

[24] Chen, J., Micali, S.: Algorand: A secure and efficient distributed ledger. Theoretical Computer Science 777, 155–183 (2019).

[25] Hyperledger Foundation: Hyperledger Caliper benchmarking tool (2023), https://www.hyperledger.org/projects/caliper, Last accessed 8 August 2024.

[26] Barger, A., Manevich, Y., Meir, H., Tock, Y.: A byzantine fault-tolerant consensus library for Hyperledger Fabric. In: Proceedings of the IEEE International Conference on Blockchain and Cryptocurrency (ICBC) 2021. pp. 1–9. IEEE (2021).

[27] Michalopoulos, F., Vavilis, S., Niavis, H., Loupos, K. (2025). Integrating a Hybrid Lightweight Consensus Algorithm in HyperLedger Fabric. In: Presser, M., Skarmeta, A., Krco, S., González Vidal, A. (eds) Global Internet of Things and Edge Computing Summit. GIECS 2024. Communications in Computer and Information Science, vol 2328. Springer, Cham. https://doi.org/10.1007/978-3-031-78572-6_12.

[28] Harris Niavis and Konstantinos Loupos. 2022. ConSenseIoT: A Consensus Algorithm for Secure and Scalable Blockchain in the IoT context. In Proceedings of the 17th International Conference on Availability, Reliability and Security (ARES '22). Association for Computing Machinery, New York, NY, USA, Article 103, 1–6. https://doi.org/10.1145/3538969.3543811.

[29] Vavilis, S., Petković, M., & Zannone, N. (2014). A reference model for reputation systems. Decision Support Systems, 61, 147–154.

DOI: 10.1561/9781638285076.ch8

Chapter 8

Intrusion Detection for IoT-based Context and Networks

By Rosella Omana Mancilla, Francesca Costantino, Cesar Caramazana Zarzosa and Juan Manuel Vera Diaz

This chapter discusses the importance of establishing robust monitoring and detection capabilities in IoT ecosystems to identify emerging cybersecurity threats, in alignment with NIST guidelines and the NIS directive. Intrusion Detection Systems (IDS) play a critical role in monitoring network traffic, identifying suspicious activities, and responding to potential threats. The chapter also addresses the limitations of traditional IDS in modern IoT environments, such as handling large volumes of data and ensuring real-time detection. To address these challenges, the ERATOSTHENES project proposes an integrated solution using Machine Learning to distinguish between normal and malicious device behaviours, complemented by Federated Learning techniques to optimize data transmission and enhance collaborative AI model development.

8.1 Introduction

To strengthen IoT ecosystems and align with the NIST guidelines [1] and NIS directive [2], it is crucial to establish monitoring and detection capabilities to identify emerging cybersecurity threats. According to NIST, intrusion detection is defined as "the process of monitoring the events occurring in a computer system or network and analysing them for signs of possible incidents, which are violations or imminent threats of violation of computer security policies, acceptable use policies, or standard security practices" [3].

By monitoring and analysing network traffic, we can ensure that each identified and authenticated device is generating legitimate activity and not acting as a shadow IoT device. Incidents may not always stem from malicious intent—employees might inadvertently attempt to access restricted areas, for example. Such events should be reported to ensure the ecosystem can respond promptly and stay secure.

Intrusion Detection Systems (IDS) are vital in establishing a robust security framework. An IDS monitors network traffic for suspicious behaviour and raises alerts when potential threats are detected. In some cases, IDS can automatically respond to malicious activity, such as blocking traffic from suspicious IP addresses. When this proactive capability is integrated, the system becomes known as an Intrusion Prevention System (IPS).

However, modern IoT ecosystems present significant challenges for traditional IDS, including the need to handle massive amounts of network data, maintain detection efficiency, and provide real-time monitoring. As highlighted in directive 51 [2], member states are encouraged to adopt innovative technologies such as Artificial Intelligence to overcome these challenges, therefore ERATOSTHENES proposes an integrated solution that uses Machine Learning techniques to adequately and efficiently classify normal behaviours or habits of devices from new types of attack from the domain point of view. Additionally, novel solutions based on Federated Learning techniques leverage the distributed properties inherent to IoT networks, thereby optimising the amount of data transmitted through the network and facilitating the collaborative generation of more accurate AI-based models.

This chapter is divided into two subsections, one for the Network Intrusion Prevention Detection System IDPS) and one for the FedLPy, their integration composes the ***Monitoring,IDS* which is a Trust Manager & Broker (TMB) submodule in charge of analysing traffic data and identifying threats (and potential threats).**

8.2 Network Intrusion Detection Prevention System

From the State of the Art, IDPS focuses on enhancing detection accuracy, scalability, and efficiency through the integration of advanced technologies such as machine learning, deep learning, and cloud computing.

One of the ERATOSTHENES project scopes is to enhance the security on communication among enrolled, and not, devices and edge, and to do so innovative approaches have been adopted to define an effective Network Intrusion Detection Protection System, including:

- Introduction of Anomaly detection
- Zero-trust on device
- Cyber-Threat Information Sharing and application of external Mitigation action (from MUD files)

Hereafter, Section 8.2.1, the studies that have suggested the innovation brought by the project.

Section 8.2.2 reports the overall architecture of the solution, and the implementation of its building blocks is listed into Section 8.2.3. It is worth mentioning that the implementation was driven by state of the art on technologies at the beginning of the project. Further studies are in place to continue to improve the proposed solution following trends on Network Intrusion Detection and Prevention.

Lastly in Section 8.2.4 the interconnections with other ERATOSTHENES modules are provided.

8.2.1 State of the Art and beyond SOTA

In today's highly interconnected world, cybersecurity threats are evolving at an unprecedented pace, posing significant risks to organizations and their digital infrastructures. The rapid expansion of Internet of Things (IoT) ecosystems and the increasing reliance on complex networks have made it more challenging to detect and mitigate potential security breaches. To address these growing concerns, the implementation of robust security measures has become essential for safeguarding sensitive information and ensuring the stability of critical systems.

One of the core components in modern cybersecurity frameworks is the Intrusion Detection and Prevention System (IDPS). An IDPS combines two essential security functions: intrusion detection, which monitors network traffic for suspicious activity, and intrusion prevention, which takes proactive steps to block or mitigate identified threats. By incorporating both detection and response capabilities, IDPS plays a pivotal role in identifying emerging cyber threats, preventing unauthorized access, and ensuring the overall integrity of the network.

Traditional signature-based IDS, faces several challenges, including:

- High false positive rates: IDS often generate false alarms by flagging benign activities as malicious, which overwhelms security teams and reduces overall effectiveness.
- Scalability: As network traffic grows, the ability to process and analyse large volumes of data in real-time becomes difficult.

- Evolving threats: Attackers continuously develop new methods, such as zero-day exploits and advanced persistent threats (APTs), that evade traditional IDS signature-based detection.
- Encrypted traffic: The rise in encrypted communications limits the visibility of traditional IDS, making it harder to inspect and detect malicious activity.

On the other hand, anomaly-based detection poses bases for detecting new or unknown threats, as it focuses on unusual behaviour rather than specific signatures with the help of the Artificial Intelligence (AI): anomaly detection is a powerful technique for detecting deviations in data, hence it could help in identifying anomalous traffic, unknown patterns than can suggest a threat is being performed. A particular AI field of study, Machine Learning (ML) can be used to build models that automatically learn what constitutes normal and abnormal behaviour.

There are three primary paradigms in machine learning:

- **Supervised learning:** The model is trained on a labelled dataset, where both input and output data are provided. The goal of supervised learning is to predict labels for new, unseen data based on the input. This approach is often used for tasks such as classifying whether an email is spam.
- **Unsupervised learning:** In this case, the dataset is unlabelled, meaning there is no predefined relationship between input and output. The model identifies patterns and relationships within the data on its own. A common problem addressed by unsupervised learning is clustering, which involves grouping similar data points together.
- **Reinforcement learning:** There is no predefined input or output data for the model to learn from. Instead, the model learns through trial and error, improving its decision-making over time based on feedback from previous actions. Reinforcement learning is commonly applied in areas like video games and robotics.

Even though heuristic methodologies on intrusion detection have been studied for more than a decade, implemented solutions are less common than signature/rule-based tools. Research is still ongoing giving space for our proposed solution. The ***ERATHOSTENES project introduces a novel approach by combining unsupervised and supervised learning to implement anomaly detection*** (details in Section 8.2.3.1). Although this method has been explored in other areas, its application to intrusion anomaly detection holds potentials [4, 5]. The idea is that by first applying a clustering algorithm to unlabelled datasets, the subsequent classifier's accuracy improves. The classification algorithms are then trained using the output from the clustering process. Later studies have been released providing similar approach in anomaly-detection [6] making our solution a valid one.

Also, the core principle of a Zero-Trust Security Model [7], "do not trust anyone, verify everyone", is that both internal and external threats exist, meaning no users or devices are automatically trusted. Instead, Zero Trust continuously verifies user identities, access privileges, and device security. Following this principle, detection capability can influence the device Trustability: when a device is generating malicious traffic to a specific/set of device/server (DOS or DDOS attacks) it could be identified as a threat to the trusted network; in terms of behaviours, this device is not behaving correctly and other members of the network should not trust it as they did, or they should be monitored and periodically verified. ***ERATOSTHENES project introduces a process to generate a behavioural score for devices that influence their trust score*** (details in Section 8.2.3.2).

8.2.2 Architecture

Internally the solution is divided into four main blocks:

- Engine + Anomaly Detection Inspector (ADI)
- Threat and Rules manager
- Score calculator
- Alert GUI

The *Engine+ADI* is the block that combines signatures-based detection and applies a Machine Learning based procedure to identify known threats and misbehaviours or anomalies in network traffic data. When a threat or potential threat is identified an alert in generated.

The *Threats and Rules Manager* collects alerts generated by the Engine+ADI and forwards them to the Alert GUI and MQTT Broker. It also applies reactions or controls received from the MUD Management Module and the CTI Agent (such as implementing new detection rules) via the MQTT Broker.

The *Score Calculator* is the block influenced by the "Zero trust" paradigm, it notifies the TMB if bad behaviour (high-priority alerts) is identified, the notification can request the update of the Trust value for the device that triggered the alert.

The *Alert GUI* is the dashboard capable of displaying alerts and events identified.

Figure 8.1 depicts the internal architecture of the IDS.

8.2.3 Implementation

Based on the WP1 output, architecture and requirements, and State of The Art, the main functionalities implemented to define the ERATOSTHENES IDS are the following:

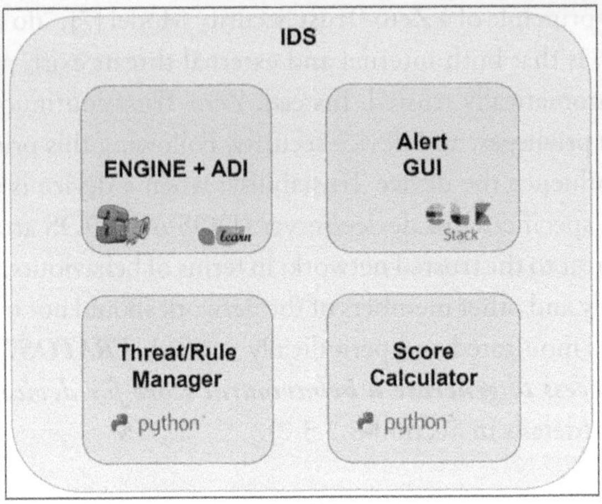

Figure 8.1. IDS internal architecture.

- Signature-based detection and anomaly-based detection
- Device Trust Monitoring
- CTI Sharing and Policy enforcement

Each functionality is implemented by a building block and the technologies used have been picked up following specific criteria: the open-source licence, community support, multi-threading/capabilities, adaptability, security, etc.

Each building block is implemented a Docker container to ensure portability, efficiency, easier management, flexibility and faster start-up. In particular the containers are managed by docker-compose.

8.2.3.1 Engine + Anomaly Detection Inspector

The Engine + ADI block ensures *signature-based detection* is enhanced with *anomaly-based detection.*

The prototype designed and implemented in the context of ERATOSTHENES, uses *SNORT version 3.*[1] as the engine that ***apply signature to identify known threats***. The selection has been influenced by the following features:

- Real-time traffic monitoring
- Can be installed in any network environment
- Open Source
- Rules are easy to implement
- Prevention can be enabled
- Great community support

1. https://www.snort.org/snort3.

- Plug-in framework, make key components pluggable (and 200+ plugins)
- Multi-threading for packet processing

The prototype inherits the macro classifications, available in Table 8.1, each of them is identified with a set of rules *and the priority level*, that represent a level of danger/risk.

- **1 – High,**
- **2 – Medium,**
- **3 – Low,**
- **4 – Very low**

Configuration of the engine is file-based: output, rules files, plugins and other option are enabled or disables, set and or modified through the snort.lua file (usual path */usr/local/etc/snort/snort.lua*).

Specific and additional customization are possible to enhance the detection, including the introduction of new detection rules and inspectors. ERATOSTHENS as initial prototype has defines custom rules per pilot and an external Inspector with the intention to be portable or can be used with other signature-based engines, such as Suricata.[2] The Inspector implements the anomaly detection proposed as the enhancement to signature-based detection.

It is developed using Python scripts: the selection was influenced by the adoption of Scikit-learn [6] library, well established for Machine Learning and Deep Learning algorithms.

Based on the SOTA described previously, ***applying anomaly detection to identify unknown threats or misbehaviours*** can be achieved by combining unsupervised and supervised learning, enhancing the detection rate during operational state. Therefore, ERATOSTHENES project introduces the following approach depicted in Figure 8.2: the upper part depict the training process, where the detection model (*ADI model*) is generated, is it the application prediction/operational time on new records/packets to determine their classification (*anomal, normal*), each have been implemented as Python scripts, details are in Tables 8.2 and 8.3.

The whole process can be divided into four phases:

- **Clustering phase:** uses an unsupervised algorithm, *K* clusters are created from an unlabelled dataset that collects the normal network behaviour.
- **Outlier detection phase:** all the outliers, from the *K* clusters, are (1) removed from the dataset because they are considered noise and will be compromising the performance of algorithms, (2) or defined as *anormal.* The resulting

2. https://suricata.io/

Table 8.1. Threat classifications.

Short name	Short description	Priority
attempted-user	Attempted User Privilege Gain	1
unsuccessful-user	Unsuccessful User Privilege Gain	1
successful-user	Successful User Privilege Gain	1
attempted-admin	Attempted Administrator Privilege Gain	1
successful-admin	Successful Administrator Privilege Gain	1
shellcode-detect	Executable Code was Detected	1
trojan-activity	A Network Trojan was Detected	1
web-application-attack	Web Application Attack	1
inappropriate-content	Inappropriate Content was Detected	1
policy-violation	Potential Corporate Privacy Violation	1
file-format	Known malicious file or file-based exploit	1
malware-cnc	Known malware command and control traffic	1
client-side-exploit	Known client-side exploit attempt	1
bad-unknown	Potentially Bad Traffic	2
attempted-recon	Attempted Information Leak	2
successful-recon-limited	Information Leak	2
successful-recon-largescale	Large Scale Information Leak	2
attempted-dos	Attempted Denial of Service	2
successful-dos	Denial of Service	2
rpc-portmap-decode	Decode of an RPC Query	2
suspicious-filename-detect	A Suspicious Filename was Detected	2
suspicious-login	An Attempted Login Using a Suspicious Username was Detected	2
system-call-detect	A System Call was Detected	2
unusual-client-port-connection	A Client was Using an Unusual Port	2
denial-of-service	Detection of a Denial of Service Attack	2
non-standard-protocol	Detection of a Non-Standard Protocol or Event	2
web-application-activity	Access to a Potentially Vulnerable Web Application	2
misc-attack	Misc Attack	2
default-login-attempt	Attempt to Login By a Default Username and Password	2

(*Continued*)

Table 8.1. Continued

Short name	Short description	Priority
sdf	Sensitive Data was Transmitted Across the Network	2
not-suspicious	Not Suspicious Traffic	3
unknown	Unknown Traffic	3
string-detect	A Suspicious String was Detected	3
network-scan	Detection of a Network Scan	3
protocol-command-decode	Generic Protocol Command Decode	3
misc-activity	Misc activity	3
icmp-event	Generic ICMP event	3
tcp-connection	A TCP Connection was Detected	4

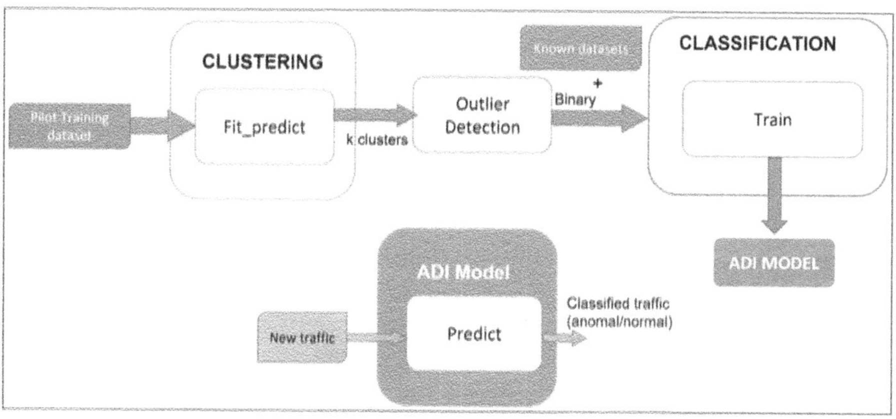

Figure 8.2. IDS anomaly detection inspector or ADI.

dataset is combined with another known dataset (for example IoT23[3] dataset or others to enhance the classification with known threats/anomalies).

- **Classification phase:** the classification algorithm is trained using the combined dataset from the previous phase. The output of this phase is the *ADI model*, a trained machine-learning model which will be used in the last phase.
- **Predict phase:** in this phase, the new incoming traffic will be analysed and classified as normal or anormal using the ADI model.

3. https://www.stratosphereips.org/datasets-iot23.

Table 8.2. IDS ADI training script details.

Script	Training
Purpose	Train the anomaly detection model with Density-Based Spatial Clustering of Applications with Noise (*DBSCAN*) for clustering and outlier detection and *Random Forest* for classification using the input dataset, or the NF-TON-IoT[4] dataset
Functionalities	• Load and preprocess the input dataset, or the NFTON-IoT dataset • Train and generate the model • Save the trained model to disk for later use
Notes	The default dataset NF-TON-IoT could be replaced with other more recent known dataset

Table 8.3. IDS ADI prediction/monitoring script details.

Script	Prediction/monitoring
Purpose	Monitor network packets from a file, in semi real-time, classify packets as anomalous or normal, and log the results.
Functionalities	Continuously read a network traffic packets from a file Extract and preprocess features from each packet Apply trained model generated by the training script to classify packets Log anomalies for further analysis

The output of this block is stored into a log file and displayed through the Alert GUI dashboard. An example of output is available hereafter. Alert's format, or fields list is configurable in the Engine configuration file.


```
{ "timestamp" : "10/02-13:31:09.494433", "pkt_num" : 160946, "proto" : "UDP", "pkt_gen" : "raw",
"pkt_len" : 60, "dir" : "C2S", "src_addr" : "192.168.8.114", "src_port" : 5353, "dst_addr" :
"224.0.0.251", "dst_port" : 5353, "service" : "unknown", "rule" : "122:23:1", "priority" : 3,
"class" : "none", "action" : "allow", "msg" : "(port_scan) UDP filtered portsweep" }
{ "timestamp" : "10/02-13:31:09.787387", "pkt_num" : 160967, "proto" : "IP", "pkt_gen" : "raw",
"pkt_len" : 40, "dir" : "C2S", "src_addr" : "192.168.8.114", "dst_addr" : "224.0.0.22", "service" :
"unknown", "rule" : "116:444:1", "priority" : 3, "class" : "none", "action" : "allow", "msg" :
"(ipv4) IPv4 option set" }
{ "timestamp" : "10/02-13:31:09.787454", "pkt_num" : 160968, "proto" : "ICMP", "pkt_gen" : "raw",
"pkt_len" : 76, "dir" : "C2S", "src_addr" : "fe80::f38:a9a0:99ec:7e11", "dst_addr" : "ff02::16",
"service" : "unknown", "rule" : "1:10000002:0", "priority" : 0, "class" : "none", "action" :
"allow", "msg" : "ICMP Traffic Detected" }
{ "timestamp" : "10/02-13:31:33.978841", "pkt_num" : 162678, "proto" : "TCP", "pkt_gen" : "raw",
"pkt_len" : 150, "dir" : "C2S", "src_addr" : "192.168.8.114", "src_port" : 53648, "dst_addr" :
"192.168.8.240", "dst_port" : 8500, "service" : "unknown", "rule" : "1:10000004:1", "priority" : 1,
"class" : "none", "action" : "allow", "msg" : "Possible SSL Flood Detected" }
{ "timestamp" : "10/02-13:31:33.987360", "pkt_num" : 162686, "proto" : "TCP", "pkt_gen" : "raw",
"pkt_len" : 52, "dir" : "C2S", "src_addr" : "192.168.8.114", "src_port" : 53648, "dst_addr" :
"192.168.8.240", "dst_port" : 8500, "service" : "unknown", "rule" : "1:10000004:1", "priority" : 1,
"class" : "none", "action" : "allow", "msg" : "Possible SSL Flood Detected" }
```


4. https://research.unsw.edu.au/projects/toniot-datasets.

Table 8.4. Few IDS alert fields' descriptions.

Variable	Description
timestamp	Timestamp of the alarm
pkt_num	Packet number
pkt_len	Length of the packet
dir	Direction of the traffic (e.g., "S2C" for server-to-client, "C2S" for client-to-server)
proto	Transport layer protocol of the risky packet.
src_addr	source IP address
src_port	source port number
dst_addr	destination IP address
dst_port	destination port number
rule	Additional information to include in the alarm.
priority	priority associated with the detection rule
class	the classification type of the event
action	the action taken (e.g., allowed, blocked, etc.)

8.2.3.2 Score Calculator

This block handles *Device Trust Monitoring* by assigning a device Monitoring Score (MS) that reflects the device's performance in terms of high-priority alerts generated. Higher priority events, which pose greater risks or signify critical actions, have a more significant impact on the device trustability score. The goal is to adjust the Trust Score of an enrolled or bootstrapped device based on detected threats or anormal behaviour, considering the ERATOSTHENES Trust framework for potential corrective measures.

Figure 8.3 illustrates the process of creating the Monitoring Score. The priority of an alert, denoted by “p”, ranges from 1 to 4, with 1 being the highest priority, see definition in Section 8.2.3.1. Alerts with $p \leq 2$ are considered the most critical and are prioritized. The TrustScore is measured on a scale from 0 to 1 and is retrieved from the TMB through an API.

After retrieving the DID of the device (through a REST API provided by the TMB), the process can be reduced into three cases:

1. CASE 1 – Priority ≤ 2 and Trust Score $= 0$

   This means that the device has the lowest value of TS and has generated high or medium-high-priority alerts.

   - The IP address is added to the IDS blacklist and traffic to and from it is blocked

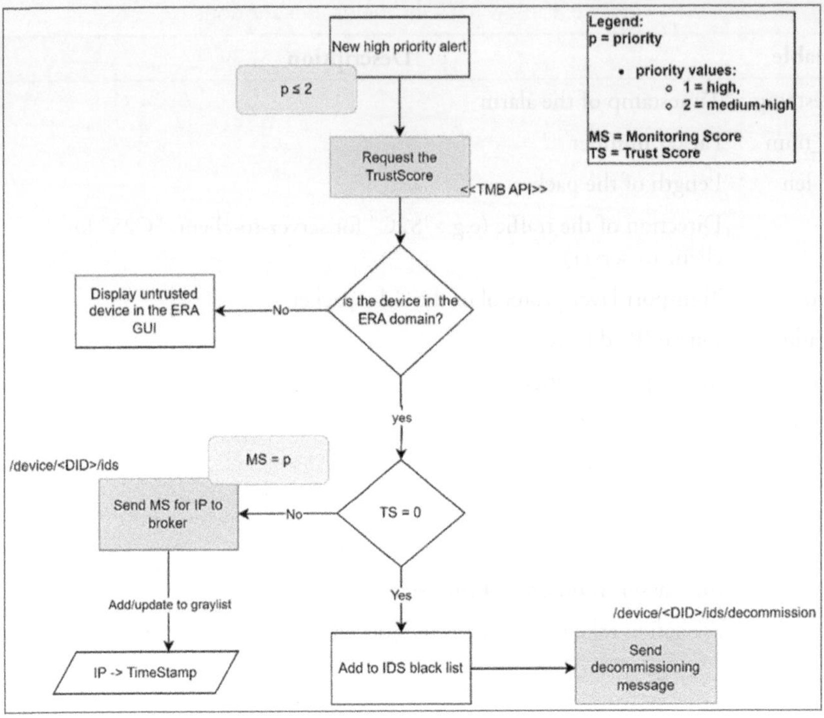

Figure 8.3. IDS monitoring score management.

- Request for decommissioning of the device through the MQTT Broker

2. CASE 2 – Priority ≤ 2 and TS $\neq 0$

   This means that the device is somehow trusted, and the generated alert could be a warning.

   - The IP address is added to the IDS *graylist*, the device is in under observation state, or quarantine period (Timestamp, IP address and MS are stored)
   - Send a message with the information related to the packet (MS and IP address) to the TMB, which will recalculate the TS based on the MS received and the weight of the MS value
   - After a tr (quarantine or under observation time) if no other alerts are generated MS is updated to 3 and sent to the Broker
   - Figure 8.4 depicts how to manage the device under quarantine period

3. CASE 3 – Priority ≤ 2 and device not bootstrapped yet

   This means that the device must be notified to the Network Administration team and the TMB

   - The packet is displayed in a panel of the IDS Alert GUI

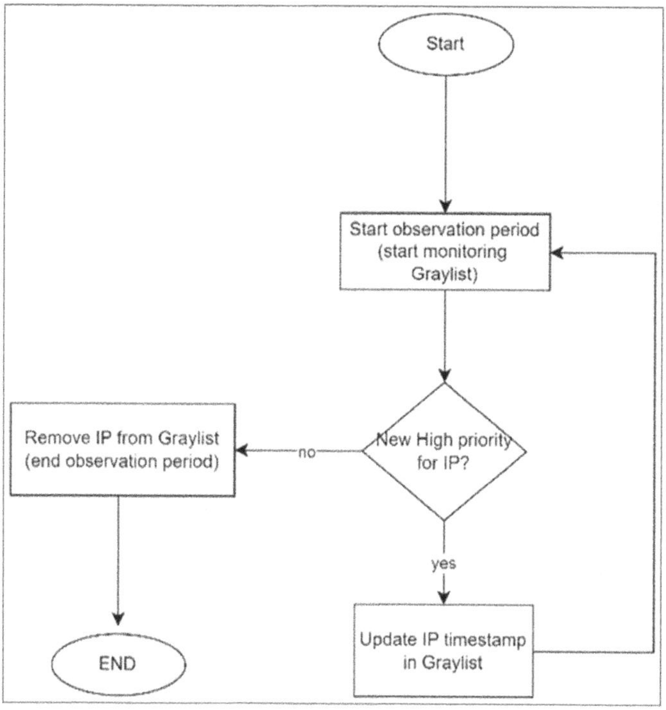

Figure 8.4. IDS under observation device management.

- Notify TMB that the new not bootstrapped device has generated high priority alert (possible control: don't accept/finish enrolment)

Table 8.5 in an example of TrustScore updates based on MonitoringScore value received: e.g. if priority of the alert $p = 1$, hence MonitoringScore MS = 1 and the current TrustScore TS = 0 then the reaction could be to request the decommissioning because the alert generated has the highest level of danger/risk and the device has the lowest level of trust.

The Score Calculator, as for the other blocks, is docker container that runs an MQTT client for Node.js (MQTT.js[5]) and sends messages to the following channels (see Table 8.6).

8.2.3.3 Threat and Rule Manager

This block handles and implements the *CTI sharing and policy enforcement* functionality, mainly:

- Forwarding alerts on detected threat to the CTI Agent
- Applying policy enforcement when received by the MUD Manager Module

5. https://github.com/mqttjs/MQTT.js.

Table 8.5. Example of IDS Monitoring Score values and Trust Score update/reaction.

MonitoringScore	Current TrustScore	Updated TrustScore/reaction
1	0	Request decommissioning
1	0.5 (middle)	0
1	1	0
2	0	Request Decommissioning
2	0.5 (middle)	0
2	1	0.5
3	0	0.5
3	0.5	1
3	1	Same value – no update

Table 8.6. IDS Score Calculator communication channels.

Topic	**/device/<DID>/ids**
Message payload	Monitoring score, IP and/or DID, Json formatted data
Description	The IDS shares Monitoring Score for a specific IP/DID, requesting recalculation of its Trust Score
Topic	**/device/<DID>/ids/decommission**
Message payload	IP and/or DID, Json formatted data
Description	The IDS shares Monitoring Score for a specific IP/DID requesting decommissioning

As for the Score calculator this block is a Docker container that runs an MQTT client for Node.js, MQTT.js [1].

The block handles alerts, generated by the *Engine+ADI*, with *high* or *medium high* priority level (p <= 2), generate a Json string, following specific format, and forward them to the *ThreathInfoSharing* channel, as depicted in Figure 8.6 in the detection block.

When a new MUD file is generated or an update is shared among the CTI stakeholders, if it contains relevant information regarding enforcement policy at network traffic level, this block will receive a policy, through the broker channel *threat/ID/threatMudMSPL* or *device/ID/mudMSPL*. The policy will be parsed, and action will be taken such as adding a detection rule for the Engine. Policies are written in MSPL, so the Threat and Rule Manager block implement a library that translate MSPL data into SNORT rules.

Table 8.7. IDS Threat and Rule manager communication channels.

Topic	**threat/ID/threatMudMSPL**
Message payload	The translated Threat MUD file associated to the threat
Description	The IDS subscribes to this channel to receive the result of the retrieval and translation of a Threat MUD file
Topic	**device/ID/mudMSPL**
Message payload	The translated MUD file associated to the device
Description	The IDS subscribes to this channel to receive the retrieval and translation of a MUD file

8.2.3.4 Alert GUI

Additional block is the *Alert Graphical Interface* (GUI), introduced to display in real-time the alert generated through a smart and user-friendly dashboard, for network administrators' further analysis.

This block is implemented with several docker containers that together is called *Elastic stack*, aka ELK (Elasticsearch, Logstash and Kibana) with three open-source projects[6]:

- *Elasticsearch is a search and analytics engine*
- *Logstash is a server-side data processing pipeline that ingests data from multiple sources simultaneously, transforms it, and then sends it to a "stash" like Elasticsearch*
- *Kibana lets users visualize data with charts and graphs in Elasticsearch.* [7]

Important are the Logstash configuration file *logstash.conf* and the Kibana dashboard designed specifically for ERATOSTHENES IDS functionalities.

The *logstash*.conf mention the input file, where the alerts are stored, the filtering and/or translation of the data and lastly the output, which is Elasticsearch.

The Dashboard includes mainly the following panels:

- A panel that lists all the alerts generated by the *Engine+ADI*
- A panel for statistical data over the type of the protocols involved.
- A panel for statistical data over the type of threat class detected (see Table 8.1)
- A panel with the list of IPs that are considered *Untrusted* (devices that generate high priority alerts while being not enrolled into ERATOSTHENES)
- All the panel can be queried or filtered for further analysis.

6. Basic License

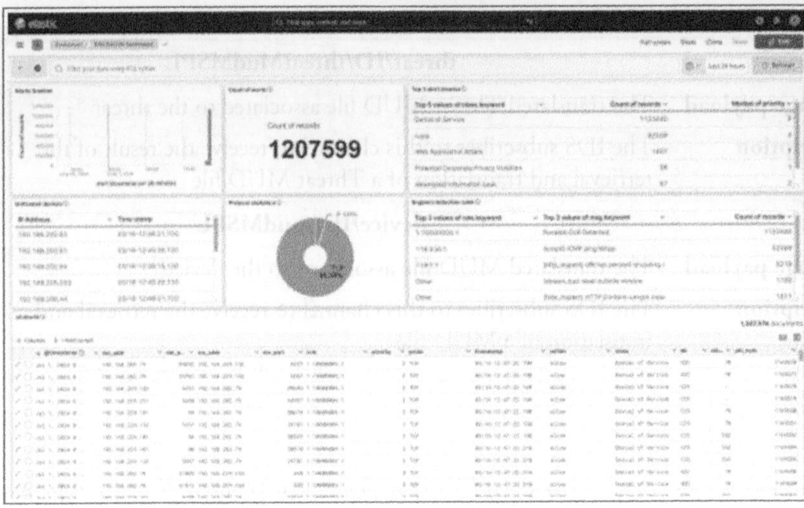

Figure 8.5. IDS alert GUI dashboard.

8.2.4 Interaction with Other ERATOSTHENES Tools

As stated previously, the IDS is part of the *Monitoring,IDS*: the interconnection with the FedLPy is also described in Section 3.4. Briefly, the two solutions share the *Alert GUI* block to display alerts: specific configuration on the Logstash container are in place to achieve this integration.

Also, as part of TMB, it interacts with other submodules, in particular with the Trust Manager and Broker, CTI Agent and MUD Management Module:

- Whit the first one, it communicates for *Device Monitoring* functionality – when the IDS define a device behavioural score, the *MonitoringScore* (MS), it is sent to the TMB, which could influence the device trustability, details are available in Section 8.2.3.2.
- With the second one, it communicates for the *CTI sharing* functionality – CTI Agent is notified of all the high priority event detected, see 8.2.3.3.
- With the latter, for Policy enforcement - the MUD Management Module generates new policy to be parsed and applied by the IDS, such as detection rules or blocking rules, see 8.2.3.3.

The three types of interaction are depicted in Figure 8.6: all the communication are done via MQTT broker, and the specific channels description are available within each block subsection.

8.2.5 Preliminary Results

The preliminary tests and validations conducted have provided us with a solid foundation to proceed confidently with the development and refinement process.

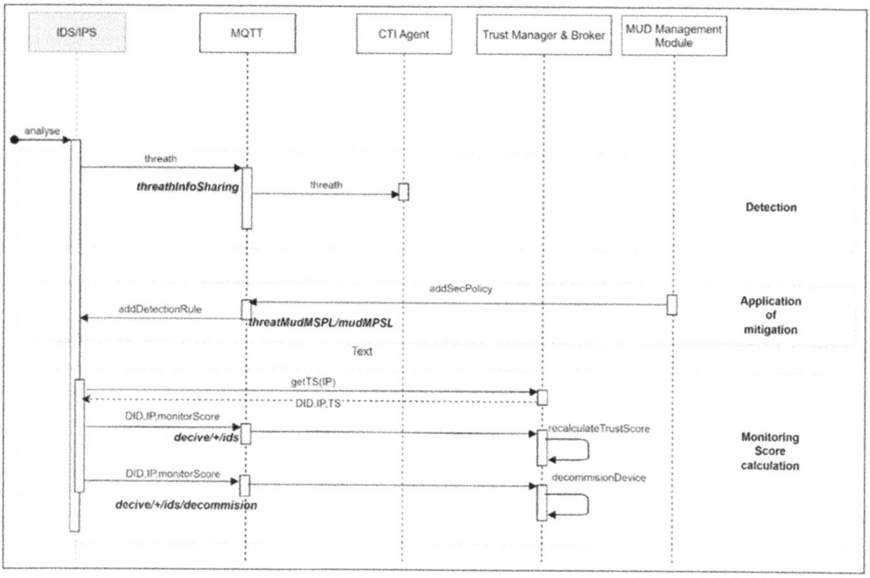

Figure 8.6. IDS interaction with other ERATOSTHENES modules.

These initial assessments have yielded encouraging results, even if slightly significant, demonstrating the viability of the core concepts of the Anomaly Detection Inspector, and highlighting areas where further improvements that leads to the reported solution. The accuracy observed across various testing scenarios not only validate the direction we've taken but also reinforce our confidence in achieving the desired outcomes.

8.2.5.1 ADI Tests

In a preliminary version of the prototype the ADI was implemented as a stand-alone solution (a separate container) used to assess the benefit of the proposed approach for the anomaly detection:

- For the clustering phase the Density-Based Spatial Clustering of Applications with Noise (DBSCAN) has been selected also because it simplifies the transformation of the dataset into a binary one during the Outlier detection phase.
- Several classifications algorithms have been used for comparison, Random Forest, Decision Tree, Support Vector Machine and Logistic Regression

Two test sessions have been performed using same dataset (part of NF-TON-IoT), the first only using the classification algorithms the second using the proposed approach:

- DBSCAN parameters n – the minimum number of points (a threshold) clustered together for a region to be considered dense and ε – a distance measure

Table 8.8. Comparison of the ADI with NF-TOM-IoT without/with clustering.

	NF-ToN-IoT	
	Classification	**Clustering + Classification without outliers**
Decision Tree	Confusion matrix: TN=5995, FP=6, FN=3, TP=18870 Accuracy: 0.9996381764	Confusion matrix: TN=5774, FP=3, FN=5, TP=18843 Accuracy: 0.9996751269
Random Forest	Confusion matrix: TN=5999, FP=2, FN=2, TP=18871 Accuracy: 0.9998391895	Confusion matrix: TN=5774, FP=2, FN=2, TP=18846 Accuracy: 0.9997969543
Support Vector Machine	Confusion matrix: TN=5993, FP=8, FN=11, TP=18862 Accuracy: 0.9992361502	Confusion matrix: TN=5774, FP=3, FN=6, TP=18842 Accuracy: 0.9996345178
Logistic Regression	Confusion matrix: TN=5784, FP=217, FN=132, TP=18741 Accuracy: 0.9859692851	Confusion matrix: TN=5583, FP=194, FN=10, TP=18838 Accuracy: 0.991715736

that will be used to locate the points in the neighbourhood of any point: $n = 2 * D$ where D is the number of features used, and $\varepsilon = 0.5$.

- The NF-TON-IoT dataset is split into 70% for training and 30% for testing, in the second test the division is made after the outlier detection phase, where the outliers are removed leaving a test dataset with 24625 record to classify.

The tests have provided a slight benefit on the accuracy, see Table 8.8. From these results, consortium worked on the implementation of an inspector that could be integrated with a signature-based engine and that can provide prediction on whether they could potentially be a threat or not, on new traffic, details are in Section 8.2.3.1.

Hereafter a recap on the measures used to compare the results: the confusion matrix and the accuracy that report a quick overview of the distribution of False Negative (FN), False Positive (FP), True Negative (TN) and True Positive (TP).

TP = true positive – Classified as anomal correctly
TN = true negative – Classified as normal correctly
FP = false positive – Wrongly classified as anomal

FN = false negative – wrongly classified as normal

The accuracy score is defined as the total number of correctly predicted records over the total number of records:

$$A = \frac{TP + TN}{Tot}$$

8.3 FedLPy

The Internet of Things (IoT) can be defined as a network of interconnected objects and devices, which can send and receive data collected by sensors. In this context, the concept of distributed processing emerges when the devices responsible for sensing, sending and receiving these data are also endowed with the capacity to process the data they collect. The concept of distributed learning arises when these devices are also invested with the capacity to learn from the data, which they have collected through the utilization of Machine Learning (ML) techniques. Furthermore, when this learning, acquired through Artificial Intelligence (AI) based models, is disseminated across all devices in the IoT network, such that all devices adhere to the same model based on collaborative learning, this is designated as Federated Learning (FL).

This section will provide a comprehensive account of the implementation of an FL subsystem (henceforth designated as FedLPy) within the ERATOSTHENES system, along with an exposition of the model generated thereby and its deployment in a distributed anomaly detection analysis of network traffic.

8.3.1 State of the Art and Beyond SOTA

One of the primary challenges associated with IoT networks is their susceptibility to security threats. Any malicious entity can potentially gain access to the IoT network and infect one or more devices with the objective of compromising communication between devices, limiting the functionality of the distributed system, or extracting data or information from other devices within the network. Thus, monitoring the network traffic flows of these devices should be done to assess possible malicious events.

As detailed in [8] the core motivations for the implementation of a continuous risk assessment system within a network can be attributed to the following factors:

- Maintaining situational awareness of all devices in the network.
- Maintaining an understanding of threats to act accordingly.

This monitoring provides continuous assessment of the network, enabling organisations to stay ahead of cyber threats through real-time visibility of devices operating on the network. There are several approaches to address continuous risk assessment [9, 10], with AI-based systems being one of the most widely used today [9–18]. The two principal approaches followed in the literature are: *(i)* the detection of anomalies within the network flow received by a device and *(ii)* the detection of potentially malicious packets and their categorisation according to known attack categories.

The technique presented in [19] represents a novel approach to the collaborative training of ML models for the detection of network threats. It does so by exploiting the distinctive topologies of IoT networks based on client-server schemes. This collaborative learning approach, also known as federated learning [20–23], is an AI algorithm training technique in which each participant trains an AI model with a topology shared among the different participants using data from their own device. The trained models are then sent to a central server, which aggregates all models into a global one. Finally, the global model is shared with each participant.

The FL approach offers several advantages over classical training, in which data from all clients are sent to a central server for model training.

- The bandwidth consumed in data transfer is lower, as only model weights are sent over the network, and even only increments or compressed versions of the models can be sent.
- The time required for model training is reduced, as there is no longer a need to iterate over all available data in a sequential manner.
- The data used to train the models never leaves the device, thereby maintaining the privacy of the data. Furthermore, the global model can be protected against inference attacks using differential privacy techniques.

8.3.2 Architecture

The FedLPy package implements an FL framework for the continuous detection of malware packages in IoT networks, to be used within the ERATOSTHENES system.

As illustrated in Figure 8.7 the component is mainly comprised of two modules: *(i)* a Federated Learning module (FL Server and FL Client) that implements a system for the decentralised training of AI models using raw network traffic data, and *(ii)* a Continuous Assessment module (CA Server and CA client) that exploits this AI model for the online detection of potential attacks.

1. The **Federated Learning module** represents the core component of FedLPy, providing the functionality for orchestration and communication between

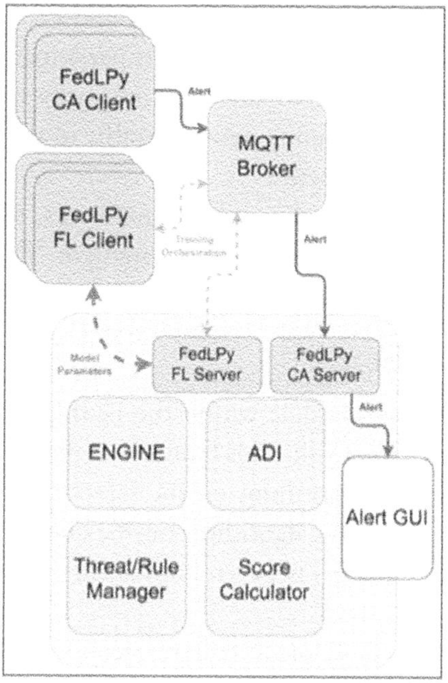

Figure 8.7. FedLPy within ERATOSTHENES architecture.

federated clients and a server. Particular emphasis is placed on the establishment of secure connections and the utilisation of privacy-preserving techniques.

2. The **Continuous Assessment module** provides the infrastructure for model inference on an ongoing basis, monitoring network traffic, forwarding packets through the AI model, and classifying them as either benign or malicious. It also considers the temporal aspect of Distributed Denial-of-Service attacks (DDoS) and generates a risk score for each individual sample. Additionally, it generates metadata about potential threats and notifies a server, which is integrated with the Alert GUI component of ERATHOSTENES.

The modules are independent of one another, although they share the same source code and present a very similar structure. This approach ensures that the entire component remains operational even in the event of a single module malfunction, while simultaneously facilitating the integration of the modules into a unified system.

8.3.3 Implementation

The FedLPy system is implemented as a Python module. As previously stated, this component is composed of two sub-modules: (i) The Federated Learning submodule is responsible for deploying and preparing the required resources for the process, as well as orchestrating, communicating, and executing the various steps involved in the process across the different agents participating in it. (ii) The Continuous Assessment sub-module employs the previously trained model with the objective of monitoring the incoming network traffic to the devices, thereby alerting to any incoming threats to them.

To exploit the distributed typology of IoT networks, both sub-modules have been implemented following the client-server paradigm. The implementation carried out for each of the parts within each sub-module is detailed below.

8.3.3.1 Federated Learning

The Federated Learning sub-module within the FedLPy component is based on the well-known Flower[7] framework. This framework allows the implementation of powerful model aggregation algorithms on the server side, provides the freedom to implement one's own training algorithms on the client side, and also manages the process of message exchanges between both agents for the transfer of weights between them.

Furthermore, additional functionalities have been incorporated into the component to facilitate process orchestration techniques and the registration and monitoring of the global model throughout the training process. The first of the additional features is the orchestration process, which is carried out by deploying an MQTT server. This server defines several topics that trigger different events during the process, such as the beginning of a training round. The second feature is achieved by deploying an MLFlow lite server to track models on the client side. This server has the minimum functionality necessary to track the models received by the clients and decide which model is used in the Continuous Assessment sub-module.

As illustrated in Figure 8.8, the process comprises three principal stages, which are conducted in a repetitive sequence. These stages are subdivided into the following actions:

1. **Model Broadcasting**:
    a. The FL Server publishes an initialization message to the MQTT broker under the topic "Start Training".
    b. The FL Server broadcasts the initial model weights to all participating devices.
2. **Model Training on Edge device**:
    a. Each FL Client fits the model locally using its own private data for a certain number of epochs.

---

7. https://flower.ai/.

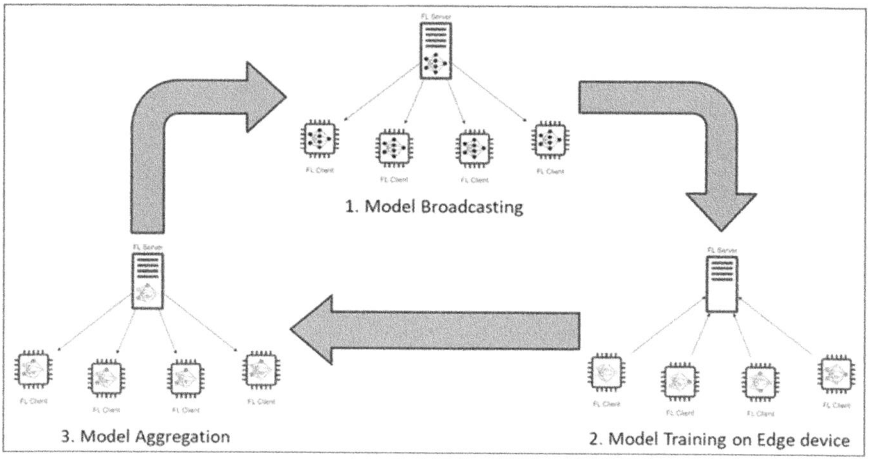

Figure 8.8. FedLPy training loop.

Table 8.9. Federated learning related used MQTT Broker topics.

Topic	**device/DID/Learning/Start**
Message payload	None
Description	Represents the start of the Federated Learning process of the Machine Learning algorithms for Threat detection.

   b. All FL Clients then send the result back to the FL Server.

3. **Model Aggregation**:
   a. The FL Server aggregates all received model weights and evaluates the performance of the model on a public dataset.
   b. The FL Server sends the final version of the model back to all devices.
   c. Each FL client evaluates the performance of the model on its own private datasets and logs the model in its MLFlow server.
   d. This process is executed in a loop until several fixed rounds is completed.

Since FedLPy is designed to run on IoT devices, the AI model is lightweight, ensuring that it is expressive enough to fit the data while keeping the number of parameters to the minimum. This reduces the computational cost on the devices – which usually do not have a lot of computational power – and avoids communication bottlenecks when transmitting the updates.

Training is carried out with labelled traffic data from IoT networks. The samples are raw packets without any preprocessing. Since, by definition, Federated Learning is decentralized, datasets remain always at the edge devices, preventing sharing sensitive information and minimizing the risk of data leakage.

Table 8.10. FL system configuration.

Variable	Description
Num rounds	Number of federated rounds.
Num epochs	Number of local epochs in each round.
Min available	Minimum number of clients necessary to trigger the process.
Min fit	Minimum number of clients required in a training round.
Fraction fit	Percentage of clients that participate in a training round.
Broker name	Address of the MQTT broker.
Topic	MQTT topic to trigger the process.

The FL system can be deployed with different setups by modifying the values of the configuration file that contains the common variables for all participating devices. These variables are related to the training itself and to the orchestration. In Table 10 some of the most important variables are described.

8.3.3.2 FL Client

FL Client agents are responsible for training the model provided to them by the FL Server with their local and proprietary data. Subsequent to the training process, the fitted weights are transmitted back to the server. Ultimately, once the aggregation process is completed on the server side, the new weights are evaluated and registered on the MLFlow Lite server deployed on the device.

The entire process is comprised of distinct blocks that are interconnected, as depicted in Figure 8.9. Each block is responsible for a specific function, as outlined below:

- The **Deserialize Model** block is responsible for receiving the serialized model weights for transmission over the gRPC network, deserializing them and loading the received weights into the defined model structure.
- The **Model Training** block implements the algorithms necessary for training the model. These algorithms comprise functions for processing the data used for training and for optimizing the model.
- The **Serialize Model** block is responsible for the inverse process of the "Deserialize Model" block. It extracts the weights from the model and serializes them for transmission through the gRPC channel.
- The **Model Evaluation** block assesses the efficacy of the global model that is received following the aggregation process conducted by the FL Server. This model is then registered in the deployed MLFlow server and placed into production if, following the evaluation process, it is determined to be the optimal model to date.

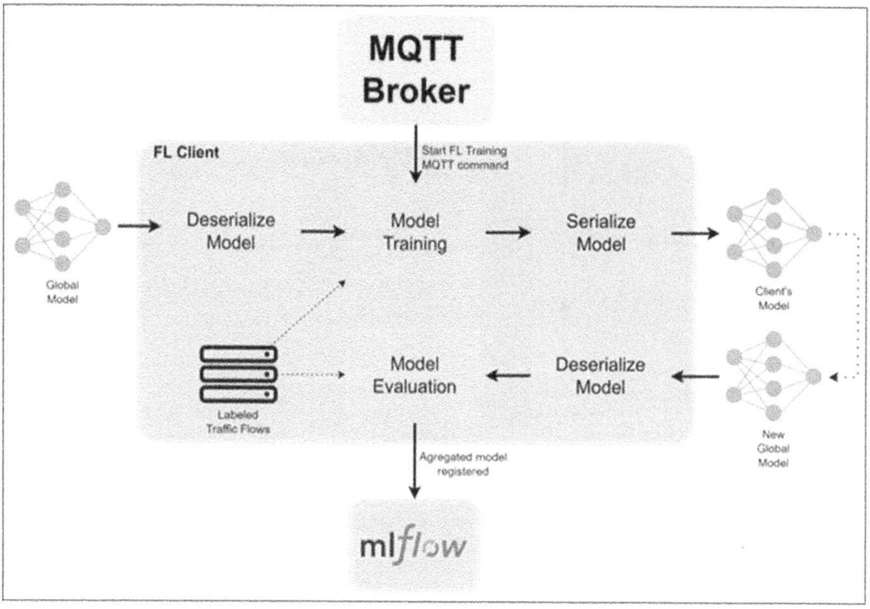

Figure 8.9. FL Client functional block.

8.3.3.3 FL Server

The FL Server agent oversees the global management of the federated learning process, orchestrating the distinct phases that comprise it and aggregating the weights of the models received from clients through the utilization of diverse techniques.

The component is subdivided into four distinct blocks (see Figure 8.10), each of which is responsible for a specific function.

- The **Global Model Evaluation** block is responsible for assessing the performance of the global model generated following the aggregation process. This enables the progress of FL to be monitored. It is noteworthy that, at the initial stage of the process, the evaluated model (either a random weight model or a pre-trained model) is the initial model. Subsequently, the order is transmitted via the MQTT broker to the FL Clients, who then initiate the federated learning process on their respective systems.
- The **Serialize Model** block performs the inverse operation of the Deserialize Model block. It extracts the weights from the model and serializes them for transmission through the gRPC channel.
- The **Deserialize Model** block is responsible for receiving the serialized model weights for transmission over the gRPC network. It then deserializes them and loads the received weights into the defined model structure.
- The **Models' Aggregation** block is responsible for the consolidation of all received model weights, thereby ensuring the preservation of the knowledge

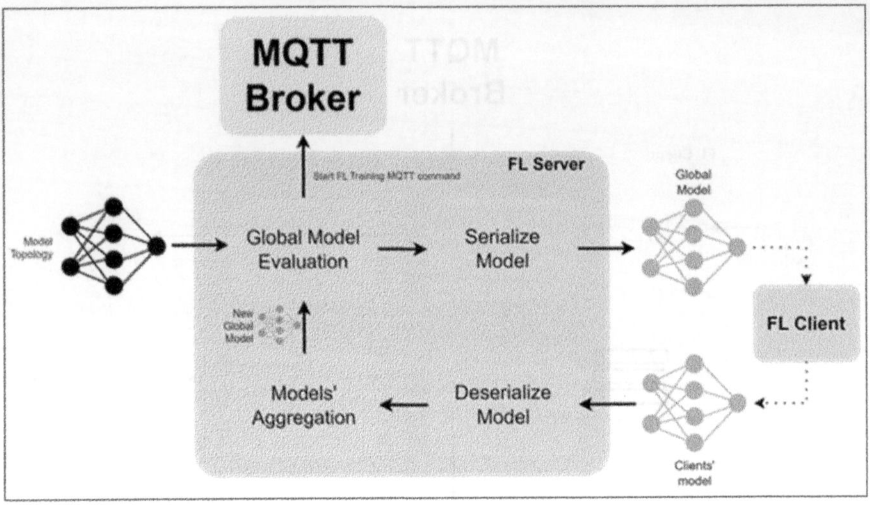

Figure 8.10. FL Server functional block.

acquired by each FL client. The most utilized algorithms are FedAvg [20] and FedAdam [23].

8.3.3.4 Continuous Assessment

The Continuous Assessment (CA) Module of FedLPy is responsible for analysing online traffic in the network and detecting possible DDoS attacks on edge using the federated trained global ML model. It works in parallel to the Federated Learning module, following an analogous design where instead of for training, the models are used for inference.

The Continuous Assessment (CA) Module of FedLPy is designed to monitor network traffic and identify potential DDoS attacks at the edge using a globally trained FL model. It operates alongside the Federated Learning module, utilizing the models for inference rather than training. The CA component consists of two main submodules: a detection system (CA Client agent) that sends alarm messages with threat metadata when a client is targeted, and an alarm collection system (CA Server agent) that compiles all risk notifications into a single log report. The CA Client is typically paired with an FL Client to maximize FedLPy's capabilities, and similarly, the CA Server is paired with an FL Server. However, clients that did not participate in the training can still benefit from the CA system if they receive an updated model at any time during the assessment part.

Analogously to the Federated Learning system, the Continuous Assessment module loads a configuration file that specifies the setup. In Table 8.11, some of the variables that are contained in this file are described.

Table 8.11. CA system configuration.

Variable	Description
Threshold	Minimum probability of malicious packet to trigger an alert.
Topic	MQTT root topic to publish alarm messages.
Model path	Path to the MLFlow repository where the latest model from the FL module is stored.
Log path	Path to the log file where the CA Server merges all messages from clients.
Broker name	Address of the MQTT broker. Not necessarily the same as in the FL system.

8.3.3.5 CA Client

The Continuous Assessment subsystem for clients performs the traffic analysis and threat detection on device by running a loop with the following operations:

1. **Loading the latest available model:** The CA client uses the best performing model from the Federated Learning component of FedLPy. This requires checking periodically the most recent model stored in the client's local MLFlow repository and loading it when an update is required.
2. **Data preprocessing block:** This block preprocesses raw data to the input format of the neural network.
3. **Model inference:** This block feeds forward the input traffic through the loaded model, which outputs the probability of a packet being malicious, in range [0,1].
4. **Risk evaluation:** This block takes the outputs of the inference to further discern, considering the frequency of malicious packets, if the client is being targeted or not. The instantaneous risk, $r(t)$, is calculated as the Exponential Weighted Mean Average (EWMA) filtering [24] of the probabilities of being a threat from the current and past received network packets, according to the following formula:

$$r(t) = (1 - \varepsilon) * r(t - 1) + \varepsilon * (1 - p)$$

With ε being the weighting factor, in range [0,1], and p the probability of benign packet from the model, in range [0,1]. By default, ε is set to 0.02, which implies a higher focus on the history of inferences rather than the risk probability of single samples.

The risk $r(t)$ value is then compared against a threshold that can be configured to control the tolerance of the module to positive threats – a low threshold will imply many detections.

Table 8.12. Alarm message taxonomy.

Variable	Description
Date	Timestamp of the alarm.
Risk	Risk value of the packet.
Client ID	Identifier of the attacked device.
Client IP	IP address of the attacked device.
Protocol	Transport layer protocol of the risky packet.
Service	Service of the risky packet.
Length	Length of the risky packet.
Source port	Source port of the risky packet.
Destin port	Destination port of the risky packet.
Info message	Additional information to include in the alarm.

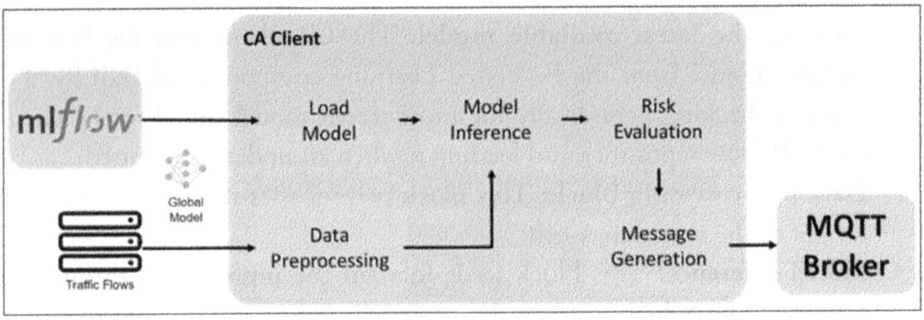

Figure 8.11. CA Client functional block.

5. **Alarm message generation:** If a packet is deemed risky, an alarm message is generated with information about the attacked client and the packet that triggered it. This message presents the taxonomy defined in Table 8.12.
6. **Alarm publishes:** Finally, this alarm message is published to the MQTT broker under the specified topic for the server to gather.

The aforementioned elements are represented in Figure 8.11, which depicts the interactions and dependencies between the different operations.

8.3.3.6 CA Server

The Continuous Assessment subsystem for the server oversees collecting all alarms published by the clients to the MQTT topic and communicating with the Alert GUI component of ERATHOSTENES.

1. **Alarm collection:** This phase entails the aggregation of all notifications transmitted to the Threat Detection topic and their subsequent storage in

Table 8.13. Continuous assessment related MQTT Broker topics.

Topic	device/DID/Threat/Detection/client-id
Message payload	Alarm message generated by the Continuous Assessment client.
Description	Root topic where alarm messages from the Continuous Assessment module are sent.

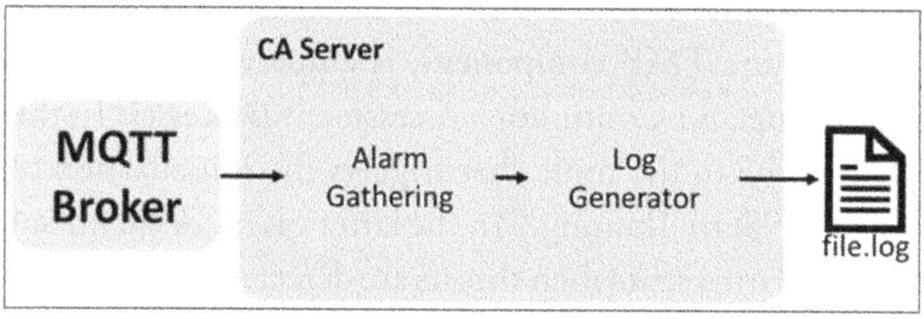

Figure 8.12. CA Server functional block.

a centralized .log file. The log file is updated on a continuous basis with the addition of new messages as they are received. Given the nature of DDoS attacks, which consist of a rapid series of small packets, clients often generate a considerable number of alarm messages in rapid succession. The MQTT broker, which facilitates communication between clients and the server, has been configured with a Quality-of-Service level of 1. This setting introduces some communication overhead for acknowledgements but ensures that no alarms are overlooked. The MQTT topic for the Continuous Assessment module employs a hierarchical structure, enabling clients to publish messages to a common topic with a unique suffix identifying themselves. This configuration allows the server to collect all messages by subscribing to the root topic, while also facilitating the creation of individual logs for specific clients by subscribing to client-level topics. For instance, clients publish messages to "Threat/Detection/<client-id>", and the server subscribes to "Threat/Detection".

2. **Alert GUI integration:** By sharing a common directory, the log file is integrated within the Alert GUI component.

Figure 8.12 illustrates the way these two operations interact with one another in order to update the .log file, which is subsequently utilized by the Alert GUI component.

8.3.4 Interaction with Other ERATOSTHENES Tools

As evidenced in Figure 8.7, the FedLPy Server component is integrated within the Intrusion Detection System (IDS), whereas the FedLPy Client component is integrated on the edge device's premises and uses the Trust Manager Broker (TMB) component to communicate with the Server. Consequently, the two principal tools with which FedLPy interacts are the MQTT Broker and the Alert GUI submodules. FedLPy's integration with these other ERATHOSTENES tools is seamless, and from its usage point of view, clients can treat it as a black box functionality within the IDS, without the need of interacting with it besides specifying its configuration.

FedLPy – MQTT Broker interaction: The ERATOSTHENES MQTT Broker, which forms part of the TMB component, is employed for the orchestration of the Federated Learning and Continuous Assessment processes. In the former case, the FL agents subscribe to the topic that triggers the initialization of the training process, for example, "Start Training." In the latter case, CA clients subscribe to the topic to publish the alarms sent when threats are detected. The CA server subscribes to the same topic, gathers all the alarms in a single file, and forwards them to the IDS.

FedLPy – Alert GUI integration: To provide ERATOSTHENES users with information regarding potential threats to edge devices, the CA Server generates a log file containing a record of all identified threats, annotated by the edge devices themselves. This log file can then be accessed by the Alert GUI, which presents users with a graphical representation of the historical status of each enrolled device.

8.3.5 Preliminary Results

This section presents the findings of the evaluation of the FedLPy component, with a particular focus on the two assigned tasks: (i) the Federated Learning task and (ii) the Continuous Assessment task. Figure 8.13 presents the topology implemented for the assessment of the component's performance. Three clients are deployed, comprising a train set (utilised for the evaluation of the Federated Learning task) and a test set (deployed for both tasks), situated alongside a server (also employed for both tasks).

To conduct this evaluation, the Aposemat IoT 23 dataset [25] was employed. This dataset comprises a set of network traffic from various IoT devices extracted by the Stratosphere lab, with each packet categorised according to a list of malicious attacks.

Furthermore, a dense neural network has been implemented with the objective of identifying whether a packet is associated with a DDoS attack.

8.3.5.1 Aposemat IoT 23 Dataset

To evaluate the proposed Proof of Concept (PoC), the raw traffic data from the IP layer, which is available in the Aposemat IoT 23 dataset, is utilised. This data is directly fed into the proposed neural network, rather than being processed through

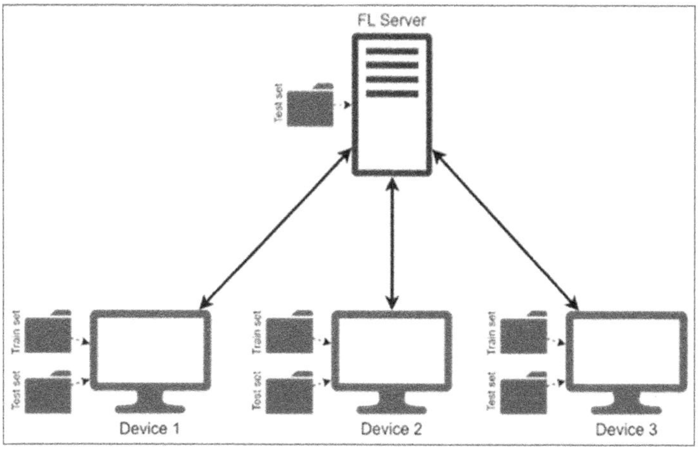

Figure 8.13. FedLPy component scheme for the evaluation of federated learning and continuous.

Table 8.14. Train-test data split per PoC participant.

	Train Set			Test Set		
	Total	**Benign**	**DDoS**	**Total**	**Benign**	**DDoS**
Server	—	—	—	21615	8121	13494
Device 1	17290	6496	10794	4327	1627	2700
Device 2	17290	6496	10794	4326	1626	2700
Device 3	17292	6497	10795	4327	1627	2700

the extraction of metadata from each packet. This approach facilitates the subsequent deployment of the model in a continuous assessment scenario, as there is no requirement for the raw inputs to be pre-processed.

Regarding the construction of the train and test sets, only the Benign and DDoS attack packets are considered, with the objective of better aligning the specifications of the PoC. Given the extensive data set available, only the captures "CTU-IoT-Malware-Capture-7-1", "CTU-IoT-Malware-Capture-34-1" and "CTU-IoT-Malware-Capture-35-1" are considered. These captures were selected based on the quantity and quality of the flows corresponding to the defined list of attacks.

Once the aforementioned traffic flows have been processed, the train-test split obtained is as presented in Table 8.14. It can be observed that the FL server has only test samples, whereas the FL clients have both, training and test samples, that are equally balanced.

It is crucial to highlight that the FL Server does not possess a training set, as the model employed in this procedure is only trained on the device premises locally.

The FL Server's sole function is to aggregate the different versions of the received model. The test set is utilised to assess the performance of the aggregated model.

8.3.5.2 Proposed AI Model

The deep learning-based model implemented to address the task of detecting potentially malicious events within the provided traffic flows is composed of an input layer designed to be fed with data of size 1505, which consists of the concatenation of simple packet metadata (protocol, service, packet length, source port and destination port) next to the raw IP packet. The model comprises a set of five fully connected layers, with sizes of 512, 256, 128, 64 and 16, respectively. The final layer is of size 1 and provides the probability of the packet being malicious.

8.3.5.3 Federated Learning Results

The assessment of the Federated Learning task utilising the FedLPy component is conducted in two distinct phases.

- A traditional learning training process is conducted on each device, utilizing the training data stored on that device. Subsequently, the resulting models are evaluated on the distinct test sets of each participant (server and clients).
- A federated learning training is conducted on the three devices, with the resulting data aggregated in the FL server. Subsequently, the global model is evaluated on each of the test sets.

Traditional learning

The traditional training approach for each of the devices involves 100 epochs of training with a batch size of 100 samples. The Binary Cross Entropy function is employed as the function loss, while the Binary Accuracy serves as the model metric function. The model optimization is regularized with a learning rate of 1e-3.

Table 8.15 presents the results of the experiment, highlighting that, on average, approximately 98.9% binary accuracy is achieved for all test sets evaluated with each model trained on each device.

The results of this experiment demonstrate that, despite the favourable outcomes achieved by each trained model when tested on the same set of data, the accuracy levels vary between models. This indicates that the models exhibit effective generalization capabilities for this problem, however, they are not suitable for use as a general model due to their lack of homogeneous behaviour.

Federated learning

The training phase for the federated learning experiment comprises 10 rounds of server model aggregation, with each round involving 10 epochs of training across all devices and a batch size of 100 samples. The Binary Cross Entropy function is

Table 8.15. Traditional learning results.

		Tested with			
		Server	**Device 1**	**Device 2**	**Device 3**
Model from	**Server**	—	—	—	—
	Device 1	98.94%	98.88%	98.82%	98.88%
	Device 2	98.98%	98.98%	98.95%	98.98%
	Device 3	98.98%	98.98%	98.98%	98.98%

Table 8.16. Federated learning results.

		Tested with			
		Server	**Device 1**	**Device 2**	**Device 3**
Model from	**Server**	99.98%	99.95%	99.97%	99.99%
	Device 1	99.98%	99.95%	99.97%	99.99%
	Device 2	99.98%	99.95%	99.97%	99.99%
	Device 3	99.98%	99.95%	99.97%	99.99%

employed as the function loss, while the Binary Accuracy function is utilised as the model metric function. The model is regularised using a learning rate of 1e-3.

Table 8.16 demonstrates that, in this instance, the aggregated model shared by each FL client (device) ensures uniform behaviour for each test set. About Binary Accuracy, an average accuracy of 99.97% is achieved, which represents a 1% improvement over the traditional learning approach.

8.3.5.4 Continuous Assessment Results

Once the federated global model has been trained, the alert system implemented in the Continuous Assessment block is evaluated. As previously stated, this block is responsible for generating a log file in which the alerts generated by the different devices included in the ERATOSTHENES system are collected. The file is presented below as an example, showing the different fields that compose the message. Among these fields, it should be noted the date on which the packet was received, the risk of that packet being a DDoS attack, the client that received that packet and metadata related to the packet received.


```
2024-07-12 07:18:28,645 - {"date": "12/07-07:18:28.331364", "risk": 0.8421232539984038, "client_id":
2, "client_ip": "172.19.0.4", "proto": "tcp", "service": "unknown", "pkt_len": 60, "src_port":
57568, "dst_port": 23, "msg": "Possible DDoS attack detected."}
2024-07-12 07:18:28,991 - {"date": "12/07-07:18:28.679537", "risk": 0.7952990876725874, "client_id":
1, "client_ip": "172.19.0.2", "proto": "udp", "service": "dns/domain", "pkt_len": 67, "src_port":
45981, "dst_port": 53, "msg": "Possible DDoS attack detected."}
```

2024-07-12 07:18:29,012 - {"date": "12/07-07:18:28.708525", "risk": 0.8316813925007899, "client_id": 3, "client_ip": "172.19.0.5", "proto": "tcp", "service": "unknown", "pkt_len": 60, "src_port": 43332, "dst_port": 23, "msg": "Possible DDoS attack detected."}
2024-07-12 07:18:29,045 - {"date": "12/07-07:18:28.741926", "risk": 0.8452807889173497, "client_id": 2, "client_ip": "172.19.0.4", "proto": "tcp", "service": "unknown", "pkt_len": 60, "src_port": 60764, "dst_port": 23, "msg": "Possible DDoS attack detected."}
2024-07-12 07:18:29,397 - {"date": "12/07-07:18:29.086249", "risk": 0.7993931059191356, "client_id": 1, "client_ip": "172.19.0.2", "proto": "udp", "service": "dns/domain", "pkt_len": 67, "src_port": 59488, "dst_port": 53, "msg": "Possible DDoS attack detected."}

Acknowledgements

References

[1] NIST, "Cybersecurity Framework," [Online]. Available: https://www.nist.gov/cyberframework.

[2] "DIRECTIVE (EU) 2022/2555 OF THE EUROPEAN PARLIAMENT AND OF THE COUNCIL on measures for a high common level of cybersecurity across the Union.," 2022. [Online]. Available: https://eur-lex.europa.eu/eli/dir/2022/2555/oj.

[3] P. M. K. Scarfone, "Guide to Intrusion Detection and Prevention Systems (IDPS)," National Institute of Standards and Technology (NIST), 2007.

[4] Y. E. A. E. M. L. O. Y. E. A. Ouafae EL AISSAOUI, "Combining supervised and unsupervised machine learning algorithms to predict the learners' learning styles," *Procedia Computer Science*, vol. 148, pp. 87–96, 2019.

[5] Wienand A. Omta, Roy G. van Heesbeen, Ian Shen, Jacob de Nobel, Desmond Robers, Lieke M. van der Velden, René H. Medema, Arno P.J.M. Siebes, Ad J. Feelders, Sjaak Brinkkemper, Judith S. Klumperman, Marco René Spruit, Matthieu J.S. Brinkhuis and David A. Egan, "Combining Supervised and Unsupervised Machine Learning Methods for Phenotypic Functional Genomics Screening," *SLAS Discovery*, vol. 25, no. 6, pp. 655–664, 2020.

[6] Y.-A. L. B. O. C. Y. K. F. O. G. B. Fabrizio Carcillo, "Combining unsupervised and supervised learning in credit card fraud detection," *Information Sciences*, vol. 557, 2021.

[7] D. B. Evan Gilman, Zero-Trust Network, O'Reilly Media, Inc.

[8] K. Dempsey, N. Chawla, J. L., R. Johnston, A. Jones, A. Orebaugh, M. Scholl and K. Stine, Information security continuous monitoring (ISCM) for Federal Information Systems and Organizations, NIST, 2011.

[9] M. Aljabri, S. S. Aljameel, R. M. A. Mohammad, S. H. Almotiri, S. A. F. M. Mirza and H. S. Altamimi, "Intelligent techniques for detecting network attacks: review and research directions," *Sensors*, 2021.

[10] R. Vinayakumar, M. Alazab, K. P. Soman, P. Poornachandran, A. Al-Nemrat and S. Venkatraman, "Deep learning approach for the intelligent intrusion detection system.," *IEEE Access*, 2019.

[11] R. Vinayakumar, K. P. Soman and P. Poornachandran, "Applying convolutional neural network for network intrusion detection.," *International Conference on Advances in Computing, Communications and Informatics (ICACCI)*, pp. 1222–1228, 2017.

[12] V. Dutta, M. Choraś, M. Pawlicki and R. Kozik, "A deep learning ensemble for network anomaly and cyber-attack detection.," *Sensors*, 2020.

[13] M. Ahmad, Q. Riaz, M. Zeeshan, H. Tahir, S. A. Haider and M. S. Khan, "Intrusion detection in internet of things using supervised machine learning based on application and transport layer features using UNSW-NB15 data-set.," *EURASIP Journal on Wireless Communications and Networking*, 2021.

[14] A. Aleesa, M. Younis, A. A. Mohammed and N. Sahar, "Deep-intrusion detection system with enhanced UNSW-NB15 dataset based on deep learning techniques.," *Journal of Engineering Science and Technology*, pp. 711–727, 2021.

[15] T. M. Booij, I. Chiscop, E. Meeuwissen, N. Moustafa and F. T. Den Hartog, "ToN_IoT: The role of heterogeneity and the need for standardization of features and attack types in IoT network intrusion data sets.," *IEEE Internet of Things Journal*, 2021.

[16] S. K. Nukavarapu and T. Nadeem, " Securing edge-based IoT networks with semi-supervised GANs.," *IEEE International Conference on Pervasive Computing and Communications Workshops and other Affiliated Events (PerCom Workshops)*, 2021.

[17] R. Alghamdi and M. Bellaiche, "Evaluation and selection models for ensemble intrusion detection systems in IoT," *IoT*, 2022.

[18] M. Rashid, J. Kamruzzaman, T. Imam, S. Wibowo and S. Gordon, "A tree-based stacking ensemble technique with feature selection for network intrusion detection," *Applied Intelligence*, 2022.

[19] P. Tian, Z. Chen, W. Yu and W. Liao, "Towards asynchronous federated learning based threat detection: A DC-Adam approach," *Computers & Security*, 2021.

[20] B. McMahan, E. Moore, D. Ramage, S. Hampson and B. A. Arcas, "Communication-efficient learning of deep networks from decentralized data," *Artificial intelligence and statistics*, 2017.

[21] T. M. H. Hsu, H. Qi and M. Brown, "Measuring the effects of non-identical data distribution for federated visual classification," *arXiv preprint arXiv:1909.06335*, 2019.

[22] T. Li, M. Sanjabi, A. Beirami and V. Smith, "Fair resource allocation in federated learning," *arXiv preprint arXiv:1905.10497*, 2019.

[23] S. Reddi, Z. Charles, M. Zaheer, Z. Garrett, K. Rush, J. Koneènı, S. Kumar and H. McMahan, "Adaptive federated optimization," *arXiv preprint arXiv:2003.00295*, 2020.

[24] J. S. Hunter, "The exponentially weighted moving average," *Journal of quality technology*, 1986.

[25] S. Garcia, A. Parmisano and M. J. Erquiaga., "Zenodo," 2020. [Online]. Available: https://zenodo.org/records/4743746.

[26] A. K. Sahu, S. Sharma, M. Tanveer and R. Raja, "Internet of Things attack detection using hybrid Deep Learning Model.," *Computer Communications*, 2021.

DOI: 10.1561/9781638285076.ch9

Chapter 9

Digital Twins for Secure Software Updates to Maintain IoT Device Trustworthiness

By Rustem Dautov, Hui Song and Shukun Tokas

Software updates are critical in maintaining the security and reliability of IoT devices, acting as a key response strategy to address identified vulnerabilities and enhance trust scores. In dynamic IoT environments, devices can become susceptible to new threats, and without timely updates, their trustworthiness diminishes. Ensuring regular and secure software updates is thus essential to protect these devices from exploitation, maintain their functionality, and safeguard the broader network they are part of.

The Trusted Computing Group (TCG) has developed the Guidance on Secure Software Updates in Embedded Systems [1], a reference architecture that outlines the key steps required to manage software updates securely. This includes secure development, signing, distribution, installation, and post-installation verification. While the TCG Guidance provides a solid foundation for ensuring the security of updates, it remains a general framework that does not specify how to implement a fully integrated solution. In practice, the individual steps of the update lifecycle are often addressed separately, resulting in disjointed approaches and gaps in the security and functionality of updates.

Our approach introduces Digital Twins as a powerful solution to enhance the software update lifecycle. Digital Twins provide real-time, virtual representations of IoT devices, allowing for continuous monitoring of device status and contextual properties. This integration allows the Digital Twin to act as a central point for managing software updates, ensuring timely delivery, guaranteed installation through the Desired-Reported Property pattern, and granular control over which devices receive the updates. Digital Twins also support scalability, enabling efficient management of software updates across large fleets of IoT devices. Additionally, Digital Twins ensure state persistence, allowing devices to return to their desired state following updates, recoveries, or rollbacks.

The expected benefits of this approach are manifold. By leveraging Digital Twins, IoT device updates can be more timely, reliable, and precise, with reduced service disruption and enhanced security. The ability to integrate updates with real-time contextual information ensures that updates are tailored to each device's needs, increasing operational efficiency. This approach represents an adaptable and scalable solution to the challenges of secure software updates in modern IoT ecosystems.

9.1 Introduction

In the rapidly advancing domain of connected IoT devices, the significance of secure software updates (SSUs) cannot be overestimated. These devices, ranging from low-level resource-constrained IoT sensors to more capable edge gateways, are integral to many modern industries, including the ones represented by the ERATOSTHENES use cases: Smart Healthcare, Connected Vehicles and Industry 4.0. In all these domains, ensuring the security and reliability of the software that governs these devices is paramount for system functionality. To this end, this chapter outlines the design and implementation of the SSU mechanism in ERATOSTHENES, highlighting its critical role in maintaining the integrity and efficacy of IoT devices, drawing upon the principles established in the 'Guidance for Secure Update of Software and Firmware on Embedded Systems' by the Trusted Computing Group (TCG).

9.1.1 Reference Architecture: Secure Software Update Lifecycle

The SSU lifecycle consists of five essential steps designed to ensure that software updates are applied safely, maintaining the security and functionality of the system. These steps are typically referenced from the TCG Guidance, which provides a reference architecture rather than prescriptive instructions on how to implement specific solutions. This flexibility allows developers to adapt the principles to their needs, but it often results in disjointed implementations of the lifecycle steps, rather than a unified, holistic approach. Schematically depicted in Figure 9.1, the SSU lifecycle includes the following steps:

1. **Secure Development:** This step focuses on the secure creation of the software update itself. It involves following security best practices during the design and development stages to ensure that the software is free of vulnerabilities and prepared for safe distribution.
2. **Secure Signing:** Once developed, the software update is cryptographically signed to guarantee its authenticity and integrity. This step ensures that the update comes from a trusted source and has not been altered or tampered with before distribution.
3. **Robust Distribution:** The signed update is securely distributed to devices. This involves ensuring that the update is delivered to the correct devices in a reliable manner, preventing unauthorised interception or modification during transmission.
4. **Secure Installation:** After distribution, the update is securely installed on the device. This step ensures that the update is applied without errors or security risks, maintaining system stability and trust.
5. **Post-installation Verification:** Following installation, this step ensures that the update was successfully applied and that the system is functioning correctly. It verifies the integrity of the new software and checks that the device's trust and security parameters remain intact.

While the TCG Guidance outlines these steps as key elements of a secure update lifecycle, it does not dictate how to build or implement these processes. As a result, in practice, organisations often implement individual steps in isolation, without integrating them into a cohesive, end-to-end architecture. This fragmented approach can weaken the overall security posture, as the lack of coordination between steps may introduce vulnerabilities or gaps in the update process.

9.1.2 Proposed Approach at a Glance: Why Digital Twins?

Digital Twins (DTs) can significantly enhance the SSU lifecycle by acting as a centralised, real-time reference for the status of installed software across IoT devices. By mirroring the physical device in a virtual environment, DTs provide a comprehensive view of each device's software, making the update process more efficient and reliable. When combined with other tools, DTs enable a streamlined approach to managing updates, improving the delivery, control, and verification of software changes. These practical benefits are summarised as follows:

- **Timeliness** is a key benefit of using DTs. By continuously collecting real-time contextual information from IoT devices, DTs ensure that software

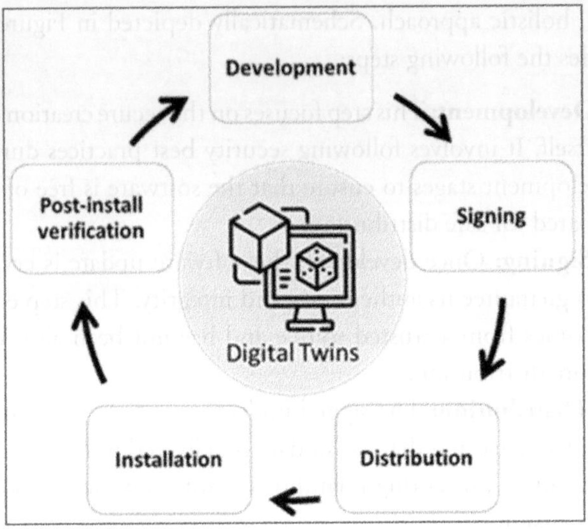

Figure 9.1. Secure software lifecycle supported by the digital twins.

updates are delivered promptly. This real-time insight allows the system to push updates with minimal service disruption and downtime, as updates are deployed when conditions are optimal for each device, such as when it is idle or less critical to operations.

- **Guaranteed delivery** is facilitated by the use of the Desired-Reported Property pattern. In this approach, the desired state (new software version) is sent to the DT, while the device reports back its current state. Even if a device is temporarily offline, the DT keeps track of the desired state. As soon as the device comes back online, the system ensures the update is installed, guaranteeing no missed updates regardless of device availability.
- **Granular control** over the update process is another advantage. DTs allow for precise management of updates, whether targeting a single device, specific groups, or an entire fleet. The cyber-physical-social context of each device can be taken into account, ensuring that updates are deployed only when suitable. For example, more critical devices can receive updates first, or updates can be staggered based on geographical location, device type, or operational role.
- **Scalability** is greatly enhanced by DTs. They enable the management of large fleets of devices, potentially consisting of hundreds or even thousands of devices. By providing a digital representation of each device, updates can be deployed and monitored across vast networks, ensuring all devices receive the correct updates while keeping track of their individual statuses.
- **A sandbox environment** is another significant benefit. DTs provide the capability to test updates in a virtual space before pushing them to the physical

devices. This allows organisations to validate updates in a safe, isolated environment, identifying potential issues before they affect the real-world devices. This mitigates risks and ensures that updates are fully functional before deployment.

- **State persistence for upgrades and recovery** is another critical feature of DTs. By keeping the history of the twin updates, the system can restore a device to its desired state following an upgrade or recovery process. This ensures that if an update fails or a device requires a recovery, it can seamlessly return to its correct configuration, maintaining the continuity of operations.

These benefits will be further revisited in this section with a more detailed explanation of how the proposed DT-based approach can implement them. Noteworthy, this approach is by no means a complete, standalone solution for the SSU lifecycle. Rather, it serves as an end-to-end point of integration, where various existing tools and approaches that address individual steps of the SSU lifecycle can converge. DTs act as a centralised framework that ties together different components, such as secure signing tools, robust distribution systems, and post-installation verification mechanisms. While it provides a unified view and control of the update process, this approach can and should be further extended and complemented with additional tools. For example, enhanced security mechanisms, automated verification systems, and advanced simulation tools can be incorporated to strengthen specific stages of the lifecycle, ensuring a more robust and holistic update management system.

9.1.3 Positioning within ERATOSTHENES

ERATOSTHENES's vision is to build a robust and secure ecosystem for devices, ensuring that each device operates reliably and securely throughout its lifecycle. This ecosystem aims to safeguard application data, ensure the uninterrupted provisioning of business services, and maintain compliance with applicable regulatory requirements. SSUs are essential for implementing of this vision, enabling the seamless and safe evolution of device capabilities while protecting against emerging cyber-threats. In this context, SSUs ensure that vulnerabilities are patched promptly, reducing the risk of malicious interference or malfunction, thus aligning with the TCG's emphasis on maintaining device integrity through timely and trustworthy updates.

In the context of ERATOSTHENES, a core pillar is the use of SSUs as a reaction strategy to an event that reduces the trust level of an IoT device. Thus, the SSU mechanism is one of the possible instruments that ERATOSTHENES users can leverage in order to bring the IoT devices back into a trustworthy state.

Therefore, the scope of this research effort encompasses the development and implementation of a comprehensive SSU framework across all IoT devices within the ERATOSTHENES network. This includes conducting thorough security assessments of existing devices, integrating secure update mechanisms, and establishing an automated and secure software delivery system. More specifically, the SSU process can be triggered after a failed trust assessment, i.e., when the actual calculated trust score of an IoT device is lower than the expected score. This essentially signifies the need to identify potential vulnerabilities and apply mitigation measures.

9.2 Conceptual Architecture of the Secure Software Update Mechanism

We now proceed with the design of the SSU functionality, as depicted in Figure 9.2. In this architecture, we distinguish between stakeholders and functional elements (i.e., software components).

9.2.1 Main Stakeholders

The main stakeholders of this architecture are the following:

- **Device Manufacturer** plays a crucial role in the overall ERATOSTHENES ecosystem, not only by producing the IoT hardware but also by developing the associated software. The expected version of the software stack to be deployed for each device model is specified as part of the MUD profile [9]. The device manufacturer may either develop the software themselves or subcontract trusted third parties (**Software Developer**) to ensure specialised expertise and security. Regardless of the chosen development approach, the integrity and security of the software updates remain paramount. The manufacturer (or a trusted third party acting on its behalf) sign the software updates with a private key, ensuring that each update can further be authenticated and verified. The corresponding public key is embedded in the manufactured IoT devices, enabling the high-end devices to verify the authenticity of updates upon receipt.[1] This cryptographic method ensures that only verified, untampered updates are installed, maintaining the security and reliability of the device.
- **System administrator** in the context of ERATOSTHENES possesses in-depth knowledge of the application domain and its specific security-related requirements and is thus responsible for providing information on

1. Please note that this approach primarily applies to relatively capable IoT devices that have the sufficient computing capabilities for asymmetric cryptography.

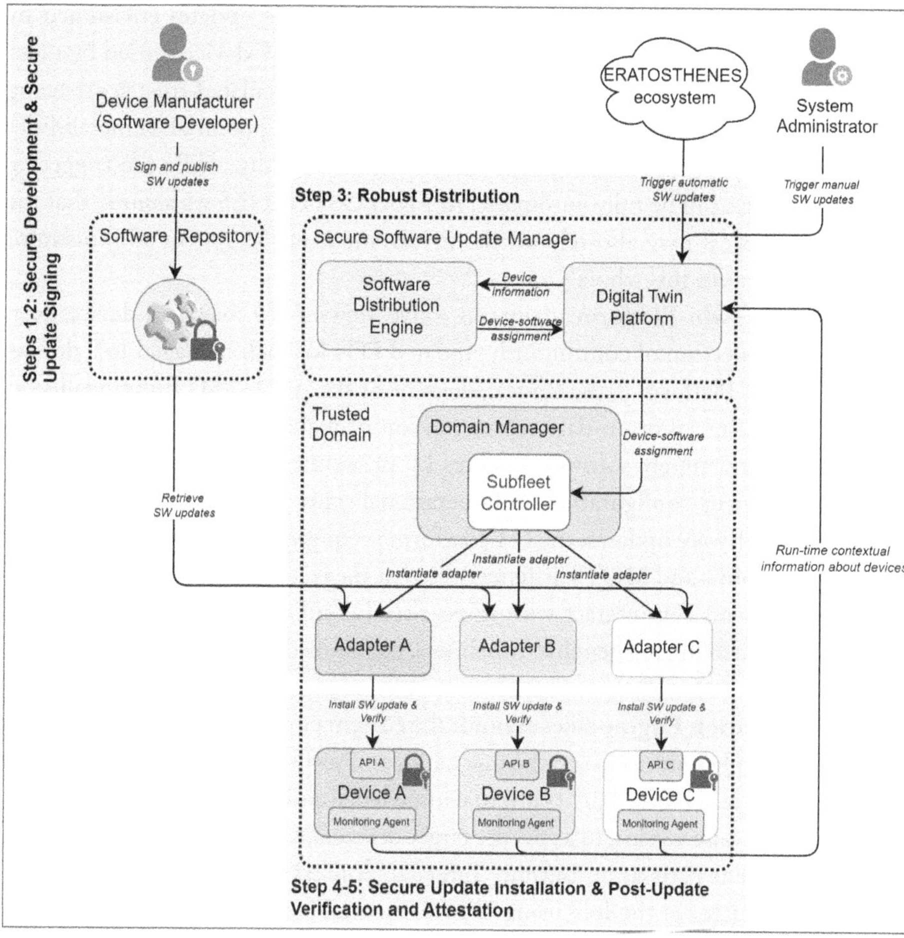

Figure 9.2. Conceptual architecture of the secure software update mechanism.

domain-specific threats and vulnerabilities for risk assessment. In addition to these responsibilities, the system administrator also oversees the SSU process and ensures that software patches are applied correctly and securely across all devices. Using the DT Platform, the system administrator can manually trigger updates if needed, to provide timely response to emerging threats or vulnerabilities.

9.2.2 Main Functional Elements

The main functional elements of the architecture are the following:

- **ERATOSTHENES ecosystem** collectively represents the rest of the ERATOSTHENES components which may trigger the SSU process. More specifically, the main reason for automatic software updates envisioned by ERATOSTHENES is a reduced trust score of an IoT device caused by identified vulnerability in the existing software. The calculated trust score being lower than expected signifies the need to identify potential vulnerabilities and apply necessary mitigation measures. Noteworthy, while the triggering of updates can be fully automatic, in ERATOSTHENES we assume that the SSU process may also rely on the involvement of the system administrator who oversees this whole process.

- **Digital Twin Platform** maintains a live view of the managed device fleet, i.e., a collection of continuously updated DTs for each managed IoT device. The DT Platform is the central element of the whole SSU functionality, as it maintains an up-to-date representation of managed devices. This enables secure and timely software updates by providing a comprehensive view of each device's configuration and operational state. For the automatic triggering of software updates, the DT Platform is equipped with APIs (e.g., HTTP entry-points and MQTT listeners), so that the rest of the ERATOSTHENES components can interact with it. As already outlined, the use of DTs introduces the following benefits: timeliness, guaranteed delivery, granular control, scalability, a sandbox environment, and state persistence.
- **Distribution Engine** takes as input the current contextual information about managed IoT devices – on the one hand, and software assignment constraints – on the other. Based on its internal knowledge and rules, it then assigns a specific software version to a specific target device, i.e., generates device-software assignment pairs as an output. Targeted, context-aware assignment of software updates in the IoT using DTs is essential for ensuring that each device receives updates tailored to its specific configuration and operational environment. This approach minimises the risk of incompatibility and maximises the effectiveness of updates.
- **Subfleet Controller** is deployed and runs within the ERATOSTHENES trusted domain (i.e., close to devices in the secure network domain) and is responsible for interaction with the DT Platform on behalf of a subfleet of devices (e.g., a subfleet of connected healthcare gateways in remote patient monitoring). It receives software update commands from the central DT Platform through its northbound interface and propagates them to the downstream IoT devices via its southbound interface using device- or platform-specific Adapters. This setup ensures efficient and secure dissemination of updates, tailored to the specific needs of local devices, while maintaining synchronisation with the central management system.
- **Software Repository** serves as a central distribution point of SSUs for devices. This repository can be a private server managed by the manufacturer

or a public cloud-based service, such as Docker Hub,[2] which is widely used for distributing containerised applications. Acting as a central hub, the repository ensures that updates are securely stored and can be accessed programmatically by the adapters and/or devices. Secure protocols like HTTPS are employed to protect the integrity of the data in transit, and access control mechanisms are in place to restrict update uploads and modifications to authorised personnel only.

- **Adapters** are device- or platform-specific software components responsible for interacting with devices and enacting the actual software updates on devices. They are instantiated and run along-side the subfleet controller in the trusted domain and depending on the type of devices in its sub-fleet, the subfleet controller will instantiate a corresponding adapter. These adapters are tailored to the unique characteristics and protocols of each device type or platform within the IoT fleet. By interfacing directly with the devices through standardised or proprietary APIs, they ensure that updates are deployed efficiently and securely.
- **Devices** are diverse IoT assets that ERATOSTHENES already deals with (e.g., healthcare gateways, smart vehicle onboard units, and smart industrial appliances), as well as a wider range of network-connected IoT devices with similar characterises. In ERATOSTHENES, we primarily focus on relatively capable devices equipped with sufficient hardware capabilities (e.g., network bandwidth, CPU, storage). Devices expose some APIs specific to their hardware platform, network interfaces, OS, software stack, etc., which are used by the Adapters to enact the software update process.
- **Monitoring Agents** run on the devices and serve to collect real-time contextual information. These agents gather data on device status, operational parameters, environmental conditions, and other relevant metrics. This information is then transmitted back to the central DT Platform where it is represented as reported properties in DTs. By continuously updating these properties, the platform maintains an accurate and dynamic DT model of each device, facilitating informed decision-making for the following SSU activities, as well as for stateful recovery.

9.2.3 Triggering Software Updates with the Desired-Reported Property Pattern

The **Desired-Reported Property** pattern in DTs is a key mechanism for managing and synchronising the state of physical assets and their virtual counterparts, as

2. https://hub.docker.com/

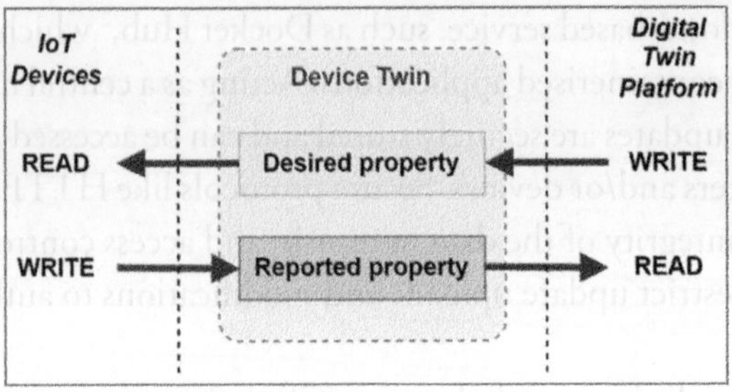

Figure 9.3. Desired-reported property pattern in digital twins.

depicted in Figure 9.3. This pattern involves two primary elements:

- **Desired Properties:** These are the target states or configurations that the System Administrator wants the physical asset to achieve. They are set within the DT and serve as directives for how the asset should be configured or operated. For instance, in the context of SSUs, the desired property might be the target software version to be deployed.
- **Reported Properties:** These reflect the current state or configuration of the physical asset as detected and communicated by sensors or monitoring systems. The reported properties are continuously updated to provide a runtime status of the asset's condition. Continuing with the SSU example, the reported property would be the current software version that the device is running. Reported properties, and especially evidence on the correct device configuration (which entailed evidence on the device's correct software version running), is achieved through the trusted computing enablers of ERATOSTHENES.

The interplay between these two properties allows for effective monitoring and control. When a discrepancy is detected between the desired properties and the reported properties, the DT Platform can trigger actions to align the physical asset with the desired state. This might involve sending commands to the asset to adjust its configuration (e.g., upgrade the software version), or it might involve alerting operators to take corrective actions. This pattern is particularly valuable in the ERATOSTHENES use case scenarios requiring precise control and automation, such as telemedicine using remote patient monitoring, smart manufacturing, and intelligent vehicle services. It ensures that the DT remains an accurate and actionable representation of the physical asset, enabling proactive maintenance, optimisation, and fault detection.

9.2.4 Context-Aware Software Assignment

Software assignment using DTs in devices leverages detailed digital representations of physical devices, incorporating multi-dimensional contextual properties, to assign software updates efficiently. More specifically, the cyber-physical-social context of monitored devices encompasses several dimensions [2]. The cyber aspects include the traditional hardware and software properties of the devices. Physical aspects refer to environmental conditions such as the device's location, surrounding temperature, and time of day, which can also affect device performance and availability. Social aspects involve the actual human user, considering factors like specific medical conditions, usage patterns, and service subscription types, all of which influence how the device is used and monitored.

Target conditions for software updates can be defined in two primary ways, each offering different levels of control and flexibility. One option is for the **Device Manufacturer (Software Developer)** to specify the conditions, such as identifying the security vulnerability the update addresses and listing the specific device models that are affected and require the patch. This ensures that the update is applied where it is most needed, addressing known issues in the devices it was designed to protect. Another, more flexible approach is for the System Administrator to manually define the target conditions. By leveraging their knowledge and experience, the Administrator can take a more fine-grained approach, tailoring the update deployment based on the contextual properties of each device. These properties, collected and maintained by the DT Platform, allow the Administrator to consider factors such as device location, usage patterns, and current operational state. This method enables highly targeted updates, ensuring that the right devices are updated at the right time, maximising both security and operational efficiency.

In both cases, the distribution engine uses these context-aware DT representations to match target software requirements with the appropriate devices. This can be implemented in three possible scenarios:

- **One-to-One Scenario:** the distribution engine assigns a specific software update to a single device based on its unique contextual properties. For example, if a DT of a particular device indicates that it requires a firmware update to fix a known vulnerability, the Distribution Engine will push the update directly to that specific device using its unique ID as the target condition. The Desired-Reported Property pattern is used to confirm the device reaches the desired state after the update, ensuring the device operates securely and effectively after the installation.
- **One-to-Many Scenario:** the Distribution Engine assigns software updates to a group of devices sharing certain contextual properties. For instance, a hospital might have several patient monitoring systems that require an update to enhance data encryption protocols. The DTs of these monitors, which may include similar models or devices within the same department, will indicate they all need the update. The Distribution Engine identifies

these commonalities and assigns the update to all relevant devices, ensuring consistency and efficiency. So if a vulnerability is identified in more than one device, a patch can be applied to all of them at once. This approach facilitates the update process across multiple devices, leveraging batch processing capabilities to maintain high standards of data security.

- **One-to-All Scenario:** the Distribution Engine broadcasts a software update to all devices within the network. This is typically done for critical updates, such as a security patch addressing a widespread vulnerability. For example, if a new regulation requires enhanced cyber-security measures across all IoT devices, the DTs provide the necessary contextual properties to ensure each device is eligible and capable of receiving the update. For example, if a vulnerability is identified for a single device of a specific model, a patch can be applied to all other devices of this type in a scalable and timely manner. The Distribution Engine then ensures that this update is deployed across the entire fleet of devices, leveraging the DTs to monitor and validate the update process.

In each of these scenarios, the Desired-Reported Property pattern is used to confirm the devices reach the desired state after the update, to make sure they operate securely and effectively after the installation.

9.3 Implementing the Software Management Lifecycle

The described conceptual architecture for SSUs in ERATOSTHENES is aligned with the already mentioned TCG Guidance. The software update lifecycle is part of the runtime phase of the ERATOSTHENES architecture. It is expected that the secure device domain is already established, with the IoT devices enrolled and the domain manager up and running.

The SSU lifecycle begins with the development step, which employs secure coding practices. Updates are cryptographically signed to verify their authenticity and integrity, ensuring that only verified updates can be installed on the device. The distribution step ensures updates are assigned and delivered securely, using encrypted communication channels and secure servers to prevent interception or tampering. In the deployment phase, devices must authenticate the updates before installation. This involves verifying the cryptographic signatures to confirm the update is from a trusted source and has not been altered. Post-deployment, the verification and attestation step involves validating the update's integrity and functionality, monitoring for any issues or anomalies that might arise. All these lifecycle steps are also included in Figure 9.2 as grey boxes in the background. In the following subsections, we will look into each of these steps in more detail, describing how the proposed ERATOSTHENES SSU functionality implements them.

9.3.1 Step 1: Secure Development of Software Updates

In ERATOSTHENES, developing software patches can take place in response to reduced trustworthiness levels of devices. Thus, it is seen as part of the response mechanism to identified vulnerabilities. Implementing secure development for devices goes beyond the official scope of ERATOSTHENES, thus, we assume that developers and service providers follow best practices for secure software development. Essential practices include: incorporating secure coding practices throughout the software development lifecycle to avoid vulnerabilities like buffer overflows and SQL injection; regular code reviews and the use of static analysis tools are essential for early detection of vulnerabilities; conducting extensive security testing, including penetration testing, to identify and mitigate potential issues before deployment; employing robust cryptographic measures to protect data, and ensure that software updates are signed and verified to maintain integrity [9, 11].

9.3.2 Step 2: Secure Signing of Software Updates

In the first place, implementing secure update signing for IoT devices (depicted in Figure 9.4 as a simplified sequence diagram) requires robust key management and thorough signing of software updates. In ERATOSTHENES, we assume that Device Manufacturers generate and manage a pair of cryptographic keys: a private key for signing updates and a corresponding public key for verifying them. The private key is stored securely, while the public key is embedded within the IoT devices during the manufacturing process, enabling these devices to verify the authenticity of received updates. For the devices capable of symmetric cryptography, it can be the case that a symmetric SSU key is established in each device during the manufacturing process.

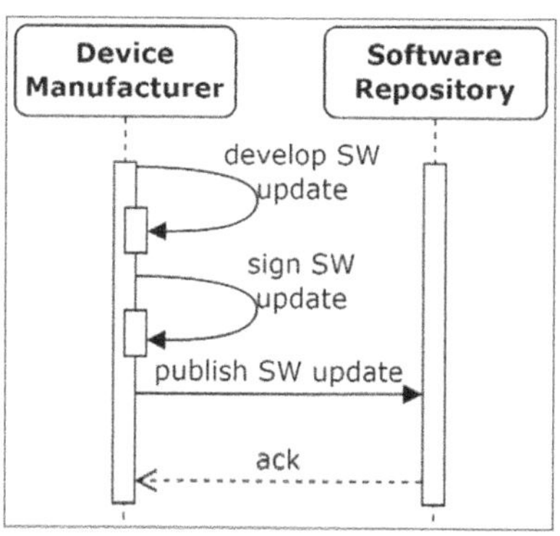

Figure 9.4. Steps 1–2: Secure development and signing of software updates.

When a software update, such as a Docker container or a binary executable file, is prepared for deployment following the secure development phase, the manufacturer uses their private key to create a digital signature. This process involves generating a hash of the update file and encrypting this hash with the private key. The resulting digital signature is then attached to the software update package. For updates involving Docker containers, the process is similar. The entire container image is signed by hashing its content and creating a digital signature. Devices that run Docker can verify the container signature before deploying it, ensuring that the container has not been altered. After generating a digital signature using the private key, the signed software updates are securely uploaded to the designated software repository, which can be a private server managed by the Device Manufacturer or a public cloud-based service. At this point, the signed software update, coupled with its signature, is ready for secure distribution to the devices.

9.3.3 Step 3: Robust Distribution

To implement robust distribution of software updates for IoT devices (Figure 9.5), leveraging DTs and the Desired-Reported Property pattern is essential. As previously explained, DTs provide real-time virtual representations of each IoT device, capturing their current status, including operating system, software version, execution traces, and other critical data. The Distribution Engine uses the detailed information from DTs to determine which devices need updates [3]. By comparing the desired state (i.e., the latest software version) with the reported state (i.e., the current software version on the device), the engine can identify discrepancies and target the necessary updates.

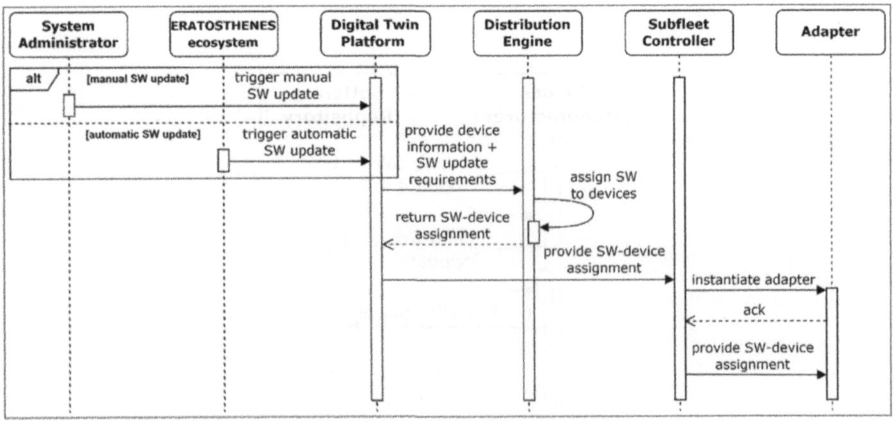

Figure 9.5. Step 3: Robust distribution of software updates.

For a single device (i.e., one-to-one scenario), the Distribution Engine checks the DT's reported properties and pushes the update if the device is not up to date. For a subset of devices (i.e., one-to-many scenario), the engine filters devices based on specific criteria, such as those running an outdated version or those with a particular operating system. It then pushes the update to this group, ensuring all selected devices meet the desired state. For fleet-wide updates (i.e., one-to-all scenario), the engine initiates a fan-out distribution to all devices. This ensures uniformity across the entire network, with each device's DT confirming receipt and installation of the update, maintaining consistent software versions across the fleet.

The distribution itself takes place over secure channels, ensuring data integrity and preventing unauthorised access. The process includes continuous monitoring of the update status, using the DTs to track progress and verify successful installations.

9.3.4 Step 4: Secure Update Installation

Secure installation of software updates on IoT devices (Figure 9.6) requires addressing the diversity in hardware architectures, operating systems, execution environments, network interfaces, and APIs. This implementation relies on specific software Adapters developed for each device type, ensuring a seamless installation process tailored to the unique requirements of each device [3, 4].

In addition to the Adapters, the Subfleet Manager is another important software component installed within the same secure domain as the devices. It coordinates and manages the update process across a diverse range of IoT devices, ensuring that each device receives the appropriate updates securely and efficiently. The Subfleet Manager acts as intermediary between the central SSU server (i.e., DT Platform)

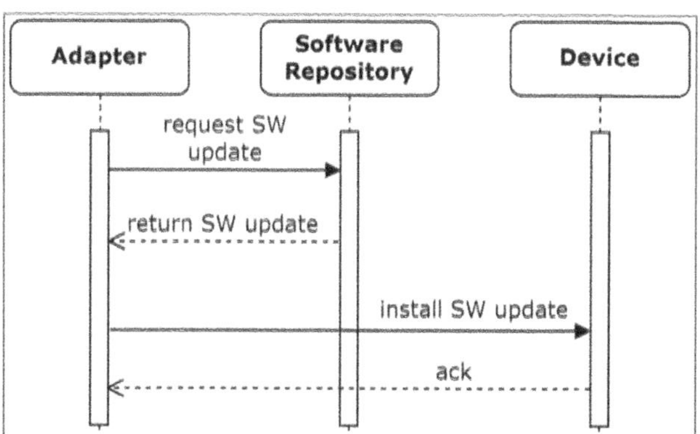

Figure 9.6. Step 4: Secure installation of software updates.

and the IoT devices; its main task is to receive software update commands from the DT Platform on the northbound interface and to route them to the assigned device on its southbound interface [5]. Upon receiving a command, the Subfleet Manager identifies the specific Adapter required for the target device type and instantiates it accordingly. It then forwards the software update command to the designated Adapter, which then enacts the correct and secure execution of the update process.

The installation process varies depending on the device type but generally involves securely transferring the update package to the device and initiating the installation process via the corresponding API. The Adapter handles specific commands and procedures required for installation on different operating systems and execution environments. It monitors the installation process in real-time to ensure it completes successfully without interruptions or errors.

Before installation, the Adapter may perform signature verification by fetching the update package from the secure repository and using the device's embedded public key to verify the attached digital signature. This ensures that the update is from a trusted source and has not been tampered with. If verification fails, the installation is aborted, and the issue is logged.

9.3.5 Step 5: Post-Update Verification and Attestation

This is the last step in the SSU cycle (Figure 9.7). Local attestation involves verifying the integrity of software updates directly on the device. Each device is equipped with a public key from the manufacturer. These keys are essential for verifying the authenticity and integrity of installed software updates, which are signed with the manufacturer's private key. Before a software update is installed, the device uses this public key to verify the digital signature of the update. This verification ensures that the update has not been tampered with and is indeed from a trusted source.

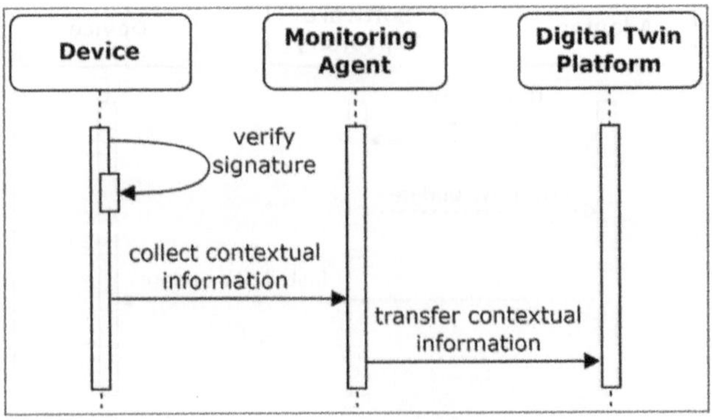

Figure 9.7. Step 5: Post-update verification and attestation.

This process can be automated and performed periodically, ensuring the software's continuous integrity.

To further enhance security, continuous monitoring is implemented using device-side Monitoring Agents. These agents run on each device, collecting run-time information such as current software versions, execution traces, and other relevant metrics. This data is sent to the DT Platform at regular intervals. The platform uses this information to maintain an up-to-date virtual representation of each device, enabling real-time monitoring and detection of anomalies or discrepancies.

The continuous monitoring system allows for proactive security measures, as any deviations from expected behaviour can be quickly identified and addressed. By leveraging local attestation supported by continuous monitoring, a robust framework is established to ensure the security and integrity of software updates in devices, thereby safeguarding user data and device functionality.

9.4 Proof of Concept

Following the described architecture, the proof-of-concept implementation focuses on adoptability and integrability. Therefore, we have taken an architectural design approach to improve aspects of coupling to application-specific details and separation of concerns. Given the cyber-physical nature of managed IoT devices within the distributed fleet, three main design decisions underpin the design and implementation of the SSU mechanism:

- **Decoupled architecture:** Managed IoT devices may unexpectedly crash, unpredictably lose network connection, and then reappear online. To accommodate such ad-hoc behaviour and prevent bottlenecks, communication between software components is implemented using pub-sub messaging based on MQTT.
- **Asynchronous communication:** For the same reason, it is important that any software updates initiated are guaranteed to be delivered to target devices regardless of how long they stay offline. This also means that the status of each device is continuously monitored and stored to apply the required changes when it gets back online. This can be implemented using the described Desired-Reported Property pattern, which enables real-time monitoring of devices and comparison of reported properties against desired ones.
- **Hierarchical architecture and extensibility:** To prevent single points of failure and distribute the workload within the managed fleet of heterogeneous

devices, devices with similar interfaces are grouped together [3]. This introduces an extra layer of filtering and load-balancing functionality between the centralised SSU engine and numerous devices within the managed fleet. Thanks to this hierarchical architecture, where generic functionality is separated from device-specific implementations, the SSU engine will be able to accommodate new types of devices in the future.

In addition to these main requirements, the design and implementation of the SSU mechanism were driven by several non-functional requirements, such as the availability of a graphical user interface (GUI), user friendliness, and the intention to re-use existing software libraries.

To implement the conceptual architecture of the SSU functionality depicted in Figure 9.2, several software components were developed. These elements correspond to the main functional elements of the conceptual architecture, which we describe in more detail in the following subsections.

9.4.1 Digital Twin Platform: Eclipse Ditto

As the technological baseline on top of which we developed the SSU functionality, we used Eclipse Ditto[3] – an open-source framework for building DTs of Internet-connected devices with extensible modelling and built-in querying languages.

As already explained, by using a device management platform, edge application [12] providers can remotely provision, monitor, and maintain their devices, as well as push software updates either manually or in an automated manner whenever a new version is released. In recent years, all these tasks have been underpinned by the prominent concept of DTs. Simply put, DTs are virtual models designed to accurately reflect physical objects equipped with various sensors related to certain aspects of their functionality. They enable the creation of rich digital models of anything physical or logical, from simple assets or products to complex cyber-physical environments. The collected sensor data is relayed to a processing system and applied to the DT.

Furthermore, Ditto acts as middleware, providing an abstraction layer for IoT solutions interacting with physical devices via the DT pattern. It can be seen as a toolkit, providing core functionality (e.g., meta-model, database, different messaging protocols and connectors, REST APIs, etc.), while some other features must be developed by users on top of it (e.g., domain-specific DT models, graphical user interfaces, device-side monitoring agents, etc.). Being part of a larger open-source ecosystem, it can be relatively easily integrated with other technologies from

3. https://eclipse.dev/ditto/

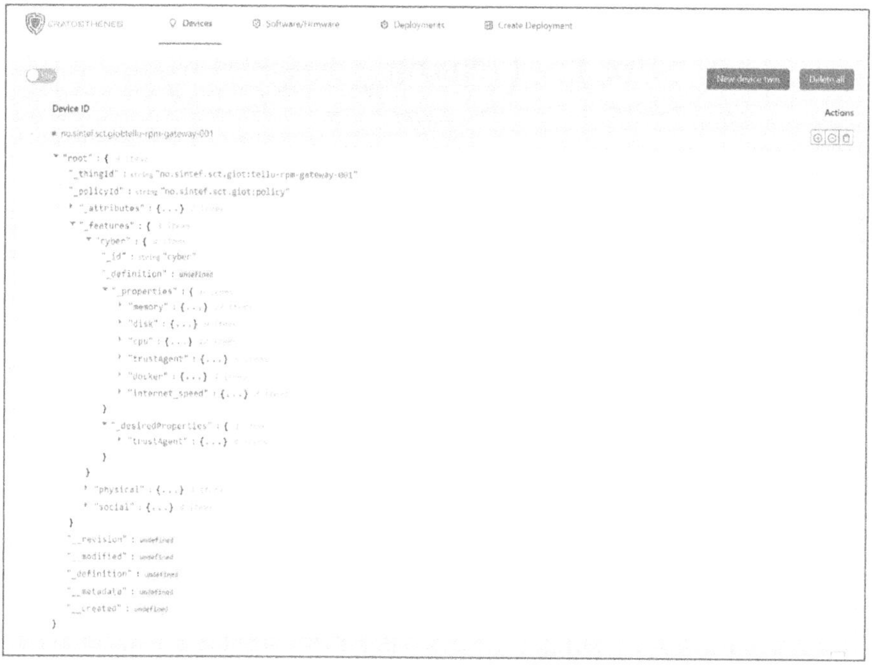

Figure 9.8. Front-end interface of the DT Platform for secure software updates.

the Eclipse stack, including various communication protocols, pub-sub messaging, and load balancing. Some of these extensibility capabilities are demonstrated in Figure 9.8, which includes the GUI of the extended DT Platform in the context of ERATOSTHENES. More specifically, the screenshot includes the basic SSU functionality accessible to the System Administrator via a DT representation in the context of the Smart Healthcare use case on connected healthcare gateways.

9.4.2 Software Assignment Engine: Ditto Meta-Model + Resource Query Language

Ditto offers developers an extensible meta-model [2] (depicted in Figure 9.9) that, in its simplest form, enables modelling physical entities, referring to them as **Things**, using a JSON schema with the following key concepts:

- **Thing** is the top-level modelling concept for describing physical assets.
- **Definition** is included in every **Thing** (and optionally in **Features**) and essentially represents a URI linking to an external Web of Things (WoT) model.[4]

4. https://www.w3.org/TR/wot-thing-description/

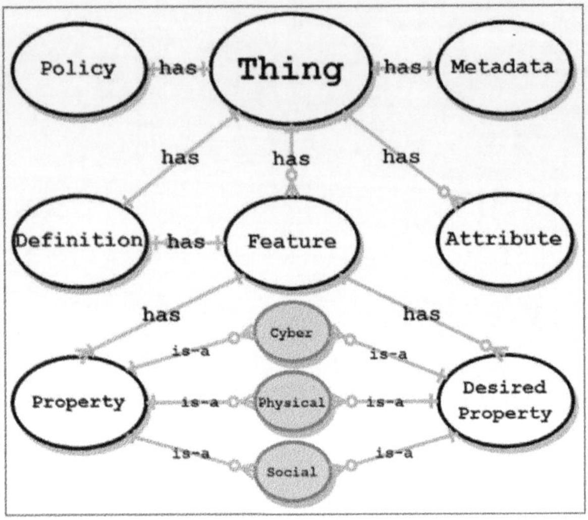

Figure 9.9. Digital twin meta-model capturing the multi-dimensional device context (an extension to Eclipse Ditto) [2].

It describes how a **Thing** is structured and what behaviour/capabilities can be expected in an interoperable and standard manner.

- **Policy** enables fine-grained access control configuration. A specific policy defines who and how can access a specific resource.
- **Metadata** is Ditto's internal field to store technical information, e.g., version or creation/modification timestamps.
- **Attributes** are used to model rather static properties of a **Thing**, i.e., values that do not change as frequently as **Features**. They can be of any type and can be used to search for **Things**.
- **Features** are the central modelling concept to capture all run-time data and functionality of a **Thing** in a given application system. Users are allowed to define their own **Features** or extend existing WoT definitions. This is a key enabler for modelling the multi-dimensional context through more fine-grained **Properties**.
- **Properties** are used within **Features** to model individual run-time indicators of a **Thing**, e.g., to manage the status, the configuration, or any fault information. Each **Property** can be either a simple scalar value or a complex JSON object. By using **Properties**, it is possible to implement the prominent Desired-Reported Pattern widely adopted in DTs, wherein sensor measurements are reported upstream while desired configuration updates are pushed downstream until eventually **Properties** and **DesiredProperties** are in sync. As explained, this is the main mechanism for monitoring the state of the deployed software and managing the deployment.

A simplified example of a DT definition (i.e., a connected medical gateway) used by the SSU mechanism is depicted in Listing 9.1. The DT includes all main elements, including the multi-dimensional features. Note the **properties** and **desired_properties** fields, which are used for twin synchronisation and trigger the update procedure of the outdated **software_component_01**.

```
"thingId": " no.sintef.sct.giot:tellu-rpm-gateway-001",
 "policyId": " no.sintef.sct.giot:policy",
 "attributes": {
        "type": "physical_device"
        "manufacturer": "RPM Inc.",
        "cpu_model": "Broadcom BCM2711"
        "platform": " linux/arm/v8",
        "ip_address": "192.168.32.5",
        "os": {
            "name": "Debian",
            "description": " Debian GNU/Linux 11 (bullseye)",
            "version": "11"
        }
 },
 "features": {
      "cyber": {
           "properties": {
                "trustAgent": {
                     "container_image": "trust-agent"
                     "container_status": "running",
                     "container_version": "0.1"
                },
                "docker": {
                     "server_version": "27.2.1"
                }
           },
           "desired_properties": {
                " trustAgent": {
                     "container_image": "trust-agent"
                     "container_status": "running",
                     "container_version": "0.2"
                }
           }
      },
      "physical": {...},
      "social": {...}
      }
 }
```

Listing 9.1. A simplified example of a personal healthcare gateway DT.

Eclipse Ditto also offers its users the Resource Query Language (RQL) to search for and manage these DTs efficiently. Using RQL's logical operators, we can perform precise assignments of software updates to IoT/Edge devices based on their DT data. One-to-one assignment involves updating a specific device by querying its unique ID. For instance, if a critical update is needed for a particular device identified by its ID, RQL allows us to target and update just that device:

```
eq(thingId,"no.sintef.sct.giot:tellu-rpm-gateway-001")
```

Listing 9.2. One-to-one assignment.

One-to-many assignment leverages RQL to identify and update multiple devices that meet certain contextual requirements. This might include updating devices running an outdated software version, devices running on a specific OS, devices deployed in a particular location, or devices used by patients with a premium subscription:

```
and(eq(features/cyber/properties/trustAgent/container_image,"trust-agent"),
    in(features/cyber/properties/trustAgent/container_version,"0.1","0.2"))
eq(attributes/os/version,"11")
eq(features/physical/properties/location,"hospital")
eq(features/social/properties/subscription,"premium"))
```

Listing 9.3. One-to-many assignment.

One-to-all assignment involves updating an entire class of devices. By querying devices in the fleet, we can efficiently distribute the update to ensure all relevant devices are up to date:

```
eq(attributes/type,"physical_device")
```

Listing 9.4. One-to-all assignment.

This way, Eclipse Ditto's meta-model and RQL enable accurate and efficient assignment of software updates, enhancing the reliability and security of devices.

9.4.2.1 Subfleet Controller and Adapters

We now discuss the actual installation of software updates onto the managed devices. The design emphasises generality and extensibility, ensuring compatibility with diverse device types and allowing effortless introduction of new device categories. Currently, the system supports three different types of high-end devices (all based on Smart Healthcare use case on remote patient monitoring):

- **Docker:** This type involves any device equipped with a Docker Engine, hosting a software component as a Docker container.
- **Linux SSH:** This category encompasses devices operating on a Linux operating system with open SSH access, wherein the software components operate as basic shell scripts.
- **Device-specific HTTP API (Axis Camera):** Specifically for Axis cameras,[5] the software components run as apps within the camera, utilising the camera's REST API for deployment and lifecycle management.

5. https://www.axis.com/products/network-cameras.

For each of these three, there is an **Adapter**, which oversees the device, handling connection, status checking, basic device info collection related to SSUs, and the actual installation of the updates. Once active, all the Adapters will subscribe to any possible downstream commands from the DT Platform. Whenever there is a software update that requires actions on one of the devices, the Adapter will launch the action on the corresponding device through the device-specific APIs.

We use the Docker Adapter as an example [8]. For devices that support a Docker environment, a software component operates as a Docker container. The essential requirement is for the device to enable the Docker Engine, which provides a REST API for communication. This Adapter operates on the Domain Manager in the same local network with the target device. It utilises the REST API to remotely communicate with the Docker Engine on the device. The device DT holds key information such as the device's IP and the Docker Engine API port. This information allows the Adapter to call the info method of the Docker Engine to retrieve additional metadata about the device, including CPU architecture, OS distribution, and Docker version. This method also serves as a ping operation, ensuring the device is connected.

For installing a software update, the Adapter performs several sequential steps. It begins by downloading the Docker image using the URL provided in the device twin. Following this, it invokes the **loadImage** method of the Docker Engine to upload the image package into the device. To start the software, the Adapter calls **runContainer**, launching a Docker container from the loaded image. Given that loading an image and initialising a container may be time-consuming, the Adapter maintains continuous communication with the Docker Engine.

9.4.2.2 Device-side Monitoring Agents

As previously explained, Monitoring Agents are deployed on devices to collect contextual information, which is then sent to the DT Platform. This information includes hardware and software status, environmental conditions, and user interactions, creating a comprehensive overview of each device's state and performance. By providing real-time data, Monitoring Agents close the monitoring loop, enabling continuous oversight and proactive management of the device fleet.

One of the key functionalities of the Monitoring Agents is to track the successful installation and execution of software updates. They verify that updates have been applied correctly and that the updated software operates as intended. This may involve checking for any installation errors, verifying the integrity of the installed software, and monitoring the device's performance post-update. By doing so, they will ensure that updates do not disrupt device functionality or compromise user safety.

Currently, these Monitoring Agents are implemented using Influx Telegraf[6] and are installed as Docker containers. Influx Telegraf is a highly versatile data collection agent that can gather a wide range of metrics and events from the host devices. Running these agents as Docker containers provides a consistent and isolated environment, simplifying deployment and management across diverse hardware and software configurations. Looking ahead, the goal is to develop more lightweight Monitoring Agents that can perform the same functions with reduced resource consumption.

9.5 Summary

The proposed approach leverages Digital Twins to enhance the SSU lifecycle, offering a robust, scalable framework for managing software updates across large fleets of IoT devices. Digital Twins provide a real-time, up-to-date view of each device's status, acting as a central integration point for various tools and processes involved in secure updates. This approach ensures timeliness by using real-time contextual information to deliver updates with minimal disruption and downtime. The use of the Desired-Reported Property pattern guarantees that updates are installed even if devices are temporarily offline, as they are applied once the devices come back online.

The system also offers granular control over the update process, allowing for targeted updates based on the cyber-physical-social context of each device. This ensures updates are distributed to specific devices or groups as needed, offering flexibility and precision. Furthermore, the approach supports scalability, enabling the management of updates across fleets of hundreds or thousands of devices efficiently. The integration of a sandbox environment allows for updates to be tested in a virtual space before deployment, reducing risks.

In addition to facilitating updates, the Digital Twin Platform ensures state persistence, allowing devices to be restored to their desired state following updates, recoveries, or rollbacks. However, it is important to note that this approach is not a complete solution but rather an integration point for other existing tools and methodologies. While it enhances the SSU lifecycle, it can be further extended and complemented by additional tools to provide a more comprehensive solution to

6. https://www.influxdata.com/time-series-platform/telegraf/.

SSUs. This flexibility makes it an adaptable and valuable approach in the dynamic landscape of secure IoT device management.

References

[1] D. Liberty, W. Ibrahim, M. Streets, B. J. L. Jaeger, M. Wiseman, D. Krahn, G. Proudler, S. Hanna, M. Areno, S. Lee, I. McDonald, D. Challener, A. Seema, P. England, R. Spiger, D. Wilkins, J. Quévremont, Q. Thareau and R. Pal, "TCG Guidance for Secure Update of Software and Firmware on Embedded Systems," 2020.

[2] R. Dautov and H. Song, "Context-Aware Digital Twins to Support Software Management at the Edge," in *International Conference on Research Challenges in Information Science*, 2023.

[3] R. Dautov, H. Song and N. Ferry, "A light-weight approach to software assignment at the edge," in *2020 IEEE/ACM 13th International Conference on Utility and Cloud Computing (UCC)*, 2020.

[4] N. Ferry, H. Song, R. Dautov, P. H. Nguyen and F. Chauvel, "Model-based continuous deployment of SIS," in *DevOps for Trustworthy Smart IoT Systems*, N. Ferry, H. Song, A. Metzger og E. Rios, Red., Now Publishers Inc., 2021, p. 59–93.

[5] H. Song, R. Dautov, N. Ferry, A. Solberg and F. Fleurey, "Model-based fleet deployment of edge computing applications," in *Proceedings of the 23rd ACM/IEEE International Conference on Model Driven Engineering Languages and Systems*, 2020.

[6] R. Dautov, H. Song and N. Ferry, "Towards a sustainable IoT with last-mile software deployment," in *2021 IEEE Symposium on Computers and Communications (ISCC)*, 2021.

[7] R. Dautov, S. Distefano and R. Buyya, "Hierarchical data fusion for smart healthcare," *Journal of Big Data*, vol. 6, p. 1–23, 2019.

[8] R. Dautov and H. Song, "Towards agile management of containerised software at the edge," in *2020 IEEE Conference on Industrial Cyberphysical Systems (ICPS)*, 2020.

[9] Ayyoob Hamza, Dinesha Ranathunga, Hassan Habibi Gharakheili, Matthew Roughan and Vijay Sivaraman, "Clear as MUD: Generating, validating and applying IoT behavioral profiles," *Proceedings of the 2018 Workshop on IoT Security and Privacy*, p. 8–14, 2018.

[10] Rafiq Ahmad Khan, Siffat Ullah Khan, Habib Ullah Khan and Muhammad Ilyas, "Systematic literature review on security risks and its practices in secure software development," *IEEE Access*, 10, p. 5456–5481, 2022.

[11] Lynn Futcher and Rossouw Von Solms, "Guidelines for secure software development," *Proceedings of the 2008 Annual Research Conference of the South African Institute of Computer Scientists and Information Technologists on IT Research in Developing Countries: Riding the Wave of Technology*, p. 56–65, 2008.

[12] Mehdi Kherbache, Moufida Maimour and Eric Rondeau, "Digital twin network for the IIoT using eclipse ditto and hono," *IFAC-PapersOnLine*, 55, 8, p. 37–42, 2022.

DOI: 10.1561/9781638285076.ch10

Chapter 10

Tracing Techniques for Connected Medical Devices

By Vaios Bolgouras, Georgios Petychakis, Aristeidis Farao, Apostolis Zarras and Christos Xenakis

Integrating Connected Medical Devices (CMDs) into modern healthcare systems has enhanced clinical workflows and improved patient care through real-time data sharing. However, this digital evolution introduces significant security and privacy risks. Ensuring the integrity and trustworthiness of these devices is critical, as vulnerabilities may compromise patient safety and the healthcare infrastructure. This chapter investigates the role of tracing technologies in safeguarding CMDs, specifically in monitoring security and performance across both high-end and low-end devices. Advanced tracing tools like the extended Berkeley Packet Filter (eBPF) enable continuous monitoring and anomaly detection in high-end CMDs. In contrast, resource-constrained low-end CMDs necessitate a balance between security and performance through tailored tracing solutions. We explore static and dynamic properties vital for maintaining device integrity, such as secure boot processes and real-time operational data, and discuss the unique challenges of securing low-end devices with limited resources. Beyond device-level monitoring, tracing technologies contribute to the broader security lifecycle, enabling early detection of vulnerabilities, regulatory compliance, and forensic analysis in case of a breach. The chapter concludes with insights into future trends in CMD tracing technologies, addressing emerging threats while maintaining a balance between security, performance, and resource efficiency.

10.1 Introduction

Integrating CMDs into modern healthcare systems has fundamentally changed the patient care, diagnosis, and treatment landscape. These devices, from wearable health monitors to complex implantable technologies, enable real-time monitoring, data collection, and communication with healthcare providers, supporting more accurate clinical decisions and personalized care. As the healthcare industry embraces the digital revolution, CMDs play a pivotal role in bridging the gap between patient needs and medical expertise, often functioning autonomously or as part of larger medical systems [1]. However, the growing reliance on these devices is not without challenges, particularly in security and privacy.

The increased connectivity and functionality of CMDs introduce new vulnerabilities, making them an attractive target for cyberattacks. These devices often handle sensitive patient data, including personal health information, which must be protected to ensure patient privacy [2]. Furthermore, the integrity and availability of CMDs are critical; any compromise in their functionality can have dire consequences, especially when a device is responsible for life-sustaining tasks such as monitoring vital signs or delivering medication. Thus, ensuring the trustworthiness of CMDs is paramount, and the ability to detect, respond to, and mitigate potential threats is a central concern for healthcare providers, regulatory bodies, and device manufacturers alike.

The challenge of securing CMDs is compounded by the diversity of devices in use today. High-end devices, such as those used in hospitals for intensive monitoring, have significant computational resources and advanced capabilities, making them well-suited to sophisticated security solutions. These devices can support robust security protocols and complex tracing mechanisms, enabling continuous system behavior monitoring [3]. In contrast, low-end devices, such as wearable monitors or home-use medical equipment, are often constrained by limited processing power, memory, and battery life. These resource limitations make it difficult to implement traditional security solutions, necessitating the development of tailored approaches that balance security needs with operational efficiency [4].

Tracing technologies have emerged as a critical solution in this context, continuously monitoring CMDs' behavior. Tracing refers to observing a device's operations in real time, recording static properties (e.g., secure boot processes) and dynamic behaviors (e.g., system calls, network activity, and performance metrics). By tracking this data, tracing technologies enable early detection of anomalies or deviations from expected behavior, providing valuable insights into the device's operational integrity and security posture. These insights are essential for maintaining the trustworthiness of CMDs, allowing for proactive responses to potential threats before they can impact patient care.

For high-end CMDs, tracing is often implemented using sophisticated technologies like the extended eBPF, which allows for deep system monitoring at the kernel level. eBPF provides a flexible and efficient means of tracking a wide range of system activities, including network traffic, filesystem changes, and process executions, without introducing significant performance overhead [5]. This capability makes it particularly well-suited for high-end medical devices requiring robust security and high performance.

On the other hand, low-end devices present unique challenges regarding tracing. These devices often operate on RTOS, designed to manage time-sensitive tasks with minimal delay [6]. Tracing on low-end devices must account for the limited computational resources available, ensuring that monitoring activities do not interfere with the device's primary functions. Static tracing methods, which monitor predefined behaviors such as boot integrity, and dynamic tracing methods, which observe real-time performance, must be carefully balanced to maintain security and operational efficiency.

This chapter delves into the critical role of tracing technologies in ensuring the security and integrity of CMDs across both high-end and low-end devices. Towards this direction, the ENTRUST framework is proposed, specifically designed to establish trust in CMDs through a robust architecture that integrates real-time monitoring, attestation, and verification mechanisms. It provides a comprehensive approach to managing the security of CMDs by leveraging tracing technologies to assess the behavior and operational integrity of these devices continuously. A key focus of ENTRUST is to address the specific challenges and solutions associated with tracing in different device categories, providing a comprehensive overview of the techniques and technologies that support secure device operation. By exploring the technological underpinnings of ENTRUST's tracing approach, the chapter sheds light on the importance of continuous monitoring for maintaining the trustworthiness of CMDs in an increasingly connected healthcare ecosystem. Additionally, this chapter addresses how tracing fits into the broader context of CMD security, operational assurance, and compliance with regulatory standards, ensuring that healthcare systems can continue to rely on these devices without compromising patient safety.

10.2 Tracing

Tracing is indispensable in the ENTRUST framework, serving as a core component for monitoring and ensuring the security, privacy, and integrity of CMDs. As CMDs become more critical to healthcare delivery and patient management, their secure operation must be continuously assessed to detect potential threats, identify vulnerabilities, and ensure compliance with strict regulatory standards. The complexity of this task is heightened by the diversity of CMDs, which range from powerful hospital-grade devices to more resource-constrained wearable or home-use devices. ENTRUST addresses this challenge by leveraging tailored tracing technologies that meet the specific needs of both high-end and low-end devices.

In ENTRUST, tracing is defined as continuously observing and recording a device's behavior, including its static properties (e.g., secure boot sequences) and dynamic operations (e.g., runtime performance and network activity). The goal is to establish a comprehensive, real-time understanding of the device's operational state, which can then be used to verify the integrity of the device, ensure compliance with security policies, and detect any abnormal or unauthorized behaviors that could indicate a security breach. Tracing is a defensive measure and a proactive tool, enabling early detection of vulnerabilities and potential exploits before they can compromise the device or the broader healthcare network. For CMDs, tracing typically involves monitoring a wide range of system components, including hardware, software, network interfaces, and application layers. By tracing these components, ENTRUST can gather critical data as the foundation for trust assessments. These assessments evaluate the device's overall security posture, determining whether it meets the required trust level for operation within a healthcare network. If a device's behavior deviates from expected norms or an anomaly is detected, ENTRUST's tracing mechanisms provide the necessary evidence to trigger corrective actions, such as isolating the device, applying software patches, or updating security configurations.

One of the most significant advantages of tracing technologies within ENTRUST is their ability to adapt to different CMDs, offering tailored solutions for high-end and low-end devices. High-end CMDs, such as hospital monitoring systems and complex diagnostic equipment, benefit from sophisticated tracing technologies like the eBPF. These technologies enable deep inspection of system operations, allowing for comprehensive monitoring of kernel-level activities, network communications, filesystem access, and process execution. High-end devices often have the computational resources to support these advanced tracing capabilities, making it possible to maintain continuous and detailed monitoring without degrading the device's performance. Conversely, low-end devices, typically used in less resource-intensive settings, require more efficient and lightweight tracing solutions. These devices, such as wearable heart monitors or glucose sensors, often operate with limited processing power, memory, and energy resources, necessitating a careful balance between security monitoring and performance efficiency. In such cases, tracing focuses on monitoring key system activities without overloading the device's limited resources. Techniques such as static tracing, where predefined behaviors are monitored, or dynamic tracing, where real-time performance is observed, are carefully applied to ensure that security is maintained without impacting the device's primary functions.

ENTRUST's tracing solutions are not limited to monitoring the internal operations of CMDs but also extend to interactions with external systems. CMDs frequently communicate with other devices, cloud platforms, and healthcare networks to share data, receive updates, or relay real-time information to clinicians. These interactions can introduce additional security risks, especially if the communication channels are not adequately protected. To address this, ENTRUST's tracing technologies monitor network traffic and data exchanges, ensuring that all communications are secure, encrypted, and in line with the device's trust policies. This holistic approach to tracing not only safeguards the device itself but also the broader network in which it operates. Additionally, the integration of tracing technologies within the ENTRUST framework supports forensic analysis in the event of a security incident. By maintaining detailed logs of system operations and interactions, ENTRUST enables investigators to trace back through the device's activities, identifying the root cause of an attack or failure. This forensic capability is essential for understanding how and why a device was compromised, allowing for more targeted remediation efforts and improving the overall security of the CMD ecosystem.

10.2.1 Tracing in High-End Devices

High-end CMDs are typically found in hospitals and include complex diagnostic tools, advanced imaging systems, and real-time monitoring equipment. These devices are integral to critical care and rely on robust computational resources to perform complex functions such as processing large amounts of data, maintaining real-time patient monitoring, and integrating with broader healthcare information systems. Given their critical nature and data sensitivity, high-end CMDs demand highly effective and continuous monitoring mechanisms to ensure they remain secure and trustworthy throughout their operational lifecycle.

eBPF is a powerful technology adopted in the ENTRUST framework to provide sophisticated tracing capabilities for high-end devices. Originally designed for packet filtering in network operations, eBPF has evolved into a versatile tool that allows for deep inspection of a system's behavior by monitoring events at the kernel level. eBPF operates within the operating system kernel, making it possible to observe a wide range of system activities without requiring modification of the core application code or causing significant performance overhead. One of the key advantages of eBPF in high-end devices is its ability to execute user-defined programs in a secure, isolated environment within the kernel. This means that developers and system administrators can create custom monitoring functions tailored to the specific needs of a device. These programs can track events such as system calls, process execution, network activity, and filesystem interactions in real time. By tracing these events, eBPF helps ensure that the device operates as intended and that no unauthorized or anomalous behavior occurs.

In ENTRUST, eBPF supports real-time security monitoring and trust assessments for high-end CMDs. Its ability to dynamically track system behavior at the kernel level provides deep visibility into the device's operational state, allowing for the detection of potential security breaches or system malfunctions before they escalate into critical failures. The versatility of eBPF makes it especially well-suited for devices that require continuous monitoring and rapid response to emerging threats, as is often the case with life-critical medical equipment. Below we present some of the key benefits of eBPF for high-end devices:

Deep System Visibility. eBPF allows for detailed monitoring of kernel-level events, offering visibility into the operating system's inner workings. This is particularly useful for identifying low-level security issues, such as privilege escalation attacks, unauthorized system calls, or attempts to modify critical system files. eBPF can also be used to monitor performance metrics, such as CPU and memory usage, which ensure that high-end devices operate efficiently without being affected by potential malware or performance degradation.

Low Overhead Monitoring. Unlike traditional monitoring tools, eBPF operates with minimal overhead, ensuring that the performance of high-end devices is not significantly impacted by the tracing processes. This is crucial in the medical context, where high-end CMDs must perform complex tasks in real time, such as monitoring patients' vital signs or processing medical images, without experiencing slowdowns or interruptions due to security monitoring processes. The efficiency of eBPF results from its ability to run directly within the kernel, avoiding the need for frequent context switches between the kernel and user space. This reduces the resource consumption associated with tracing activities, making monitoring a wide range of system events possible without overwhelming the device's computational resources.

Programmability and Flexibility. One of eBPF's most significant advantages is its programmability. System administrators and developers can write custom eBPF programs to track specific events or behaviors relevant to a particular device or use case. This flexibility allows eBPF to be adapted to the unique requirements of high-end CMDs, whether they are monitoring patient data in real time or processing sensitive medical information. The flexibility of eBPF programs allows for creating highly targeted tracing mechanisms that focus on critical areas of the system, such as monitoring the integrity of executable code, network packet flows, or interactions between different software components.

Security and Isolation. eBPF runs in a highly secure and isolated environment within the kernel, ensuring that the tracing programs cannot interfere with the device's normal operation. This isolation is critical in medical devices, where any disruption in the system's functionality could have serious consequences for patient care. Additionally, eBPF's execution model ensures that user-defined programs are strictly controlled regarding what they can access and modify within the system, reducing the risk of introducing new vulnerabilities through tracing activities.

Real-Time Threat Detection. eBPF provides real-time insights into system behavior, enabling immediate detection of security anomalies such as unexpected process creation, unauthorized access attempts, or suspicious network activity. This real-time detection is essential for high-end CMDs, which must respond rapidly to any potential threats to maintain their operational integrity and ensure the safety of their patients. By continuously monitoring the device's activity, eBPF can trigger alerts or automated responses, such as isolating the device from the network, rolling back to a safe configuration, or initiating a security audit to identify and mitigate the threat.

Integration with Broader Security Tools. eBPF is often integrated with other security tools and frameworks to provide a comprehensive security posture for high-end CMDs. For example, data collected through eBPF tracing can be fed into machine learning algorithms or Artificial Intelligence (AI)-based anomaly detection systems, which analyze the data for patterns of malicious activity or performance issues. This integration allows for more proactive threat detection and response.

Figure 10.1 represents the architecture for integrating tracing in high-end within the ENTRUST framework. The architecture is structured into various layers corresponding to specific components and functionalities of the high-end device. It is organized based on trust boundaries, defined as Hardware, Trusted, and Untrusted regions. This delineation ensures secure operations and protection against potential threats. At the base of the architecture lies the hardware layer, which consists of the high-end device's physical components and includes a Physical Unclonable Function (PUF). The PUF is a unique hardware identifier, providing a strong foundation for device attestation and preventing hardware-level tampering. The secure bootloader is positioned above the hardware layer, which verifies the integrity and authenticity of the device's software components before allowing the system to

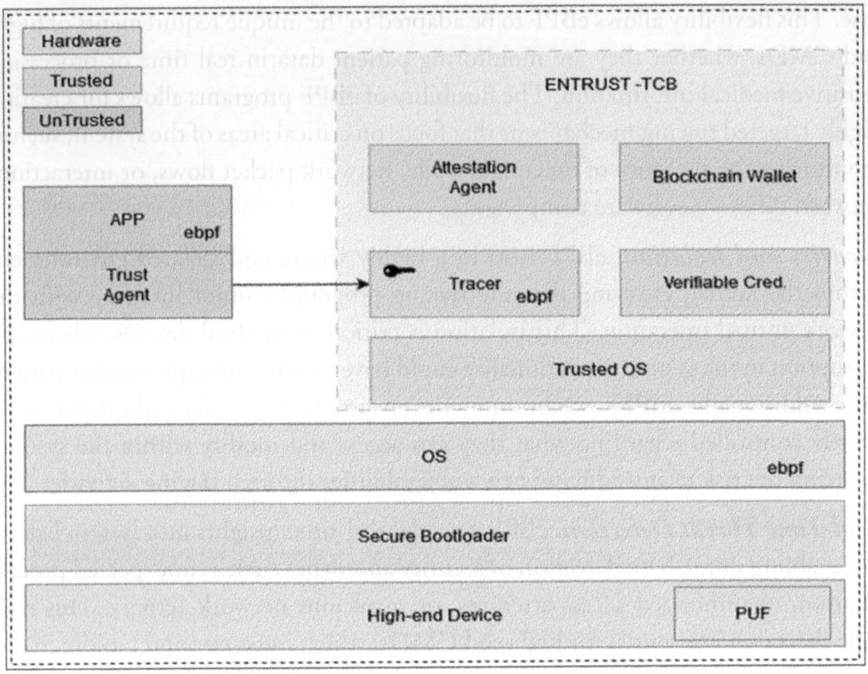

Figure 10.1. Architectural overview of the ENTRUST tracing mechanism for high-end devices.

boot. This ensures that only trusted software components are loaded during startup, establishing a secure foundation for subsequent operations. The operating system (OS) layer forms the core of the software environment and is depicted with the eBPF technology integrated within it. eBPF is a flexible and low-overhead tracing mechanism that monitors kernel-level and application-level activities. This capability is critical for maintaining system integrity and detecting anomalous behaviors that could indicate security breaches or misconfigurations. Above the OS layer is the untrusted application layer, which includes two key components: the Application (APP) and the Trust Agent. The Trust Agent acts as an intermediary, communicating directly with the eBPF-based Tracer to send and receive security-related information, ensuring that the application behaves as expected. This layer is considered untrusted until the Tracer verifies the application's behavior as part of the system's continuous monitoring and trust evaluation process.

The right section of Figure 10.1 showcases the Trusted Computing Base (TCB) within the ENTRUST framework. The TCB encompasses trusted software components running within a secure environment. These include the Attestation Agent, responsible for validating the security posture and integrity of the device, and the eBPF-based Tracer, which continuously monitors the CMD's behavior. The Tracer interacts with the Trust Agent in the untrusted layer, gathering data on system operations to provide a comprehensive view of the device's state. Additionally, the Blockchain Wallet component securely manages cryptographic credentials and supports secure transactions, while the Verifiable Credentials module stores cryptographically signed credentials that verify the CMD's identity and trustworthiness. Together, these components ensure that all activities within the TCB are securely managed and isolated from potentially compromised elements in the untrusted sections of the device. The Trusted OS, forming the base of the TCB, provides a secure execution environment for the attestation and verification processes. It ensures that sensitive operations are isolated from potentially untrusted or compromised components in the application layer and the standard OS environment, preserving the integrity of the device's security functions.

10.2.2 Tracing in Low-end Devices

While high-end CMDs benefit from robust computational resources supporting advanced tracing technologies like eBPF, low-end CMDs present different challenges. Often used in wearables, home monitoring systems, and other resource-constrained environments, these devices are essential for personalized care and remote health monitoring. However, they operate under stringent processing power, memory, and energy consumption limitations. This necessitates a more efficient and lightweight approach to tracing that ensures security without compromising the device's primary functionality. Low-end CMDs often run on Real-Time Operating Systems (RTOS) designed to manage time-critical tasks with minimal delays. RTOS is ideal for CMDs prioritizing responsiveness, such as monitoring vital signs or controlling drug delivery systems. However, the limited resources of these devices make it impractical to implement resource-intensive tracing technologies like those used in high-end devices. Therefore, tailored solutions are required to balance security and performance while addressing the unique needs of low-end CMDs.

In low-end CMDs, RTOS plays a central role in managing device operations, ensuring that tasks are executed with precise timing to meet the stringent requirements of healthcare applications. For instance, a wearable heart monitor that tracks a patient's vital signs in real time must respond immediately to changes in heart rate or oxygen levels without delay. In such cases, any additional processes, such as tracing or security monitoring, must not interfere with the device's real-time performance. RTOS is designed to prioritize tasks, ensuring that critical functions, like monitoring and reporting vital signs, are given higher priority over less time-sensitive operations. This prioritization is crucial when incorporating tracing technologies, as security monitoring must coexist with the device's core functionality without causing performance bottlenecks.

The primary challenge of tracing in low-end CMDs is maintaining an optimal balance between security and resource efficiency. Given that these devices have limited processing power and memory, the overhead introduced by tracing activities must be minimal to avoid slowing down or disrupting the device's core functions. Furthermore, many low-end CMDs are battery-powered, meaning that energy consumption is a critical consideration. Any additional computational tasks, such as continuous tracing, could drain the device's battery faster, reducing its operational lifespan and requiring more frequent recharging or maintenance.

Another significant challenge is the reduced flexibility in implementing complex tracing mechanisms due to the hardware constraints of low-end devices. These devices often lack the advanced processing capabilities required for deep inspection of system behaviors, making it necessary to adopt more lightweight tracing solutions that focus on essential aspects of the system's operation.

Static and dynamic tracing techniques are commonly used to address the limitations of low-end CMDs, each offering distinct advantages depending on the specific use case.

Static Tracing. Static tracing involves monitoring predefined, unchanging aspects of the system, such as the integrity of the boot process, configuration settings, and firmware updates. These are typically fixed properties that do not change frequently and can be monitored efficiently without constant real-time inspection. For example, static tracing can ensure that the device's boot sequence follows a secure process, verifying the integrity of the firmware before allowing the device to operate. One of the key benefits of static tracing is its low overhead. Since it only tracks predefined, infrequent events or system states, static tracing consumes fewer resources than dynamic tracing, making it well-suited for low-end CMDs with limited processing power and memory. However, static tracing is less effective for detecting real-time security issues, such as runtime anomalies or unauthorized network communications, which may occur during the device's operation.

Dynamic Tracing. In contrast to static tracing, dynamic tracing focuses on monitoring the real-time behavior of a device during its operation. This type of tracing is particularly useful for detecting anomalies, such as unexpected system calls, abnormal network activity, or deviations from expected performance patterns. Dynamic tracing provides a more comprehensive view of the system's operational state, allowing for the detection of potential security threats as they occur. However, dynamic tracing introduces higher overhead than static tracing, as it requires continuous real-time monitoring of the system's behavior. For low-end CMDs, this presents a challenge, as their limited resources may not be able to support such intensive monitoring without impacting the device's performance. To mitigate this, dynamic tracing in low-end devices is often applied selectively, focusing on key system activities

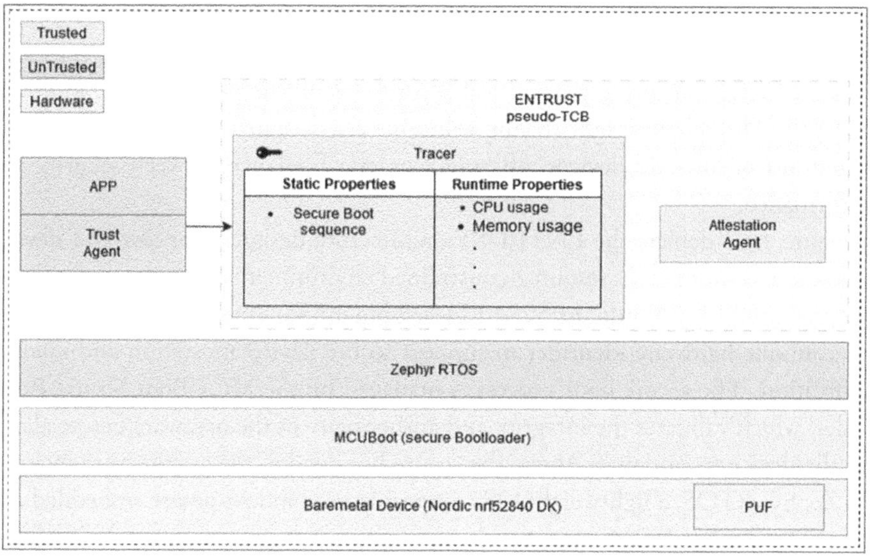

Figure 10.2. Architectural overview of the ENTRUST tracing mechanism for low-end devices.

most critical to the device's security, such as monitoring network traffic or task execution.

One of the most critical aspects of implementing tracing in low-end CMDs is finding the right balance between performance and security. In resource-constrained environments, monitoring every aspect of the system in real time is not feasible, as this would quickly overwhelm the device's processing capabilities and reduce its operational efficiency. Instead, a hybrid approach is often employed, combining static and dynamic tracing elements. For example, a low-end CMD may use static tracing to secure its boot process and firmware. In contrast, dynamic tracing is applied intermittently to monitor network activity or detect unusual behaviors during the device's operation. This approach allows continuous security monitoring without excessive demands on the device's limited resources. Additionally, event-driven tracing can further reduce the overhead associated with dynamic tracing. This approach triggers dynamic tracing only when specific events or conditions are met, such as when the device detects a sudden spike in network traffic or an unexpected system call. This ensures that tracing activities are focused on periods of high risk, minimizing the impact on the device's performance during normal operation.

To meet the unique needs of low-end CMDs, the ENTRUST framework incorporates lightweight tracing solutions designed specifically for resource-constrained environments. One such solution is the *Segger SystemView*, a real-time tracing tool commonly used in RTOS embedded systems and devices. SystemView allows for the efficient monitoring of real-time processes, task execution, and interrupt handling without introducing significant overhead. By leveraging tools like SystemView, ENTRUST can provide real-time visibility into the operation of low-end CMDs, ensuring that critical security events are detected and addressed promptly. These lightweight tracing solutions are designed to operate within the limitations of low-end devices, offering a practical balance between security and performance.

Figure 10.2 depicts the ENTRUST architecture designed for low-end devices structured to function in resource-constrained environments. The device hardware is represented by a Nordic nrf52840 Development Kit (DK) and a PUF, providing a unique hardware identifier to support secure device attestation and identity verification. The secure boot process is managed by the MCUBoot Secure Bootloader, which validates the integrity and authenticity of the firmware before allowing the device to initialize. Above the secure bootloader, the architecture includes the Zephyr RTOS, a lightweight OS commonly used in low-power embedded systems. The Zephyr RTOS manages the device's core operations, providing a foundation for real-time task scheduling, efficient resource management, and secure communication protocols. Zephyr allows the device to perform critical monitoring and control functions with minimal overhead, which is essential given the limited computational resources in low-end CMDs. The central component of this architecture is the ENTRUST Tracer, which is housed within a pseudo-Trusted Computing Base (pseudo-TCB). The Tracer monitors two categories of properties: *(i)* Static Properties and *(ii)* Runtime Properties. Static Properties include elements that do not change during operation, such as the secure boot sequence, ensuring that the device's initial state is verified and trusted. Runtime Properties cover dynamic aspects like CPU usage, memory consumption, and other real-time metrics that reflect the device's current state and performance. This dual monitoring approach allows the Tracer to detect anomalies at startup and during operation, providing comprehensive security coverage. To the left, Figure 10.2 shows the Trust Agent and the APP components. The Trust Agent interacts directly with the Tracer to communicate relevant security information, facilitating continuous monitoring and evaluation of the application's behavior. This ensures the device adheres to its security policies throughout its operational lifecycle. The architecture also includes the Attestation Agent within the pseudo-TCB, which validates the integrity and security posture of the device based on the evidence collected by the Tracer. The Attestation Agent's role is to generate verifiable claims regarding the device's trustworthiness, which can then be used to communicate its security status to external entities.

In healthcare, low-end CMDs are commonly used in applications such as remote patient monitoring, wearable health devices, and home-use diagnostic tools. These devices play a critical role in providing continuous care for patients outside of traditional clinical settings, often collecting vital health data that is transmitted to healthcare providers for analysis.

Wearable Heart Monitors. These devices continuously track a patient's heart rate and can alert healthcare providers if an irregular heartbeat is detected. Static tracing ensures the device's firmware is secure, while dynamic tracing monitors real-time data transmission to ensure that sensitive health information is not intercepted or altered.

Glucose Monitors. For patients with diabetes, wearable glucose monitors provide real-time feedback on blood sugar levels. Tracing in these devices focuses on maintaining the integrity of data transmissions, ensuring that readings are accurate and securely communicated to the patient's healthcare provider.

Home-Use Diagnostic Tools. Low-end CMDs used in home diagnostics, such as blood pressure monitors or pulse oximeters, require efficient tracing to ensure that their measurements are reliable and that abnormal readings are transmitted securely.

Tracing low-end CMDs presents unique challenges due to their limited resources and real-time operational requirements. By employing a combination of static and dynamic tracing, along with lightweight tools such as Segger SystemView, ENTRUST ensures that these devices can be monitored effectively without compromising performance. This approach allows low-end CMDs to remain secure and trustworthy, even in resource-constrained environments.

10.3 Impact

The use of tracing technologies in CMDs within the ENTRUST framework profoundly impacts the security, functionality, and trustworthiness of these devices. Tracing plays an essential role in safeguarding patient safety, ensuring regulatory compliance, and maintaining the overall integrity of the healthcare system. As CMDs become more deeply integrated into healthcare delivery, the need for robust monitoring solutions like tracing has grown, making these technologies crucial for operational assurance and long-term trust.

One of the most immediate impacts of tracing technologies is enhancing security across CMDs, particularly in protecting patient data and maintaining device functionality. Tracing provides a powerful tool for real-time threat detection, allowing healthcare organizations and device manufacturers to continuously monitor CMDs for signs of security breaches, unauthorized access, or other abnormal behavior. In high-end devices, tools like the eBPF allow for deep system monitoring at the kernel level, providing immediate insight into system events such as unauthorized system calls, unexpected process execution, or malicious network traffic. The real-time nature of eBPF's monitoring capabilities ensures that potential security threats can be identified and addressed before they escalate into serious incidents, helping to prevent data breaches or system failures that could have catastrophic consequences for patient care.

For low-end devices with more limited resources, tracing solutions like static and dynamic tracing offer a more focused approach to security monitoring. By concentrating on key events such as secure boot verification or abnormal task execution, tracing ensures that these devices remain secure even in resource-constrained environments. The ability to detect anomalies early in low-end CMDs is particularly critical, as these devices often serve in less supervised environments, such as patient homes or remote monitoring setups, where direct oversight by healthcare professionals is limited.

The operational assurance of CMDs is another key area where tracing technologies have a significant impact. These devices often operate in real-time, managing or monitoring critical patient functions where reliability and uptime are essential. Tracing helps ensure that CMDs function properly by continuously monitoring system performance, detecting performance degradation, and verifying the integrity of key system components. In high-end CMDs, such as imaging equipment, surgical robots, or intensive care unit monitoring systems, performance monitoring through tracing can prevent system bottlenecks or failures that could interrupt critical medical services. Tracing enables healthcare providers to proactively maintain these systems, ensuring that performance remains within acceptable thresholds and that any emerging issues are addressed before they affect patient care. Low-end CMDs, such as wearable monitors or at-home diagnostic tools, also benefit from tracing by ensuring they function as intended over extended periods. For instance, dynamic tracing allows these devices to detect unusual system behavior or communication errors that might indicate a fault. This ensures that patients relying on these devices for continuous monitoring receive accurate and reliable readings, preventing delays in care or misdiagnoses due to faulty data collection or transmission.

In the healthcare sector, ensuring compliance with regulatory standards is critical for device manufacturers and healthcare providers. CMDs are subject to strict regulations regarding patient data handling, device operations' integrity, and network communications security. Tracing technologies are pivotal in helping organizations meet these regulatory requirements by providing continuous monitoring, generating audit logs, and offering real-time evidence of compliance. For example, tracing can ensure that CMDs comply with data protection regulations such as the General Data Protection Regulation (GDPR) by monitoring and securing the transmission of sensitive patient data. By continuously observing how a device handles data, tracing can provide assurance that privacy policies are being followed and that data is encrypted, anonymized, or securely transmitted as required by law. Furthermore, post-market surveillance regulations often require manufacturers to demonstrate that their devices operate securely and reliably after deployment. Tracing provides the necessary data for manufacturers to perform regular security assessments and issue software updates or patches to address new vulnerabilities. This ensures that CMDs comply with evolving regulatory requirements throughout their operational lifecycle.

In the event of a security breach or device malfunction, the ability to perform forensic analysis is critical for identifying the root cause of the problem and determining how to prevent future incidents. Tracing technologies enable comprehensive forensic analysis by capturing detailed logs of system activities, network communications, and interactions between CMDs and external systems. These logs serve as a vital resource for investigating security incidents or device failures, allowing for reconstructing events that led to the issue. For high-end devices, eBPF's kernel-level tracing capabilities provide detailed insights into system behavior, making it easier to pinpoint the exact moment and cause of a security breach or system failure. This level of visibility is invaluable for incident response teams, as it allows them to trace the problem back to its origin, whether it was a malicious attack, a software bug, or a hardware failure. By providing a clear timeline of events, tracing helps to reduce the time required to diagnose and resolve issues, minimizing the impact on patient care. In low-end devices, where resources are more limited, event-driven tracing can still provide critical forensic data in the event of an incident. By recording key events such as boot sequences, task execution, or network communications, tracing ensures that investigators have access to the information they need to perform a thorough post-incident analysis. This capability is particularly important for CMDs that operate in remote or unsupervised environments, as it allows security teams to analyze incidents after the fact and implement preventive measures to protect against future occurrences.

Ultimately, the impact of tracing technologies on healthcare delivery and patient safety cannot be overstated. By ensuring that CMDs remain secure, reliable, and compliant with regulatory standards, tracing directly contributes to improved patient outcomes and more efficient healthcare services. The ability to detect and respond to security threats in real time enhances the trust that healthcare providers, patients, and regulators place in CMDs, leading to broader adoption and integration of these devices in clinical care. This means safer, more reliable care for patients, particularly those who rely on CMDs for critical monitoring or treatment. Whether a hospital-based device that tracks vital signs in an intensive care unit or a wearable sensor that monitors glucose levels in a diabetic patient, the security and functionality provided by tracing technologies ensure that these devices can be trusted to perform their roles effectively. From a healthcare delivery perspective, tracing technologies support the scalability and efficiency of digital health solutions. As healthcare systems continue to evolve and integrate more connected devices, tracing will play an essential role in managing the security and operational reliability of CMDs at scale. Tracing helps healthcare providers manage complex systems while reducing the risks associated with device malfunctions, data breaches, or regulatory non-compliance by providing the tools to monitor large numbers of devices in real time.

10.4 Future Developments or Challenges

As the healthcare industry continues to adopt and integrate CMDs into patient care, the role of tracing technologies will become even more crucial. However, with the evolving landscape of medical technology and cybersecurity threats, several key developments and challenges will shape the future of tracing solutions for CMDs. These factors will influence how devices are monitored and the broader implications for patient safety, regulatory compliance, and the operational efficiency of healthcare systems.

One of the most significant challenges facing the future of CMD security and tracing is the increasing complexity of devices and their growing interconnectivity within healthcare networks. As CMDs become more advanced, with new features and capabilities added, they are expected to handle more sensitive data and perform more complex tasks. Devices will no longer operate in isolation but will instead be part of an interconnected network that includes hospital systems, cloud platforms, wearable technologies, and even smart home devices. This interconnectivity raises new concerns for tracing technologies. Tracing solutions must evolve to monitor the internal operations of individual devices and their interactions with external systems. The potential for cross-device vulnerabilities increases as CMDs communicate with a broader range of devices and networks. A breach in one device could serve as an entry point for attacks on the entire network, making it critical that tracing technologies provide visibility into the device's external communications and interactions with other systems. Additionally, as CMDs become more complex, the volume of data generated by tracing technologies will increase significantly. This data must be managed effectively to avoid overwhelming healthcare providers and security teams. Future developments in tracing will need to focus on intelligent data management, including advanced filtering and prioritization techniques, to ensure that only the most critical events are highlighted for further investigation. Moreover, tracing tools must integrate more deeply with security information and event management (SIEM) systems to provide healthcare organizations with a comprehensive view of their device ecosystems.

10.4.1 Resource Constraints in Low-End Devices

While high-end CMDs will benefit from increasing computational power and more advanced tracing capabilities, low-end devices will continue to face resource constraints that limit the types of tracing technologies that can be deployed. Wearables and other small, low-power devices are becoming more prevalent in healthcare, providing continuous monitoring of patients in remote settings. These devices typically operate on limited processing power, memory, and battery life, making it difficult to implement continuous or resource-intensive tracing. The challenge for future developments in low-end CMD tracing will be to create ultra-lightweight tracing solutions that can provide effective monitoring without consuming significant device resources. This may involve the development of more efficient algorithms for event-driven tracing, where monitoring is only triggered by specific events or conditions rather than running continuously. Additionally, advancements in edge computing may allow some of the computational burden associated with tracing to be offloaded from the device to nearby processing nodes, such as smartphones or home hubs, thereby extending the device's operational life without compromising security. Another promising avenue for development is adaptive tracing, where the tracing level can be dynamically adjusted based on the device's current workload, energy levels, or operational status. For example, a low-end, fully charged CMD that does not actively monitor the patient could run more intensive tracing activities. In contrast, during periods of high demand or low battery, the tracing could be scaled back to essential activities only.

10.4.2 Integration of AI and Machine Learning in Tracing

One of the most exciting developments in the future of CMD tracing is integrating AI and machine learning (ML) into tracing solutions. AI and ML algorithms can analyze vast amounts of data generated by tracing activities and identifying patterns, anomalies, and potential security threats that may be too subtle or complex for traditional detection methods. These technologies will play a critical role in predictive analysis, enabling healthcare providers and device manufacturers to identify potential vulnerabilities before they are exploited or device malfunctions before they impact patient care. AI-driven tracing solutions will allow real-time anomaly detection, providing more proactive security and operational monitoring. For example, AI algorithms could learn the normal operational patterns of a CMD and then flag any deviations from these patterns that may indicate a security breach or malfunction. These algorithms could also prioritize the most critical events, reducing the workload on security teams and ensuring that threats are addressed promptly.

Using AI and ML in tracing will also facilitate automated incident response. In the event of a detected anomaly or breach, AI-driven tracing solutions could automatically take predefined actions, such as isolating the affected device from the network, rolling back software to a secure version, or alerting the security team for further investigation. This level of automation will be crucial as the number of CMDs deployed in healthcare continues to grow, making manual monitoring and response increasingly impractical.

10.4.3 Regulatory and Ethical Challenges

As tracing technologies become more sophisticated and integrated into CMDs, they will also face increasing scrutiny from regulatory bodies and ethical considerations. Tracing technologies must operate within a framework that balances security and privacy. While the continuous monitoring of CMDs is essential for detecting security threats, it also raises concerns about the privacy of the device user (often the patient) and the healthcare providers interacting with these devices. Regulatory bodies such as the *U.S. Food and Drug Administration (FDA)* and the *European Union Agency for Cybersecurity (ENISA)* are likely to impose stricter guidelines on how tracing data is collected, stored, and used. These guidelines must address the need for transparency in tracing activities, ensuring that device manufacturers and healthcare providers know what data is being collected and how it is being used. This is particularly important in light of regulations like the General Data Protection Regulation (GDPR), which imposes strict requirements on the handling of personal data. Furthermore, the ethical implications of tracing must be considered, particularly in scenarios where CMDs are used in vulnerable populations, such as elderly patients or individuals with chronic conditions. Future developments in tracing will need to ensure that patient autonomy and informed consent are maintained, allowing patients to control how their data is monitored and shared. The design of tracing systems must consider the ethical responsibility to protect patient privacy while providing the security necessary to ensure device safety and functionality.

10.4.4 Scalability and the Future of Connected Healthcare

As CMDs proliferate across healthcare systems worldwide, scalability will become a significant challenge for tracing technologies. Healthcare providers are already deploying increasing numbers of CMDs in hospitals, clinics, and patient homes, and this trend is only expected to accelerate with the rise of personalized medicine and remote care. Tracing technologies will need to scale to monitor vast networks of devices without overwhelming security teams or healthcare infrastructure. The future of connected healthcare, often called Healthcare 4.0, envisions a world where CMDs are integrated into large-scale, interconnected systems that communicate seamlessly across hospital networks, cloud platforms, and even smart city infrastructures. In this environment, tracing solutions will need to evolve to provide end-to-end visibility into the behavior of CMDs within these complex ecosystems. This will require advancements in distributed tracing, where data from multiple CMDs across different locations and platforms are collected, correlated, and analyzed to provide a comprehensive picture of the healthcare system's overall security and performance. Additionally, future developments in blockchain or distributed ledger technologies (DLT) could enhance tracing by providing immutable, verifiable records of device activity, further ensuring the integrity of CMDs within interconnected healthcare systems.

10.5 Conclusion

As CMDs become integral to modern healthcare, the need for robust security measures, such as tracing technologies, has never been more critical. This chapter has highlighted the indispensable role of tracing in ensuring the security, privacy, and operational integrity of CMDs, particularly as these devices evolve in complexity and capability. Tracing provides early detection of anomalies by continuously monitoring device behavior, safeguarding patient safety and the broader healthcare ecosystem from potential cyber threats. For high-end CMDs, advanced tracing mechanisms like eBPF offer deep system insights and comprehensive security monitoring without compromising device performance. Conversely, low-end CMDs face unique challenges due to resource constraints, requiring lightweight, efficient tracing solutions that balance security with operational efficiency. Both categories benefit from tailored tracing strategies that enable proactive security management and regulatory compliance. Looking ahead, integrating AI and machine learning into tracing technologies will enable more intelligent and predictive security measures, enhancing real-time threat detection and automated response. As the healthcare landscape continues to evolve, CMDs will play an increasingly central role in personalized care, making it essential that tracing technologies adapt to new threats and emerging healthcare needs. In conclusion, tracing technologies will continue to be pivotal in maintaining the trustworthiness of CMDs in an ever-connected healthcare environment. Tracing supports the future of digital healthcare by ensuring that these devices remain secure, reliable, and compliant, promoting safer and more efficient patient care across diverse healthcare settings.

Acknowledgments

This research has been funded from the European Union's research and innovation programme ENTRUST, under grant agreements No.101095634.

References

[1] B. Iantovics, *The CMDS Medical Diagnosis System,* Ninth International Symposium on Symbolic and Numeric Algorithms for Scientific Computing (SYNASC 2007), Timişoara, Romania, 2007, DOI: 10.1109/SYNASC.2007.40.

[2] P. A. H. Williams, A. Woodward, *Cybersecurity vulnerabilities in medical devices: a complex environment and multifaceted problem*, Medical Devices (Auckland, N.Z.), Auckland, New Zealand, 2015, DOI: 10.2147/MDER.S50048.

[3] S. D. Baker, J. Knudsen, D. Ahmadi, *Security and safety for medical devices and hospitals*, Biomedical Instrumentation & Technology, Maryland, USA, 2013, DOI: 10.2345/0899-8205-47.3.208.

[4] M. Tavakolan, I. A. Faridi, *Applying an Energy-Aware Security Mechanism in Healthcare Internet of Things*, 2020 International Conference on Computational Science and Computational Intelligence (CSCI), Las Vegas, USA, 2020, DOI: 10.1109/CSCI51800.2020.00192.

[5] S. Magnani, F. Risso, D. Siracusa, *A Control Plane Enabling Automated and Fully Adaptive Network Traffic Monitoring With eBPF*, IEEE Access, New Jersey, USA, 2022, DOI: 10.1109/ACCESS.2022.3202644.

[6] A. Godunov, F. N. Chemerev, *Tracing Tools for «Baget» Family RTOS*, Proceedings of the Institute for System Programming of RAS, Moscow, Russia, 2019, DOI: 10.15514/ispras-2019-31(4)-1.

DOI: 10.1561/9781638285076.ch11

Chapter 11

Securing the Software Supply Chain: Innovations and Approaches

By Apostolis Zarras, Evangelos Haleplidis, Christos Xenakis and Apostolos Fournaris

In modern software development, applications are built using diverse components sourced externally, such as open-source libraries, cloud services, and hardware, which introduce significant security risks into the software supply chain. High-profile incidents like the Log4j and SolarWinds attacks have demonstrated the severe impact of vulnerabilities in this interconnected ecosystem. Traditional security measures focus heavily on open-source components, often overlooking hardware and firmware, which are equally susceptible to threats. This chapter introduces RESCALE, a comprehensive framework designed to address these challenges through a security-by-design approach. RESCALE integrates advanced static and dynamic security testing tools with blockchain technology, creating a Trusted Bill of Materials that provides both hardware and software components transparency, traceability, and immutability. By incorporating cutting-edge security assessments and leveraging blockchain for the secure recording of results, RESCALE ensures a holistic and resilient supply chain, safeguarding against known and emerging threats in today's complex cybersecurity landscape.

11.1 Introduction

In modern software development, applications are no longer built entirely from scratch; they consist of various components from multiple sources integrated into the *Software Development Lifecycle (SDLC)*. Many of these components are not developed in-house. Still, they are used as-is, which, while accelerating time to market by leveraging pre-existing functionality, introduces significant security risks. This software supply chain, comprised of external hardware, infrastructure, operating systems, drivers, open-source scripts, CI/CD tools, and even cloud services, is inherently complex and often untrustworthy. The traditional security assessment methods applied to in-house development must address the intricate vulnerabilities posed by this external integration.

High-profile incidents, such as the Log4j vulnerability [1] and the SolarWinds supply chain attack [2], have starkly illustrated the potential devastation of supply chain breaches. Attacking a single component in the supply chain can compromise many downstream software products, exponentially magnifying the impact. As cybersecurity experts increasingly anticipate future large-scale attacks to target the software supply chain, there is an urgent need for a holistic approach that addresses both hardware and software security [3].

Much of the attention on securing the software supply chain focuses on open-source solutions, perceived as a primary vulnerability. However, this perspective overlooks the broader scope of the problem. A comprehensive view must account for all aspects of the SDLC, including hardware and firmware, which also follow distinct supply chains. Hardware vulnerabilities, such as side-channel attacks [4] and transient execution attacks [5], as well as hardware Trojans [6], can compromise not only individual systems but also the software built upon them. The interconnectedness of hardware and software supply chains demands that security-by-design principles be applied across the entire ecosystem to mitigate risks.

One emerging solution is the *Software Bill of Materials (SBOM)* [7]. This formal document tracks the components of a software product and their supply chain relationships. SBOMs provide visibility into third-party components, particularly open-source libraries, and help organizations manage compliance and dependency tracking. Although some of the existing SBOM standards can disclose vulnerabilities, the majority fail to provide comprehensive security information for the listed components and fail to address the hardware supply chain. Furthermore, robust mechanisms are lacking to protect SBOMs from *Confidentiality, Integrity, and Availability (CIA)* attacks.

This chapter proposes RESCALE, an innovative approach to securing software supply chains through a holistic, security-by-design methodology. By integrating cutting-edge security assessment tools with blockchain technology, RESCALE aims to create a resilient and trustworthy supply chain framework that can withstand the evolving threat landscape.

11.2 Background

The ever-evolving software and hardware development landscape presents new challenges in maintaining a secure supply chain. The potential for vulnerabilities grows as the software industry increasingly relies on third-party components, hardware integrations, and open-source solutions. These weaknesses, if exploited, can disrupt entire ecosystems, as evidenced by high-profile incidents like the Log4j and SolarWinds attacks. Ensuring the security of both hardware and software components across the SDLC is crucial. This section will explore various approaches and methodologies for testing vulnerabilities, ensuring firmware security, applying formal verification techniques, and addressing hardware vulnerabilities at the processor level for a comprehensive supply chain security framework.

11.2.1 Security Testing and Vulnerability Assessment

Security testing is essential for uncovering vulnerabilities and weaknesses within software, networks, and systems. By employing various techniques, security experts can identify potential threats, estimate the likelihood of exploitation, and evaluate the overall risk landscape of an application. For example, vulnerability scanning detects known vulnerabilities and loopholes, helping establish a security baseline. Popular tools include OpenVAS, Nessus, Burp Suite, Tripwire, Qualys, and Metasploit.

Security scanning, another critical approach, is designed to uncover misconfigurations and vulnerabilities within applications, networks, and systems. Both manual and automated tools, such as Nmap, Wireshark, and Zenmap, are commonly utilized for this type of testing. In contrast, penetration testing simulates real-world cyberattacks against an application, system, or network in a controlled environment. Conducted by certified security experts, this test is critical for identifying previously unknown vulnerabilities, including zero-day threats and business logic flaws. Tools frequently used for penetration testing include W3af, Aircrack-ng, John the Ripper, OWASP ZAP, and the comprehensive Kali Linux suite.

Once vulnerabilities are identified, security risks are classified (i.e., Critical, High, Medium, and Low) through a risk assessment, usually using the *Common Vulnerability Scoring System (CVSS)*. Tools such as SpiraPlan, A1 Tracker, RM Studio, Isometrix, and CheckIt assist in this process. Based on these assessments, mitigation strategies and security controls are prioritized and recommended.

11.2.2 Firmware Security

Firmware serves as the crucial interface between a computer's hardware and software, abstracting many low-level, hardware-specific details to enable the seamless development and execution of software across multiple systems. However, positioning firmware below the software layer poses significant security challenges, often requiring dedicated solutions. Several tools and frameworks have been developed to detect vulnerabilities at the firmware level, thereby reducing the potential attack surface for hackers.

One such solution is *Avatar* [8], an event-based arbitration framework that facilitates communication between an emulator and a physical target device. Avatar enables complex dynamic analysis of embedded firmware, supporting various security tasks such as reverse engineering, malware analysis, vulnerability discovery, vulnerability assessment, backtrace acquisition, and root-cause analysis of known vulnerabilities.

Another solution, *Charm* [9], enhances the dynamic analysis of device drivers in mobile systems. Charm's key innovation is remote device driver execution, allowing device drivers to run in a virtual machine. In contrast, the mobile device is used solely for servicing low-level and infrequent I/O operations through a low-latency, customized USB channel. This approach isolates the analysis from the mobile device, enabling more efficient and thorough testing.

Similarly, *PROSPECT* [10] supports dynamic code analysis of embedded binary code within arbitrary analysis environments. By transparently forwarding peripheral hardware access requests from the original host system to a virtual machine, security analysts can run and analyze the embedded software without requiring intimate knowledge of the embedded peripheral hardware components.

While these tools have collectively advanced the state of dynamic firmware analysis, they still face significant challenges. Dynamic testing or fuzzing of embedded firmware is often constrained by hardware dependencies and limited scalability, contributing to the ongoing vulnerability of IoT devices. Additionally, these solutions demand substantial expert knowledge and manual effort to set up and operate, further hindering their scalability and practical application in real-world scenarios.

11.2.3 Formal Verification

Formal verification plays a pivotal role in the development of complex information systems. It is a systematic process that uses mathematical reasoning to ensure that a system's design specification remains consistent throughout the implementation process. One of the most widely adopted techniques for formal verification is the *Symbolic Model Verifier (SMV)*. Despite its success in commercial designs,

SMV has limitations, particularly in handling the size and complexity of verifiable designs [11].

Formal verification requires engineers to adopt a different mindset from traditional testing methods. While simulation relies on empirical testing—using trial and error to explore combinations of inputs and uncover potential errors—this approach can be time-consuming and incomplete. Engineers typically create numerous input scenarios in simulation, focusing on trying to break the design rather than ensuring it behaves as intended in all situations. In contrast, formal verification is both mathematical and exhaustive, allowing engineers to verify the correct behavior of the design comprehensively.

Several tools are commonly used in formal verification. *Coq*[1] is a formal proof management system that provides a formal language for writing mathematical definitions, executable algorithms, and theorems and an environment for developing machine-checked proofs semi-interactively. Similarly, the *HOL* interactive theorem prover [2] is a proof assistant for higher-order logic, offering a programming environment where theorems can be proved and proof tools developed. *ACL2*[3] is another software system comprising a programming language, an extensible theory in first-order logic, and an automated theorem prover. *Isabelle*[4] is a generic proof assistant that enables the expression of mathematical formulas in a formal language, providing tools to prove these formulas in a logical calculus. Initially developed at the University of Cambridge and the Technical University of Munich, Isabelle has since benefited from global contributions from various institutions and individuals. Despite the maturity of formal verification tools, some technologies need to catch up in this area.

11.2.4 Identify Vulnerabilities at the Processor Level

For many years, secure system design has been built on a foundational assumption: hardware is inherently trustworthy. However, recent research has revealed that this assumption is flawed and that hardware often represents the weakest link in the security of commodity supply chains. Worse still, the hardware/software interface is inadequately specified, with a notable absence of microarchitectural contracts. This gap frequently leads to new security vulnerabilities as software unintentionally violates assumptions silently made by hardware.

1. https://coq.inria.fr/
2. https://hol-theorem-prover.org/
3. https://www.cs.utexas.edu/users/moore/acl2/
4. https://isabelle.in.tum.de/

From Rowhammer [12] to cache side-channel attacks [13] and from Spectre [14] and Meltdown [15] to RIDL/MDS [16], it has become clear that modern hardware presents a vast attack surface. Attackers can exploit this surface to mount attacks compromising real-world systems' integrity and confidentiality. Sadly, our understanding of these hardware-level vulnerabilities remains limited. Researchers continuously discover new vulnerabilities, and vendors respond with long embargo periods to develop solutions that minimize disruption. These solutions often include patches for CPU microcode, hypervisors, operating system kernels, compilers, and browsers.

This cycle of vulnerability disclosure and patch deployment is ongoing, with newly discovered issues sometimes refining or complementing existing vulnerabilities. As a result, new *"spot"* mitigations are frequently applied to real-world systems. However, the fragmented landscape of mitigations, especially in the last five years since the disclosure of Spectre and Meltdown, has led to a chaotic state of security for systems. Practitioners aiming to protect their systems against known (N-day) vulnerabilities face many mitigation techniques, complex dependencies, and unclear applicability and security guarantees.

More concerning is that even when deploying all vendor-recommended mitigations for a specific hardware/software stack, experts find it difficult, if not impossible, to quantify the residual attack surface. This challenge exists even when ignoring the complex interactions between N-day vulnerabilities or any yet-to-be-disclosed zero-day vulnerabilities. The current state of the art reflects this fragmented status quo [17]. While individual efforts often focus on specific attack variants [18], there remains a critical lack of comprehensive techniques to systematically assess the security of a hardware/software stack. Furthermore, developing strategies that can offer robust security guarantees against zero-day vulnerabilities is still an unmet need.

11.3 Methodology

RESCALE considers supply chain security a holistic issue that must be addressed by integrating hardware and software components within the software application supply chain. This approach establishes a chain of trust among the various elements within the supply chain. Unlike recent efforts focusing solely on the software aspects of supply chain security, RESCALE incorporates hardware and firmware components, which serve as the backbone of software application DevSecOps and the overall SDLC. Recognizing this, RESCALE adopts the *Bill of Materials (BOM)* as a conceptual vehicle for conveying supply chain information, leveraging established BOM standards (e.g., SPDX, CycloneDX, and SWID) while enhancing this construct with supply chain trust for each link within the chain.

On top of that, RESCALE introduces the *Trusted Bill of Materials (TBOM)*, which lists the components of an application and their dependencies and includes information about the security tests performed, their outcomes, and the guidelines followed in conducting these tests. To ensure trust, the TBOM is linked to a public Blockchain 2.0 (e.g., Ethereum, Cardano), where the results of the security tests are recorded and secured, with the TBOM itself integrated as a digital asset. The security of each TBOM component is guaranteed through cryptographic measures. In contrast, the non-repudiation of the security tester/evaluator and the test results are ensured by storing a smart contract on the blockchain. Acting as proof of responsibility, this contract uses the TBOM hash as its asset. As a result, the RESCALE trusted and secure TBOM-based supply chain ensures high levels of traceability, immutability, and authenticity, all inherited from its blockchain association, while supporting trusted updates.

The abovementioned concept is built around an advanced static and dynamic security testing mechanism, activated whenever a software or hardware asset is generated and utilized. This testing mechanism is part of a broader security assessment and assurance process, resulting in a TBOM. The process consists of two modules: the static code analysis module and the dynamic testing module. The RESCALE static code analysis module, after evaluating a given software component (referred to as an asset) within the supply chain (e.g., third-party proprietary code or open-source software library), produces a trusted report, known as the *Static Supply Chain Component Guarantee (SSCG)*. The SSCG includes details such as *(a)* the tests performed, *(b)* the test results (whether vulnerabilities were discovered or not), *(c)* the tester's/evaluator's ID, and *(d)* the asset's version. The SSCG is linked to the component's entry within the TBOM of the final software application (the endpoint of the supply chain).

Similarly, after evaluating a given hardware or software component within the supply chain, the RESCALE dynamic testing module produces a trusted report known as the *Dynamic Supply Chain Component Guarantee (DSCG)*. This report is linked to the component's TBOM entry within the final software application or hardware implementation.

The RESCALE security testing modules establish a trusted, secure supply chain via the TBOM. Following the latest NIST guidelines, RESCALE introduces two key entities in the supply chain and BOM establishment: the software/hardware component producer and the software/hardware component consumer. The producer integrates existing components with newly developed code to create a new product, whether a final application or a component (e.g., a library) for other products. In addition to existing components, the producer controls their code and executable code (e.g., binaries or hardware netlists) from prior components. To contribute to the RESCALE trusted secure supply chain, the producer uses the static code analysis module, generates the SSCG for the new component, and securely includes it in the TBOM. However, other applications cannot use the component directly in the RESCALE model. It must first be further assessed and marked as a candidate for the supply chain.

To make a candidate component a full TBOM entry in the RESCALE supply chain, it must be adopted or used by a consumer (another component of the supply chain or the final application). The consumer characterizes the candidate component as a third-party asset (proprietary or open-source) and performs a security audit. Initially, the SSCG guidelines are validated for compliance with existing standards and the consumer's security policy. After passing this initial check, the component undergoes dynamic testing within the RESCALE sandbox environment, tailored to the component type (e.g., hardware, processor, firmware, OS, driver, etc.). If the component passes all security tests, its DSCG outcome is linked to its SSCG, and the component becomes part of the consumer's TBOM. The dynamic testing process only occurs when a consumer first uses the component as the evaluator. The evaluator records the DSCGs on a public blockchain and secures them with a smart contract, with the software/hardware TBOM as its asset. This blockchain transaction, concatenated with the SSCG, legitimizes the component for integration into other applications, and future consumers can use the component without re-evaluating it unless the evaluation period has expired or the component has been updated.

We acknowledge that many open-source and proprietary components may lack the producer's security guarantees or static code analysis. In the absence of an SSCG, and if the consumer's security policy permits, the consumer can perform static code analysis using the RESCALE module to generate an SSCG for inclusion in the supply chain. In this case, the component will still undergo dynamic testing to receive the DSCG, and both the SSCG and DSCG will be stored on the blockchain. Figure 11.1 depicts RESCALE's security assessment process.

11.3.1 Security and Trust in the TBOM-based Supply Chain

The RESCALE trusted supply chain is structured around secure TBOM constructs, combining the *Hardware Bill of Materials (HBOM)* and SBOM. Each recorded component (as a BOM entry) is associated with the related SSCG and DSCG, along with proper authenticity information about every component created or used in the supply chain.

To achieve a high level of trust, the information in the TBOM must maintain integrity and be genuine, unforgeable, and authentic. Existing BOM standards, particularly for SBOM components, often rely on unverified attestations with security assumptions related to the *Uniform Resource Identifier (URI)*, the primary identifier

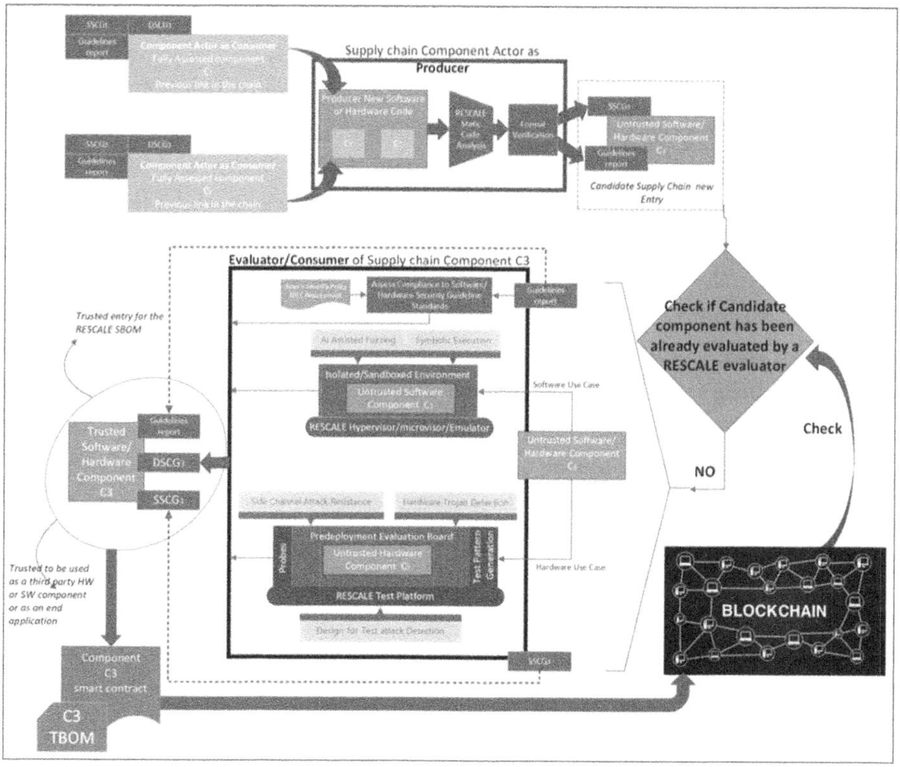

Figure 11.1. RESCALE security assessment process.

for a software component within an SBOM. Within the BOM, these URIs are presumed to act as contact points or identifiers for the manufacturer. The assumption is that the manufacturer's attestation and trust are established through conventional security protocols like TLS/SSL, with associated public key certificates validated when the URI is accessed.

However, this reliance on domain names poses challenges, as domain names can be hacked or mismanaged, especially by entities outside the control of the BOM producer or consumer. This weakness implies that the current BOM authentication process lacks the robustness required for a truly trusted system. This is even more critical in RESCALE, as the TBOMs carry vital information regarding the security testing performed on each component, including the SSCG, DSCG, guidelines, and associated vulnerabilities.

RESCALE aims to provide a trust framework capable of acting as a trust attestation for the hardware and software component stack in any supply chain or end software/hardware application through the TBOM. To succeed, the BOM information must be authentic, accountable, attributable to the component's producer and evaluator, and non-repudiable. In RESCALE, we extend the functionality of

BOM validation tools, such as the OWASP Dependency Graph, by adding trust capabilities, including formal verification processes, reputation systems, and secure building blocks like centralized or decentralized registries/ledgers. A key activity for ensuring authenticity in BOM entries is linking them to public blockchains (Blockchain 2.0 and beyond) to complement URIs. When a TBOM is created, the software or hardware solution producer associates the TBOM with a smart contract on the blockchain. This contract uses the TBOM as a blockchain asset; it binds the TBOM with the producer, product version, TBOM validity period, component assessment periods, TBOM hash, TBOM ownership, and component IDs.

Each producer in RESCALE acts as a consumer for third-party components used in their products. If any component lacks a DSCG (or SSCG), meaning it has not been evaluated yet, the producer, acting as a consumer, takes on the role of evaluator. For these components, the producer retrieves the SSCG from the component's TBOM blockchain entry, generates the DSCG, and stores it in their own TBOM. The evaluated component's SSCG, DSCG, and guidelines are then added to the product's TBOM. Additionally, the producer/evaluator creates a smart contract on the blockchain that includes the TBOM as an asset and records the components they have evaluated. This blockchain contract ID is forwarded to the evaluated component's creator. Thus, whenever this component is used in the future, it will provide the SSCG along with the blockchain smart contract ID of the evaluator. The consumer can review all the security testing details by accessing this smart contract. The security testing can be trusted since blockchain entries are unforgeable and immutable. RESCALE will also implement a reputation-based trust system for evaluators to enhance trust further.

A crucial aspect of the overall trusted supply chain is the unique, unforgeable identification of a software or hardware component and its associated TBOM. In RESCALE, the software TBOM includes a digital signature of the software (using its hash value) and a digital certificate of the software author. This process complements the RESCALE blockchain mechanism and is tied to the blockchain's unique ID, as described earlier.

For hardware TBOMs, a fundamental challenge is establishing an indisputable physical-to-digital association between a piece of hardware and its related certifications. This issue is addressed in various ways, depending on the hardware characteristics and the desired security level. Solutions may range from traditional Public Key Infrastructure (PKI) approaches, which resemble the software TBOM process, to QR-code stamping on the device. In RESCALE, we will explore existing techniques to establish a low-requirement hardware "identity" through hardware fingerprinting (e.g., via Physically Unclonable Functions, etc.), identifying appropriate fingerprinting methods for certain hardware classes, and formalizing processes and formats to create this association. Ultimately, a unique hardware ID will be generated and added to the RESCALE blockchain, digitally signed, and incorporated into the TBOM.

11.3.2 Management of Trustworthy Updates

Building on the trust mechanism, blockchain technology ensures the traceability of hardware and software components used in the supply chain of a given application. TBOM smart contracts contain information about the assessed components, their version, and the validity period of the assessment. In RESCALE, we provide a trust validator mechanism that evaluates a software or hardware application's overall correctness, security, trustworthiness, and TBOM. A crucial aspect of this process is determining, via blockchain entries in the TBOM, whether a component has been updated. If an update is identified, the TBOM entry for that component must be updated with a new blockchain entry ID (linked to the new smart contract). Once the updated component has successfully passed the static and dynamic security tests and has new SSCG and DSCG reports, the associated product will be updated with the new component version.

When a software or hardware solution—whether the end product of the supply chain or an individual component—undergoes an update, it must be statically and dynamically retested following the RESCALE testing approach. Until the updated solution passes these tests, it cannot be considered a fully trusted component of the RESCALE trusted supply chain. Instead, it reverts to a candidate component status after the static code analysis. The existing blockchain smart contract for the product has been updated to indicate that an update exists, and the TBOM has been revised to a new version. A new blockchain smart contract is linked to the updated solution version. Since the component is now in candidate status, consumers of the solution will act as evaluators, and they will link the new blockchain smart contract ID (of the updated solution) within their own TBOM.

11.4 Security Testing

The complexity of modern software and hardware supply chains demands rigorous security testing to ensure the integrity and resilience of systems. As software and hardware components are sourced from multiple vendors and integrated into the SDLC, vulnerabilities at any stage of the supply chain can compromise the entire system. Security testing is critical in identifying these vulnerabilities, mitigating risks, and strengthening the overall security posture of an application.

11.4.1 Static Code Security Testing

The RESCALE static code security testing provides a comprehensive static code analysis module, incorporating innovative static code analyzers for both source code and binary files. This module combines traditional code analysis engines with *Deep Learning (DL)*-based techniques to offer accurate vulnerability assessments for the most popular programming languages (e.g., C, C++, Java, Python). Traditional analysis engine results enhance the DL analyzer's training process, improving its ability to detect code vulnerabilities.

Static code analyzers generate alarm reports based on rule-based techniques and graph-based control flow analysis. While effective, these approaches often produce a high volume of false alarms, undermining user trust in the analyzer and its results. This issue is addressed in RESCALE by integrating *Machine Learning (ML)* and DL techniques into the static code analysis flow, following the latest research trends. Additionally, reinforcement learning algorithms are deployed to improve the accuracy of the ML/DL models. If component distribution during assessment is necessary, RESCALE adopts federated learning techniques to ensure privacy for both the components and transmitted data. These models are then applied to post-classify generated alerts, identifying false positives and allowing the static analyzers to filter out or assign low risk to these alerts, thus enhancing the accuracy of the analysis through a multiparametric fusion approach.

Beyond improving static code analysis, RESCALE utilizes DL-based classification to identify whether data processed in transit or storage is sensitive or non-sensitive. Based on this classification, appropriate security and cryptography operations are recommended to protect the data. The RESCALE static code analyzers are linked to developed security and cryptography primitive blocks (software or hardware libraries), which, based on the data classification, guide the developer in achieving high data security during design time. Sensitive data insecurity is another type of vulnerability that must be addressed.

RESCALE also introduces an intelligent vulnerability exposure engine based on symbolic execution. Although various static analysis tools, such as Coverity, Parasoft, and Klocwork, exist, most suffer from high false positive rates due to their reliance on simpler syntactical and semantic analysis rather than symbolic execution. While symbolic execution tools like JPF (for Java) and Otter (for C) are available, they struggle to scale to real-world applications. RESCALE overcomes these limitations by offering a formal verification solution for software.

Given a software component, RESCALE's intelligent vulnerabilities exposure engine verifies whether the program satisfies specific properties (i.e., assertions embedded in the code). A property is satisfied if no feasible execution path leads to violating the corresponding assertion. RESCALE either proves the property holds or provides a counterexample demonstrating a violation. This verification process involves symbolic interpretation, which combines the explicit exploration of all feasible execution paths with a symbolic representation of input variables. Through this approach, RESCALE delivers an intelligent code quality assessment framework that remains active throughout the entire software development and maintenance lifecycle.

11.4.2 Dynamic Testing

Apart from the above static code analysis, the RESCALE security testing toolbox includes the RESCALE Dynamic Testing Module, which features specialized ML/DL-based fuzzers capable of performing black-box or gray-box dynamic testing. These fuzzers use ML/DL techniques to generate and update the appropriate test vector inputs through a reinforcement learning process, which acts as the corpus for the fuzzer's mutation or evolution mechanism. These ML/DL techniques are complemented by symbolic execution analyzers to generate proper constraints on the input corpus data as aligned by the ML/DL analyzers. In the second stage of the RESCALE dynamic testing approach, we provide tools and mechanisms to discover security vulnerabilities in the supply chain's hardware (or firmware) and software components. Different dynamic testing approaches address these issues per component type within the RESCALE supply chain.

11.4.2.1 Hardware and Software Side Channel Security Testing

For side-channel vulnerabilities, RESCALE offers dedicated platforms capable of performing hardware power and electromagnetic emission side-channel trace collection. These traces are assessed using in-house RESCALE assessment libraries focusing on *(a)* generic non-specific leakage assessment through high-order t-tests and *(b)* dedicated profile-based side-channel attack assessment, similar to hardware penetration testing. A dedicated side-channel trace collection and analysis platform for hardware IP cores, combined with COTS side-channel trace collection tools, is enhanced with specialized DL trace analysis software. In addition to power consumption and electromagnetic emission side-channel leakage analysis, RESCALE explores timing leakages, particularly in software components handling sensitive information (e.g., cryptographic keys). Finally, the platform also identifies potential hardware Trojans by detecting abnormalities during computation.

11.4.2.2 Chip-Level Security/Vulnerability Testing

Given the diverse and often untrusted hardware supply chain, the risk of hardware Trojan injection at various stages (designers, testing facilities, foundries, etc.)

is a significant threat. RESCALE addresses this using ML/DL test vector generation techniques, such as *Automatic Test Pattern Generation (ATPG)* and ML/DL side-channel analysis from the Hardware Side Channel Assessment toolbox. This multiparametric approach increases the likelihood of triggering hardware Trojans and detecting timing or power consumption anomalies that reflect such triggers. Additionally, RESCALE assesses vulnerabilities in hardware chips that could be exploited post-design, such as those stemming from the on-chip Design-for-Test infrastructure, which may expose sensitive information through scan-chain-based attacks.

11.4.2.3 Firmware Dynamic Testing

To address growing concerns around the security of embedded systems, RESCALE provides an accurate analysis of firmware binaries, even when source code or hardware documentation is unavailable. A dynamic analysis framework is developed that orchestrates the execution of an emulator together with real hardware. A special software proxy allows firmware instructions to be executed in the emulator while I/O operations are channeled to the physical hardware. This approach facilitates large-scale firmware analysis and uncovers new security insights into embedded devices and their firmware.

11.4.2.4 Operating System and Processor Security Testing

To identify vulnerabilities at the processor level (e.g., transient execution errors) and operating system vulnerabilities specific to certain processors, RESCALE offers dedicated lightweight Virtual Machine-like environments based on QEMU/Gem5 hypervisors/emulators equipped with appropriate sensors/detectors. These environments capture vulnerabilities in a sandbox, focusing on microarchitectural attacks, such as cache attacks, processor architecture-based side-channel attacks, and fault injection attacks like Rowhammer. Furthermore, security sensors will be integrated into the QEMU-based processor kernel emulation to identify embedded OS kernel vulnerabilities, which could impact the end software solution using these kernel modules in its supply chain.

11.4.2.5 Cloud/Container/Microservice Security Testing

RESCALE also considers container-based security aspects. From a RESCALE perspective, microservices introduced in a container are treated as supply chain components and handled accordingly, following the RESCALE trusted supply chain establishment process. A cloud service, which relies on multiple microservices, is treated like software and hardware component-based supply chains and is associated with a TBOM. Dynamic testing within a container (i.e., a provided microservice) is conducted by placing the container in a sandbox environment (e.g., mine sandbox environments) and monitoring system call behavior through system call interpolation analysis. This technique is enhanced with anomalous behavior analyzers using Deep Learning models to detect unknown, anomalous interactions between the tested container and its external environment. Fuzzing techniques developed for software executables will be adapted for container security testing when applicable.

11.4.3 Supply Chain Trust Orchestrator and Continuous Security Assurance

The RESCALE *Trust Orchestrator (TrustOR)* acts as the primary handler of the TBOM for a given hardware or software solution. TrustOR has a dual role in the RESCALE project. First, it generates the RESCALE TBOM by utilizing the security assessment results from static and dynamic testing (producing the relevant SSCG, DSCG, and guidelines as previously described). Second, it validates existing TBOMs. TrustOR automatically processes software and hardware, orchestrating the necessary RESCALE components to generate the appropriate TBOM. This includes utilizing RESCALE's asset modeling features and sharing mechanisms with relevant initiatives such as the DBoM consortium,[5] which focuses on developing an infrastructure for supply chain attestation and TBOM sharing. As a TBOM generator, TrustOR orchestrates the security testing of software or hardware solutions. As a consumer of software or hardware components, TrustOR identifies whether a component is a candidate or a fully integrated RESCALE supply chain entry. If it is still a candidate, TrustOR manages all necessary evaluator operations, including dynamic testing, recording information on the RESCALE public blockchain, and ultimately incorporating the component into the end solution's TBOM.

Beyond the above capabilities, TrustOR addresses the need for continuous security assessment at runtime, going beyond the static TBOM information of a given software or hardware component. Since the vulnerability landscape evolves rapidly and zero-day vulnerabilities are constantly discovered, relying solely on the TBOM for security may be insufficient. From the time of security testing to when a TBOM may need to be updated or replaced, new vulnerabilities could emerge that are not reflected in the existing TBOM. To mitigate this, RESCALE integrates TrustOR with a *continuous security assurance platform*, which monitors the security status of software in real time. If new vulnerabilities are detected, the platform triggers a TBOM update process.

The RESCALE TrustOR, in conjunction with the continuous, evidence-based security assurance platform, provides comprehensive safety, security, and privacy

5. https://dbom.io/

assessments for all software or hardware solutions' assets (i.e., components) (e.g., network, compute, data, processes). The RESCALE model-based assessments go beyond the security testing platform and incorporate continuous, evidence-based evaluations of safety, security (confidentiality, integrity, availability), and privacy for software and hardware components. This process supports the following modalities: *(a)* dynamic testing based on the RESCALE security testing platform, *(b)* penetration testing, *(c)* runtime monitoring, *(d)* certificate-based assessments that evaluate the relevance and impact of existing certifications (and the evidence underpinning them) on the overall risk posture of the software or hardware solution, and *(e)* hybrid analysis that combines assessments from different modalities.

Finally, the proposed solution programmatically integrates with various architectural components of a system via appropriate probes (e.g., event captors, test tools), enabling RESCALE's risk identification capabilities and orchestrating its continuous risk assessment capabilities.

11.5 Field of Applications

The strategies and innovations presented in RESCALE provide a comprehensive solution to securing the software supply chain across various industries. RESCALE offers significant advancements for protecting complex supply chains in critical infrastructure, aerospace, automotive, healthcare, financial services, and cloud computing by addressing hardware and software vulnerabilities.

Critical infrastructure sectors, such as energy, telecommunications, transportation, and water management, rely heavily on intricate software and hardware systems to manage essential services. These systems are increasingly integrated with third-party software components, open-source libraries, and connected devices, all contributing to a significantly expanded attack surface. The RESCALE framework addresses these vulnerabilities by providing enhanced traceability through the TBOM, which allows granular tracking of hardware and software components, ensuring that all third-party components are rigorously tested and verified. In addition, by utilizing blockchain for immutable security records, RESCALE ensures that once a component has been certified, its security assessment remains tamper-proof. This feature is particularly valuable in protecting critical infrastructure systems, where any compromise could have severe consequences. Furthermore, RESCALE incorporates dynamic risk mitigation tools, which continuously monitor critical system components in real-time, allowing for proactive identification and resolution of emerging vulnerabilities. In this way, critical infrastructure systems benefit from increased resilience against known and zero-day supply chain attacks.

The ***aerospace and defense industries***, characterized by highly sensitive and complex systems, demand the most rigorous security measures. The reliance on diverse hardware and software components integrated across various platforms introduces significant risks to the supply chain, where compromised components could lead to catastrophic failures. RESCALE offers a holistic security approach by encompassing both hardware and software supply chains, ensuring that each component—from processors to software drivers—undergoes comprehensive security assessment. Using blockchain-backed TBOMs, enables the aerospace and defense sectors to maintain an auditable and trustworthy record of each component's security status. This capability mitigates the risk of introducing malicious or compromised components into mission-critical systems, providing assurance and traceability. The security-by-design methodology embedded in RESCALE allows these industries to meet stringent regulatory requirements and standards while ensuring their systems remain resilient in increasingly sophisticated cyberattacks.

The transition toward autonomous and connected vehicles has increased the complexity of software and hardware integrations in the ***automotive industry***. Relying on multiple suppliers for components such as sensors, communication modules, and onboard control systems introduces new cybersecurity challenges. RESCALE provides a robust solution by offering supply chain transparency through its TBOM mechanism, enabling automakers to track each component used within vehicle systems. This traceability ensures that all hardware and software components are rigorously assessed for security vulnerabilities, safeguarding against potential cyberattacks, such as remote vehicle hijacking or disabling critical safety features. Furthermore, RESCALE's dynamic testing tools, tailored for automotive systems, ensure the integrity of firmware, a crucial aspect of connected vehicle security. By enabling automakers to meet functional safety and cybersecurity standards, RESCALE helps reduce non-compliance risk, protecting manufacturers from costly regulatory penalties while enhancing overall vehicle security.

Industrial Control Systems (ICS), which play a crucial role in automating manufacturing, energy production, and logistics processes, face unique cybersecurity challenges due to their reliance on interconnected devices, including *Programmable Logic Controllers (PLCs)* and SCADA systems. While highly efficient, these systems are highly vulnerable to cyberattacks, especially when embedded firmware and hardware components are sourced from various suppliers. RESCALE enhances the security of ICS environments by providing comprehensive firmware and hardware testing, which helps to identify and mitigate vulnerabilities that could disrupt operations. The framework's continuous security compliance monitoring tools enhance system security by providing real-time assessments, ensuring that ICS operators can promptly detect and address new vulnerabilities before they can be exploited. Additionally, RESCALE supports IoT device security within industrial settings by securing the integration of connected devices into the ICS supply chain, thereby preventing common attack vectors, such as botnet infections and data breaches, from compromising critical industrial processes.

The rapid adoption of connected medical devices, electronic health records (EHRs), and telemedicine platforms has introduced new cybersecurity risks in the ***healthcare industry***. The sensitive nature of healthcare data and the potential consequences of compromised medical devices make supply chain security a priority for healthcare providers. RESCALE addresses these concerns by offering comprehensive security assessments for medical devices and healthcare systems. The framework's static and dynamic testing modules ensure that each medical device, whether implantable or used within a hospital setting, undergoes rigorous security assessments to prevent unauthorized access and potential tampering. Additionally, RESCALE ensures the confidentiality and integrity of healthcare data through cryptographic measures, providing compliance with regulatory standards such as GDPR and HIPAA. By continuously monitoring system components for compliance and updating the TBOM with new vulnerability assessments, RESCALE ensures that hospitals and healthcare providers maintain high levels of security and trust in their systems, safeguarding patient data and medical treatments' safety.

Financial institutions face some of the highest cybersecurity risks, given the sensitive nature of the data they handle and the value of the transactions they process. The financial sector's reliance on third-party software, cloud services, and hardware for tasks such as transaction processing, fraud detection, and data analytics introduces significant risks to the security of these systems. RESCALE strengthens cybersecurity for financial services by providing a comprehensive supply chain risk management solution. Through the TBOM, financial institutions can track every component in their software stack, ensuring that third-party software, open-source tools, and hardware are thoroughly assessed before being integrated into critical systems. RESCALE's dynamic testing and AI-based predictive security services enable financial institutions to detect abnormal patterns and potential fraud indicators in real time, enhancing the security of banking operations. Additionally, the framework's automation of compliance audits ensures that financial systems meet the strict requirements of regulations such as PCI-DSS and PSD2, while the immutable blockchain-backed records provide a trusted foundation for regulatory assurance.

Finally, ***cloud providers and data centers*** form the backbone of modern IT infrastructure, handling vast amounts of sensitive data and facilitating critical operations for organizations across the globe. However, the complexity of cloud environments, which often involve virtual machines, containers, and microservices, creates significant security challenges. RESCALE addresses these challenges by providing comprehensive security testing and continuous assessment tools for cloud and data center environments. The framework's container security testing ensures that microservices and containers, frequently used in cloud operations, are thoroughly vetted for vulnerabilities, reducing the risk of attacks such as container escapes or privilege escalation. RESCALE's side-channel attack detection tools add another layer of security by identifying vulnerabilities in software and hardware components, such as timing attacks or cache-based side-channel leaks, which are becoming increasingly prevalent in cloud environments. By automating the security testing of these components and continuously updating the TBOM with new vulnerability information, RESCALE ensures that cloud and data center services remain secure, even in the face of emerging threats.

11.6 Conclusion

RESCALE offers a comprehensive solution to the growing security challenges in software and hardware supply chains. By integrating static and dynamic security testing with blockchain technology, RESCALE ensures that every component, whether software, hardware, or firmware, undergoes rigorous assessment, resulting in a resilient and trustworthy supply chain. The innovative use of a Trusted Bill of Materials tracks each component's security status and secures the integrity of this information through blockchain, providing an immutable record that enhances transparency and accountability across the supply chain. RESCALE's holistic approach addresses vulnerabilities that traditional methods often overlook, such as hardware flaws and supply chain complexity. Its capability to continuously monitor and update components in real time positions RESCALE as a forward-thinking framework capable of mitigating existing and emerging threats. By adopting RESCALE, organizations can ensure their systems' integrity, security, and compliance, significantly reducing the risk of supply chain attacks and enhancing the overall cybersecurity posture.

Acknowledgments

Funded by the European Union (Grant Agreement Nr. 101120962, RESCALE Project). Views and opinions expressed are however those of the author(s) only and do not necessarily reflect those of the European Union or the Health and Digital Executive Agency. Neither the European Union nor the granting authority can be held responsible for them.

References

[1] R. Hiesgen, M. Nawrocki, T. C. Schmidt and M. Wählisch, "The Race to the Vulnerable: Measuring the Log4j Shell Incident," in *Network Traffic Measurement and Analysis Conference*, 2022.

[2] R. Alkhadra, J. Abuzaid, M. AlShammari and N. Mohammad, "Solar Winds Hack: In-depth Analysis and Countermeasures," in *International Conference on Computing Communication and Networking Technologies*, 2021.

[3] P. Ladisa, H. Plate, M. Martinez and O. Barais, "SoK: Taxonomy of Attacks on Open-Source Software Supply Chains," in *IEEE Symposium on Security and Privacy*, 2023.

[4] F.-X. Standaert, "Introduction to Side-Channel Attacks," *Secure Integrated Circuits and Systems*, 2010.

[5] W. Xiong and J. Szefer, "Survey of Transient Execution Attacks and their Mitigations," *ACM Computing Surveys*, 2021.

[6] K. Xiao, D. Forte, Y. Jin, R. Karri, S. Bhunia and M. Tehranipoor, "Hardware Trojans: Lessons Learned after One Decade of Research," *ACM Transactions on Design Automation of Electronic Systems*, 2016.

[7] B. Xia, T. Bi, Z. Xing, Q. Lu and L. Zhu, "An Empirical Study on Software Bill of Materials: Where we Stand and the Road Ahead," in *International Conference on Software Engineering*, 2023.

[8] J. Zaddach, L. Bruno, A. Francillon and D. Balzarotti, "AVATAR: A Framework to Support Dynamic Security Analysis of Embedded Systems' Firmwares," in *Network and Distributed System Security Symposium*, 2014.

[9] S. M. S. Talebi, H. Tavakoli, H. Zhang, Z. Zhang, A. A. Sani and Z. Qian, "Charm: Facilitating Dynamic Analysis of Device Drivers of Mobile Systems," in *USENIX Security Symposium*, 2018.

[10] M. Kammerstetter, C. Platzer and W. Kastner, "PROSPECT: Peripheral Proxying Supported Embedded Code Testing," in *ACM symposium on Information, computer and communications security*, 2014.

[11] F. Copty, A. Irron, O. Weissberg, N. Kropp and G. Kamhi, "Efficient Debugging in a Formal Verification Environment," *International Journal on Software Tools for Technology Transfer*, vol. 4, 2003.

[12] O. Mutlu and J. S. Kim, "Rowhammer: A Retrospective," *Transactions on Computer-Aided Design of Integrated Circuits and Systems*, 2019.

[13] F. Liu, Y. Yarom, Q. Ge, G. Heiser and R. B. Lee, "Last-Level Cache Side-Channel Attacks are Practical," in *IEEE Symposium on Security and Privacy*, 2015.

[14] P. Kocher, J. Horn, A. Fogh, D. Genkin, D. Gruss, W. Haas, M. Hamburg, M. Lipp, S. Mangard, T. Prescher, M. Schwarz and Y. Yarom, "Spectre Attacks: Exploiting Speculative Execution," *Communications of the ACM*, 2020.

[15] M. Lipp, M. Schwarz, D. Gruss, T. Prescher, W. Haas, J. Horn, S. Mangard, P. Kocher, D. Genkin, Y. Yarom, M. Hamburg and R. Strackx, "Meltdown: Reading Kernel Memory from User Space," *Communications of the ACM*, 2020.

[16] S. Van Schaik, A. Milburn, S. Österlund, P. Frigo, G. Maisuradze, K. Razavi, H. Bos and C. Giuffrida, "RIDL: Rogue In-Flight Data Load," in *IEEE Symposium on Security and Privacy*, 2019.

[17] P. Jattke, V. Van Der Veen, P. Frigo, S. Gunter and K. Razavi, "Blacksmith: Scalable Rowhammering in the Frequency Domain," in *IEEE Symposium on Security and Privacy*, 2022.

[18] E. Barberis, P. Frigo, M. Muench, H. Bos and C. Giuffrida, "Branch History Injection: On the Effectiveness of Hardware Mitigations Against Cross-Privilege Spectre-v2 Attacks," in *USENIX Security Symposium* , 2022.

DOI: 10.1561/9781638285076.ch12

Chapter 12

Cybersecurity Challenges and Pitfalls in 6G Networks

By Aristeidis Farao, Vaios Bolgouras, Apostolis Zarras and Christos Xenakis

The transition from 5G to 6G networks aims to improve connection speeds and intelligence levels. 6G is expected to support machine-type communications and ultra-reliable low-latency communications while enhancing mobile broadband services by integrating cutting-edge technologies. These advancements can potentially transform sectors, including healthcare and autonomous transportation systems; however, they bring security challenges. The open, distributed, and user-centric nature of 6G—marked by numerous connected devices, decentralized networks, and complex interactions between systems—makes traditional centralized security models inadequate. This shift introduces a broader attack surface with increased vulnerability to threats like API exploitation, data privacy violations, interception risks, and insider attacks. Applying blockchain and Self-Sovereign Identity (SSI) technologies is a promising approach to addressing the security concerns associated with 6G. These technologies provide decentralized and cryptographically secure systems that match the changing requirements of 6G. Blockchain technology ensures immutability, transparency, and tamper-proof record-keeping across the network. Through smart contracts, it enforces security measures and validates API communications while safeguarding data integrity among the distributed nodes of 6G. In parallel, SSI supports managing identities where users possess authority over their verified identities, ensuring privacy protection and secure access control, diminishing the likelihood of identity theft or unauthorized access. The combination of blockchain and SSI addresses security issues in 6G. Incorporating blockchain and smart contracts can minimize the risks associated with API vulnerabilities. This integration allows only authorized users and devices to interact with APIs, while SSI provides verifiable credentials that confirm users' identities and prevent unauthorized access to APIs. Although the 6G distributed architecture expands the attack surface, it can be protected using the blockchain's decentralized security enforcement mechanisms, where nodes can effectively verify each other's settings and activities. Moreover, the immutability feature provided by blockchain and the selective disclosure capabilities offered by self-sovereign identity help protect the privacy and integrity of data, ensuring that confidential information remains secure even when there are risks of interception. This chapter explores how blockchain and self-sovereign identity can tackle the security issues in 6G, analyzing how these technologies can shape a secure 6G infrastructure.

12.1 Introduction

The advent of the 6G marks a significant leap forward in telecommunications, promising to reshape how industries, devices, and individuals connect and communicate. Building on top of 5G, 6G aspires to offer ultra-high speeds, ultra-low latency, and ubiquitous connectivity, driving the development of futuristic applications (e.g., autonomous vehicles). At this transformation's backbone lies a sophisticated and user-friendly Service-Based Architecture (SBA), which is open, distributed, and user-centric, enabling seamless integration of devices and services into a unified network. The open and distributed nature of the 6G network represents a paradigm shift from the relatively centralized architecture of previous generations. While this shift benefits flexibility, scalability, and support for a vast array of use cases, it also exposes the network to new cybersecurity threats. By increasing interconnectivity among network functions, services, and third-party applications, the 6G SBA amplifies the risk of vulnerabilities across various network layers. Particularly, 6G networks will rely on Application Programming Interfaces (APIs) to enable communication between disparate services and functions, opening up more potential attack vectors. Thus, misconfigured or insecure APIs may be gateways for attackers, allowing unauthorized access to sensitive data and critical network infrastructure. Works on 5G SBA have already demonstrated the vulnerability of

APIs [1–3], a risk that is expected to grow as 6G becomes more complex and interconnected significantly [4].

Beyond the inherent API vulnerabilities, the openness of 6G also raises concerns about data privacy and interception [5, 6]. In this new architecture, data flows more freely between network nodes, users, and third-party service providers. Without robust encryption protocols and strict access controls, sensitive information could be susceptible to interception by malicious actors through man-in-the-middle (MitM) attacks or unauthorized access points [7]. As more entities access different components of the 6G network, the potential for data breaches and privacy violations rises. Another critical challenge that 6G's distributed nature introduces is expanding the network's attack surface. Unlike 4G and 5G, which rely on centralized core networks, 6G distributes core network functions across multiple edge nodes, cloud environments, and virtualized infrastructure. This decentralization is crucial for delivering low-latency services and optimizing network efficiency, but it also creates numerous potential points of vulnerability [8, 9]. Each edge node, cloud server, or virtualized function becomes a cyberattack target. One of the most pressing threats in this environment is the risk of Distributed Denial of Service (DDoS) attacks. In such attacks, malicious actors flood specific nodes or network functions with excessive traffic, causing widespread disruptions or even complete network outages.

Moreover, the distributed nature of the 6G SBA complicates the enforcement of consistent security policies across the network. In centralized architectures, security protocols could be more easily implemented and managed from a single location. However, each node or service may require individual security configurations in a distributed environment. The shift toward a user-centric model in 6G also introduces novel security concerns. With 6G, users will gain unprecedented control over network resources and services, customizing configurations and privacy settings to suit their needs. While this empowers users and enhances the overall user experience, it also increases the likelihood of misconfigurations. Improperly configured network slices, insufficient security settings, or weak authentication practices can create significant vulnerabilities [10]. In addition, 6G will significantly increase the amount of sensitive personal data being transmitted and processed across the network, raising critical privacy concerns. As more industries adopt 6G technology—particularly sectors like healthcare, finance, and transportation—user data will include highly sensitive information, such as health records and financial transactions. This data must be adequately protected from unauthorized access or misuse, requiring the implementation of cutting-edge privacy-preserving technologies such as blockchain and Self-Sovereign-Identity (SSI). Balancing robust privacy protections with the seamless user experience that 6G promises will significantly challenge network designers and regulators.

12.2 Security Constraints and Vulnerabilities in 6G SBA Core Network

The security constraints and vulnerabilities of the 6G SBA core network are vast and multifaceted. This stems from the shift toward a more open, distributed, and user-centric architecture, which introduces numerous complexities and risks. As 6G becomes more advanced and interconnected, the potential attack surface expands significantly, creating opportunities for cyber threats to exploit weaknesses in the system. In analyzing these challenges, examining how API vulnerabilities, distributed architecture, data privacy, and user misconfigurations contribute to the overall security risks facing 6G networks is crucial.

12.2.1 API Vulnerabilities

The development of 6G introduces significant advances in network architecture, but with it comes an increased reliance on APIs [11], which presents opportunities and security challenges. APIs are critical for enabling the open and distributed nature of 6G, allowing different services, applications, and network functions to communicate seamlessly [12]. However, this openness also makes APIs prime cyberattack targets [13].

API vulnerabilities can arise from weak authentication mechanisms, inadequate encryption, or insecure communication channels. The consequences of API attacks include but are not limited to data exposure, compromised authentication mechanisms, and service interruptions [14]. In the context of 5G and beyond, works have already revealed that insecure APIs have been a point of exploitation [1, 4, 15], and with 6G, these vulnerabilities are expected to be even more pronounced [16, 17]. In particular, as APIs will serve as interfaces within the network and with third-party services, the security challenges multiply, necessitating stringent security protocols at every layer. API attacks can take various forms, such as MitM attacks, where an attacker intercepts data during transmission between services, or API injection attacks, where malicious code is inserted into the API request to manipulate data or compromise the system. These threats underscore the importance of implementing robust encryption, authentication, and access control measures. End-to-end encryption is essential to ensure that data transmitted through APIs is protected from eavesdropping or tampering, while strong authentication mechanisms, such as OAuth or mutual TLS, can help prevent unauthorized access. Moreover, API vulnerabilities can become even more concerning in distributed network environments like those seen in 6G, where services are spread across multiple edge nodes and cloud infrastructures. Each API call made between services represents a potential point of failure.

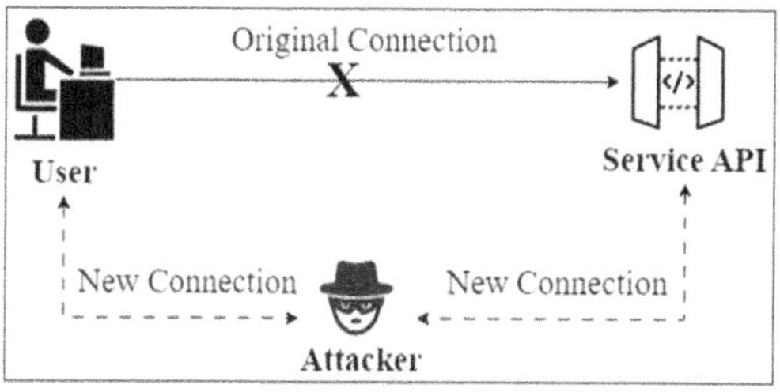

Figure 12.1. Cybersecurity attack in API.

The following are the most common cybersecurity attacks that can exploit APIs (see Figure 12.1) in 5G and beyond networks [4, 19]:

- MitM Attacks: the attacker intercepts the data transmitted between different network components, such as between the core network and third-party applications. This can lead to data breaches, manipulation of messages, or session hijacking. In 5G and beyond networks, as APIs are more widely used for communication between network slices, edge computing, and other services, MitM attacks can be more prevalent without proper encryption.
- API Injection Attacks: an attacker inserts malicious data or code into API requests, leading to unintended behavior or compromising network services. With the growing complexity of APIs in 6G, particularly those managing real-time data flows and edge computing services, injection attacks could lead to critical infrastructure disruptions.
- DoS and DDoS Attacks: an API is overwhelmed with a large volume of requests, causing it to slow down or crash, making the service unavailable to legitimate users. In a DDoS attack, multiple compromised devices (e.g., a botnet) are used to flood the API. Given that networks support many devices, including IoT and edge devices, APIs are particularly vulnerable to DDoS attacks that target the availability of network functions. Unprotected APIs can serve as easy entry points for such attacks, leading to disruptions in service.
- Broken Authentication and Session Management: APIs often manage authentication and session tokens to verify users and services. If attackers gain access to session tokens due to insecure APIs, they can hijack user sessions, impersonate legitimate users, and gain unauthorized access to sensitive network services. Broken authentication can occur if APIs fail to manage user credentials and tokens securely or if session expiration is not handled properly. Where there are diverse and distributed access points across devices, the risk of broken authentication increases.
- Cross-Site Scripting (XSS): attackers inject malicious scripts into an API response, which can then be executed in the user's browser. In scenarios where APIs serve web applications or user interfaces, an attacker can exploit

vulnerabilities in API responses to inject malicious code. This can lead to session hijacking, redirection to malicious websites, or stealing sensitive data. XSS is especially dangerous when APIs are exposed to third-party services, a common feature in 6G networks.

- Replay Attacks: an attacker intercepts valid API requests and resends them to the server, attempting to replicate valid actions or requests. Without mechanisms like timestamps or nonce (a random number used only once), replay attacks can exploit API sessions, such as resubmitting a payment request or gaining repeated access to services. Replay attacks can be especially dangerous in 6G environments where real-time data transfers, such as autonomous vehicle communication, rely on API exchanges.

12.2.2 Distributed Architecture and Increased Attack Surface

The distributed architecture of 5G and 6G networks significantly widens the attack surface, presenting new cybersecurity challenges [5]. 5G and 6G adopt a decentralized approach where core network functions are distributed across various edge nodes. This transformation introduces operational advantages like lower latency, enhanced scalability, and more flexible service deployment. However, it also opens up many potential entry points for cyberattacks. As each node, server, and API becomes a critical network component, attackers have more opportunities to exploit vulnerabilities, disrupt services, or steal data [20].

In 6G, where services are widely distributed across edge nodes and cloud environments, a DDoS attack targeting a key node could cause significant disruptions to critical network services. As 5G and 6G networks rely heavily on edge computing to deliver low-latency services, particularly for various applications [21] (e.g., autonomous driving), the impact of a DDoS attack could be devastating. By targeting the edge, attackers can disrupt data flow between devices and the cloud, degrade service performance, or cause complete service outages [22]. Moreover, 6G will further increase reliance on edge infrastructure, meaning that the attack surface for DDoS attacks will continue to expand. It has already been emphasized that 5G/6G networks need robust DDoS protection mechanisms, including AI-driven traffic filtering, anomaly detection, and adaptive firewalls [23, 24]. These technologies can help detect malicious traffic patterns early and mitigate the effects of DDoS attacks. AI and machine learning can analyze network traffic in real time, identifying anomalies that may indicate an ongoing attack [25, 26].

Moreover, the distributed edge computing environment, which brings network services closer to the user, also increases the number of potential targets for attackers. The more edge nodes that exist, the more points of vulnerability an attacker can target [27]. Unlike a centralized system where security can be more easily managed, distributed architectures create a challenge in implementing and enforcing consistent security policies across every node. Edge nodes may not have the same level of security or processing power as centralized cloud systems, making them more vulnerable to attacks. If an edge node is compromised, an attacker could access sensitive data, disrupt services, or even infiltrate the broader network. Securing edge nodes requires ensuring each node is properly configured, regularly updated, and equipped with strong access control measures [28].

Implementing consistent security policies across a distributed architecture is a significant challenge. In a 5G/6G network, different nodes and servers may be owned or operated by different entities, each with its own security protocols. Ensuring that security policies are enforced uniformly across these disparate infrastructures is crucial to maintaining the integrity of the overall network. This challenge is compounded by the fact that 6G networks will support various services with varying security requirements [29]. Some services, like those handling sensitive data, will require stringent security measures, including strong encryption, while others may prioritize low-latency or high-throughput performance over security. Therefore, orchestration tools are essential in ensuring that the right security policies are applied to each part of the network, depending on the service it delivers [30]. Automated orchestration and management tools powered by AI can help address this challenge by dynamically configuring and enforcing security policies across the network. These tools can ensure that security measures such as encryption, authentication, and access control are consistently applied across different network slices, cloud environments, and edge nodes.

Finally, in 6G networks, many core network functions will be virtualized and deployed as Virtualized Network Functions (also known as VNFs). On the one hand, this approach offers greater flexibility and scalability; on the other hand, it introduces new cybersecurity risks. Virtualization layers can become targets for attackers who may attempt to compromise the hypervisor or exploit vulnerabilities in VNFs to gain access to underlying network resources. This risk is particularly pronounced in 6G, where VNFs are expected to handle increasingly complex tasks (e.g., managing AI-driven services). Ensuring the security of VNFs requires robust isolation mechanisms to prevent attackers from moving laterally within the network and continuous monitoring for vulnerabilities at the virtualization layer [31].

12.2.3 Data Privacy and Interception Risks

In 5G and 6G networks, data privacy and interception risks are key concerns due to the scale and complexity of the infrastructure. As mobile networks evolve to accommodate a massive number of connected devices and the diverse services that characterize 6G, ensuring the protection of user data becomes more challenging.

The transition to SBA introduces new vulnerabilities and opens up various points where sensitive data can be intercepted or exposed. These risks require comprehensive security measures, as increased network nodes and distributed services magnify the potential attack surface.

One of the primary privacy concerns in 6G networks is the sheer volume of personal data transmitted and processed across the network [32]. As 6G enables more advanced applications (e.g., autonomous vehicles), the data generated from these services grows exponentially. Much of this data is personal or sensitive [33]. If improperly secured, malicious actors can intercept this data during transmission or be compromised at storage points across the network. In 6G, a distributed architecture shifts much of the data processing to the network's edge—closer to the end-user devices [34]. While this reduces latency and enhances performance, it also introduces more points of vulnerability. Each edge node becomes a potential target for attackers looking to intercept data as it moves between devices and the core network. In addition to edge nodes, network slices pose privacy risks if not properly secured [35]. Network slicing allows operators to allocate virtualized resources to different services or customers based on their needs, enabling faster, more tailored service delivery. However, with multiple network slices running simultaneously, each tailored for a specific use case, a security flaw in one slice could expose data traversing the entire network. Attackers could potentially exploit vulnerabilities in a low-security slice to gain access to more sensitive slices, compromising user data or even intercepting critical information such as authentication credentials.

Beyond malicious attacks, data interception can also occur due to poorly implemented security protocols or weak encryption standards. As more data flows across diverse and distributed infrastructure, it is crucial that strong encryption protocols are applied consistently [36]. Another layer of risk comes from quantum computing, which, although not yet widely available, could eventually break many of the encryption algorithms currently in use. As 6G networks are expected to be operational well into the future, the post-quantum security of encryption methods must be considered. Quantum computers could theoretically decrypt intercepted previously thought secure data, posing a significant future risk. The evolving nature of 6G networks also means that traditional identity and access management strategies may not be sufficient to protect against data interception. As the number of devices and users connecting to the network increases, ensuring that only authorized entities access data and services becomes more complex.

12.2.4 User Misconfiguration and Insider Threats

The introduction of 6G networks, with their advanced capabilities such as ultra-low latency, high-speed data transfer, and massive connectivity, presents transformative potential for various industries. However, the complexity of these networks also creates numerous security vulnerabilities that must be addressed. While much attention is paid to external threats (see above), user misconfigurations and insider threats remain significant and often underestimated risks. The aftermath of such a threat includes but is not limited to unintentional data breaches. In the context of 6G, the challenges posed by user misconfigurations and insider threats will likely grow.

The most common vulnerability in modern networks is human error, often misconfigurations [37]. This risk is heightened in complex, decentralized networks like 6G because the architecture requires multi-layered configurations, each with its own set of protocols and security mechanisms. Misconfigurations can occur when settings related to network access, data encryption, or firewall rules are incorrectly applied, inadvertently creating backdoors for cyberattacks [38–42]. In addition, The SBA and network slicing inherent to 6G present additional risks. In SBA, individual services are separated into microservices, each requiring its own configuration and security settings [43]. The entire network's security posture may be compromised if any of these services are misconfigured. Additionally, network slicing, which allows for creating multiple virtual networks on top of a single physical infrastructure, requires precise configuration to ensure each slice is properly isolated and secure. A single misstep in the configuration process [43] can expose sensitive data across different network slices or grant access to unauthorized entities, causing potentially widespread damage. Cloud misconfigurations [44] account for 15% of initial attack vectors in security breaches—the third most common initial attack vector in breaches. On average, these types of data breaches take 186 days to identify and yet another 65 to deal with. Misconfigurations like this cost companies around 3.86 million dollars in total costs [45]. Besides the unintentional misconfigurations, insider threats pose a serious risk to 6G networks. These occur when individuals with authorized access to the network misuse their privileges, either intentionally to cause harm or unintentionally through negligence [46]. The potential for insider threats is substantial in 6G, where millions of devices and users will be connected. Insider threats are particularly dangerous because they often come from trusted individuals with legitimate access to sensitive areas of the network, making detection more difficult.

12.3 Candidate Technologies

At this point, we present the technological pillars that jointly can provide a robust solution for the 6G network ecosystem. The proposed solutions have been designed on the grounds of well-established technologies (i.e., Blockchain, Smart Contracts, and SSI) with proven security properties.

12.3.1 Blockchain

Blockchain [47] is a decentralized, distributed ledger technology that enables secure, transparent, and immutable record-keeping of transactions across multiple participants without the need for a central authority or intermediary. Blockchain networks can be public, private, consortium, or hybrid. Public blockchains are decentralized and open to anyone, with no central authority, where anyone can participate in the consensus process. On the other hand, private blockchains are restricted and governed by a single organization, making them more centralized and suitable for enterprise use where control over participants is needed. Consortium blockchains are semi-decentralized, where a group of organizations collectively manage the blockchain, offering a balance between openness and control, often used in industries like finance or supply chains. Finally, hybrid blockchains combine elements of both public and private models, allowing certain data to be publicly accessible while keeping sensitive information private, enabling flexibility and control in specific use cases like healthcare or government services.

Blockchain's security is underpinned by cryptographic techniques such as hashing and digital signatures. Every participant on the blockchain network has a pair of public and private keys used to sign and verify transactions. These digital signatures ensure that only the rightful owner of a private key can authorize a transaction, providing a robust form of authentication. In addition, blockchain networks rely on consensus mechanisms [48] to validate transactions. These mechanisms ensure that only legitimate transactions are added to the blockchain and that the network is resilient to attacks. For 6G networks, which are expected to handle vast amounts of data and devices, blockchain's security features can help authenticate devices, secure data exchanges, and ensure that communication between network nodes remains tamper-proof. The consensus mechanism is the process by which blockchain networks agree on the ledger's state. These mechanisms are critical to ensuring that the blockchain remains decentralized and secure. Consensus mechanisms ensure that all nodes in the network agree on the transactions being added to the blockchain, thus maintaining the system's integrity.

Blockchain [49] works by creating a chain of blocks, each containing a list of transactions. Every block is cryptographically linked to the previous block, forming an unalterable chain of records. This cryptographic linkage, combined with the distributed nature of blockchain, provides enhanced security, transparency, and trust. The most defining feature of blockchain is its decentralized nature. Unlike traditional centralized databases that rely on a single entity to manage and validate transactions, blockchain networks operate on a peer-to-peer basis. Each node in the network maintains a copy of the entire blockchain, ensuring that the system remains operational even if some nodes go offline or attempt to manipulate data. Decentralization removes the need for intermediaries, reducing costs and the potential for manipulation or fraud. Another critical feature is the use of smart contracts [47, 49]. These are self-executing contracts with the terms of the agreement directly written into code. They automatically execute and enforce the contract's terms when predefined conditions are met. Smart contracts enable automation of transactions and processes, reducing the need for intermediaries and enhancing efficiency. In 6G networks, smart contracts could manage resource allocation, automate service provisioning, or enforce network security policies, providing real-time, trustworthy execution without human intervention.

Another critical feature is immutability, which refers to the fact that once data is recorded on the blockchain, it cannot be altered or deleted. This is achieved through the use of cryptographic hashing. Each block in the chain contains a unique cryptographic hash of the previous block, linking them together to ensure any attempt to alter the data in a block would require changing all subsequent blocks. Such a task would require controlling more than 50% of the network's computing power [50] This feature is critical for applications that require reliable and tamper-proof records (e.g., supply chain management, where tracking the origin and authenticity of products is mandatory). In 6G networks, immutability could be used to maintain accurate logs of data exchanges, device authentication, or even service provisioning. In addition, Blockchain promotes transparency by making all transaction data visible to every participant in the network. Each node maintains a complete copy of the ledger, and the transactions are verified by the consensus of the network participants before being added to the blockchain. While public blockchains are fully transparent, where all transaction details are viewable, permissioned blockchains used in enterprises can restrict access to certain information, allowing for a more controlled form of transparency. This transparency builds trust between participants, even when they do not know or fully trust one another. In telecommunications and 6G, blockchain can create a transparent environment for managing decentralized resources, such as network slices, or for enabling seamless, trust-based interactions between devices in IoT ecosystems.

12.3.2 Self-Sovereign-Identity

Self-Sovereign Identity [47], also known as SSI, is an example of a decentralized identity management system. Thanks to this, individuals or organizations can take ownership of and control their digital identities. As an additional benefit, SSI makes it easier to engage in selective attribute disclosure, a method for minimizing the disclosure of personal information. Additionally, it provides features that protect users' privacy, such as anonymity and the inability to be linked to an individual. With SSI, no central authority keeps ownership of users' data, which eliminates the

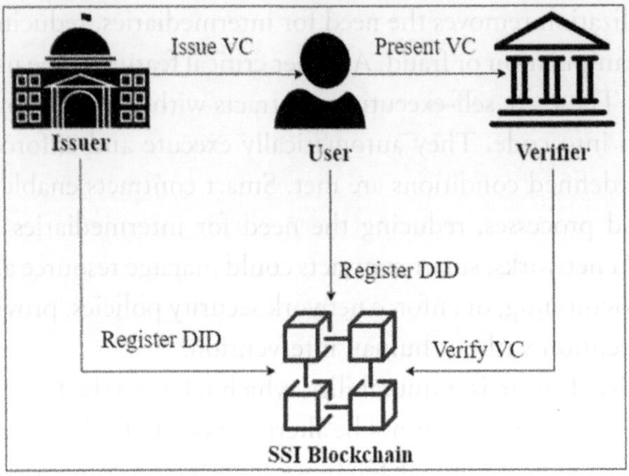

Figure 12.2. SSI functionalities.

requirement to provide it to other people when they request it. The user is the one that carries their data, and because of the encryption and distributed ledger technology that underpins it, the user can make assertions about its identity, which other entities can verify with cryptographic certainty. With the help of SSI, stakeholders in the 6G networks can exchange verified data in a way that is both automated and respectful of their privacy. This technique eliminates the need for manual data verification processes, which not only helps to prevent the disclosure of confidential information but also saves time. SSI is built on the foundation of Verifiable Credentials, also known as VCs. VCs were defined by the World Wide Web Consortium (W3C) as tamper-evident credentials with authorship that can be cryptographically confirmed [51]. This proposal was published as a formal recommendation. VCs can enhance interoperability and selective disclosure of information pertaining to its holders.

An issuer, a user, and a verifier are the three types of participants actively involved in the SSI framework (see Figure 12.2). Two fundamental features constitute the SSI: *(i)* the issuance of VC and *(ii)* the verification of VC. VC Issuance is the initial functionality that allows the user to obtain a VC from the issuer while acting in the holder's role. VC consists of tamper-evident claims and information that provide cryptographic proof of the authenticity of its issuer. *Claims* are statements a holder makes, such as the holder's birth year. Every VC is issued on the Decentralized Identifiers (DIDs) of its holder and issuer, serving as a public key within the blockchain ecosystem. A DID is a globally unique identifier. It is made up of a string of letters and numbers and is directly associated with a pair of public and secret keys simultaneously. Using the private key, the holder can access and manage their data. The holder is the only entity who should be aware of the private key, and its information should never be disclosed to any other individual. Concerning DIDs, the private key enables holders to demonstrate ownership and authorize authorization to share particular data. Blockchain, on the other hand, is a distributed ledger that maintains the public key that is connected with the DID of the VC's issuer public key. This public key can be safely shared with anybody to send and receive data. VCs that have been issued are stored in a secure manner in a digital identity wallet. This wallet is the location (for example, a mobile app) where holders maintain their VCs [52]. It is not possible to host these just within cell phones; rather, certain implementations permit their hosting within trusted computers.

The second functionality is VC Verification, in which the holder (acting as the prover) must demonstrate to the verifier that he holds accurate attributes without necessarily exposing the values included within those attributes. Establishing that the corresponding user is, in fact, in control of the provided identity is how this objective is accomplished through the utilization of zero-knowledge proofs. The verifier must check the Blockchain to view the VC's issuer (i.e., the DID of the VC's issuer) to validate the legitimacy of the venture capital. This can be done without the need to contact the issuer. When presenting a VC, the prover has the ability to choose which claims to reveal and which to keep hidden. An additional benefit of SSI is that it can accomplish unlinkability because the user uses a unique DID for each presentation.

12.4 Facing the Challenges

Blockchain and SSI technologies hold tremendous potential in addressing the cybersecurity challenges faced by 6G networks. These next-generation networks bring unprecedented speed, connectivity, and automation but also present new vulnerabilities, including identity management, data privacy, and system integrity. Security becomes an essential concern as 6G networks aim to create an open, distributed, and user-centric environment. In this section, we will explore how blockchain and SSI can be used to tackle the key cybersecurity challenges inherent in the evolving landscape of 6G networks.

12.4.1 Addressing the API Vulnerabilities

API vulnerabilities have been a persistent security issue in modern networks and are expected to pose even greater risks in 6G. APIs are essential communication bridges between applications, devices, and services in highly interconnected and distributed environments. As 6G networks introduce more open and decentralized interfaces, poorly secured APIs could become prime targets for attackers, enabling them to intercept sensitive data, manipulate services, or execute malicious code.

On the one hand, Blockchain's inherent decentralization and transparency can significantly enhance the security of API interactions in 6G networks. By using a distributed ledger, Blockchain can verify and record every API transaction, ensuring that each interaction between devices or services is cryptographically signed and time-stamped. This means that unauthorized modifications to API requests and responses can be easily detected, as all interactions are recorded in an immutable ledger accessible to network participants. Blockchain also offers the potential for smart contract-based APIs. Smart contracts can enforce predefined rules and security policies on API transactions. These contracts can automatically ensure that only authorized devices, applications, and users can access certain APIs. This would eliminate many common API vulnerabilities, such as unauthorized access, excessive data exposure, and parameter tampering, often exploited in traditional networks.

On the other hand, SSI is crucial in securing API access by providing a decentralized approach to identity management. In an SSI model, users and devices control their own cryptographically verified identities without needing a central authority. In the context of APIs, SSI can ensure that only authenticated and authorized entities gain access to the network's APIs. By integrating SSI, 6G networks can ensure that each API request is associated with a verifiable, cryptographically secure identity. This eliminates the risk of unauthorized devices or users accessing sensitive APIs, as each API request must be accompanied by verifiable credentials stored in decentralized identity wallets. Furthermore, since users have complete control over their identity data, the risk of identity theft or impersonation through compromised API endpoints is minimized.

12.4.2 Securing Distributed Architecture and Mitigating Increased Attack Surface

One of the defining characteristics of 6G networks is their distributed architecture, which significantly expands the network's attack surface. With numerous devices, edge nodes, and services distributed across the network, traditional security models that rely on centralized control are ineffective.

In a blockchain-based system, there is no single point of failure; instead, security is enforced collectively by all participants in the network. This decentralized security model is particularly effective in environments like 6G, where data and devices are spread across multiple nodes. Each 6G device or edge node could participate in the blockchain network, where security policies, configurations, and access controls are transparently managed and enforced through consensus. Using Blockchain's peer-to-peer validation, network participants can collectively verify the authenticity of each device, transaction, and service in real time, ensuring that no compromised device can subvert the network's integrity.

In traditional networks, a central authority manages identity verification, which becomes a bottleneck in decentralized environments. However, SSI can eliminate this bottleneck by giving each user and device control over their own VCs, which can be securely stored and shared without relying on a centralized authority. In 6G networks, SSI enables decentralized authentication across all devices and nodes, ensuring that only verified participants can access network resources and perform transactions. As SSI credentials are cryptographically secure, they can be validated by any party in the network, preventing unauthorized access. SSI also allows for granular access control, where devices and users can selectively share specific credentials to gain access to particular services. This reduces the attack surface, as entities only expose the minimal necessary information to perform a transaction, making it harder for attackers to exploit the system.

12.4.3 Addressing Data Privacy and Interception Risks

Data privacy and interception risks are heightened in 6G networks due to the sheer volume of sensitive data being transmitted across the network. In addition to the potential for data breaches, there is the risk of eavesdropping, where attackers intercept data as it moves between devices, edge nodes, or applications. Given the reliance on edge computing and multi-access edge networks, data no longer resides in centralized data centers but is processed closer to the user, increasing its vulnerability to interception.

Blockchain's immutability and encryption mechanisms offer strong guarantees for ensuring the integrity and confidentiality of data in 6G networks. By recording each data transaction in an immutable ledger, Blockchain ensures that any attempt to modify or tamper with data is immediately detectable. This is particularly valuable in 6G environments where data might traverse multiple edge nodes before reaching its final destination. Furthermore, Blockchain can facilitate data encryption, ensuring that only authorized entities can access the transmitted information. Even if an attacker intercepts the data in transit, they cannot decrypt it without the proper cryptographic keys, which are securely managed through blockchain-based key distribution systems.

Next, one of the key features of SSI is its focus on data minimization and user control over personal information. In an SSI framework, users can selectively share only the necessary attributes required to perform a transaction, minimizing the risk of data exposure. This feature is invaluable in the context of 6G networks, where personal data is constantly being transmitted between devices, applications, and services. SSI allows users to control what information is shared and with whom, using cryptographically verifiable claims. This ensures that even if an attacker gains access to the transmitted data, they cannot infer sensitive information, as only minimal and necessary data points would be revealed.

As 6G networks introduce unprecedented connectivity, speed, and decentralization, they also bring cybersecurity challenges. Blockchain and SSI technologies offer powerful solutions to address these issues by providing decentralized, cryptographically secure frameworks for managing identities, securing data, and enforcing security policies. Blockchain's immutability, transparency, and distributed consensus mechanisms make it an ideal solution for securing API interactions, enforcing decentralized security policies, and maintaining data integrity in 6G networks. Meanwhile, SSI empowers users and devices with control over their identities, reducing the risk of unauthorized access and protecting personal data through selective disclosure and cryptographic proofs. Together, these technologies offer a robust, decentralized security architecture that aligns with the distributed, open nature of 6G networks. By integrating Blockchain and SSI, 6G networks can become more resilient, secure, and privacy-preserving, laying the foundation for a safer and more trustworthy digital future.

Acknowledgments

This Chapter has received funding from the European Commission's Horizon Europe programs under grant agreements No. 101131292 (AIAS) and No. 101139031 (SAFE6G).

References

[1] Tang, Q., Ermis, O., Nguyen, C. D., De Oliveira, A., & Hirtzig, A. (2022). A systematic analysis of 5g networks with a focus on 5g core security. IEEE Access, 10, 18298–18319.

[2] Dolente, F., Garroppo, R. G., & Pagano, M. (2023). A Vulnerability Assessment of Open-Source Implementations of Fifth-Generation Core Network Functions. Future Internet, 16(1), 1.

[3] Wehbe, N., Alameddine, H. A., Pourzandi, M., & Assi, C. (2024). Empowering 5G SBA security: Time series transformer for HTTP/2 anomaly detection. Computers & Security, 104114.

[4] Porambage, P., Gür, G., Osorio, D. P. M., Liyanage, M., Gurtov, A., & Ylianttila, M. (2021). The roadmap to 6G security and privacy. IEEE Open Journal of the Communications Society, 2, 1094–1122.

[5] Nguyen, V. L., Lin, P. C., Cheng, B. C., Hwang, R. H., & Lin, Y. D. (2021). Security and privacy for 6G: A survey on prospective technologies and challenges. *IEEE Communications Surveys & Tutorials*, *23*(4), 2384–2428.

[6] Wang, M., Zhu, T., Zhang, T., Zhang, J., Yu, S., & Zhou, W. (2020). Security and privacy in 6G networks: New areas and new challenges. *Digital Communications and Networks*, *6*(3), 281–291.

[7] Kazmi, S. H. A., Hassan, R., Qamar, F., Nisar, K., & Ibrahim, A. A. A. (2023). Security concepts in emerging 6G communication: Threats, countermeasures, authentication techniques and research directions. *Symmetry*, *15*(6), 1147.

[8] Kehelwala, J., Siriwardhana, Y., Hewa, T., Liyanage, M., & Ylianttila, M. (2024, June). Decentralized Learning for 6G Security: Open Issues and Future Directions. In *2024 Joint European Conference on Networks and Communications & 6G Summit (EuCNC/6G Summit)* (pp. 1175–1180). IEEE.

[9] Ferrag, M. A., Friha, O., Kantarci, B., Tihanyi, N., Cordeiro, L., Debbah, M., ... & Choo, K. K. R. (2023). Edge learning for 6G-enabled Internet of Things: A comprehensive survey of vulnerabilities, datasets, and defenses. *IEEE Communications Surveys & Tutorials.*

[10] Mao, B., Liu, J., Wu, Y., & Kato, N. (2023). Security and privacy on 6g network edge: A survey. *IEEE communications surveys & tutorials*, *25*(2), 1095–1127.

[11] Beyond bit-pipes – new opportunities on the 6G platform, Ericsson, Online: https://www.ericsson.com/en/reports-and-papers/ericsson-technology-review/articles/6g-platform [Last access: 23/9/2024].

[12] 6G Security – drivers and needs, Ericsson White Papers, Online: https://www.ericsson.com/49c1cd/assets/local/reports-papers/white-papers/2024/6g-security-drivers-and-needs.pdf [Last access: 23/9/2024].

[13] Oliveira, D. S., Lin, T., Rahman, M. S., Akefirad, R., Ellis, D., Perez, E., ... & Brun, Y. (2018). {API} blindspots: Why experienced developers write vulnerable code. In *Fourteenth Symposium on Usable Privacy and Security (SOUPS 2018)* (pp. 315–328).

[14] Khan, M. S., Siam, R. S. F., & Adnan, M. A. (2024). A framework for checking and mitigating the security vulnerabilities of cloud service RESTful APIs. *Service Oriented Computing and Applications*, 1–22.

[15] Bjerre, S. A., Blomsterberg, M. W. K., & Andersen, B. (2022, October). 5G attacks and countermeasures. In *2022 25th International Symposium on Wireless Personal Multimedia Communications (WPMC)* (pp. 285-290). IEEE.

[16] Siriwardhana, Y., Porambage, P., Liyanage, M., & Ylianttila, M. (2021, June). AI and 6G security: Opportunities and challenges. In *2021 Joint European Conference on Networks and Communications & 6G Summit (EuCNC/6G Summit)* (pp. 616–621). IEEE.

[17] Je, D., Jung, J., & Choi, S. (2021). Toward 6G security: technology trends, threats, and solutions. *IEEE Communications Standards Magazine*, *5*(3), 64–71.

[18] Martin-Lopez, A., Segura, S., & Ruiz-Cortés, A. (2022, November). Online testing of RESTful APIs: Promises and challenges. In *Proceedings of the 30th ACM Joint European Software Engineering Conference and Symposium on the Foundations of Software Engineering* (pp. 408–420).

[19] Soltani, S., Shojafar, M., Amanlou, A., & Tafazolli, R. (2024). Intelligent Control in 6G Open RAN: Security Risk or Opportunity?. *arXiv preprint arXiv:2405.08577*.

[20] Ramezanpour, K., & Jagannath, J. (2022). Intelligent zero trust architecture for 5G/6G networks: Principles, challenges, and the role of machine learning in the context of O-RAN. *Computer Networks*, *217*, 109358.

[21] Alotaibi, B. (2023). A survey on industrial Internet of Things security: Requirements, attacks, AI-based solutions, and edge computing opportunities. *Sensors*, *23*(17), 7470.

[22] Uddin, R., Kumar, S. A., & Chamola, V. (2024). Denial of service attacks in edge computing layers: Taxonomy, vulnerabilities, threats and solutions. *Ad Hoc Networks*, *152*, 103322.

[23] Cunha, J., Ferreira, P., Castro, E. M., Oliveira, P. C., Nicolau, M. J., Núñez, I., ... & Serôdio, C. (2024). Enhancing Network Slicing Security: Machine Learning, Software-Defined Networking, and Network Functions Virtualization-Driven Strategies. *Future Internet*, *16*(7), 226.

[24] Karatisoglou, M., Farao, A., Bolgouras, V., & Xenakis, C. (2022, June). BRIDGE: BRIDGing the gap bEtween CTI production and consumption. In *2022 14th International Conference on Communications (COMM)* (pp. 1–6). IEEE.

[25] Petihakis, G., Farao, A., Bountakas, P., Sabazioti, A., Polley, J., & Xenakis, C. (2024, July). AIAS: AI-ASsisted cybersecurity platform to defend against adversarial AI attacks. In *Proceedings of the 19th International Conference on Availability, Reliability and Security* (pp. 1–7).

[26] Pantelakis, V., Bountakas, P., Farao, A., & Xenakis, C. (2023, August). Adversarial machine learning attacks on multiclass classification of iot network traffic. In *Proceedings of the 18th International Conference on Availability, Reliability and Security* (pp. 1–8).

[27] Xiao, Y., Jia, Y., Liu, C., Cheng, X., Yu, J., & Lv, W. (2019). Edge computing security: State of the art and challenges. *Proceedings of the IEEE*, *107*(8), 1608–1631.

[28] Ravidas, S., Lekidis, A., Paci, F., & Zannone, N. (2019). Access control in Internet-of-Things: A survey. *Journal of Network and Computer Applications*, *144*, 79–101.

[29] Zhang, Z., Xiao, Y., Ma, Z., Xiao, M., Ding, Z., Lei, X., ... & Fan, P. (2019). 6G wireless networks: Vision, requirements, architecture, and key technologies. *IEEE vehicular technology magazine, 14*(3), 28–41.

[30] De Sousa, N. F. S., Perez, D. A. L., Rosa, R. V., Santos, M. A., & Rothenberg, C. E. (2019). Network service orchestration: A survey. *Computer Communications, 142*, 69–94.

[31] Repetto, M. (2023). Adaptive monitoring, detection, and response for agile digital service chains. *Computers & Security, 132*, 103343.

[32] Tripi, G., Iacobelli, A., Rinieri, L., & Prandini, M. (2024). Security and Trust in the 6G Era: Risks and Mitigations. *Electronics, 13*, 2162.

[33] Hexa-X and data protection evolution in 6G, Ericsson Blog, Online: https://www.ericsson.com/en/blog/2023/10/hexa-x-and-data-protection-evolution-in-6g [Last access:23/9/2024].

[34] Ishtiaq, M., Saeed, N., & Khan, M. A. (2021). Edge computing in IoT: A 6G perspective. *arXiv preprint arXiv:2111.08943.*

[35] Singh, V. P., Singh, M. P., Hegde, S., & Gupta, M. (2024). Security in 5G Network Slices: Concerns and Opportunities. *IEEE Access.*

[36] Wang, Y., Kang, X., Li, T., Wang, H., Cheng, C., & Lei, Z. (2023). SIX-Trust for 6G: Towards a Secure and Trustworthy Future Network. *IEEE Access.*

[37] Petihakis, G., Kiritsis, D., Farao, A., Bountakas, P., Panou, A., & Xenakis, C. (2023, August). A Bring Your Own Device security awareness survey among professionals. In *Proceedings of the 18th International Conference on Availability, Reliability and Security* (pp. 1–10).

[38] Yungaicela-Naula, N. M., Sharma, V., & Scott-Hayward, S. (2024). Misconfiguration in O-RAN: Analysis of the impact of AI/ML. *Computer Networks*, 110455.

[39] Muñoz, A., Farao, A., Correia, J. R. C., & Xenakis, C. (2021). P2ISE: preserving project integrity in CI/CD based on secure elements. Information, 12(9), 357.

[40] Suciu, G., Farao, A., Bernardinetti, G., Palamà, I., Sachian, M. A., Vulpe, A., … & Xenakis, C. (2022). SAMGRID: security authorization and monitoring module based on SealedGRID platform. *Sensors, 22*(17), 6527.

[41] Kalderemidis, I., Farao, A., Bountakas, P., Panda, S., & Xenakis, C. (2022, August). GTM: Game Theoretic Methodology for optimal cybersecurity defending strategies and investments. In Proceedings of the 17th International Conference on Availability, Reliability and Security (pp. 1–9).

[42] Farao, A., Panda, S., Menesidou, S. A., Veliou, E., Episkopos, N., Kalatzantonakis, G., … & Xenakis, C. (2020). SECONDO: A platform for cybersecurity investments and cyber insurance decisions. In Trust, Privacy and Security in Digital Business: 17th International Conference, TrustBus 2020,

Bratislava, Slovakia, September 14–17, 2020, Proceedings 17 (pp. 65–74). Springer International Publishing.

[43] Scalise, P., Boeding, M., Hempel, M., Sharif, H., Delloiacovo, J., & Reed, J. (2024). A Systematic Survey on 5G and 6G Security Considerations, Challenges, Trends, and Research Areas. *Future Internet, 16*(3), 67.

[44] 40+ Alarming Cloud Security Statistics for 2024, strongdm, Online: https://www.strongdm.com/blog/cloud-security-statistics#:~:text=just%20internal%20mistakes.-,Cloud%20misconfigurations%20account%20for%2015%25%20of%20initial%20attack%20vectors%20in,another%2065%20to%20deal%20with. [Last access: 23/9/2024].

[45] PurpleSec, 2024 Cybersecurity Statistics, The Ultimate List Of Cybersecurity Stats Data, & Trends, Online: https://purplesec.us/resources/cybersecurity-statistics/ [Last access: 23/9/2024].

[46] Pandey, D., Goyal, S., Bhaumik, K., Suneja, S., Sharma, M., & Dadheech, P. D. (2024). A Systematic Review of Security Issues in 6G Networks and Communication. *Security Issues and Solutions in 6G Communications and Beyond*, 1–11.

[47] Farao, A., Paparis, G., Panda, S., Panaousis, E., Zarras, A., & Xenakis, C. (2024). INCHAIN: a cyber insurance architecture with smart contracts and self-sovereign identity on top of blockchain. *International Journal of Information Security, 23*(1), 347–371.

[48] Bamakan, S. M. H., Motavali, A., & Bondarti, A. B. (2020). A survey of blockchain consensus algorithms performance evaluation criteria. Expert Systems with Applications, 154, 113385.

[49] Voudouris, A., Farao, A., Panou, A., Polley, J., & Xenakis, C. (2024, July). Integrating Hyperledger Fabric with Satellite Communications: A Revolutionary Approach for Enhanced Security and Decentralization in Space Networks. In *Proceedings of the 19th International Conference on Availability, Reliability and Security* (pp. 1–8).

[50] Sayeed, S., & Marco-Gisbert, H. (2019). Assessing blockchain consensus and security mechanisms against the 51% attack. *Applied sciences, 9*(9), 1788.

[51] World Wide Web Consortium (W3C).: Verifiable credentials data model v1.1. Online: https://www.w3.org/TR/vc-data-model/ [Last Access: 23/09/2024]

[52] Farao, A., Veroni, E., Ntantogian, C., & Xenakis, C. (2021). P4G2Go: a privacy-preserving scheme for roaming energy consumers of the smart grid-to-go. Sensors, 21(8), 2686.

DOI: 10.1561/9781638285076.ch13

Chapter 13

Towards a Framework and Methodology Adherent to the EU Cyber Resilience Act - The CERTIFY Project (Extended Version)

By Sara Nieves Matheu Garcia, Stefano Sebastio, Matteo Molé, Roberto Cascella and Antonio Skarmeta

The rapid expansion of the Internet of Things (IoT) has led to a critical increase in the volume of connected devices, introducing significant security and privacy challenges across industries. As devices become embedded in essential systems and daily life, their inherent vulnerabilities can have far-reaching impacts. Addressing these risks, the European Union's Cyber Resilience Act (CRA) proposes rigorous requirements for establishing a baseline for the cybersecurity of IoT products through their entire lifecycle. The CERTIFY project offers a comprehensive framework that aligns with CRA's objectives, enabling IoT stakeholders to manage cybersecurity from initial design to decommissioning. The CERTIFY's lifecycle methodology encompasses phases such as secure design, bootstrapping, continuous monitoring, update management, and eventual decommissioning or repurposing. A key element of the CERTIFY's approach is the use of standardized security practices and tools, including the extended Manufacturer Usage Description (MUD) framework and advanced cryptographic solutions. These elements ensure that device behavior adheres to security policies and that updates are both transparent and traceable, facilitated by blockchain and other distributed ledger technologies. The CERTIFY architecture also enables real-time risk assessment, with dynamic threat detection and rapid response to vulnerabilities, helping maintain a secure operational state. Through the deployment of active monitoring and security intelligence sharing, CERTIFY improves resilience against emerging cyber threats and promotes compliance with evolving regulations like the CRA. This chapter examines the CERTIFY's methodology and highlights its application through use cases, such as a connected cabin system, to illustrate the framework's effectiveness in addressing CRA regulatory and operational challenges. The CERTIFY project represents a proactive, holistic approach to IoT security, empowering stakeholders to respond to the demands of an interconnected world and establish lasting, lifecycle-oriented security for IoT ecosystems.

13.1 Introduction

Envisioned decades ago, ubiquitous computing [1] is now a consolidated reality, as digital products are no longer confined to business settings but are seamlessly integrated into consumer and critical application environments. Smart and Internet of Things (IoT) devices are not only embedded in homes and workplaces, but they also underpin essential functions across sectors like healthcare, transportation, and energy. Given the widespread role of these devices and the rapid development cycles focused on cost reduction, they have become prime targets for cyber threats. High-profile attacks—such as those affecting the Colonial Pipeline oil system [2], Marriott hotels [3], and major hospital systems in the United States [4]—are stark examples of the vulnerabilities that connected devices introduce when security practices are inadequate. These incidents underscore the need for robust regulatory frameworks and security protocols that protect devices and systems throughout their lifecycle.

In fact, cyber incidents were historically not disclosed unless they were causing major impacts to the public until the entry into force of recent regulations [5, 6] and [7]. From that point on an already galloping trend manifested more openly, also allowing the appearance of public reporting services (e.g., [8] and [9]). Cybercrime continues to grow, with global annual costs projected to exceed 15.63 trillion euros by 2029 [10]. In response to this alarming trend, the European Commission proposed the Cyber Resilience Act (CRA) [11] in September 2022, with the goal of strengthening cybersecurity and resilience across all products with digital components. By placing responsibility on manufacturers to secure devices throughout their entire lifecycle, the CRA seeks to ensure that devices are secure by design, fit for purpose, and protected against emerging threats.

In this context, the Horizon Europe CERTIFY project [12]—active security for connected device lifecycles—presents a cohesive approach to managing IoT device security. The CERTIFY's mission is to provide a methodological, technological, and organizational framework that ensures security throughout the lifecycle of connected devices. The project's efforts align closely with current EU regulations, particularly the CRA, by developing and testing practical use cases that support regulatory objectives. This regulatory alignment is crucial, as it positions CERTIFY to not only demonstrate compliance but also to address real-world security challenges by fostering coherence with the evolving EU policy landscape.

The CERTIFY's methodology encompasses the entire lifecycle of a connected device, from its initial design and risk assessment to secure decommissioning or repurposing. The project's approach is based on the security by design principle, which incorporates security protocols and cryptographic controls at the outset. By embedding these measures during the design and development stages, CERTIFY ensures that devices are prepared to handle threats before deployment. Once a device is deployed, CERTIFY facilitates secure bootstrapping, continuous monitoring, and adaptive reconfiguration to maintain device integrity and security, even as new vulnerabilities emerge. This approach mitigates risks in real-time and minimizes the need for costly and complex retroactive measures.

A defining aspect of the CERTIFY's framework is its collaborative approach, allowing multiple stakeholders—such as auditors, manufacturers, and end-users—to contribute to a shared security ecosystem. The framework supports ongoing communication and feedback loops that improve risk assessment and response times. Through advanced technologies such as the extended Manufacturer Usage Description (MUD) [13] files and Zero Trust Architecture principles, CERTIFY provides stakeholders with a secure, and standardized method for managing device interactions and enforcing access controls. This integrated approach allows stakeholders to monitor, update, and reconfigure devices as needed, creating a flexible security model that adapts itself to changes in the threat landscape. Furthermore, the CERTIFY's architecture enables Distributed Ledger Technology (DLT), such as blockchain, which records every event, update, or configuration change related to the device, providing an immutable and transparent record that reinforces trust among users and regulatory bodies.

The project's engagement with policy and standardization activities throughout the EU demonstrates its commitment to regulatory alignment. The CERTIFY's consortium actively participates in discussions on cybersecurity regulations, ensuring that the project's solutions and use cases reflect current legal requirements and contribute valuable feedback to the regulatory process. This approach not only strengthens the project's alignment with EU policies but also enables sharing challenges linked to their practical roll out, for instance the broader industry's need for guidance on implementing the CRA's requirements in practical settings. The CERTIFY's use cases demonstrate a variety of scenarios, from connected cabins in aviation to smart manufacturing systems and tracking of artworks, where high levels of connectivity and data sensitivity demand rigorous security practices. Each scenario illustrates how the CERTIFY's lifecycle management can support compliance and protect devices from real-world threats.

In this chapter, we delve into the CERTIFY project's lifecycle methodology and its alignment with the objectives of the CRA. Section 13.2 outlines the CERTIFY framework, detailing its structured approach to IoT lifecycle management. In Section 13.3, we present a comprehensive use case—the connected cabin system in aviation—as a demonstration of the CERTIFY methodology in a high-connectivity, high-security environment. Section 13.4 discusses initial observations on the feasibility of deploying CERTIFY as a pilot framework aligned with CRA requirements, exploring how its approach addresses regulatory and operational challenges. Finally, Section 13.5 concludes with insights into the broader implications of CERTIFY for IoT security, regulatory compliance, and the advancement of secure, resilient IoT ecosystems.

13.2 The CERTIFY Project

The CERTIFY's goal is to provide to IoT stakeholders (e.g., auditors, manufacturers, users, Information Sharing and Analysis Centers - ISACs), with tools and strategies they need to ensure a high level of security. The project takes a collaborative and decentralized approach, helping stakeholders identify, assess, and respond to security threats throughout the lifecycle of connected devices. A key point of the CERTIFY approach is the sharing of security information and evidence among relevant parties, allowing for continuous risk assessments and faster responses to new vulnerabilities.

The project is based on international standards and frameworks such as MUD files and Zero Trust architecture [14]. These foundations enable CERTIFY to support ongoing security evaluations, enabling stakeholders to detect threats in real-time, securely update devices, and reconfigure them as necessary. The CERTIFY's focus is on providing security by design and ensuring that it can be monitored and updated securely as new risks emerge. This holistic approach also facilitates future recertification processes by streamlining the collection of security evidence throughout the operational life of a device.

13.2.1 Certify Framework

An abstract representation of the CERTIFY framework is depicted in Figure 13.1, where, for the sake of clarity, only the main interactions are reported.

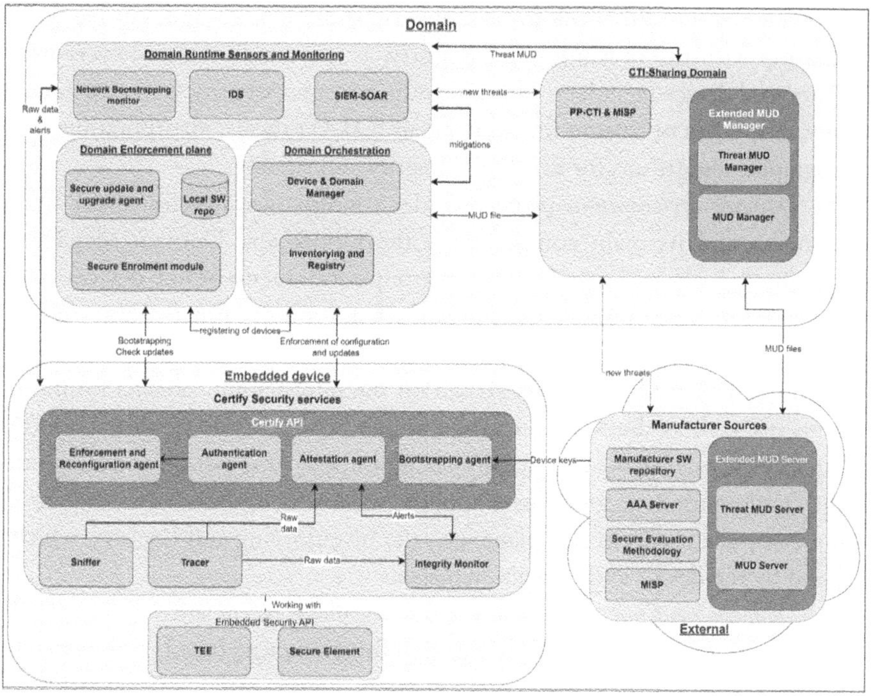

Figure 13.1. CERTIFY architecture.

The CERTIFY architecture is organized into six "domains" or "planes" based on the functionality.

The *Embedded device* plane provides the CERTIFY security services built on top of hardware functionalities to instantiate and maintain a secure environment. It characterizes the IoT platform by means of the API (Application Programming Interface) and services of CERTIFY. The CERTIFY security services include elements needed to support operations such as configuration, bootstrapping, upgrading, and monitoring. Instead, the low-level components part of the embedded security API, i.e., the Secure Element (SE) [15] and the Trusted Execution Environment (TEE) [16], provide the necessary enablers to guarantee the security of the processes inside the IoT Device.

The *Domain enforcement* plane includes services for the secure deployment of the device within the domain and the application of updates on the device. One core component of this plane is the Secure Enrollment module, responsible for the registration of the devices in the domain and the issuance of the required cryptographic material to enable the creation of Direct Anonymous Attestation (DAA) [17] signatures. Instead, the Secure update and upgrade agent provides a graphical user interface where security administrators can visualize registered software and devices, upload the software to the repository, and trigger the software update process. It also provides features to check for available updates. This component has a close relationship with the Inventory and Registry, as it is used to record every event, firmware, and device metadata. This integration ensures security, transparency, and an unbroken chain of trust in the over-the-air (OTA) process, incorporating secure cryptographic algorithms for firmware integrity and signing.

The *Domain orchestration* plane provides coordination functionalities within the domain, and its main component is the Device and Domain Manager. It focuses on the high-level management of groups or domains of IoT devices. These groups could be based on various criteria, such as location, functionality, or other attributes. In particular, the Device and Domain Manager coordinates enforcement and reconfiguration of IoT devices based on the information received from other components such as the MUD manager or the SIEM-SOAR (Security Information and Event Management - Security Orchestration, Automation and Response). All the configurations (e.g., policies applied, version of updates) are stored in the second component part of this plane, i.e., the Inventorying and Registry, which is managed by the device and domain manager.

The *Domain runtime sensors and monitoring* plane offers software-based solutions for monitoring, detection, and decision functionalities based on the information received from the device and other domain components. The Network Bootstrapping Monitor and the Intrusion Detection System (IDS) receive data from the CERTIFY API in the IoT device regarding the network activity in different phase of the lifecycle. They generate an alert if the network bootstrapping behavior differs from the expected one or if a threat has been detected at runtime, respectively. Alerts are sent to the SIEM-SOAR component for aggregation and correlation analysis with other raw data and alerts. Also, this plane interacts with the Cyber Threat Intelligence plane, since discovered threats can be shared with the MISP (Malware Information Sharing Platform), and possible mitigations can be received in the form of threat MUD files.

The *Cyber Threat Intelligence (CTI)* plane provides services for ensuring privacy-preserving security information sharing like vulnerabilities, mitigations or recommended configurations. A central pillar of this plane is constituted by the Privacy-Preserving CTI (PP-CTI) system, which is responsible for anonymizing sensitive data and attributes in cyber threat reports. For responding to identified threats, the PP-CTI combines the MUD [7] with the Threat MUD server [10] as threat signaling mechanism. The MUD is a standardized software description defined by the Internet Engineering Task Force (IETF) Request for Comment (RFC) 8520, that allows IoT manufacturers to advertise device specifications and supported communication patterns. In particular, CERTIFY extends the MUD model to accommodate finer-grained security aspects and diverse security policies. These encompass extended network access control, channel protection, data protection,

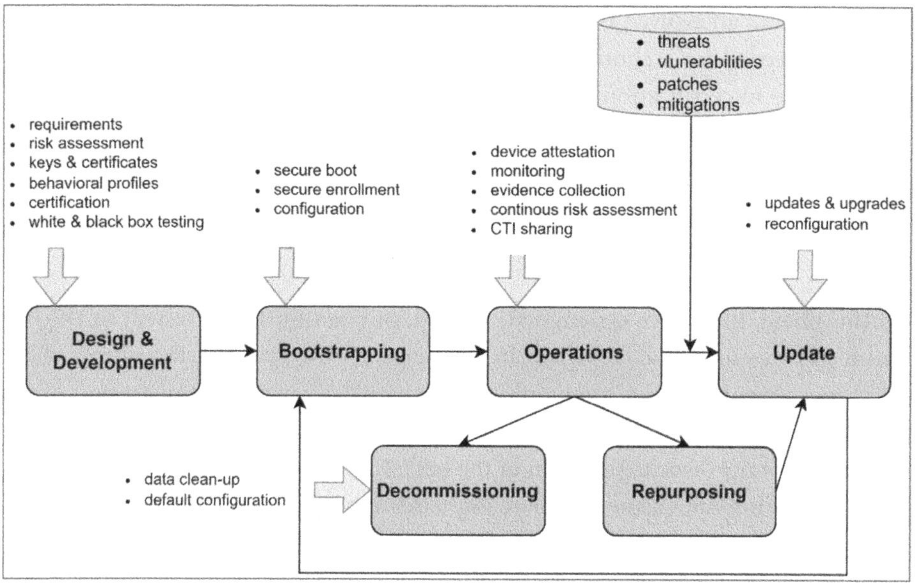

Figure 13.2. CERTIFY lifecycle methodology.

and authorization policies [8]. In this regard, while a standard MUD server offers guidelines for allowed or restricted network activities for each device, a Threat MUD server would allow to incorporate real-time or near real-time threat information as provided by the PP-CTI.

Finally, the external plane integrates all the manufacturer services that, even if not strictly part of the framework, are exploited by CERTIFY. In particular, it includes services for security assessment and certification, CTI sharing, device authentication, and MUD generation and storage.

13.2.2 Certify Lifecycle Methodology

The CERTIFY lifecycle (pictorially represented in Figure 13.2) starts with the design and deployment of the device. At that time requirements are considered, the risk assessment is performed considering the target application domain, and a certification may be requested. Moreover, keys, certificates and behavioral profiles used during the enrollment are built and securely stored by the manufacturer (some information is stored on the device while others remotely). Once deployed, the device bootstrapping takes care of the secure boot, enrollment, and configuration in the domain. During operations, device attestation and monitoring are performed to identify the presence of any suspicious event. New threats, vulnerability and patches may be identified by exploiting internal and external information. These may summon update, upgrade and reconfiguration. Changes performed on the device and an evolved threat landscape are also considered while collecting the evidence needed for a continuous risk assessment and the potential need to trigger a device re-certification. A complete lifecycle includes also the case of device repurposing (i.e., when it no longer fulfills a given purpose) and decommissioning (requiring the proper application of data cleaning policies and default reconfiguration).

13.2.2.1 Manufacturing: Design and Development

In this phase, the device is designed, created, programmed, and tested, so the initial level of security is established. In this stage, all the actors in the supply chain (i.e., component designer, integrator, software and library developer) are part of the process, while the manufacturer is responsible for carrying out the initial security evaluation of the device. Adoption of the best security practices for design, production and testing can ensure adequate implementation.

In this area, there is vast research and documentation effort to summarize all existing attacks. Nonetheless, many more are found continuously. Furthermore, there is difficulty in defining a common standard methodology to describe how security evaluation and certification must be done. The wide variety and heterogeneity of methodologies, mechanisms, standards, and products generates a complex landscape of solutions. Therefore, it is quite unclear which security aspects should be considered to guarantee an adequate security level. In this context, performing a comprehensive comparison is unfeasible, as different schemes use their own metrics, especially when products are evaluated under different national schemes or approaches, or when they include some subjective or difficulty calculating metrics (e.g., Common Weakness Scoring System, CWSS, uses likelihood). The Cybersecurity Act (CSA) and the CRA present a pioneer initiative to foster a European Cybersecurity assessment of product and services. These regulations, in addition to the directive on security of network and information systems (NIS) [18] and the General Data Protection Regulation (GDPR) represent the four main pillars for cybersecurity in Europe.

However, as new vulnerability and threats are continuously discovered, defining a comprehensive and common standard methodology for cybersecurity testing, evaluation and certification becomes cumbersome. On the one hand, the wide variety of standards, certification schemes, and requirements hardens the goal of an objective comparison on the security achieved by products and a comparison between certified products. On the other hand, the intended use and context (regulation, domain, etc.) determine the security level required for a particular product and requirements to be considered. This problem is exacerbated by the out-of-date certificates offering a false sense of security due to zero-day vulnerabilities and evolving threats. The dynamism inherent to security makes necessary agile and dynamic approaches to manage the security of a product throughout its lifecycle. Consequently, it is also necessary to consider continuous assessment and adopt dynamic labels capable of showing in real time the actual security level. Current certification schemas and approaches are not neglecting this dynamism, however Common Criteria (CC), Commercial Product Assurance (CPA) or Certification de Sécurité de Premier Niveau (CSPN), to name a few, require a complete recertification in case of a security change, involving high money losses and time [19].

Toward this end, CERTIFY considers a security evaluation and certification approach based on modelling, allowing to test the design of the device from the very beginning and automating the security evaluation process as indicated in previous section, combining security testing and risk assessment towards an objective and automated assessment. In CERTIFY, the secure evaluation methodology is supported by the Cyberpass tool,[1] a cloud-based platform taking as input security requirements and suggesting an evaluation methodology that starts with the self-declaration/self-assessment, allowing the manufacturer to answer the questionnaire based on these security requirements.

Although in general the results of the security assessment are used only to certify the security of the device, CERTIFY explores approaches to benefit from this information during the deployment and operation of the device. In this sense, the evaluation results can be embedded in a behavioral profile associated to different levels of security with some recommendations (polices) to consider during the operation phase of the product. This profile reduces the attack surface to the allowed behaviors, and it can be also used to monitor suspicious behaviors during the operation phase. This activity interoperates and makes use of the results of the previous evaluation. Indeed, the behavioral profile designed in CERTIFY, which is based on extending the MUD standard [20, 21] is generated from the security results containing both security recommendations from the manufacturer and from the security certification to perform a secure deployment. In particular, the use of MUD is being extended to create augmented security profiles, to govern the intended communications of IoT devices throughout their lifecycle.

Once the certification process is finished, the MUD is signed by the Certification Authority (CA), and the manufacturer can publish it on its MUD server to be accessible to any buyer of the product. The MUD URL together with the device identity is then stored inside the device for its secure deployment.

To provide support for the following phases of the lifecycle, CERTIFY adopts formally proven authentication and cryptographic protocols and robust isolation mechanisms enabled by open hardware architectures and trusted computing

1. https://www.cyber-pass.eu/

standards. The architecture of the IoT device includes three strategic enablers: the SE, the TEE, and the Embedded Security API acting as an interface for these low-level components. The SE is a dedicated secure and physical tamper-resistant micro-controller allowing protection against high-level software and hardware attacks. Such an element, when present, will constitute the hardware engine, assuring support for the securitization at a high level of the IoT device. While the SE provides PKCS11 functions [22] to be used by the agents to interface and invoke crypto functionalities, the TEE provides a trusted world for those applications that need it, supporting cryptographic functions and secure operations. This is necessary to execute and protect CERTIFY processes such as IoT authentication, derivation of keys or data integrity protection. The embedded security API aims to abstract access to the low level IoT security components such as the SE and the TEE. Thanks to these enablers, high-level components described in the following subsections can securely enforce certain configurations inside the IoT device, not only policies, but also software images (enforcement and reconfiguration agent), perform the secure bootstrapping and authentication of the device (bootstrapping and authentication agent), and monitoring of the IoT device behavior and configuration (attestation agent).

13.2.2.2 Bootstrapping/Deployment

The bootstrapping phase starts when the device is installed and configured in a certain context. This process usually consists of a set of procedures in which a device joins a network in a certain domain (health, house, industry…). During the bootstrapping, the cryptographic material statically configured during manufacturing of the device is used to derive dynamic credentials and keys to be used during its operation. In recent years, different botnets (e.g., Mirai [23]) have shown that the deployment of IoT devices can compromise critical infrastructures with huge economic losses. This is especially critical in certain scenarios (e.g., involving eHealth devices), which can affect users' safety. To address such security concerns, there is a need to define approaches to reduce the attack surface of the devices from the very beginning. Beyond the use of traditional cryptographic (and more recently towards post-quantum cryptographic algorithms) and access control techniques, the security aspects of IoT devices should be properly managed through a governance approach to ensure devices behave as expected. However, the specification and enforcement of such aspects can be challenging in environments where a huge number of IoT devices can communicate with each other and, sometimes, without the explicit consent from their owners.

Extended MUD files were integrated into the CERTIFY's enhanced bootstrapping to enable the safe deployment of configurations prior to the device joining the domain. Therefore, the device will not be allowed to interact with other components or to access network resources until it is not properly identified, configured, and authenticated, ensuring that the network will not be compromised once the device will access to it.

Following this strategy, CERTIFY divides the bootstrapping into three subphases, each of them involving a subset of the components reported in Figure 13.1:

1. **The factory bootstrapping.** In this phase, the cryptographic material (device keys) and the MUD URL are statically configured and securely stored in the IoT during manufacturing (if available, in the SE).
2. **The domain bootstrapping.** In this phase, the device requests to start the bootstrapping in the domain (bootstrapping agent). CERTIFY leverages the Constrained Application Protocol (CoAP) - Extensible Authentication Protocol (EAP) [24, 25] to authenticate the device and generate the keys. In particular, the bootstrapping agent acts as the EAP peer, the secure enrollment module acts as EAP authenticator, the Device and Domain Manager acts as an Authentication, Authorization and Accounting (AAA) domain server [26] and the AAA manufacturer server acts as EAP server. Moreover, CERTIFY relies on the extended MUD to securely configure the device. For this, CERTIFY adapts the IETF architecture to the MUD extension and the interactions with other components. In this sense, the Extended MUD Manager is the main entity of the CERTIFY MUD architecture. It aggregates the functionality of the MUD manager and threat MUD manager, in charge of the processes required for obtaining and parsing the MUD and threat MUD file. This component has been extended from the IETF standard and the NIST proposal. In this way, the MUD, which is stored by the manufacturer in the Extended MUD Server, is obtained and translated to MSPL policies by the Extended MUD Manager using the URL provided by the device. While the Device and Domain manager orchestrates at domain level the enforcement of the MSPL policies, the Enforcement and Reconfiguration Agent is the component responsible for the internal IoT orchestration of the activities that need to be performed. Additionally, CERTIFY also checks that the device type is authorized based on its fingerprint. While attempting to join an IoT network, each device type exhibits a characteristic fingerprint. Such a fingerprint changes by device type (hardware) and firmware version. The network bootstrapping monitor exploits such a behavioral feature of the device to build a monitor that can pose constraints on the devices that can join the network as well as request the enforcement of specific rules. As fingerprints are characterized by device type (and firmware version), we envision that the manufacturer builds such a behavioral fingerprint and includes it as part of the extended MUD file designed in CERTIFY.

3. **The domain enrollment.** In this phase, high-end devices need to verify their correct state based on the policies defined in the MUD. CERTIFY leverages the DAA protocol to authenticate the high-end device and generate appropriate policies for attestation. In the CERTIFY architecture, the Authentication agent is responsible for the creation and management of the DAA key, and the Secure Enrollment module is the DAA issuer, responsible for the issuance of the cryptographic material required to enable the creation of DAA signatures. While the extended MUD file is retrieved from the server and enforced, enhancing device security in alignment with the manufacturer's certification, the DAA allows verifying the correct state of the device based on this verifiable evidence and helps to decide whether the network should allow or not the device to join. All in all, these processes allow CERTIFY to leverage the extended MUD file information during device bootstrapping to enable the configuration of security policies before granting network access, enhancing the security posture.

Once deployed, the device can generate dynamic credentials (authentication agent) based on its identity for securely communicating with the entities inside the domain.

All the information about authorized network devices, configurations, identity certificates and upgrades are stored in the Device Inventory and Registry. In essence, this repository serves as a pivotal tool in safeguarding the security, functionality, and integrity of network devices while maintaining a comprehensive inventory of their attributes by enabling monitoring and securing device-related information.

13.2.2.3 Operations

During the **operational** phase, continuous monitoring of the device is essential due to evolving security threats and vulnerabilities that were not anticipated at design time. The device's security level changes over time, requiring re-assessment and potentially re-certification.

In the CERTIFY framework, monitors are in place to send information about the IoT device (Sniffer and Tracer). Therefore, whenever a vulnerability is detected, CERTIFY can select and apply a mitigation. This information is processed by run-time attestation (Attestation agent) and by the Integrity monitor to check the fulfillment of the security properties certified (i.e., the ones contained in the MUD) during the operational phase. Network traces are also processed by the IDS that analyses the traffic in real-time and alerts about potential threats. Detection rules are periodically updated with new known signatures and new rules can be added to customize the solution to customers' and users' needs. The detection is enriched with an anomaly detection procedure that analyses offline datasets of network traffic to identify potential misbehavior and anomalies in the usage of the network. These events can be further processed with more advanced, and computationally expensive, solutions by the SIEM-SOAR that could also correlate multiple events identified in the network and on the device under analysis.

The SIEM-SOAR tool combines the typical functionalities of Security Information and Event Management (SIEM) and Security Orchestration, Automation and Response (SOAR) systems. While the SIEM allows for the collection and analysis of security events and contextual data, the SOAR enables the centralized handling of threat intelligence and automates responses to security incidents, significantly reducing reaction times and limiting potential damage. Given alerts details, the SIEM-SOAR identifies and applies the most appropriate reaction (e.g., publish information, request an update, apply a mitigation by reconfiguring system, network or device, or even check for threat MUD file from the Extended MUD Server). Then the Device and Domain Manager coordinates the mechanisms to enforce mitigations and updates on the IoT Device. If an update is required, the secure update and upgrade agent orchestrates the software update based on the information contained in the local software repository, Manufacturer software repository, and Inventorying and Registry. In any case, the Enforcement and Reconfiguration agent is in charge of enforcing the configuration on the IoT device.

By linking runtime detection with mitigation actions suggested by manufacturers, threat databases, or certification authorities, CERTIFY ensures timely protection against identified vulnerabilities. This is facilitated by an extended threat MUD. CERTIFY combines manufacturing-phase security evaluation with runtime metrics to continuously assess security. The system can deny network access if critical risks are detected, and adjust device configurations as needed to maintain security.

CERTIFY also promotes continuous communication among stakeholders by integrating external security information about new vulnerabilities, updates, patches, and potential zero-day attacks with domain-specific data. The framework integrates mechanisms to share security information with manufacturers and other interested parties in a privacy-preserving (PP) way through the PP-CTI component [27]. In particular, the PP-CTI includes data mining techniques such as suppression, generalization, K-Anonymity, T-Closeness, L-Diversity and Differential Privacy [28–30]. PP-CTI interfaces with the Malware Information Sharing Platform (MISP)[2] where vital threat information is shared, and other valuable cybersecurity insights. Furthermore, PP-CTI & MISP integrates an access control layer, featuring identity management software such as Fiware Keyrock [31]. This

2. https://www.misp-project.org/

allows CERTIFY to decide which entities can send or receive specific data, further enhancing data security and privacy. The information could then be accessed by other CTI providers and the manufacturer (MISP manufacturer). In the same way, new threats and alerts can be received and exchanged among these sources.

13.2.2.4 Updating

Traditionally, IoT security has been hindered by a "set and forget" approach, where manufacturers and service providers configure devices but rarely update their firmware. This practice represents a significant obstacle to long-term IoT security. To overcome this, OTA [32] software updates are essential for maintaining the security of IoT devices over time. This necessity is reinforced by various standards and recommendations, including those from the European Union Agency for Cybersecurity (ENISA), which has emphasized the importance of regular software updates in enhancing the security and reliability of connected devices [33, 34].

However, the process of updating software on IoT devices introduces its own set of cybersecurity challenges [35–37], particularly for devices with limited resources. In response to this, the IETF published RFC 9019 [38], which defines a standardized architecture for firmware updates in IoT environments. CERTIFY builds on these guidelines, incorporating OTA components that adhere to RFC 9019's framework. To further enhance security, CERTIFY integrates advanced blockchain technology, which records every event related to firmware updates and device metadata. This ensures transparency, immutability, and a continuous chain of trust throughout the OTA process. Secure cryptographic algorithms are employed to verify firmware integrity and to sign firmware updates, ensuring that the software is authentic and untampered.

The updating phase in CERTIFY encompasses the procedures for deploying software updates or patches provided by manufacturers, as well as configuration tasks required to address newly identified threats. These procedures involve multiple components, including the enforcement and reconfiguration agent, secure update and upgrade agent, device and domain manager, inventory and registry, and software repository. The secure update-and-upgrade agent provides a graphical user interface (GUI) where security administrators can manage registered devices and software. This interface allows administrators to upload new software to the software repository, register it with the Device and Domain Manager, and trigger updates. It also includes features to check for available updates and initiate the upgrade process, making the management of software versions straightforward and efficient. The software repository serves as a storage hub where software packages are stored, organized, and managed. This repository allows users to access, download, and update applications and libraries, facilitating the distribution of software across devices. By centralizing the management of software packages, the repository ensures that updates are delivered efficiently and securely to all connected devices within the network.

Finally, to enhance the transparency and traceability of the update process, CERTIFY framework employs DLTs such as blockchain. This provides a transparent ledger that tracks software versions and any known vulnerabilities, allowing manufacturers to be represented as individual blockchain nodes. Through this approach, information about software components can be securely shared between stakeholders. Although interoperability issues with various DLT implementations persist, CERTIFY is exploring the use of interledger technology to link different DLT systems into a cohesive, secure framework for managing updates.

13.2.2.5 Decommissioning & Repurposing

The decommissioning phase in the CERTIFY lifecycle methodology represents the final stage in the life of a connected device, where it is either retired or repurposed. This phase is critical to ensuring that once a device has reached the end of its operational life or it is no longer able to meet security requirements, all security-sensitive data and configurations are effectively and securely handled. The focus during decommissioning is on safeguarding the network and preventing any residual vulnerabilities that might remain if the device were simply discarded without proper protocols.

A device may be decommissioned for several reasons: it may no longer meet the security standards required for its operational environment, it may be incompatible with essential software updates due to hardware limitations, or a vulnerability may have been discovered that cannot be mitigated through available patches. In all these cases, the decommissioning process begins by performing a comprehensive analysis to determine whether the device can be repurposed for a different or less security-critical role, or if it must be fully decommissioned and removed from service.

When a device is slated for decommissioning, CERTIFY emphasizes the importance of secure data erasure. This involves permanently wiping all sensitive data stored on the device, including cryptographic keys, certificates, and any stored configurations or logs. Simply restoring the device to factory settings is not sufficient in most cases, as residual data might remain accessible. CERTIFY ensures that the decommissioning process includes a thorough, verifiable data destruction procedure, employing cryptographic techniques or secure overwriting methods to guarantee that no information can be recovered.

For devices that are repurposed rather than fully decommissioned, CERTIFY provides a framework for reconfiguring the device for a different role within the network. This may involve reassigning the device to a domain with lower security requirements or reconfiguring its functionality to handle fewer sensitive tasks. Repurposing a device can often extend its operational life and reduce costs, but it must be done in a way that ensures the device is still capable of meeting the security standards necessary for its new role.

If a device is determined to be unsuitable for repurposing, the final step in the decommissioning phase is its secure removal from the network. DLT technology used in the CERTIFY's framework provides a transparent and immutable record that verifies the device's decommissioning and ensures compliance with all relevant security policies. This record could not only include confirmation that all sensitive data was securely erased, but also the steps taken to prevent the device from re-entering the network or being reused in an unauthorized manner.

13.3 Connected Cabin System – CERTIFY Use Case

Next generation aircrafts foresee the presence of a multitude of IoT-based connected devices supporting new and enhanced services in the cabin, e.g., smart screen, galley, lavatory, seat, and light. This evolution will usher in the era of intelligent aircraft cabin. The expected benefits from such a scenario encompass: (i) a personalized experience for passengers, e.g., customized In-Flight-Entertainment (IFE) and seating configurations; (ii) opportunities for airlines in delivering targeted retail offers; and (iii) optimized operations and Prognostics and Health Management (PHM) applications, thanks to a detailed overview on the aircraft status and passenger preferences built through distributed and connected sensors.

This environment is characterized by a high volume of data per second – GBs up to TBs (considering all the sensors in the aircraft) – and by a heterogeneous set of devices. Communications is performed by means of wired (e.g., the Ethernet-based AFDX – ARINC 664, CAN bus, ARINC429) or wireless connectivity (e.g., IEEE 802.11, ECMA-368, IEEE 802.15.3). The device heterogeneity is also reflected in the different capabilities to host services. It is worth noting that the devices considered in this scenario are part of the cabin system and therefore do not require any specific safety assessment. However, they must still meet the related certifications, guidance, and regulations for airworthiness (e.g., from RTCA, EUROCAE [39], FAA [40] and EASA [41]) such as the AC 20-168 and the RTCA DO-313 "Certification Guidance for Installation of Non-Essential, Non-Required Aircraft Cabin Systems & Equipment (CS&E)". Therein it is required to verify the security of the wired and wireless systems, by adopting a design approach that will prevent any unintended change to the systems during operations. The emphasis is given to hardware, software, network, and data in consideration of the potential challenges related to the inclusion of Commercial Off the Shelf (COTS) components where alternative methods and processes are needed to perform the required tests and evaluations. All in all, there is a clear need to protect these devices throughout their lifecycle and generate appropriate evidence.

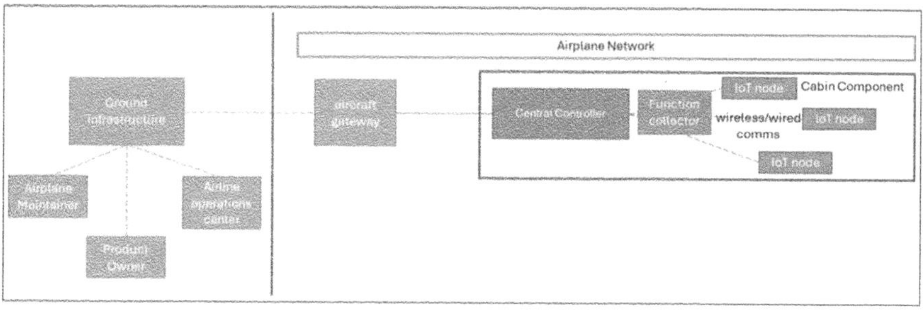

Figure 13.3. High-level block diagram of the CERTIFY use case for the connected cabin system.

The CERTIFY use case considers an environment constituted by two different classes of devices deployed in the cabin, plus a set of infrastructural remote services hosted by the component and system manufacturer, and airline. The on-board devices are: i) IoT node devices having a small footprint in terms of "Size, Weight, Power and Cost" (*low-SWaP-C*) and ii) high-end embedded central controller devices able to host more complex software services and manage entire functionalities in the cabin. These two classes of embedded devices have respectively been exemplified in the project by a custom RISC-V based node and an off-the-shelf high-end embedded board based on the ARM instruction set. Moreover, an aircraft gateway oversees the communications to/from the aircraft. This heterogeneous architecture requires a trade-off analysis on the cybersecurity services and functionalities of the CERTIFY framework that can be deployed. Figure 13.3 pictorially represents the use case.

For demonstrating the CERTIFY functionalities, three different scenarios covering multiple stages of the product lifecycle have been introduced. Namely, installation of a new component, operations and monitoring, and replacement and repurposing. In the following, we briefly recall the scenarios later referenced in Section 13.4 where the approach taken by CERTIFY for these scenarios matches the EU CRA.

Scenario 1 – Installation of a new component. A new component needs to be installed in the cabin. This could exemplify the adoption of a new smart component (e.g., a smart coffee machine) in the cabin. To not compromise the cybersecurity posture of the system the performed process must include bootstrapping, initial update, and customization for the specific deployment environment by considering the secure configuration defined by the product owner/manufacturer during the product evaluation for the original certificate. Moreover, if the new component is a replacement for a previously installed one, secure decommissioning, including reset and wipe out of any sensitive data, must be performed by the maintenance operator.

Scenario 2 – Operations and monitoring. Data is periodically collected in the cabin with a frequency that is dependent on application and services, e.g., for monitoring, optimization, and preventive maintenance. Moreover, it is worth considering that connecting passengers' devices, as well as the presence of a wireless network, generate a wider attack surface. Similarly, external infrastructures can upload data for onboard connectivity experience and In-Flight Entertainment (IFE) services. Moreover, maintainer and product owner may also need the availability of a remote connectivity to perform device reconfigurations. All these operations demands for vulnerability management and anomaly detection throughout the entire operations of product and system.

Scenario 3 – Replacement and repurposing. In case a cabin system component has a failure, to minimize the downtime, a compatible replacement Line-replaceable unit (LRU) could be retrieved from the same manufacturer and repurposed for the specific target system. Airline, maintainer, product owner, and maintenance operator are all involved to manage different steps of the process. It is important to check that the device has all the characteristics needed to be repurposed before using it. Indeed, the new deployment may request a different amount of resources to host services and security features. Therefore, the new usage must be among the ones foreseen and certified by the manufacturer so that proper reconfiguration can be implemented.

13.4 Towards a CERTIFY Pilot for the European Cyber Resilience Act

Looking at the current cybersecurity policy landscape it was quite straightforward to make a connection between CERTIFY and the CRA due to the scope of its application and its strong impact on IoT products. CRA also revolutionizes the cybersecurity ecosystem by imposing requirements, both at the product and process level, with significant implications over the entire product lifecycle.

The CRA could officially enter into force by the end of 2024, after being proposed by the European Commission at the end of 2022, and after being adopted by the European Parliament in March 2024. The objective of the CRA is to establish a minimum level of cybersecurity for all digital devices (both software and hardware) sold in the EU internal market. In order to achieve that, the CRA sets to:

- facilitate the secure development of products with digital elements and their components;
- define cybersecurity rules for placing products on the market;
- define requirements for the design, development, and production of products;

- define requirements for the vulnerability handling process;
- establish rules on market surveillance and enforcement;
- establish more or less stringent proof of conformity depending on the category the products fall in (i.e., self-declaration, third-party assessment, etc.).

To understand the implications of the CRA developments, the Connected Cabin Systems use case of CERTIFY is chosen as a reference with the intent to consider the large scope of its three scenarios, as well as the security challenges, and the complexity of the set of actors involved. It is quite clear that the CRA is a very horizontal piece of legislation with common cybersecurity requirements for all products, regardless of sector or field of application. Most of the devices involved in the Connected Cabin se case would most likely fall under the CRA scope (e.g., IoT nodes, central controllers, aircraft gateway). Indeed, Article 2 of the CRA text says that the regulation applies to products with digital elements made available on the market, which includes a direct or indirect logical or physical data connection to a device or network.

The remaining of the section develops further the ambitious and challenging task of trying to pave the way for a pilot on the CRA offered by the CERTIFY project. The challenge is mainly due to the fact that the CRA is not yet adopted, even though the text is stable, many aspects still need to be defined, and quite several key aspects will be postponed to delegated and implementing acts. Thus, the analysis herein presented might need to be revised when the details and the actual application of the CRA will occur after a transition period.

In addition, CERTIFY remains a research project, so both from a product and regulation perspective, we still need to go through complex revision cycles. Moreover, we do not claim to perform any conformance test, nor do we plan to undergo a certification process within the context of this exercise, nor the CERTIFY framework pretends to be an answer to the complex issue of conformity assessment.

In conclusion, we believe we discuss the CERTIFY use case in the context of the CRA to bring a better understanding of the project impact being developed in close alignment with the reality of the industry, the law, and its evolution. In other words, each technical advancement of the project should be performed keeping in mind what regulatory context it will face, facilitating rather than making more difficult the adherence to such regulatory context. The CERTIFY framework can be a step toward alignment with the CRA and its implementation.

13.4.1 Use Case Analysis for the CRA

This section discusses the CRA in the context of the three scenarios discussed in Section 13.3.

Scenario 1: The CRA ambitiously aims to make cybersecurity a primary perspective in the design, development, and production of products with digital elements. In essence, as has been stated in several policy fora, the successful implementation of the CRA would assure a security by design approach for each manufacturer that makes products available in the EU market. This could be achieved by making sure that several basic cybersecurity requirements are respected and that, ultimately, products made available do not have any known vulnerability. In CERTIFY, this step is carried out through the automation tool *CyberPass* which streamlines the conformity assessment process based on the ETSI EN 303 645 standard [34]. It is important to note that this latter standard was highlighted by the *CRA Requirements Standards Mapping study* [42] conducted by ENISA and the European Commission's Joint Research Centre since it maps to most of the CRA essential requirements. Strictly speaking, the scenario in question focuses on secure bootstrapping and customization of a cabin component into the network. Similarly to the essential requirements of the CRA, an initial set of basic requirements is pushed on the component to be part of the network. In addition, CERTIFY provides a certificate of the secure state of the newly added component, which should ideally facilitate further demonstration of regulatory compliance.

Scenario 2: The scenario on *operations and monitoring* is probably the most interesting for a CRA pilot. It touches upon several pillars and angles of the CRA, but more precisely on the provisions related to lifecycle and vulnerability management. If, for instance, a rogue device injects false data and or takes harmful actions within the cabin, the CERTIFY framework will be able to monitor and spot that. It goes without saying that, in case a vulnerability is detected, one or more digital products within the systems might no longer be compliant with the CRA, or at least be impacted by a "known exploited vulnerability". Clearly, the CRA requires market operators to take action, stressing their need to assure support all along the lifecycle of a product (being for product and service support, updates, or mitigation responses).

Moreover, this scenario taps into part of the CRA essential requirements that insist on processes and not only on products: such requirements call for the vulnerability handling processes put in place by manufacturers to ensure the cybersecurity of products with digital elements during the time the product is expected to be in use. In particular, there should be clear processes and formal policies showing that the manufacturer can immediately take corrective measures. Indeed, once a vulnerability is discovered, the manufacturer must promptly perform the necessary actions to bring a product with digital elements or the manufacturer's processes into conformity, or alternatively withdraw or recall the product, as appropriate. The CERTIFY methodology includes collection, identification, and decision, and coupled

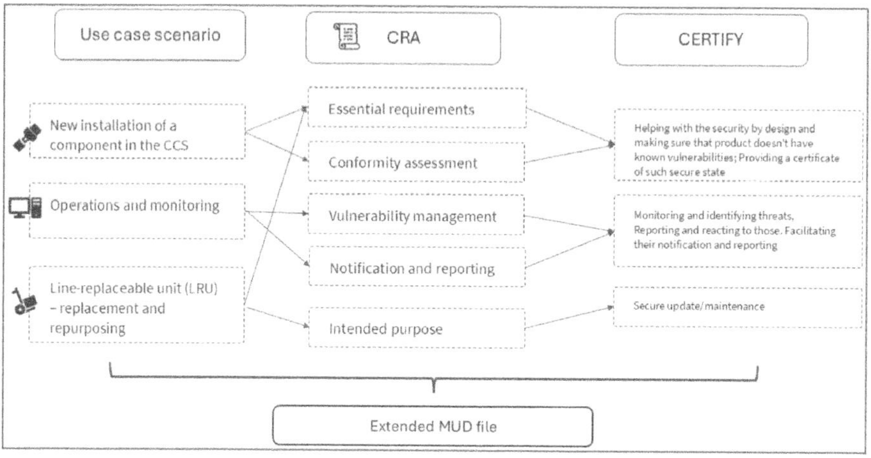

Figure 13.4. The CERTIFY cybersecurity lifecycle methodology and framework aligned with recent EU regulation: the CRA example.

with its real-time monitoring capabilities (e.g., SIEM-SOAR, IDS, runtime attestation, MUD), allows for the identification and handling of any anomalous behavior while placing its user in a better spot to comply with cybersecurity regulations.

Scenario 3: The last scenario is the Line-replaceable Unit (LRU) one. Here again, the CRA is quite explicit in the obligation to support and update digital products. However, one of the peculiar aspects of this scenario is the eventuality of repurposing a device within a network for a different use or functionality. The CRA text calls for an assessment of the intended use of a product with digital elements. In other words, the new potential purpose of a network component should already be foreseen by the market operators as the CRA calls on them to be familiar with the intended use of a product, as well as with its "foreseeable use and misuse". Repurposing a component within a system is therefore a perfect test-based scenario to assess the emergence of new intended uses. Finally, the operator should always adopt a risk-based approach to continuously assess this eventuality and make sure that new device usage does not lead to harmful and previously unforeseen consequences

Figure 13.4 pictorially represents the link between the use case, the CRA and the CERTFIY project.

13.4.2 The Role of the Extended MUD File

During the design of the CERTIFY methodology, the usage of the extended MUD file emerged as the cohesive element for the three scenarios. Each actor can collaboratively contribute, update and provide a state of the security of the system. The usage of the MUD file (and particularly its extension considered in CERTIFY) meets the spirit of many of the regulatory provisions contained in the CRA text.

Such a tool would help with the dispatching of newly discovered vulnerabilities as well as their mitigation. The enforcement of the latest MUD file policies would support the creation of evidence of a secure state of the system, providing a basis to build on for notification and reporting purposes.

The legislator has underlined several times how market operators should systematically document relevant cybersecurity aspects concerning products with digital elements, including vulnerabilities of which it becomes aware and any relevant information provided by third parties, and shall, where applicable, update the cybersecurity risk assessment of the products. In addition, the CRA introduces complex notification and reporting rules concerning exploited vulnerabilities and severe incidents (with some novelty elements such as a *Single Reporting Platform or* a *Single Point of Contact* for manufacturers).

Moreover, the extended MUD file would enhance the possibility of collaboration with all the stakeholders, encouraging cooperation and cohesion toward IoT security. All these ingredients combine well with the need for cooperation with the stakeholders involved in the notification and vulnerability handling procedures, e.g., CSIRTs (Computer Security Incident Response Teams), ENISA, Single Point of Contacts. Ideally, the extended MUD file could also be a good starting point to build the conformance documentation (being itself or third-party-assessed).

13.5 Conclusions

While European regulations advance cybersecurity by imposing measures to manage it throughout the lifecycle of a device, it is still not clear how to implement such cybersecurity lifecycle management in an efficient and coordinated manner. In response to this problem, this chapter provides an introduction and comprehensive overview of the general architecture of CERTIFY.

CERTIFY gets inspiration from recent EU initiatives such as the Cybersecurity Act and the Cyber Resilience Act the core role covered by certification, lifecycle management and information sharing. Indeed, in its framework CERTIFY considers: (i) current certification status and reports, as baseline for describing the security profile of a device including security controls, policies, recommended configuration (by means of the extended MUD) and assurance level according to domain of deployment; (ii) behavioural profile, as a way of describing the expected functioning of the device; (iii) threat modelling and risk assessment, that from a baseline built at design time is continuously updated thanks to the information sharing and the usage of the threat MUD; (iv) change impact analysis, to dynamically understand, from internal and external information, how changes in the threat landscape, and applied security controls and policies may impact the security posture of the system; v) recertification from testing results, by leveraging a complete assessment of the reached security level and exploiting the artifacts collected throughout the device lifecycle to request and support an agile recertification process in case the device should not meet anymore the requested Security Assurance Level (SAL).

This chapter discusses the CERTIFY project in the context of the CRA. In particular, the Connected Cabin Systems use case is analyzed with the intent to shed some light about the challenges and impact of the implementation of the CRA in a real industrial case.

The holistic methodology adopted by CERTIFY ensures that the CERTIFY architecture is suited to address the complexities of managing the security lifecycle of IoT devices, offering robust security, privacy, and adaptability in an ever-evolving digital landscape.

Acknowledgements

Research partially supported by the EU through the Horizon research and innovation program CERTIFY (grant agreement no. 11069471) and the Swiss SERI (grant agreements no. 22.00165 and 22.00191). The European Commission's and Swiss SERI's support for the production of this publication does not constitute an endorsement of the contents, which reflects the views of the authors only, and neither the Commission nor the Swiss Confederation can be held responsible for any use which may be made of the information contained therein.

References

[1] M. Weiser, "Ubiquitous Computing," *Computer*, vol. 26, no. 10, pp. 71–72, Oct. 1993, doi: 10.1109/2.237456.

[2] Tech Target, "Colonial Pipeline hack explained: Everything you need to know." Apr. 2022. [Online]. Available: https://www.techtarget.com/whatis/feature/Colonial-Pipeline-hack-explained-Everything-you-need-to-know.

[3] TechCrunch, "Hotel giant Marriott confirms yet another data breach." Jul. 2022. [Online]. Available: https://techcrunch.com/2022/07/06/marriott-breach-again/.

[4] TechHQ, "The way cybercrime can kill." Dec. 2022. [Online]. Available: https://techhq.com/2023/12/hospital-cyberattack-ardent-health-systems-down-er-shut/.

[5] U.S. Securities and Exchange Commission (SEC), "Cybersecurity Disclosure."

[6] European Commission, "What is a data breach and what do we have to do in case of a data breach?" 2016. [Online]. Available: https://commission.europa.eu/law/law-topic/data-protection/reform/rules-business-and-organisations/obligations/what-data-breach-and-what-do-we-have-do-case-data-breach_en.

[7] C. Boggini, "Reporting cybersecurity to stakeholders: A review of CSRD and the EU cyber legal framework," *Comput. Law Secur. Rev.*, vol. 53, p. 105987, 2024, https://doi.org/10.1016/j.clsr.2024.105987.

[8] European Union Agency for Cybersecurity (ENISA), "CIRAS." 2023. [Online]. Available: https://ciras.enisa.europa.eu/.

[9] European Repository of Cyber Incidents, "EuRepoC." Nov. 2022. [Online]. Available: https://eurepoc.eu/.

[10] "Global cybercrime estimated cost 2029," Statista. Accessed: Oct. 31, 2024. [Online]. Available: https://www.statista.com/forecasts/1280009/cost-cybercrime-worldwide.

[11] European Commission EUR-Lex – 52022PC0454, "REGULATION OF THE EUROPEAN PARLIAMENT AND OF THE COUNCIL on horizontal cybersecurity requirements for products with digital elements and amending Regulation (EU) 2019/1020 (Cyber Resilience Act)." 2019. [Online]. Available: https://eur-lex.europa.eu/legal-content/EN/TXT/?uri=celex:52022PC0454.

[12] CERTIFY, "aCtive sEcurity foR connecTed devIces liFecYcles." [Online]. Available: https://doi.org/10.3030/101069471.

[13] E. Lear, D. Romascanu, and R. Droms, "Manufacturer Usage Description Specification (RFC 8520)." Accessed: Feb. 12, 2019. [Online]. Available: https://tools.ietf.org/html/rfc8520.

[14] Rose, S., Borchert, O., Mitchell, S. and Connelly, S., "Zero Trust Architecture." Special Publication (NIST SP), National Institute of Standards and Technology, Gaithersburg, MD, 2020. [Online]. Available: 10.6028/NIST.SP.800-207.

[15] Kaur, H., & Kaur, K., "Secure elements for IoT devices: A survey," vol. 176, no. 102918, 2021.

[16] S. P. a. N. Santos, "Demystifying Arm TrustZone: A Comprehensive Survey," *ACM Comput Surv.*, vol. 51, no. 6, pp. 1–36, 2019.

[17] E. Brickell, J. Camenisch, and L. Chen, "Direct anonymous attestation," in *Proceedings of the 11th ACM conference on Computer and communications security*, in CCS '04. New York, NY, USA: Association for Computing Machinery, Oct. 2004, pp. 132–145. doi: 10.1145/1030083.1030103.

[18] EUR-Lex, "Directive (EU) 2016/1148 of the European Parliament and of the Council of 6 July 2016 concerning measures for a high common level of security of network and information systems across the Union (NIS directive)." 2016. [Online]. Available: https://eur-lex.europa.eu/eli/dir/2016/1148/oj.

[19] S. N. Matheu, J. L. Hernández-Ramos, A. F. Skarmeta, and G. Baldini, "A Survey of Cybersecurity Certification for the Internet of Things," *ACM Comput. Surv. CSUR*, vol. 53, no. 6, pp. 1–36, 2020.

[20] S. N. Matheu et al., "Security Architecture for Defining and Enforcing Security Profiles in DLT/SDN-Based IoT Systems," *Sensors*, vol. 20, no. 7, p. 1882, Jan. 2020, doi: 10.3390/s20071882.

[21] S. N. Matheu, J. L. Hernandez-Ramos, S. Perez, and A. F. Skarmeta, "Extending MUD profiles through an Automated IoT Security Testing Methodology," *IEEE Access*, pp. 1–20, 2019, doi: 10.1109/ACCESS.2019.2947157.

[22] "PKCS #11 Specification Version 3.1." Accessed: Oct. 25, 2024. [Online]. Available: https://docs.oasis-open.org/pkcs11/pkcs11-spec/v3.1/csd01/pkcs11-spec-v3.1-csd01.html.

[23] C. Kolias, G. Kambourakis, A. Stavrou, and J. Voas, "DDoS in the IoT: Mirai and Other Botnets," *Computer*, vol. 50, no. 7, pp. 80–84, 2017, doi: 10.1109/MC.2017.201.

[24] F. Bersani and H. Tschofenig, "The EAP-PSK Protocol: A Pre-Shared Key Extensible Authentication Protocol Method (RFC 4764)."

[25] ACE Working Group, "EAP-based Authentication Service for CoAP," *IETF Datatracker*. 2024. [Online]. Available: https://datatracker.ietf.org/doc/html/draft-ietf-ace-wg-coap-eap-10.

[26] J. Vollbrecht et al., "AAA Authorization Framework (RFC 2904)." 2000.

[27] H. Cavusoglu, H. Cavusoglu, and S. Raghunathan, "Efficiency of Vulnerability Disclosure Mechanisms to Disseminate Vulnerability Knowledge," *IEEE Trans. Softw. Eng.*, vol. 33, no. 3, pp. 171–185, Mar. 2007, doi: 10.1109/TSE.2007.26.

[28] D. Slijepčević, M. Henzl, L. D. Klausner, T. Dam, P. Kieseberg, and M. Zeppelzauer, "k-Anonymity in practice: How generalisation and suppression affect machine learning classifiers," *Comput. Secur.*, vol. 111, p. 102488, Dec. 2021, doi: 10.1016/j.cose.2021.102488.

[29] T. Ha, T. K. Dang, T. T. Dang, T. A. Truong, and M. T. Nguyen, "Differential Privacy in Deep Learning: An Overview," in *2019 International Conference on Advanced Computing and Applications (ACOMP)*, Nov. 2019, pp. 97–102. doi: 10.1109/ACOMP.2019.00022.

[30] F. Piccialli and Z. Lyu, "The Security of Medical Data on Internet Based on Differential Privacy Technology," *ACM Trans. Internet Technol.*, vol. 21, Mar. 2020, doi: 10.1145/3382769.

[31] Fiware Keyrock, "Fiware Keyrock API." [Online]. Available: https://fiware-idm.readthedocs.io/en/latest/index.html.

[32] S. E. Jaouhari and E. Bouvet, "Secure firmware Over-The-Air updates for IoT: Survey, challenges, and discussions, Internet of Things," *Internet Things*, vol. 18, 2022.

[33] "ENISA Baseline Security Recommendations for IoT |OWASP IoT Top 10 2018 Mapping Project." Accessed: Oct. 25, 2024. [Online]. Available: https://scriptingxss.gitbook.io/owasp-iot-top-10-mapping-project/mappings/enisa-baseline-security-recommendations-for-iot.

[34] "ETSI EN 303 645 Cybersecurity for Consumer Internet Of Things," TÜV SÜD. Accessed: Oct. 25, 2024. [Online]. Available: https://www.tuvsud.com/en/resource-centre/stories/etsi-en-303-645-cybersecurity-for-consumer-internet-of-things.

[35] N. S. Mtetwa, P. Tarwireyi, A. M. Abu-Mahfouz, and M. O. Adigun, "Secure Firmware Updates in the Internet of Things: A survey," in *2019 International Multidisciplinary Information Technology and Engineering Conference (IMITEC)*, Nov. 2019, pp. 1–7. doi: 10.1109/IMITEC45504.2019.9015845.

[36] Q. Wang, Y. Zhu, and L. Cheng, "Reprogramming wireless sensor networks: challenges and approaches," *IEEE Netw.*, vol. 20, no. 3, pp. 48–55, May 2006, doi: 10.1109/MNET.2006.1637932.

[37] S. Brown and C. J. Sreenan, "Software Updating in Wireless Sensor Networks: A Survey and Lacunae," *J. Sens. Actuator Netw.*, vol. 2, no. 4, Art. no. 4, Dec. 2013, doi: 10.3390/jsan2040717.

[38] B. Moran, H. Tschofenig, D. Brown, and M. Meriac, "A Firmware Update Architecture for Internet of Things," Internet Engineering Task Force, Request for Comments RFC 9019, Apr. 2021. doi: 10.17487/RFC9019.

[39] "EUROCAE," Eurocae. Accessed: Oct. 25, 2024. [Online]. Available: https://www.eurocae.net/.

[40] FAA, "Federal Aviation Administration." [Online]. Available: https://www.faa.gov/.

[41] EASA, "European Union Aviation Safety Agency." [Online]. Available: https://www.easa.europa.eu/en.

[42] "Cyber Resilience Act Requirements Standards Mapping - Joint Research Centre & ENISA Joint Analysis," ENISA. Accessed: Oct. 25, 2024. [Online]. Available: https://www.enisa.europa.eu/publications/cyber-resilience-act-requirements-standards-mapping.

DOI: 10.1561/9781638285076.ch14

Chapter 14

Developing a Near-real Time AI-based Network Intrusion Detection System

By Dimitrios Sygletos, Dimitra Papatsaroucha and Evangelos K. Markakis

The rapid growth of the Internet in recent years has allowed technological advancements, including communication fields by enabling global connectivity in real time, which has broken down geographical barriers and allows communication with anyone, anywhere, at any time. The size of the network data and the corresponding information that gets transmitted though communication channels have significantly increased as a result of these improvements, while technological advancement creates concerns regarding the security of data during transactions, since even simple transactions contain sensitive information. The security of the data is constantly under threat, while cyber-crimes are evolving to be more effective and complicated to detect. However, cyber security techniques are under constant enhancement as well. Researchers are investigating and employing a variety of approaches to secure computers and networks in order to protect systems and data. Among the suggested approaches resides the development of systems that analyze the network, monitor for signs of malicious activity, and trigger an alert when they detect potential threats, namely Network Intrusion Detection Systems (NIDSs). Machine Learning (ML) and Deep Learning (DL) techniques were introduced into NIDSs to enhance detection efficacy and potentially identify unknown attacks, namely zero-day attacks. ML and DL models are trained with network traffic data in order to learn to identify patterns of malicious and benign activity. A challenge of this approach is that ML and DL models should always be trained and tested with modern network traffic in order to achieve improved detection results, while models should also be evaluated in realistic network environments. Although there are numerous studies across the literature that propose and develop NIDS solutions, the majority of them don't deploy the model after training into a realistic network for validation or they use outdated datasets for the training of the model. This chapter proposes a NIDS that incorporates a DL model and an in-house dataset developed, which portrays modern network traffic. The dataset was typically divided into training and testing sets and ML metrics such as Accuracy, Recall, Precision and F1-score were used to evaluate the models' performance during the training and testing phase, while the NIDS was also deployed in a realistic network and was evaluated in near-real time conditions. The proposed solution showcased promising results by achieving over 97% rate on the accuracy evaluation metric during the training phase and over 90% when deployed in a realistic network environment and evaluated during a near-real time scenario.

14.1 Introduction

Cybercrime is defined as any illegal activity performed through the internet utilizing networks or electronic devices with the intention of inflicting damages to the system's infrastructure, tampering with the data and intercepting information among others. Such crimes include data breaches, fraud, identity theft, computer viruses, and more. As reported in the annual report by the European Union Agency for Cybersecurity (ENISA) [1] for 2023, an increase has been observed in the quantity as well as consequences of cyberattacks. In accordance with ENISA, throughout the halfway of year 2022, there were less than a thousand cyberattacks reported global and in the European region; however, during the first half of 2023, this number rose to more than 2500 reported cyberattack incidents. Moreover, according to [2], the inflicted damage worth will be 9.5 trillion USD globally in 2024 and the cost will grow by 15 percentage for the year of 2025, reaching 10.5 trillion USD.

Researchers are working to develop solutions to this global pandemic of cybercrime. Among the main goals is to develop systems that monitor for potential malicious activities that target networks or connected devices. Intrusion Detection Systems (IDS) [3] have been the main topic of several studies, since this approach shows great potential to protect against and/or mitigate a number of cybercrime-related issues. These systems monitor the network for indications of malicious activity and trigger an alert when they identify potential risks. They are divided into two categories: Network intrusion detection systems (NIDS), and Host Intrusion Detection Systems (HIDS). NIDSs [4] monitor for malicious activity and unauthorized access on networks, while HIDSs [4] monitor on devices that produce logs or metrics, seeking indicators of suspicious behavior to identify abnormal activities.

NIDS have two methods to detect intrusions: Signature-Based [3] and Anomaly-Based [3]. Systems that maintain intrusion signatures in their database and compare incoming traffic are referred to as signature-based detection systems. However, this type of system has a disadvantage as it cannot identify unknown intrusion traffic that may constitute a cyber-attack. Conversely, anomaly-based detection methods are able to detect and notify regarding unknown intrusion traffic because they can use various Machine Learning (ML) and Deep Learning (DL) algorithms that are trained with a network dataset to identify patterns of malicious traffic. ML as a subset of Artificial Intelligence (AI) utilizes mathematical algorithms in many research domains [5]. This method can acquire knowledge from the data and generalize to unfamiliar data, thus perform tasks without having previously been directly programmed. However, this method has also some drawbacks, such as the false positive alarm. This alert occurs when the system detects suspicious behavior and responds accordingly, however the identification of this behavior as malicious is a false alarm. In order to address this issue, the Deep Learning (DL) technique has been developed as a subset of ML that is manufactured with Neural Networks (NNs).

NNs are artificial neurons that aim to imitate the complicated procedure of decision-making by taking inspiration from the architecture and functions of the human brain. DL models are capable of simulating a decision similar to the human brain, adapting to novel patterns and continuously learn from their failures [5]. One of the most recent and effective methods to detect intrusions and novel attacks in NIDS is the utilization of DL methods. The term "novel attacks" refers to unknown or new threats that have the ability to exploit vulnerabilities in the network or in the machines. In addition, attackers often attempt to "hide" their traces, but by employing DL techniques in NIDS patterns and behaviors that are being suggestive of cyberattacks can be identified.

ML and DL enable NIDSs to identify patterns that serve as normal and malicious behavior traffic baseline of the system and, therefore, detect anomalies. However, the drawback of this method is that traffic may be misclassified as benign or malicious, respectively. In addition, most of the case studies that utilize ML and DL, adopt an outdated network traffic dataset for the training of the models while they lack deploying the NIDSs in realistic environments for evaluating Near-Real Time network intrusion detection, such as in [6] and [7].

Considering all the previously mentioned statistics and reported issues from [2] and [1] as well as current studies and solutions identified in the literature, this chapter introduces an Anomaly-based NIDS, since this detection method can identify intrusions and novel attacks. The proposed solution utilizes the DL capabilities of Convolutional Neural Networks (CNN), such as the generalization to new unseen data, the scalability to process very large datasets and the decision-making complexity in real time, to make predictions about the network traffic in near-real time. A recent in-house developed dataset was utilized for the training of the CNN model. This dataset reflects modern network activity and contains recent traffic patterns, behaviors, and threats with the aim to accomplish developing a more robust and accurate model that can address some of the modern difficulties that cybersecurity in general and network intrusion detection in particular encounter.

The remainder of this chapter is structured as follows: the State of the Art is presented in sub-chapter 14.2, the implementation of the proposed NIDS is described in sub-chapter ??, the Model Evaluation Process is covered in sub-chapter ??, and the Conclusion and Future Work Plans are presented in sub-chapter ??.

14.2 State of the Art

Malicious network attacks become complicated to detect due to the continuous progress of cyberthreats. A wide range of software and platforms begin to utilize the ML capabilities, as they enhance their ability to detect cyberthreats. The dataset that trains an ML has a major impact on how efficiently the model detects the intrusions. Identifying those intrusions in the network at the time that they occur is one of the most essential parts to be provided by the ML models. In this section, a review of the literature is presented regarding various ML and DL models trained with a variety of datasets to compensate for the aforementioned issues.

To address some the abovementioned issues Yalei ding et al. [8] presented a CNN model that was trained with the KDD'99 dataset. The findings of the proposed paper were compared with other studies that used KDDTrain+ as the training set, and KDDTest-21 and KDDTest+ as the testing sets. For the evaluation metrics such as accuracy, detection rate, and false positive rate were measured. ML algorithms such as Random Forest (RF), and Support Vector Machine (SVM), as well as DL algorithms such as Long Short-Term Memory (LSTM) and Deep Belief Network (DBN) were utilized. The results showcased that RF obtained the highest accuracy among the ML algorithms, scoring 74.18% at KDDTest+ and 51.01% at KDDTest-21. The second highest score among the DL algorithms was achieved by LSTM with 73.18% and 49.37%, respectively. The demonstrated results showcased that the authors' proposed CNN model scored higher than all other ML and

DL algorithms that were tested across all evaluation metrics, with KDDTest+ scoring 80.13% and KDDTest-21 scoring 62.32% in terms of accuracy.

More researchers every year are progressively beginning to utilize the ML and DL since they are constantly evolving and have great potential to detect cyberthreats on the network. Thus, Pramita Sree Muhuri et al. [9] presented a novel method to classify the NSL-KDD dataset with LSTM and Recurrent Neural Networks and compared their results with various traditional ML algorithms such as RF and SVM. Their approach intergrades a Genetic Algorithm (GA) for feature selection, which offers several benefits when the consideration of many features is required to predict a class. With 122 features that were selected from the multiclass NSL-KDD dataset the results showed that traditional ML algorithms such as SVM and RF achieved a 67.20% and 80.70% score in accuracy, respectively, while the proposed model achieved 82.68%. Moreover, the addition of 99 optimal features improved the aforementioned models, with SVM reaching 68.10% and RF achieving 84.90%, while the proposed model improved significantly reaching a 93.88% in accuracy. The results demonstrated that DL algorithms outperformed ML algorithms regarding the evaluation metrics.

With the steady evolution of ML and D to detect intrusions, the authors [10] developed a DL-based NIDS, which focuses primarily on Denial-of-Service attacks (DOS). During the training phase of the DL NIDS two different datasets were used, namely: KDD'99 and CSE-CIC-IDS 2018. Moreover, two (2) additional models were developed, one with CNN and one with RNN to cope with time series data or data that includes sequences. Results demonstrated that CNN achieved a 99% accuracy with KDD'99 multiclass dataset and 91.5% accuracy with CSE-CIC-IDS 2018 multiclass dataset. On the contrary, RNN model reached a score of 93% and 65% in accuracy, when using KDD'99 and CSE-CIC-IDS 2018, respectively.

In similar vein, the authors in [11] presented a hybrid DL model for network intrusion detection with Bidirectional LSTM and CNN that were trained on the NSL-KDD and UNSW-NB15 datasets. The proposed model reached a score of 98.88% on the scale of detection rate (DR), 0.43% in FPR, and 99.22% in accuracy when trained with the NSL-KDD multiclass dataset, while with the UNSW-NB15 multiclass dataset it reached 92.5% in DR, 6.0% at FPR, and 82.08% in accuracy. These results were compared with another research model, the HAST-IDS that was trained and evaluated with the same datasets. HAST-IDS reached 95.85% in DR and 93.27% in accuracy when trained with the NSL-KDD dataset. On the contrary, when trained with UNSW-NB15 the model achieved 93.65% in DR, 9.6% in FPR and 80% in accuracy, indicating that the proposed model when trained with NSL-KDD outperformed the rest of the implementations that were used for the comparison.

Following the approach in [11], Pengfei Sun K et al. in [12] developed a DL hybrid NIDS incorporating a CNN and an LSTM model. The proposed solution was trained with the CICIDS2017 dataset, and the authors applied one hot encoding to the data in order to be used for multi-class classification. For the evaluation of the proposed model, two additional models were developed with the same input data. The first model was based on CNN, while the second was based on LSTM. The results showed that the CNN model reached 98.44% in accuracy and 93.11% in F1-score while LSTM reached 96.83% and 90.97%. On the contrary, the proposed solution, which combines CNN and LSTM, achieved 98.67% and 93.32% accuracy in F1-score in the evaluation metrics and outperformed the models that were developed based solely on either CNN or LSTM.

CIC2017 was also used by the authors in [13], who provided a highly scalable and hybrid Deep Neural Network (DNN) framework trained with a variety of datasets, which was applied in real scenarios to efficiently monitor network traffic and host level events in order to avoid possible intrusions. The topology architecture of this method had 5 layers of DNN, and the authors utilized 5 different datasets to train this hybrid DNN model, namely KDD'99, NSL-KDD, UNSW-NB15, WSN-DS, and CICIDS 2017. The proposed architecture consisted of a different input and output layer of neurons, since each dataset is multiclass and features different quantities of classes. The evaluation of the proposed framework after training showed that WSN-DS, CICIDS2017, KDD'99, NSL-KDD and UNSW-NB15 datasets achieved accuracy results of 96.4%, 95.6%, 92.5%, 78.5%, and 65.1%, respectively. According to their findings, their DNN framework outperformed various ML algorithms such as RF, SVM etc., utilizing the same multiclass datasets, in accuracy, precision, recall, and f1-score. In order to achieve real time detection of the intrusions and attacks, the authors deployed the proposed DL model into the realistic network and results showed that this hybrid and highly scalable proposed framework has the ability to constantly monitor network traffic and supply alerts whenever malicious traffic is detected in real time; however, the authors did not reveal the exact prediction rate of that traffic.

In similar vein, the authors in [14] presented a scalable and hybrid IDS. The proposed solution was developed with the Spark-ML and Convolutional-LSTM and trained with the ISCX-IDS 2012 dataset. The evaluation of the presented approach was compared with similar studies, using the same dataset. The authors' scalable and hybrid systems showed an accuracy rate of 97.29% and a false alarm rate of 0.71%. Although, additional studies had satisfactory rate of 95.31% in accuracy and 0.80% in false alarm rate, authors with their approach provided better results with this particular dataset.

The performance of bidirectional and conventional LSTM models was investigated by Yakubu Imrana et al. [15], who presented a Bidirectional LSTM model consisting of two separate LSTM modules, trained on the original and reversed input datasets correspondingly. In order to validate the effectiveness of the bidirectional LSTM model, the results were compared with a conventional LSTM model while NSL-KDD dataset was used for the training of the model. The proposed model was validated with stratified K-fold to verify the training accuracy percentage for each class. After the evaluation, results revealed that bidirectional LSTM model outperformed the conventional LSTM in evaluation metrics such accuracy, precision, recall, FAR, and f1-score. The results of the conventional LSTM were 87.26% in accuracy, 90.34% in precision, 87.26% in recall, 4.03% in FAR, and an f1-score at 88.03%, while the author's proposed model achieved 91.36%, 92,81% 91,36%, 0.88%, and 91,67%, respectively.

Moreover, the authors in [16], developed a NIDS with CNN that utilized the NSL-KDD dataset. The proposed model accomplished an accuracy of 85.83% and a loss of 1.5553% without authors providing any further information regarding the training metrics of the model, such as Recall, Precision, and F1-Score metrics. To evaluate the performance of the model after the training the authors extracted network traffic with the Python Scrapy library, but they had significant deficiency of the statistical data essential to fit characteristics of the NSL-KDD dataset. To compensate for the problem of essential characteristics they used a network analyser namely Tshark, which is the command line version of Wireshark. According to their findings, their proposed NIDS performed real time detection of the intrusions by monitoring the traffic of specific port; however, they did not supply further details regarding the model's capabilities at real time detection.

Moving one step furher, Peilun Wu et al. [17] presented a hierarchical CNN combined with a RNN model trained with two common datasets, the NSL-KDD and the UNSW-NB15. The structure of the model was divided in three blocks; each block contained the proposed model, which was the combination of RNN and CNN with different filters. Furthermore, during data pre-processing, features were converted into groups, conducting standardization of the data and stratified k-fold cross validation. The training's phase results showcased that when trained with the NSL-KDD dataset the model achieved 99.02% in detection rate (DR), 99.14% in accuracy and 0.61% in false positive rate (FPR), while when trained with UNSW-NB15 it reached 97.43%, 85.35%, and 2.89%, respectively. The proposed combined model of CNN and RNN hierarchy outperformed various ML algorithms such as RF, AdaBoost, and SVM with Gaussian Kernel (RBF) to all metrics.

In an effort to detect network intrusions, the authors of the above presented studies utilized various datasets, algorithms and combinations between of them with intend to enhance their proposed modules. However, in those case of studies, they did not specify whether their proposed models were evaluated with real network traffic captured in near real-time or real time scenarios to detect intrusion on the network. Only the proposed solution in [13] was deployed in a realistic scenario aiming for near-real time evaluation, nonetheless, the authors did not provide detailed results in their study.

According to the literature review, very few papers realistically evaluated their proposed NIDS solutions. Furthermore, although the aforementioned research studies achieved high scores between 90% and 99%, one of their shortcomings is that they used outdated multi-class datasets that do not accurately represent modern network traffic. The few of those publications that used more recent datasets for the training of their models, they used datasets that represent only a small portion of modern network traffic, while, even though they accomplished their goals with high scores between 86% and 99% in evaluation metrics such as accuracy, recall, precision, and f1-score, they did not evaluate their solutions over a realistic network in real world conditions and did not assess the capabilities of their models to identify intrusion in near real-time. Therefore, most of the reviewed studies only approximated the model's behavior after learning from the input datasets, while for the models to be fully evaluated as intrusion detection solutions they should be applied to real network scenarios.

Based on the gaps of the literature review, in this chapter an AI-based NIDS is designed and implemented that:

- is trained with an already in-house developed, recent, enhanced and modern NIDS dataset, containing not only network traffic but also logs and vulnerability assessment information about the system
- is evaluated following a realistic, near-real time evaluation process. During the evaluation phase, the NIDS is deployed in a realistic network topology and various cyber-attacks are performed, assessing near-real time performance.

14.3 Implementation

This sub-chapter discusses the structure of the proposed NIDS, the DL model utilized, and the pre-processing methodology that was followed for developing the in-house dataset that was fed to the DL model.

14.3.1 Dataset Description

Among the most common datasets utilized in recent studies for ML and DL models to detect intrusions are KDD'99 [18] and NSL-KDD [18] that are considered benchmark datasets for training ML-based NIDSs; however, the traffic included in these datasets is outdated. In addition, KDD'99 contains several duplicate records, which is among its limitations, while NSL-KDD has the disadvantage of class imbalance. Furthermore, more recent datasets have been released, such as the UNSW-NB15 [19] dataset that has been developed by the University of New South Wales (UNSW). This dataset includes network traffic that illustrate various scenarios and up to date attacks, resulting in a major upgrade compared to KDD'99 and NSL-KDD datasets. Nonetheless, the major limitation of this dataset is that the traffic was produced using a network traffic testbed and, even though the testbed was designed to mimic real-world network traffic, this simulation process led to producing a "Synthetic" network traffic dataset. Moreover, the University of New Brunswick (UNB) developed the CIC-IDS2017 [20] dataset, which is more recent than UNSW-NB15. This dataset was created in a controlled environment that mimics network traffic from the real world, both benign and malicious. In addition, the developers included interactions between different types of real users in the dataset, which was collected over the course of five days in order to improve its robustness and the accuracy of anomaly detection for the ML models. The dataset's major drawbacks are the fact that it is also a "Synthetic" network traffic dataset since it was developed in a controlled environment while it includes a significant data class imbalance between attack and normal traffic. Furthermore, the dataset's lack of heterogeneity is an additional disadvantage.

In this proposed solution, a modern, up to date, enhanced, heterogeneous, in-house developed dataset was selected for the training of the DL model of the proposed NIDS. The dataset was captured in 2022 and comprises 68 characteristics in total, 63 of which are network features and 5 are extra characteristics, such as vulnerability assessment information and logs that have been inserted to enhance the dataset. Additionally, an 80/20 split was used to divide the initial dataset, which contained approximately 16000 rows, into two different sets. 20% of the data constitutes the testing set and 80% the training set.

The network traffic flow of the dataset was captured by employing Wireshark and Tcpdump while the benign system was operated by real users who generated realistic network traffic consisting of internet browsing and interactions among various benign services. Moreover, malicious Python scripts and information stemming from the Common Vulnerability Enumeration (CVE) were utilized to generate the malicious network traffic that was captured as part of the dataset. The captured traffic data were converted into NetFlow v5 network flows by using CICFlowMeter. Eventually, the dataset contains six classes: one class represents benign traffic, and the other five classes represent malicious traffic and include cyber-attacks such as DDos Slowloris, SSH Brute Force, ICMP Ping Flood, TCP Fingerprinting, and Remote File Inclusion. The definition of the cyber-attacks that are contained in the dataset as well as the dataset labels are provided in Table 14.1 below.

The additional features that were inserted to the dataset, complementing its 63 network features, represent vulnerabilities of the physical machines. Each one of

Table 14.1. Definition of each malicious cyber-attack included in the in-house dataset.

Attack	**Attack description**
Remote File	Unauthorized file uploading to obtain system administrative rights
Inclusion	SSH Brute Force is a technique used to gain access to a remote server or a machine via SSH by guessing the right credentials
SSH Brute Force	Ping flood is a DDOS attacks that sends numerous ICMP requests resulting to reduced system performance.
ICMP Ping Flood	A high volume of HTTP requests that negatively impact a system's performance and availability.
DDos Slowloris	Network activity that examines a system to identify its operating system and/or active services of the targeted machine

those vulnerability features have a 1 or 0 value assigned to them regarding the presence of the respective vulnerability on the system. Table 14.2 below showcases the network features contained in the dataset and the importance factor rate.

14.3.2 Architecture of the Proposed DL Model

The training set of the dataset was inserted as input to the proposed CNN model, which was designed to be employed for multi-class classification. The model was trained over an epoch of 80, and the Adam optimizer, which has a low learning rate, was used to stabilize the model throughout training. The model utilizes a variety of regulations to prevent overfitting such as dropout layers, and early stopping. It additionally makes use of a model checkpoint to save the best-performing model during the training of the model. For the NIDS to be operational after training, it needs to be deployed in the network interface. To distinguish the incoming traffic between benign and malicious traffic, the traffic needs to be passed through the NIDS to predict whether it is malicious or benign.

The model input shape layer depends on the number of features included in the in-house developed dataset, which in the proposed solution were 68. The model is composed of two convolutional blocks namely two conv2D with the Rectified Linear Unit (Relu) activation function in each block, which is one of the most frequently utilized activation functions for DL Neural Networks since it doesn't activate the neurons simultaneously. Furthermore, each block has Batch Normalization, MaxPooling2D and Dropout layer. Batch Normalization is a method that helps the model to train faster and provides more stability to the model. The MaxPooling2D technique was employed for feature extraction and down sampling to ensure robustness of the model. Furthermore, the Dropout layer is a regulation form that was utilized to drop random neurons during training. The fully connected

Table 14.2. Importance Factor/Rates of dataset's features.

Features	Rates
Dst Port	1.9105
Src Port	1.6968
Bwd Header Len	1.5457
Fwd Pkts/s	1.4968
Bwd IAT Tot	1.4911
Bwd IAT Max	1.4875
Init Bwd Win Byts	1.4708
Flow IAT Max	1.45
Bwd IAT Mean	1.4422
Flow Duration	1.4343
Bwd Pkts/s	1.4049
Flow Pkts/s	1.3609
Pkt Len Max	1.334
Pkt Len Std	1.3326
Pkt Len Var	1.3326
Pkt Len Mean	1.3276
Pkt Size Avg	1.315
Flow IAT Mean	1.3086
Fwd Pkt Len Max	1.2647
Fwd Header Len	1.2646
TotLen Fwd Pkts	1.2643
Subflow Fwd Byts	1.2643
Fwd Seg Size Avg	1.262
Fwd Pkt Len Mean	1.262
Flow IAT Std	1.2432
Flow Byts/s	1.1413
Fwd Pkt Len Std	1.1071
Fwd IAT Tot	1.0659
Fwd IAT Max	1.0618
Fwd IAT Mean	0.9383
Subflow Bwd Byts	0.9105

(Continued)

Table 14.2. Continued

Features	Rates
TotLen Bwd Pkts	0.9105
Bwd Pkt Len Max	0.9105
Bwd Pkt Len Std	0.9074
Bwd Seg Size Avg	0.9036
Bwd Pkt Len Mean	0.9036
Tot Fwd Pkts	0.8955
Subflow Fwd Pkts	0.8955
Tot Bwd Pkts	0.8882
Subflow Bwd Pkts	0.8882
Bwd IAT Std	0.8605
Bwd IAT Min	0.7654
Fwd IAT Std	0.7106
Fwd Act Data Pkts	0.6886
Idle Max	0.6349
Idle Min	0.6312
Idle Mean	0.6284
VULN_4	0.6233
Fwd IAT Min	0.5794
Flow IAT Min	0.5499
VULN_5	0.5374
Active Mean	0.4929
Active Max	0.486
Active Min	0.458
Down/Up Ratio	0.3961
Idle Std	0.2128
Active Std	0.2124
SYN Flag Cnt	0.2114
VULN_3	0.1892
ACK Flag Cnt	0.1506
VULN_1	0.1412
VULN_2	0.1412
Fwd Pkt Len Min	0.137
RST Flag Cnt	0.0828

(Continued)

Table 14.2. Continued

Features	Rates
PSH Flag Cnt	0.0763
Bwd PSH Flags	0.0763
FIN Flag Cnt	0.0201
Label	Class/Category

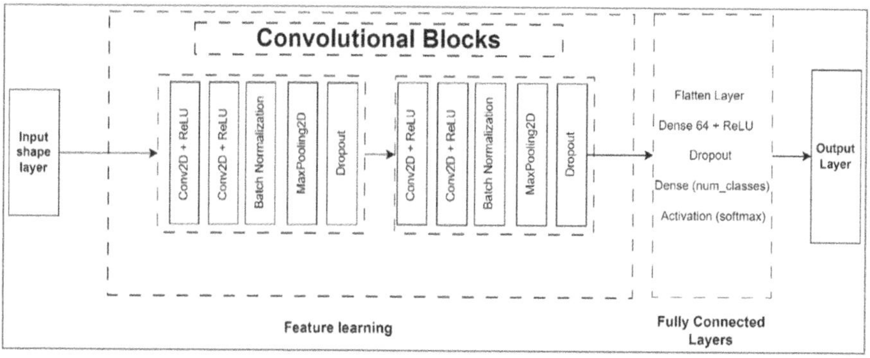

Figure 14.1. Architecture of the proposed DL model.

layer consists of a flatten layer that converts 3D tensors stemming from the second convolutional block into 1D vector. Furthermore, the fully connected Dense layer has 64 neurons, which is typically the most suitable choice of neurons for having the necessary capacity to learn from the data. Less neurons would not comprehend the complexity of the data, while more would lead to overfitting while featuring the Relu activation function and the Dropout Layer regulation form. Considering that the dataset is multi-class, the output layer has a Dense layer with a number of neurons equal to the number of classes of the dataset, i.e., six. SoftMax was the activation function used for the output layer since it categorizes the output prediction distribution over the classes and is suitable for multi-class classification. In Figure 14.1 below the model architecture is showcased.

Furthermore, Figure 14.2 below delves deep into the inner architecture of the proposed DL model and provides a visualization of the neural network which consists of an input layer, two convolutional blocks, a fully connected layer, and an output layer. The input layer contains 68 neurons, following the number of features included in the datasets. Following, each convolutional block has 2 conv2D layers with 16 neurons. In addition, the convolutional blocks include 3 more layers named Batch Normalization, MaxPooling2D, and Dropout. The fully connected layer consists of a flattened layer that converts the 3D vectors into 1D vectors, a dense layer that includes 64 neurons, and a dropout layer. Furthermore, the output

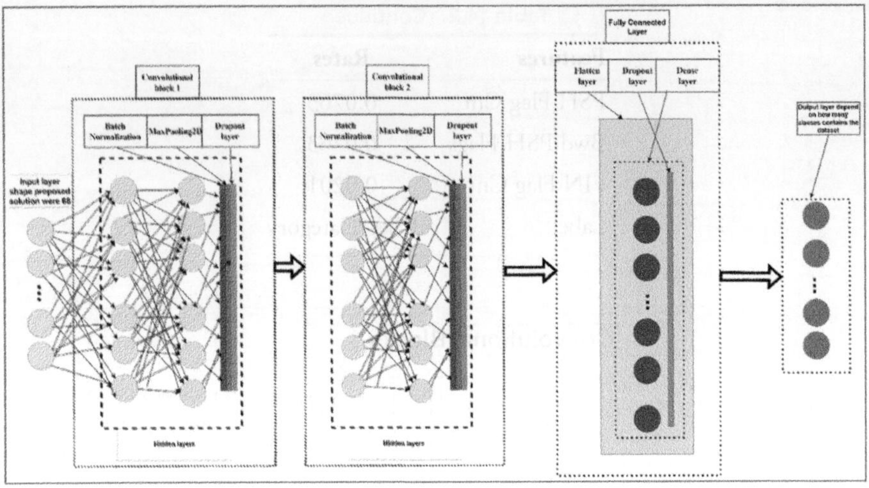

Figure 14.2. Visualization of the inner process of the proposed DL model.

layer length, i.e., the number of neurons that comprise it, depends on the classes that a dataset includes; in this case, the in-house dataset has six (6) classes.

The model operates in the following order: The input layer neurons provide inputs to the first convolutional block, which are the features derived from the dataset. The first convolutional block transforms the input data into a feature map set. This feature set is the reduced patterns, such as edges, textures, and shapes, of the input data after the implementation of the convolutional filter (kernels), while preserving the essential components of the input data. The feature map set produced by the first convolutional block is inserted into the second convolutional block, which performs the same processes as the first one and develops the final feature map set to be inserted into the fully connected layer. Following, the flattening layer of the fully connected layer converts the final feature map into one-dimensional vectors. Moreover, the fully connected layer operates as a classifier since it connects every neuron after the conversion of the flattening layer with the neurons of the output layer to produce the predictions.

14.3.3 Network Topology for Deploying the Proposed NIDS Solution

The configuration of links and nodes in a network, either physical or virtual, are referred to as the network's topology. Typically, artificial nodes consist of devices such as switches, routers, and SDN (software with network configuration functions). In an attempt to avoid interfering with the real network adapter, a virtual adapter created though VirtualBox (VM) was utilized in the proposed implementation to construct an isolated environment into which the NIDS solution was

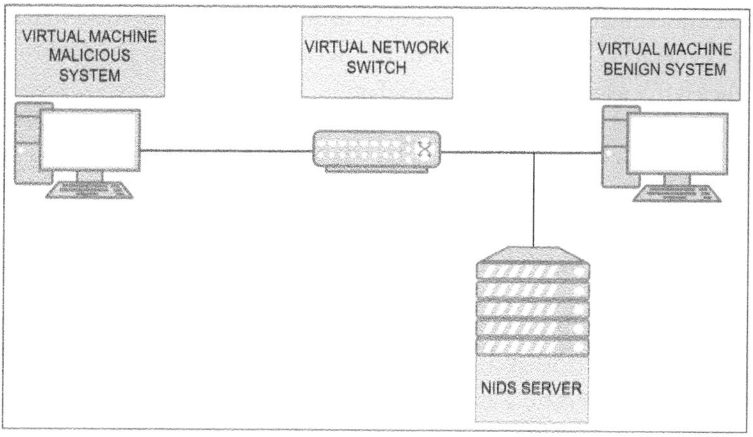

Figure 14.3. Network Topology and communication between virtual machines with host only adapter.

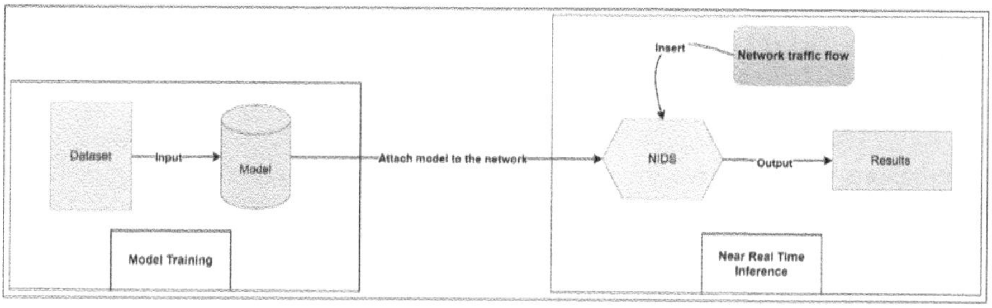

Figure 14.4. Function operation of the NIDS.

deployed. The network topology was based on a two-fold approach, i.e., a benign system that utilizes resources of network without interfering with the network, which would result in network failures or insufficient performance of the network, and a malicious system that causes network interference. The NIDS is an extra security layer on the network, which is usually placed between benign systems and switches because it is a pivotal spot to ensure the optimal ability to detect intrusions and respond to those threats, since at this position the NIDS can monitor the communication between the external incoming traffic and the internal hosts of the network. Figure 14.3 below illustrates the communication between the malicious and benign systems as well as where the proposed NIDS is placed in this topology.

Furthermore, Figure 14.4 below shows the functionality of the proposed NIDS. The first step of the process was to train the proposed DL model with the dataset and extract the model with h5 and Json format. Through the first process, the proposed NIDS establishes a baseline for both benign and malicious network behaviour. The second process is the deployment of the NIDS at the already configured isolated environment to make predictions regarding incoming network traffic.

Since the dataset includes a classification of multiple classes, the third step includes the NIDS generating predictions about the network traffic that passes through and sorting the traffic using a format of tabulate.

14.4 Evaluation

14.4.1 Aim of the Experiment

In this section, the performance of the proposed NIDS using the CNN algorithm is analyzed. The goal is to evaluate the proposed NIDS as an intrusion detection solution when deployed on a realistic network interface and assess its capacity to detect intrusions in near-real time as well as compare the performance results when the proposed solution is trained with the in-house developed dataset and a commonly used dataset stemming from the literature. The approach and results of the evaluation procedure are presented and discussed below.

14.4.2 Method

Two datasets were used for the evaluation procedure, namely the already in-house developed dataset described in the Implementation sub-chapter and the CIC-IDS2017 dataset, which is one of the most popular datasets for intrusion detection research, including up-to-date benign and malicious attacks representing real network traffic data. The CIC-IDS2017 dataset contains 8 attack types including Brute Force Attacks, Denial of Service (DoS) Attacks, Heartbleed Attack, Botnet Attack, Web Attacks, Infiltration, Port Scan, and Distributed Denial of Service (DDoS). The common denominator between the implemented datasets is in total 3 types of attacks, including a variate of DOS attack named SlowLoris, SSH Brute Force attack, and ICMP PingFlood. The proposed NIDS, i.e., the CNN model included, was trained using each dataset for multi-class classification, at the beginning of the evaluation.

The evaluation of the proposed solution included two experiments. The first experiment referring to the evaluation of the training and validation phases of the CNN model, which included the training and validation of the proposed NIDS including the collection of the results after the training and test phase and the evaluation of them using ML metrics that are described as dependent variables. Two versions of the proposed NIDS resulted from this first experiment, namely version A, trained with the already in-house developed dataset, and version B, trained with the CIC-IDS2017 dataset. The second experiment was the testing of version A and version B of the NIDS in near real-time. After the two versions of the proposed NIDS were trained, the CNN model of both versions was exported in h5 and Json format. In order to evaluate near real-time intrusion detection of the proposed solution, real network traffic was captured via CICFlowMeter and was modified to CSV so that it could be inserted in near-real time into the two versions of the trained NIDS and determine if the captured traffic was benign or malicious.

14.4.3 Variables

14.4.3.1 Fixed Variables

These values remain constant during an experiment. The fixed variables in these experiments were the DL methods, network topology, malicious and benign systems, system vulnerabilities and cyber-attacks.

14.4.3.2 Independent Variables

These variables depend on the model itself or the defined problem (in this chapter referring to network intrusion detection). In the proposed approach the independent variables are the dataset's features and values, as well as the model's architecture and parameters. Altering the independent variables forces different outcomes on the dependent variables.

14.4.3.3 Dependent Variables

Dependent variables are those that change based on the independent ones. The dependent variables of this experiment include the ML metrics that were used for the evaluation of the model, namely accuracy and loss of both training and validation phases as well as accuracy, precision, recall, and f1-score assessing the performance of the trained model.

14.4.4 Experiment Set-up

The two versions of the proposed NIDS were tested on an Oracle VM VirtualBox that was developed specifically for the experiments in order to evaluate the CNN model during training and validation phase and achieve near-real time intrusion detection. To prevent interference with the physical network adapter, a Host-only bridge adapter was utilized at VirtualBox. This virtual adapter-maintained communication between the malicious and benign systems. The first experiment set up for both systems had a 30-gigabyte disk space and 4 processors with a 100% performance limit, with the exception that the benign system had 16 GB ram with 2400 MHz and the malicious system had 4 GB ram. The operating system used for both the attacker and the victim was Kali Linux, version 2022,3. The benign system had the following characteristics: pre-installed, enabled firewall, Apache server deployed on TCP port 80, and SSH server established via port 22. The second experiment was the deployment of the two NIDS versions to achieve near-real time intrusion detection. For both NIDS versions, CICFlowMeter was utilized for capturing live network traffic. The captured traffic was then fed into the NIDS in order to achieve predictions in near real time. The malicious system used the Metasploit framework to generate malicious attacks as those that are in common between the in-house developed dataset and the CIC2017 dataset, enabling the NIDS to predict the traffic captured via CICFlowMeter in near real time.

14.4.5 Prediction

The training and validation performance results of the two versions of the proposed NIDS, i.e., version A trained with the already in-house developed multi-class dataset and version B trained with the multi-class CIC-IDS2017 dataset, are anticipated to be strongly promising since both of these datasets represent modern network traffic. Moreover, experiment results are foreseen to be over 95% at the evaluation of the training and validation phase of the proposed CNN DL model for both NIDS versions. In the second experiment, the proposed NIDS is evaluated in near real-time and positive results are expected, similar to the first experiment. It is also anticipated that version A NIDS will outperform version B NIDS due to the enhanced and heterogeneous data included in in the already in-house developed dataset.

14.4.6 Results

14.4.6.1 1st Experiment: Training and Validation of the proposed NIDS

In this section the results of the first experiment of the proposed NIDS, both version A and version B, are presented. The epochs for the proposed NIDS for version A and version B were appointed to be 80. Moreover, the CICIDS2017 dataset includes nine (9) attack types, which means that it has nine classes, while the in-house developed dataset has six (6). The two datasets contain 3 common malicious attack types, namely SSH brute force attack, Dos slowloris, and ICMP ping flood indicating that the two versions of the proposed NIDS have 3 common output layers.

The training loss for version B NIDS was 0.0863% and the validation loss was 0.0740%, while version A NIDS showcased a training loss of 0.056% and a validation loss of 0.064%. In addition, version B NIDS achieved training accuracy of 97.45% and validation accuracy of 97.85%, while version A NIDS accomplished 97.80% and 97.95%, respectively. The proposed NIDS showcased great efficiency in predicting the network traffic with each aforementioned dataset as it can be noted by the high accuracy results while both training and validation loss values

Table 14.3. Training and validation accuracy and loss of the proposed NIDS.

Model	Training loss	Training accuracy	Validation loss	Validation accuracy
Version A NIDS	0.0863%	97.80%	0.064%	97.95%
Version B NIDS	0.056%	97.45%	0.0740%	97.85%

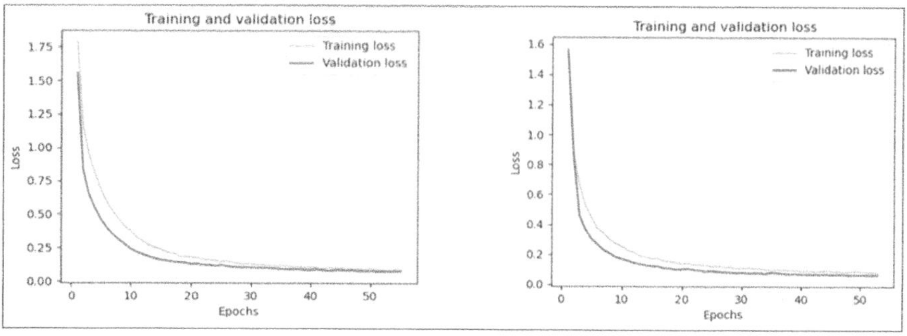

Figure 14.5. Training and validation loss of the proposed NIDS.

were minimal. Table 14.3 below illustrates the validation and training results of both versions of the proposed NIDS.

In Figure 14.5 below the training and validation loss of the proposed model are plotted; The left figure represents the training of version A NIDS and the right figure the training of version B NIDS. As explained above, the default epoch for the training of the models was 80, however, the model utilized a regulation form named Early Stopping to prevent overfitting. The CNN model on the left figure performed 53 epochs while the CNN model on the right performed 55. In Figure 14.1, the red line represents the validation loss and the green line the training loss. Moreover, the validation loss line is parallel to the training loss line for both version A and B of the NIDS, implying that there is neither under-fitting nor overfitting during the training of the proposed model.

Moreover, in Figure 14.6 below the left and right diagrams showcase a comparison between the training and validation accuracy for version A and version B NIDS, respectively, during the training of the models. The red line represents the validation accuracy and the green line the training accuracy, which are parallel during the training phase for both version A and B.

Moreover, during the training phase of both versions of the proposed NIDS, additional metrics such as accuracy, precision, recall and f1-score were collected. Version B NIDS showcased an f1-score of 97.61%, precision of 97.81%, recall of 97.83%, and accuracy of 97.41%, while version A NIDS reached 97.68%, 97.90%, 97.62%, and 97.72%, respectively. This indicates the proposed models function

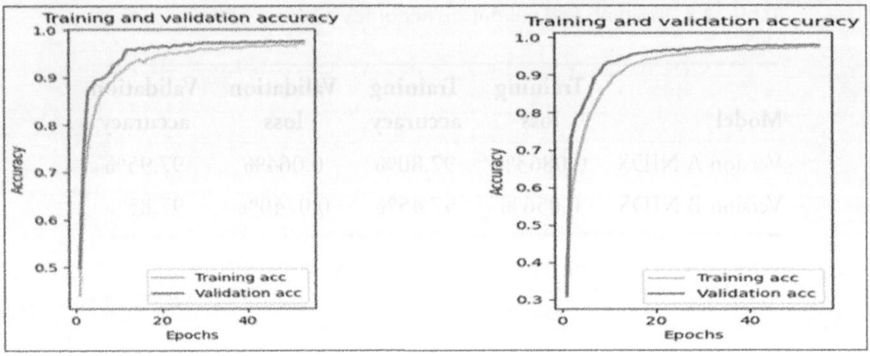

Figure 14.6. Training and validation accuracy of the proposed NIDS.

Table 14.4. Average score of DL performance metrics for multiclass classification of the proposed NIDS.

Model	Average training accuracy	Average training loss	Average prediction precision	Average prediction recall	Average prediction accuracy	Average prediction F1-score
Version A NIDS	97.80%	0.056%	97.90%	97.62%	97.72%	97.68%
Version B NIDS	97.45%	0.0863%	97.81%	97.83%	97.41%	97.61%

well since the training accuracy is high. Since the training accuracy is high, the model trains efficiently on the input datasets, while the validation accuracy represents the objective assessment of the model's capacity to generalize the inconspicuous data. In addition, the model's prediction accuracy indicates the capacity of the model to predict with effectiveness. The results of the proposed NIDS during the first experiment were obtained from the Scikit-learn[1] ML Python library. The average score results after training of versions A and B of the proposed NIDS are presented and illustrated in Table 14.4 and Figure 14.7 below.

14.4.6.2 2nd Experiment: Near-real time testing of the proposed NIDS

Network data were captured in near real time from the virtual network interface using CICFlowMeter when the malicious activities were conducted and then they were fed into the two versions of the trained proposed model. This technique led the proposed model to generate predictions in near-real time. The results showcased that version B NIDS had less than 40% of prediction accuracy in near-real

1. https://scikit-learn.org/stable/.

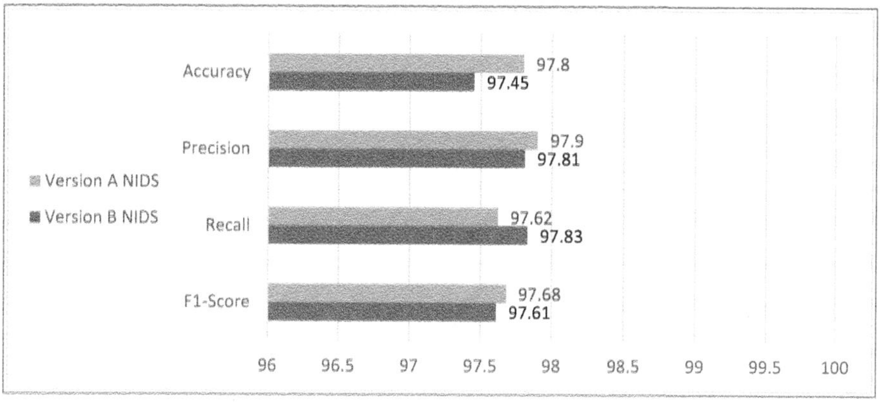

Figure 14.7. Training results of multiclass classification with CNN for the proposed NIDS.

Table 14.5. Near-real time prediction accuracy of the proposed NIDS.

Model	Prediction accuracy in near real time
Version A NIDS	90%
Version B NIDS	40%

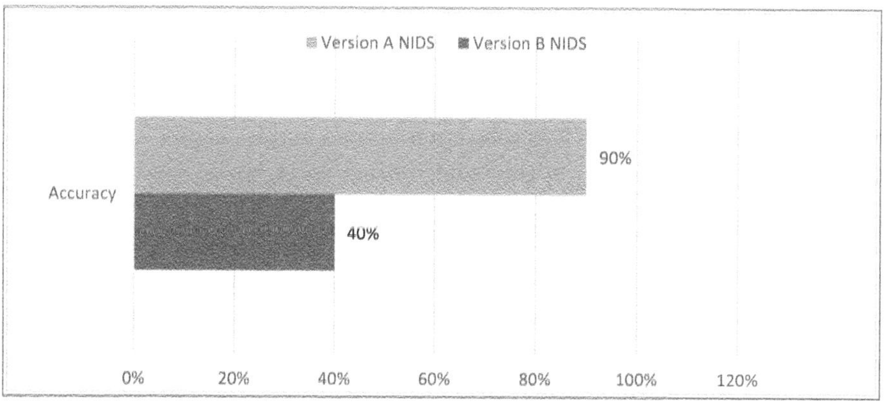

Figure 14.8. Near-real time prediction accuracy of the proposed NIDS.

time traffic when the proposed model was trained with the CIC2017 dataset and was deployed in the virtual network, despite the fact that the model's dependent variables showed great performance during the training phase. On the contrary, version A NIDS predicted accurately over 90% of the in near real time traffic, outperforming version B NIDS. The training and detection in near real time results for both NIDS versions are presented in Table 14.5 and Figure 14.8 below.

14.4.7 Discussion

After using the CNN algorithm to train the proposed DL model, the datasets results demonstrated that version A NIDS, using the in-house developed dataset, performed better than when the CIC2017 dataset was used to train the model in version B NIDS, with regard to the ML metrics presented in the dependent variables. Version A NIDS achieved more than 97% accuracy in the training phase and while those results were only slightly better than the results of version B NIDS, there were significant differences between the two versions of the NIDS when they were both deployed on the network to evaluate them for the intrusion detection in near-real time. The results indicate that when the network data were captured live from the network and fed into the trained models, version A NIDS outperformed version B NIDS in near-real time intrusion detection. This resulted because the version A NIDS utilizes an in-house dataset for the training of the CNN model, which is enhanced, heterogeneous and contains up to date modern network activity.

14.5 Conclusion

Most studies in recent literature use KDD'99 and NSL-KDD as input to train and test their ML or DL model that is part of their NIDS solution. However, these datasets are outdated, they do not represent realistic network traffic, nor they deploy their models on a realistic network to evaluate them. In order to compensate for the aforementioned issues, the NIDS solution proposed in this chapter was developed to detect intrusion in near-real-time and utilized an in-house developed, multi-class, enhanced dataset that includes modern benign and malicious network traffic. Moreover, the proposed NIDS was evaluated in a realistic scenario, during which it was assessed when trained with the in-house developed dataset and when it was trained with the CIC-IDS2017 dataset, which is a benchmark modern network traffic dataset. The proposed NIDS achieved the detection of the intrusion in near real-time, and as results demonstrate, the proposed model accomplished above 90% prediction accuracy in near real-time traffic when the model was deployed in a realistic network environment and trained with the in-housed dataset. Conversely, the CIC-IDS2017 showed remarkable performance during the training phase. However, during the deployment of the model in the network, the prediction rate was less than 40% when evaluating realistic network traffic in near real time. The NIDS proposed in this chapter performed more effectively in near-real-time traffic detection when trained with the in-house developed dataset compared to when trained with the CIC-IDS2017 dataset.

14.5.1 Limitations

The evaluation experiment performed in this chapter raised several concerns about DL methods, the development of model's necessities, and the initial processing of input data that DL needs to obtain the most efficient outcomes. Although the proposed model achieved the objective to detect intrusions in near-real time more accurately with the in-house dataset, it is possible further enhancement can be made by introducing more network traffic to the dataset.

14.5.2 Future Work

Therefore, in order to obtain more efficient results in near real-time detection, future research could utilize a variety of preprocessing techniques to enhance the input dataset. In addition, further hyper-tuning of the parameters of the model could be investigated in order to decrease the training time. Furthermore, evaluating the system by using a wide range of AI algorithms could provide additional insight into the capabilities of the proposed solution, since the proposed implementation solely explored the capabilities of the CNN algorithm.

Acknowledgement

This research initiative is supported by the European Union's Horizon Framework Programme for Research and Innovation, under the projects: INTACT (Grant Agreement No. 101168438), cPAID (Grant Agreement No. 101168407), and CoGNETs (Grant Agreement No. 101135930).

References

[1] E. U. A. for Cybersecurity et al., *ENISA threat landscape 2023 – July 2022 to June 2023*. 2023. doi: doi/10.2824/782573.

[2] Steve Morgan, " Top 10 Cybersecurity Predictions and Statistics For 2024," Northport, N.Y., Feb. 05, 2024. [Online]. Available: https://cybersecurityventures.com/top-5-cybersecurity-facts-figures-predictions-and-statistics-for-2021-to-2025/.

[3] A. Khraisat, I. Gondal, P. Vamplew, and J. Kamruzzaman, "Survey of intrusion detection systems: techniques, datasets and challenges," *Cybersecurity*, vol. 2, no. 1, pp. 1–22, 2019.

[4] S. M. Othman, N. T. Alsohybe, F. M. Ba-Alwi, and A. T. Zahary, "Survey on intrusion detection system types," *International Journal of Cyber-Security and Digital Forensics*, vol. 7, no. 4, pp. 444–463, 2018.

[5] P. P. Shinde and S. Shah, "A Review of Machine Learning and Deep Learning Applications," in *2018 Fourth International Conference on Computing Communication Control and Automation (ICCUBEA)*, 2018, pp. 1–6. doi: 10.1109/ICCUBEA.2018.8697857.

[6] A. Javaid, Q. Niyaz, W. Sun, and M. Alam, "A Deep Learning Approach for Network Intrusion Detection System," in *Proceedings of the 9th EAI International Conference on Bio-Inspired Information and Communications Technologies (Formerly BIONETICS)*, in BICT'15. Brussels, BEL: ICST (Institute for Computer Sciences, Social-Informatics and Telecommunications Engineering), 2016, pp. 21–26. doi: 10.4108/eai.3-12-2015.2262516.

[7] N. T. Van, T. N. Thinh, and L. T. Sach, "An anomaly-based network intrusion detection system using Deep learning," in *2017 International Conference on System Science and Engineering (ICSSE)*, 2017, pp. 210–214. doi: 10.1109/ICSSE.2017.8030867.

[8] Y. Ding and Y. Zhai, "Intrusion Detection System for NSL-KDD Dataset Using Convolutional Neural Networks," in *Proceedings of the 2018 2nd International Conference on Computer Science and Artificial Intelligence*, New York, NY, USA: ACM, Dec. 2018, pp. 81–85. doi: 10.1145/3297156.3297230.

[9] P. S. Muhuri, P. Chatterjee, X. Yuan, K. Roy, and A. Esterline, "Using a Long Short-Term Memory Recurrent Neural Network (LSTM-RNN) to Classify Network Attacks," *Information*, vol. 11, no. 5, p. 243, May 2020, doi: 10.3390/info11050243.

[10] J. Kim, J. Kim, H. Kim, M. Shim, and E. Choi, "CNN-Based Network Intrusion Detection against Denial-of-Service Attacks," *Electronics (Basel)*, vol. 9, no. 6, p. 916, Jun. 2020, doi: 10.3390/electronics9060916.

[11] J. Sinha and M. Manollas, "Efficient Deep CNN-BiLSTM Model for Network Intrusion Detection," in *Proceedings of the 2020 3rd International Conference on Artificial Intelligence and Pattern Recognition*, New York, NY, USA: ACM, Jun. 2020, pp. 223–231. doi: 10.1145/3430199.3430224.

[12] P. Sun et al., "DL-IDS: Extracting Features Using CNN-LSTM Hybrid Network for Intrusion Detection System," *Security and Communication Networks*, vol. 2020, pp. 1–11, Aug. 2020, doi: 10.1155/2020/8890306.

[13] R. Vinayakumar, M. Alazab, K. P. Soman, P. Poornachandran, A. Al-Nemrat, and S. Venkatraman, "Deep Learning Approach for Intelligent Intrusion Detection System," *IEEE Access*, vol. 7, pp. 41525–41550, 2019, doi: 10.1109/ACCESS.2019.2895334.

[14] M. Khan, Md. Karim, and Y. Kim, "A Scalable and Hybrid Intrusion Detection System Based on the Convolutional-LSTM Network," *Symmetry (Basel)*, vol. 11, no. 4, p. 583, Apr. 2019, doi: 10.3390/sym11040583.

[15] Y. Imrana, Y. Xiang, L. Ali, and Z. Abdul-Rauf, "A bidirectional LSTM deep learning approach for intrusion detection," *Expert Syst Appl*, vol. 185, p. 115524, Dec. 2021, doi: 10.1016/j.eswa.2021.115524.

[16] S. Wang, Z. Chen, J. Chen, and P. Zhu, "Design and Implementation of Intrusion Detection System Based on Deep Learning," in *2023 IEEE 3rd International Conference on Electronic Technology, Communication and Information (ICETCI)*, IEEE, May 2023, pp. 1495–1497. doi: 10.1109/ICETCI57876.2023.10176554.

[17] P. Wu and H. Guo, "LuNet: A Deep Neural Network for Network Intrusion Detection," in *2019 IEEE Symposium Series on Computational Intelligence (SSCI)*, IEEE, Dec. 2019, pp. 617–624. doi: 10.1109/SSCI44817.2019.9003126.

[18] M. Tavallaee, E. Bagheri, W. Lu, and A. A. Ghorbani, "A detailed analysis of the KDD CUP 99 data set," in *2009 IEEE Symposium on Computational Intelligence for Security and Defense Applications*, IEEE, Jul. 2009, pp. 1–6. doi: 10.1109/CISDA.2009.5356528.

[19] N. Moustafa and J. Slay, "UNSW-NB15: a comprehensive data set for network intrusion detection systems (UNSW-NB15 network data set)," in *2015 Military Communications and Information Systems Conference (MilCIS)*, IEEE, Nov. 2015, pp. 1–6. doi: 10.1109/MilCIS.2015.7348942.

[20] I. Sharafaldin, A. H. Lashkari, and A. A. Ghorbani, "Toward Generating a New Intrusion Detection Dataset and Intrusion Traffic Characterization," in *International Conference on Information Systems Security and Privacy*, 2018. [Online]. Available: https://api.semanticscholar.org/CorpusID:4707749.

[15] Y. Imrana, Y. Xiang, L. Ali, and Z. Abdul-Rauf, "A bidirectional LSTM deep learning approach for intrusion detection," *Expert Syst. Appl*, vol. 185, p. 115524, Dec. 2021. doi: 10.1016/j.eswa.2021.115524.

[16] S. Wang, Z. Chen, J. Chen, and P. Zhu, "Design and Implementation of Intrusion Detection System Based on Deep Learning," in *2023 IEEE 3rd International Conference on Electronic Technology, Communication and Information (ICETCI)*, IEEE, May 2023, pp. 1495–1497. doi: 10.1109/ICETCI57876.2023.10176654.

[17] R. Wu and H. Guo, "TnNet: A Deep Neural Network for Network Intrusion Detection," in *2019 IEEE Symposium Series on Computational Intelligence (SSCI)*, IEEE, Dec. 2019, pp. 617–624. doi: 10.1109/SSCI44817.2019.9003126.

[18] M. Tavallaee, E. Bagheri, W. Lu, and A. A. Ghorbani, "A detailed analysis of the KDD CUP 99 data set," in *2009 IEEE Symposium on Computational Intelligence for Security and Defense Applications*, IEEE, Jul. 2009, pp. 1–6. doi: 10.1109/CISDA.2009.5356528.

[19] N. Moustafa and J. Slay, "UNSW-NB15: a comprehensive data set for network intrusion detection systems (UNSW-NB15 network data set)," in 2015

DOI: 10.1561/9781638285076.ch15

Chapter 15

Connected Medical Devices: The Cybersecurity Nexus of the AI Act and MDR

By Maja Nisevic, Dusko Milojevic, João Rodrigues and Goncalo Cadete

The increasing use of artificial intelligence (AI) in medical devices (CMDs) and their integration in the IoMT environment offers great potential for improving healthcare delivery, but it also brings complex challenges, cybersecurity being one of the most pressing ones. This book chapter delves into how the European Union's AI Act and the Medical Device Regulation (MDR) intersect in addressing the cybersecurity aspects of AI-driven medical devices. While the MDR focuses on ensuring the safety and performance of medical devices, including cybersecurity requirements across the product lifecycle, the Artificial Intelligence Act (AI Act) introduces rigorous measures for regulating high-risk AI systems, particularly in healthcare. Accordingly, the chapter examines the alignment of these frameworks and identifies potential regulatory gaps, particularly in cybersecurity standards, risk assessment, and conformity requirements for AI-enabled CMDs. By analyzing these aspects, the chapter aims to provide insights into how the evolving EU regulatory landscape can effectively ensure the security and safety of CMDs while promoting innovation in AI-driven healthcare technologies. It also offers recommendations for harmonizing regulatory approaches to better address the unique cybersecurity risks associated with AI in medical devices.

15.1 Introduction

In an era of rapid technological advancement, the incorporation of artificial intelligence (AI) into medical devices presents exceptional opportunities alongside complex regulatory challenges. The convergence of AI with medical technology has the potential to revolutionize healthcare delivery through enhanced diagnostics, personalized treatments, and improved patient outcomes. However, this integration also raises significant concerns, cybersecurity being one of the most pressing once, emphasizing the need for a robust regulatory and risk-assessment framework to ensure patient safety and safeguard data protection.

The World Economic Forum's Global Risks Report underlines cyberattacks as a critical global risk, highlighting the increasing severity and impact of these threats [1]. The growing reliance on technology across various sectors has propelled cybersecurity to the forefront of political agendas worldwide [2, 3].

Due to abundance of valuable data and lack of maturity level regarding the cybersecurity, the healthcare sector has emerged as a primary target for cyberattacks. According to the European Union Agency for Cybersecurity (ENISA) Report on the Health Threat Landscape, the health sector ranks third in terms of the number of cybersecurity incidents, with patient data—such as electronic health records—being the most targeted asset between January 2021 and March 2023 [4]. In addition, the FBI Internet Crime Report stresses the vulnerability of the healthcare sector, identifying it as one of the most attacked critical infrastructure sectors in the US in 2023 [5]. Successful attacks on healthcare systems have the potential to disrupt hospital operations, compromise patient safety, and, in severe cases, lead to loss of life.

From the perspective of the European Union, the AI Act (AIA) and the Medical Device Regulation (MDR) are two pivotal legislative instruments addressing distinct aspects of the regulatory landscape. The AIA focuses on establishing a comprehensive framework for the development, deployment, and oversight of AI systems, with an emphasis on risk management and transparency. Contrarily, the MDR governs the safety and performance of medical devices, including those incorporating AI, placing significant emphasis on clinical efficacy and patient safety. The intersection of these regulations presents a unique challenge: *aligning the provisions of the AI Act with the requirements of the MDR to create a cohesive cybersecurity strategy.*

As AI-enabled medical devices become increasingly prevalent, ensuring their security against cyber threats is paramount to maintaining public trust and safeguarding sensitive health information. Case studies highlight the critical intersection of the AI Act and MDR, particularly in instances where AI in medical devices has given rise to compliance issues. For example, AI-driven diagnostic tools such as imaging systems must meet the MDR's General Safety and Performance

Requirements and underwent third-party conformity assessments. However, the AI Act's requirements for transparency and explainability introduce additional complexity, leading to delays in device approval as developers ensure that AI decision-making processes are interpretable by healthcare professionals [6]. Ensuring these systems are resistant to manipulation while satisfying both regulatory frameworks has proven difficult, resulting in delays and compliance issues in the early development stages [7].

This book chapter delves into the broader issue of cybersecurity in connected medical devices (CMDs) amidst the surge of cyberattacks on healthcare sector. Under the MDR, manufacturers must implement cybersecurity measures as part of the General Safety and Performance Requirements, while the AI Act introduces specific provisions on the accuracy, robustness, and cybersecurity of AI systems. Therefore, the objective of this book chapter is to explore the synergies and potential conflicts between the AI Act and the MDR in the context of CMDs cybersecurity. By analyzing the regulatory frameworks of both, it aims to identify how they can be harmonized to address the specific cybersecurity challenges posed by AI-integrated medical devices. Besides, it will delve into importance of risk management strategies and standards in this domain. Through this examination, it seeks to provide actionable insights for policymakers, industry stakeholders, and researchers navigating this complex regulatory terrain, ultimately enhancing the safety and effectiveness of AI-driven medical technologies.

15.2 The Brief Overview of the Advancements in AI and Medical Devices

Many global health systems face a widening gap between demand and capacity. This surge in demand, driven by an aging population, rising chronic conditions, and higher expectations for quality care, is exacerbated by a growing shortage of healthcare professionals. The integration of AI presents a transformative potential to address these challenges. Recent advancements in AI medical devices have greatly impacted healthcare, bringing new possibilities for improved diagnostics, personalized treatments, and enhanced patient care. In 2021, the global AI in healthcare market was valued at over 11 billion U.S. dollars, with projections indicating a significant surge in growth, anticipating the market to expand to approximately 188 billion U.S. dollars by 2030 [8]. However, these advancements also come with new challenges and considerations, particularly in cybersecurity domain.

Further research and innovation hold significant potential in this realm. One crucial focus area is the development of AI-specific cybersecurity tools and risk assessment methodologies. It is essential to investigate potential vulnerabilities of AI models, such as adversarial attacks, and develop strategies to mitigate these threats in healthcare settings to enhance device security. In addition, there is a growing need for research into explainability in AI systems as regulatory bodies increasingly seek transparent and understandable AI decision-making processes in healthcare contexts. Innovation is key to establishing dynamic regulatory frameworks that can adapt to technological advancements. This includes creating sandbox environments where new AI-enabled medical devices can be rigorously tested in real-world settings under regulatory supervision. These environments would support more effective collaboration between regulators and developers, ensuring that cybersecurity and regulatory compliance progress harmoniously with technological innovation. This section briefly stresses an overview of the recent developments in AI and medical devices.

15.2.1 AI in Medical Diagnostics and Treatment

AI has made substantial steps in medical diagnostics and treatment. Machine learning algorithms, particularly deep learning models, have demonstrated remarkable accuracy in analyzing medical images. For example, AI medical devices can now detect conditions such as diabetic retinopathy, lung cancer, and breast cancer with accuracy comparable to or exceeding that of human radiologists [9, 10]. These AI-driven tools can quickly analyze vast amounts of imaging data, providing valuable support in clinical decision-making.

Another significant advancement is the integration of AI in genomics and personalized medicine. AI algorithms can analyze genetic data to identify genetic markers associated with diseases and predict individual responses to specific treatments. This capability allows for more personalized and effective treatment plans, tailored to the unique genetic profile of each patient [11]. AI-driven platforms like IBM Watson for Oncology have been developed to assist oncologists in selecting appropriate therapies based on the latest research and patient data [12]. Likewise, a recent study highlights the significant strides made in oncology through the use of AI for cancer detection and treatment planning. The researchers developed an AI-based system that integrates genomic data and imaging to improve the accuracy of cancer diagnosis and predict patient responses to various therapies. This system has demonstrated a substantial increase in the precision of tumor classification and the identification of personalized treatment options, leading to more effective and targeted interventions [13].

15.2.2 Innovations in Connected Medical Devices

The Internet of Medical Things (IoMT) has expanded the capabilities of connected medical devices, enhancing their functionality and integration into healthcare systems. Recent innovations include wearable devices, implantable sensors, and remote monitoring systems. Wearable devices, such as smartwatches and fitness trackers, now offer advanced health monitoring features, including heart rate variability, sleep analysis, and blood oxygen levels [14]. These devices provide real-time data to both patients and healthcare providers, enabling proactive management of chronic conditions and improved patient engagement.

Implantable devices, such as pacemakers and insulin pumps, have also seen significant advancements. Modern pacemakers are now equipped with wireless communication capabilities, allowing for remote monitoring and adjustments by healthcare providers [15]. Similarly, next-generation insulin pumps feature integrated continuous glucose monitoring systems, enabling more precise insulin delivery and better diabetes management [16].

15.2.3 AI-Driven Enhancements in Device Functionality

AI is increasingly being integrated into medical devices to enhance their functionality. For example, AI algorithms are used in automated insulin delivery systems to adjust insulin dosing based on real-time glucose readings, reducing the risk of hypoglycemia and hyperglycemia [17]. AI-powered diagnostic devices, such as handheld ultrasound machines, use machine learning to provide automated image interpretation, making advanced imaging more accessible in remote or underserved areas [18].A recent study explored the use of deep learning algorithms in medical imaging for enhancing the detection and classification of various diseases. The researchers developed an AI model that analyzes chest X-rays with high accuracy, identifying subtle abnormalities indicative of conditions such as pneumonia and tuberculosis [19].

15.2.4 Challenges and Considerations

While these advancements offer substantial benefits, they also present complex challenges. The integration of AI into medical devices raises concerns about data privacy, security, and regulatory compliance. Ensuring that AI algorithms are transparent and interpretable is crucial for maintaining trust in these technologies [20]. Additionally, the interoperability of connected devices and the protection of sensitive health data remain significant concerns as the use of IoMT expands [21].

In conclusion, recent advancements in AI and medical devices are reshaping healthcare by enhancing diagnostic accuracy, personalizing treatments, and improving patient monitoring. However, harnessing these innovations also necessitate careful consideration of privacy, security, and regulatory challenges to fully realize their potential benefits.

15.3 Understanding Cybersecurity and the Cyber Threat Landscape in Healthcare

Before adopting the European Union Cybersecurity Act in 2019, the term "cybersecurity" was often used vaguely, with varying interpretations depending on the context. In both academic literature and policy discussions, cybersecurity lacked a unified definition, making it challenging to develop consistent strategies for addressing cyber threats. As noted by some scholars, cybersecurity was frequently conceptualized differently by governments, organizations, and experts, leading to fragmented approaches across sectors [22]. This ambiguity posed significant challenges to establishing cohesive cybersecurity policies, particularly in critical sectors like healthcare, where the stakes are high.

The European Union Cybersecurity Act marked a turning point by introducing the first definition of cybersecurity within the EU legislative framework. The Act defines cybersecurity as the set of activities aimed at protecting network and information systems, their users, and those affected by cyber threats. This formalization has brought much-needed clarity, enabling a more consistent and structured approach to cyber defence across member states [23]. To understand the healthcare cybersecurity landscape, it is important to explore the motivations behind malicious attacks, the associated risks, and the sector's inherent vulnerabilities.

15.3.1 Motivations and Risks

Cyberattacks on healthcare systems can be driven by a range of motivations, including financial gain, political agendas, and intellectual property theft, to mention just a few [24]. Financial incentives are particularly significant in healthcare due to the value of sensitive data. Electronic Health Records (EHRs), which include comprehensive personal and medical information, are highly sought after on the black market, with stolen records fetching between $10 and $1,000 each, depending on their detail [25, 26]. This data's value extends beyond financial theft, as it can be used for fraudulent activities such as false insurance claims [27]. In addition, ideological motives and espionage also contribute to cybercriminal activities.

15.3.2 Consequences of Cyberattacks

Successful cyberattacks can have severe implications for both healthcare institutions and patients. Financially, the costs of security breaches are substantial. According to the ENISA NIS Investments Report the median cost of significant incidents is 300,000 euros [28]. IBM's Cost of a Data Breach Report highlights that healthcare breaches have been the costliest among industries for over a decade, with costs increasing by 53.3% since 2020 [29]. Hospitals may face substantial financial burdens from patient compensation claims and regulatory fines [30]. A notable example is the Finnish psychotherapy center Vastaamo, which incurred a penalty of EUR 608,000 due to violations of the GDPR concerning the protection of personal data and the reporting of a data breach [31].

In addition to financial damage, cyberattacks can disrupt healthcare services, leading to potentially life-threatening consequences. The ransomware attack on Brno University Hospital in 2020, which led to postponed surgeries, and the attack on a German hospital that disrupted emergency services and contributed to a patient's death, underscore the critical impact of such breaches [32, 33]. Furthermore, disclosing sensitive health information can have profound and detrimental effects on patients' well-being, including adverse social perceptions, embarrassment, stigmatization, and potential harm to career prospects [34].

It is important to note that information regarding cyberattacks on hospital infrastructure is still scarce and obscured. While there are already examples of the severity of malicious attacks, such as the WannaCry ransomware attack in 2017 [35] and the Conti ransomware attack on Ireland's Health Service Executive in 2021 [36], the more comprehensive picture and information is still unknown and shrouded in mystery. This can be attributed to the reluctance of the provision of such information due to fear of reputational damage, patient compensation claims, and regulatory fines [37].

15.3.3 Physical Harm and Vulnerabilities

Cyberattacks can also result in physical harm. For example, wireless medical devices such as insulin pumps and pacemakers can be hacked to alter settings or dosage, potentially causing fatal outcomes [38]. A study by Allen et al. specifically highlights how vulnerabilities in insulin pumps could be exploited to change dosage levels, leading to severe health complications [39]. The Medtronic recall of insulin pumps due to cybersecurity vulnerabilities exemplifies the risk posed by such devices [40]. Similarly, vulnerabilities in cardiac pacemakers pose significant risks. Scholars such as He and Wu have demonstrated how cyberattacks could alter device settings, resulting in life-threatening arrhythmias or inappropriate shocks [41].

15.3.4 Cyberattack Techniques and Trends

Cybercriminals employ various techniques, including ransomware, distributed denial of service (DDoS) attacks, hijacking, remote code execution, and social engineering. Ransomware remains a prevalent threat in the healthcare sector, as highlighted by ENISA, with an upward trend in attacks [42]. In the Threat Landscape for Ransomware Attacks Report, ENISA defines ransomware as a type of attack in which threat actors seize control of a target's assets and demand a ransom to restore access to those assets [43]. Furthermore, ENISA has reported a significant increase in Denial of Service (DoS) attacks targeting the availability of systems in 2023, identifying them as one of the most prominent and rapidly growing threats [44].

15.3.5 Healthcare Cybersecurity Challenges

The healthcare sector faces unique cybersecurity challenges. Traditionally focused on patient care, healthcare institutions often lack robust cybersecurity measures. Human error is a significant factor, with many security incidents resulting from inadequate training and awareness among healthcare professionals [45]. The global shortage of cybersecurity professionals has long been recognized as a critical issue (ENISA 2020; NIST 2020), and it now looms as one of the most formidable challenges for the future [46, 47]. This crisis is starkly reflected in the ISC2 Cybersecurity Workforce Study, which reveals a staggering 26.2% increase in the global cybersecurity workforce gap since 2021, amounting to a shortfall of 3.4 million professionals required to adequately safeguard critical assets [48]. This challenge is particularly pronounced in the healthcare sector, where the stakes are immeasurably high [49]. The complexity of securing medical devices magnifies the issue, as cybersecurity specialists in this field need a distinct skill set and expertise in comparison to traditional IT security engineers or architects [50].

Legacy medical devices, which were designed before current cybersecurity threats emerged, present another major challenge. Many of these devices use outdated software and hardware, making them vulnerable to attacks. For example, some devices still operate on unsupported operating systems like Windows XP and even Windows 98 [51]. Financial constraints often prevent the updating or replacement of these devices, leaving them exposed to cyber threats.

15.4 Understanding the Nature of Connected Medical Devices (CMDs)

Modern medical devices, now capable of generating, collecting, analyzing, and transmitting health data, are increasingly connected to the Internet, forming the Internet of Medical Things (IoMT). While IoMT offers benefits such as real-time monitoring and improved patient care, it also expands potential attack surfaces. Each connected device represents a potential entry point for cyber threats, and attacks on one device can compromise the entire system [52]. With the rapid evolution of sophisticated AI-driven cyberattack techniques, the potential for malicious applications is constrained only by the ingenuity and imagination of the attacker. As these technologies advance, the scope of possible threats will continue to expand, posing unprecedented risks to IoMT environment and hospital infrastructure.

15.5 The Regulatory Framework in Focus: AIA and MDR

The AIA and the MDR pertain to regulating AI-driven medical technologies. Accordingly, the following section enters into the analysis of AIA and MDR by providing a comprehensive overview of the AIA, outlining its objectives, scope, and classification of AI systems based on risk. This will be followed by an analysis of the MDR, focusing on its requirements for the safety, performance, and compliance of medical devices incorporating AI components. In addition, analyzing the interaction between the AIA and MDR is crucial for several reasons. First, the intersection of these two frameworks is essential to ensure that AI systems used in medical devices are both innovative and safe. The AIA introduces a comprehensive framework for the classification and regulation of AI systems based on their risk to fundamental rights and safety. At the same time, the MDR focuses on the safety and performance of medical devices, including those that incorporate AI technologies. Second, AI-driven medical devices have the potential to significantly enhance patient care but also pose unique risks due to their complexity and the potential for unpredictable behaviour. Ensuring that these devices meet stringent safety and performance standards is crucial for patient safety and public trust in healthcare technologies. Therefore, the final subsection will explore the interaction between these two regulatory frameworks, highlighting areas of alignment and potential conflicts, particularly in the context of ensuring the cybersecurity and reliability of connected medical devices.

15.5.1 The AI Act

The AI Act, published in the European Journal on July 12, 2024, represents landmark legislation aimed at regulating artificial intelligence technologies across various sectors. As the world's first comprehensive legal framework dedicated to artificial intelligence, the AI Act seeks to foster the development of human-centered and trustworthy AI technologies. At the same time, it aims to safeguard individuals' health, safety, and fundamental rights from the potentially harmful impacts of AI-powered systems (Article 1(1)). Its primary goal is to mitigate risks to health, safety, and fundamental rights associated with AI systems. Notably, the AI Act adopts a sector-agnostic approach, applying uniformly across various sectors such as finance, education, transportation, and healthcare. This broad application establishes a coherent set of regulatory principles for AI systems, regardless of the specific field in which they are implemented. With its wide scope of application, the AI Act will have a significant impact on industries, including the medical devices sector, which is already navigated by the complex regulatory framework. However, it is important to acknowledge that AI is not a new player in the healthcare domain.

AI has made notable advancements in healthcare, improving diagnostic accuracy, personalizing treatment plans, and enhancing patient outcomes. AI technologies have already been integrated into medical devices for advanced imaging, predictive analytics, and even robotic surgeries. These AI-driven devices have played a crucial role in transforming medical practices, particularly in diagnosis and treatment [53]. Despite the transformative potential of AI in medical devices, these innovations are subject to strict regulatory oversight. For example, many AI-powered medical devices have been CE-marked under the now-repealed Medical Device Directive (MDD), and now must comply with the more stringent MDR, which became fully applicable in 2021 [54]. Nevertheless, scholars have pointed out that the MDR may not fully address the unique characteristics of AI technologies, particularly their autonomous decision-making capabilities and learning algorithms [55, 56].

The AI Act introduces additional regulatory obligations for medical device manufacturers, who will now be required to comply with both the MDR and the new AI Act. This dual compliance will introduce another layer of complexity to the already intricate regulatory landscape for the medical device industry. Under Article 6(1) of the AI Act, most AI-based medical devices will fall under the category of "high-risk AI systems" because medical device software classified as Class IIa or higher will need to undergo third-party conformity assessments. The Act also introduces new requirements in areas such as data governance (Article 10), record-keeping (Article 12), and human oversight (Article 14), among others, that medical device manufacturers must adhere to in addition to the MDR requirements.

While the AI Act touches upon cybersecurity concerns through several recitals and articles, it does not serve as standalone cybersecurity legislation. In Recital 76, the Act emphasizes the critical role of cybersecurity in ensuring AI systems remain secure against malicious exploitation, alterations, or disruptions that could compromise their safety, behavior, and performance. Article 15 of the Act also integrates cybersecurity with broader considerations of accuracy and robustness, prescribing that high-risk AI systems should be designed to achieve and maintain an appropriate level of cybersecurity throughout their lifecycle (AI Act, Article 15(1)). Nevertheless, some scholars argue that these cybersecurity requirements are vaguely defined and lack specific guidelines for practical implementation [57].

Moreover, the AI Act does not directly reference the cybersecurity definition provided in the Cybersecurity Act (Regulation (EU) 2019/881), a significant omission noted by experts. By not incorporating the Cybersecurity Act's definition, the AI Act may fall short of fully aligning with established cybersecurity principles, which could have strengthened the link between AI-specific and broader cybersecurity protections [58]. This omission creates further ambiguity regarding the implementation of cybersecurity requirements for high-risk AI systems and leaves open questions about how AI developers and manufacturers should integrate cybersecurity considerations into their development processes.

In conclusion, while the AI Act represents a significant step toward regulating artificial intelligence technologies, its interplay with the MDR, particularly in the context of AI-powered medical devices, raises several practical challenges. Legal uncertainty, overlapping obligations, and cybersecurity ambiguities underscore the need for detailed guidance and clear standards to help manufacturers navigate this complex regulatory landscape. Ongoing standardization efforts, alongside industrial guidelines, will be critical in supporting the practical implementation of these requirements to ensure both regulatory compliance and the safe deployment of AI systems in healthcare.

15.5.2 The Medical Device Regulation (MDR)

The Medical Devices Regulation (MDR) is one of the most critical pieces of legislation in the European Union (EU) governing the cybersecurity of medical devices. Introduced to replace the "outdated" Medical Device Directive (MDD), the MDR addresses the increasing risks posed by rapid technological advancements in healthcare, particularly in the domain of connected and software-driven medical devices. As medical devices become more integrated with digital technologies, they also become more vulnerable to cyberattacks, necessitating stronger regulatory measures. The MDR thus imposes more stringent requirements for ensuring the safety, performance, and cybersecurity of medical devices before they can be placed on the EU market or used within the EU [59].

One of the core elements of the MDR is compliance with cybersecurity rules outlined in its General Safety and Performance Requirements (Annex I). Article 5(2) of the MDR specifically mandates that manufacturers of medical devices, particularly those incorporating electronic programmable systems or software, demonstrate compliance with essential cybersecurity standards. This regulation is designed to mitigate the risks posed by cyber threats that can compromise device safety, performance, and patient data [60]. This is particularly important in light of recent trends in the healthcare sector, where cyberattacks targeting medical devices have increased, leading to potential risks to patient safety [61].

The definition of a medical device under Article 2(1) MDR is broad, encompassing a wide range of instruments, apparatuses, software, implants, and other materials intended for medical purposes. This includes devices for diagnosis, monitoring, prevention, or treatment, ranging from basic items like disposable gloves and plasters to more complex devices such as pacemakers and radiation systems [62]. This broad definition highlights the importance of cybersecurity measures across the entire spectrum of medical devices, as even seemingly simple devices can pose significant cybersecurity risks if left unprotected.

To assist manufacturers in complying with the cybersecurity requirements of the MDR, the Medical Device Coordination Group (MDCG) endorsed the Guidance on Cybersecurity for Medical Devices (MDCG 2019-16 Rev.1). This guidance provides a comprehensive framework for manufacturers to integrate cybersecurity considerations into the design and development of their devices, marking a significant step forward in implementing the MDR's cybersecurity provisions [63]. However, the dynamic nature of medical device cybersecurity has evolved significantly since the MDCG Guidance was first issued in 2019. Scholars such as Biasin and Kamenjasevic have identified areas where further refinement is necessary, including clarifying the concept of joint responsibility between different stakeholders and improving terminological consistency across the regulatory framework [64].

The introduction of the NIS2 Directive has further complicated the landscape for medical device manufacturers, adding an additional layer of regulatory complexity. NIS2, which focuses on strengthening cybersecurity for critical infrastructure sectors, intersects with the MDR in the realm of medical device cybersecurity, raising questions about how these regulations will work simultaneously (European Commission, 2023). This overlap highlight the importance of aligning various EU cybersecurity frameworks to ensure clarity and ease of compliance for medical device manufacturers. Moreover, it has become evident that updates to the MDCG Guidance will be necessary to reflect the evolving regulatory and technological landscape.

In conclusion, the MDR represents a critical regulatory advancement in ensuring the cybersecurity of medical devices. However, the rapidly changing nature of both technology and the EU's broader cybersecurity framework, such as the introduction of NIS2, presents new challenges. As scholars have noted, it is imperative to continuously refine and update both the MDR and supporting guidance documents like the MDCG Guidance to keep pace with these developments, ensuring that manufacturers can effectively navigate the complex regulatory environment and protect patient safety.

15.5.3 Discussion: The Interplay Between the AIA and MDR

The AI Act and the Medical Devices Regulation (MDR) both aim to ensure the safety, performance, and ethical use of advanced technologies in healthcare, but their approaches and focus areas reveal significant differences. The common goal of these two regulatory frameworks is to protect public health and safety while fostering innovation. Both the AI Act and the MDR address the integration of complex software systems in medical devices, including artificial intelligence (AI), to ensure that they meet high safety and quality standards.

The MDR, which came into force in 2021, focuses on ensuring the safety and performance of medical devices throughout their lifecycle. It imposes rigorous requirements on manufacturers regarding the design, testing, and post-market surveillance of devices, including those driven by AI. On the other hand, the AI Act, though addressing broader AI applications beyond healthcare, introduces specific regulations to mitigate risks associated with AI systems, especially those classified as "high-risk"—which includes most AI-driven medical devices.

Despite their complementary goals of user protection and trust-building, the AI Act and MDR adopt different approaches to risk, reflecting their distinct regulatory priorities and scopes. The MDR's device-centric framework, which focuses on the physical and technical risks associated with medical devices, is a crucial aspect of ensuring the safety, efficacy, and reliability of these devices. This rigorous approach, which includes pre-market conformity assessments, classification systems, and performance standards, aims to mitigate risks such as device malfunction, improper usage, or potential harm to patients and users. It directly addresses the medical device design and intended purpose, providing a solid foundation for user trust.

In contrast, the AI Act shifts the focus to broader societal and human-centric risks, aligning with a human-rights-based regulatory philosophy. It addresses risks arising from the deployment and operation of AI systems, such as biases in decision-making, threats to data privacy, and the erosion of transparency and accountability. Key provisions, such as those on data governance and human oversight (Article 14), aim to safeguard fundamental rights by ensuring fairness, non-discrimination, and user autonomy. It emphasizes requirements for ensuring AI systems' accuracy, robustness, and cybersecurity (Article 15), which complements but does not directly mirror the MDR's device-centric regulatory framework.

This divergence in focus—device regulation under the MDR versus human rights and societal impacts under the AI Act—creates a complex and often conflicting regulatory landscape. Stakeholders must navigate these frameworks, each with its distinct priorities: the MDR's focus on mitigating tangible risks related to the physical safety and performance of medical devices, and the AI Act's broader, more abstract emphasis on protecting human rights, ensuring fairness, and managing societal impacts of AI systems. While both frameworks aim to ensure safety and trust, the stark difference in their approaches introduces tension, as the MDR's product-centric risk management contrasts sharply with the AI Act's focus on ethical and societal risks that transcend individual devices. This creates additional challenges for stakeholders tasked with reconciling the two regulatory approaches in practice.

The amalgamation of regulations is expected to lead to increased compliance expenses for manufacturers of medical devices, as they must ensure their products meet the stringent requirements of both legal frameworks. Several scholars have already raised concerns about potential duplication and inconsistencies in the regulatory overlap between the MDR and the AI Act, which could complicate compliance efforts [65]. Moreover, the AI Act's requirements are outlined at a high level, lacking detailed specifications that would clarify their practical implementation. This lack of granularity can lead to legal uncertainty for manufacturers, who may struggle to understand how to fully comply with the overlapping regulations.

Focusing on the potential duplication of regulatory requirements, AI-driven medical devices will likely fall under both the MDR and the AI Act. For example, Article 6(1) of the AI Act classifies medical device software that falls into Class IIa or higher under the MDR as a high-risk AI system, thus triggering additional requirements under the AI Act. These include obligations related to data governance (Article 10), record-keeping (Article 12), and human oversight (Article 14), which overlap with but are distinct from MDR requirements [66]. Navigating this dual compliance could lead to increased complexity and costs for manufacturers, who will need to meet both sets of requirements without clear guidelines on how these obligations interrelate. However, there are also opportunities for harmonization, particularly in the development of industrial standards and guidance documents that bridge the regulatory gap between the MDR and the AI Act. The European Commission's standardization requests to CEN and CENELEC aim to facilitate this alignment, but the process is complex and time-consuming [87]. Moreover, the Medical Device Coordination Group (MDCG) Guidance could be revised to incorporate AI-specific risks and to provide clear direction on how manufacturers can comply with both MDR and AI Act requirements coherently. These opportunities highlight the importance of collaborative efforts between regulators, industry stakeholders, and standards bodies to streamline compliance and reduce the regulatory burden on the MedTech industry.

15.6 AI Risk Management

The purpose of a risk management framework (RMF) is to assist the organization in integrating risk management into significant activities and functions [67]. Risk management refers to the coordinated activities to direct and control an organization with regard to risk [68]. Risk is defined as the effect of uncertainty on objectives and is usually expressed in terms of:

- risk sources, i.e. elements which alone or in combination have the potential to give rise to risk;
- potential events, i.e. occurrences or changes of a particular set of circumstances;
- their consequences (or impacts), i.e. the outcome of an event, affecting objectives;
- and their likelihood, i.e. the chance of something happening [69].

Impact and likelihood can be quantitatively or qualitatively estimated, in order to assist in decision making.

An AI RMF is a framework focused on AI systems that can, for a given set of goals, generate outputs such as predictions, recommendations, or decisions influencing real or virtual environments [70].

In order to understand what risks are AI technologies subject to, the characterization of what is desirable and what is not desirable helps guide the further definition of the risks to be mitigated. This characterization can be reflected in general principles for AI systems. The OECD organization defined the Principle for Trustworthy AI [71]. As stated in this document, the objective is to "guide AI actors in their efforts to develop trustworthy AI and provide policymakers with recommendations for effective AI policies". "Countries use the OECD AI Principles and related tools to shape policies and create AI risk frameworks, building a foundation for global interoperability between jurisdictions." These principles are:

- **Inclusive growth, sustainable development and well-being** – "Stakeholders should proactively engage in responsible stewardship of trustworthy AI in pursuit of beneficial outcomes for people and the planet, such as augmenting human capabilities and enhancing creativity, advancing inclusion of underrepresented populations, reducing economic, social, gender and other inequalities, and protecting natural environments, thus invigorating inclusive growth, well-being, sustainable development and environmental sustainability [72]."
- **Human rights and democratic values, including fairness and privacy** – "AI actors should respect the rule of law, human rights, democratic and human-centred values throughout the AI system lifecycle. These include non-discrimination and equality, freedom, dignity, autonomy of individuals, privacy and data protection, diversity, fairness, social justice, and internationally recognised labor rights. This also includes addressing misinformation and disinformation amplified by AI, while respecting freedom of expression and other rights and freedoms protected by applicable international law. To this end, AI actors should implement mechanisms and safeguards, such as capacity for human agency and oversight, including to address risks arising from

uses outside of intended purpose, intentional misuse, or unintentional misuse in a manner appropriate to the context and consistent with the state of the art [73]."

- **Transparency and explainability** – "AI Actors should commit to transparency and responsible disclosure regarding AI systems. To this end, they should provide meaningful information, appropriate to the context, and consistent with the state of art:
  - o to foster a general understanding of AI systems, including their capabilities and limitations,
  - o to make stakeholders aware of their interactions with AI systems, including in the workplace,
  - o where feasible and useful, to provide plain and easy-to-understand information on the sources of data/input, factors, processes and/or logic that led to the prediction, content, recommendation or decision, to enable those affected by an AI system to understand the output, and,
  - o to provide information that enable those adversely affected by an AI system to challenge its output [74]."
- **Robustness, security and safety** – "AI systems should be robust, secure and safe throughout their entire lifecycle so that, in conditions of normal use, foreseeable use or misuse, or other adverse conditions, they function appropriately and do not pose unreasonable safety and/or security risks. Mechanisms should be in place, as appropriate, to ensure that if AI systems risk causing undue harm or exhibit undesired behaviour, they can be overridden, repaired, and/or decommissioned safely as needed. Mechanisms should also, where technically feasible, be in place to bolster information integrity while ensuring respect for freedom of expression [75]."
- **Accountability** – AI actors should be accountable for the proper functioning of AI systems and for the respect of the above principles, based on their roles, the context, and consistent with the state of the art. To this end, AI actors should ensure traceability, including in relation to datasets, processes and decisions made during the AI system lifecycle, to enable analysis of the AI system's outputs and responses to inquiry, appropriate to the context and consistent with the state of the art. AI actors, should, based on their roles, the context, and their ability to act, apply a systematic risk management approach to each phase of the AI system lifecycle on an ongoing basis and adopt responsible business conduct to address risks related to AI systems, including, as appropriate, via co-operation between different AI actors, suppliers of AI knowledge and AI resources, AI system users, and other stakeholders. Risks include those related to harmful bias, human rights including safety, security, and privacy, as well as labor and intellectual property rights.

Also important for risk management of AI systems is understanding how AI systems are designed, built, deployed, updated and finally decommissioned. In another published work from the OECD, the "OECD Framework for the Classification of AI systems", the AI lifecycle activities were defined [76]. In this document, the OECD developed a user-friendly tool to evaluate AI systems in specific contexts, from a policy perspective, to help policy makers, regulators, legislators, among others, to characterize AI systems. The AI lifecycle activities, according to five sociotechnical dimensions, are the following:

- **People and Planet:** this dimension includes several considerations about the implementers of the AI systems, the users of the AI system, the impacted stakeholders, the type of impacts on environment, societal impacts and human rights. For example, consumer protection and product safety considerations lie within this dimension. Stakeholders include all organizations and individuals involved in or affected by the AI systems [77].
- **Economic context:** the context refers to the industrial sector, business function of the organization, and the adequate AI model to be used, scale of use and maturity of the AI system [78]. It also considers the criticality of the AI system, depending on the industry, business function and environment of deployment.
- **AI model:** an AI model "is a computational representation of all or part of the external environment of an AI system – encompassing, for example, processes, objects, ideas, people and/or interactions that take place in that environment". There exists a multitude of AI models. They could be symbolic models (e.g., using human-generated logical representations), Statistical AI models (e.g., identify patterns based on data) or hybrid AI models (e.g., mixing symbolic and statistical AI models) [79].
- **Data and Input:** AI models need information in order to represent the external environment, whether it is data gathered by humans and automated tools, or expert knowledge. Data and Input refers to data that is used for training the AI model, or the input data from the environment that the AI system will process to yield outputs useful for the context of use.
- **Task & Output:** AI systems can perform the following tasks: recognition, prediction, personalization and decision-making. Depending on the level of integration with other systems, the AI system can have different levels of autonomy to perform actions on the environment. The outputs of an AI system could be recommendations, signal outputs for other systems, or even outputs for other AI systems for performing other tasks and/or actions.

This five sociotechnical dimensions were mapped to the AI system's lifecycle [80]. In the NIST AI Risk Management framework, the AI system's lifecycle were further adapted and reflects the need for risk management coordinated activities to be present throughout the AI systems' lifecycle. The AI system's lifecycle, as per NIST AI Risk Management Framework and OECD Framework for the Classification of AI Systems includes the following phases:

- **Plan and Design:** this phase is dedicated to defining the AI system's concepts, objectives, underlying assumptions, context of use and technical, legal and ethical requirements. This phase will set the path to all the subsequent phases, as the objectives, assumptions and requirements will guide decisions concerning the training of data and AI models to be used, adequate methods of validating and verifying the model training process and the correct outputs of the AI model, and also guide the evaluation of the correct behavior in production environment.
- **Collect and Process Data:** In this phase, having the objectives and requirements in mind, the processes and technologies for selection, gathering, validation and cleaning of data are selected and implemented. These data are of crucial importance since it will be used by the AI model to build a representation of the context or environment defined in the previous phase.
- **Build and Use Model plus Verify and Validate:** With processed training data, the AI model is trained in order to gain the computational representation of the external environment where the AI system will be deployed. This phase will include processes for selecting the training data set and the testing data set, accuracy tests for the trained models, and might even include training and testing several different models and selection of the best fit for the context of use. Accuracy test, comparison of several different models, validation, interpretation of the output results is included in the Verify and Validate phase. Since the two phases are very directly linked, we described them in the same paragraph.
- **Deploy/Task and Output:** In this phase, pilot testing, compatibility check with surrounding systems, verification of regulatory compliance, organizational change management, actual implementation of the system in production, monitoring of user experience and impact to the systems' environment are performed;
- **Operate and Monitor:** Once deployed, the AI system will be part of the business operations and continuous monitoring and assessment is implemented, having in mind the objectives, legal and regulatory requirements, and ethical considerations [81].

Note that the OECD framework places **People and Planet** in the center of the framework.

Some risk examples for the lifecycle phases can be found below:

- **Plan and Design:** in the planning phase, legal, regulatory and ethical requirements must be considered. Social and environmental impacts should also be considered when designing an AI system. If some of these requirements are overlooked, ignored, or even purposely discarded, then the subsequent phases, might lead to a biased AI system.
- **Collect and Process Data:** training data will influence greatly the AI system's functioning. Ultimately, it could lead, for example, to a classification model that might favor certain groups of people in an unfair way. This might be caused by unbalanced data, biased sampling of data, or corrupted/purposely changed data. Training data could include Personal Data that might not have the owner's consent to be used. Data quality plays a key role in training models. If the data has several errors, the resulting trained model might be unreliable or unsafe for use.
- **Build and Use Model:** When training AI models, if the training data is not appropriately fed to the AI model, and if there is not much testing data for evaluating the "correctness of the model", overfitting or underfitting will most certainly lead to wrong AI outputs. AI architecture models could be adequate in certain scenarios, but inappropriate in others. The selection of the wrong architecture model can lead to unintended bias of the system, leading to biased outcomes.
- **Operate and Monitor:** Real-world scenarios always have unexpected situations. These situations could feed some input to the AI system, leading to dangerous behaviors. An AI system must be up-to-date and continuously trained with up-to-date data. Model drift happens when there is no mechanism for monitoring the adequacy of the model with regards to the changing AI system environment. This can lead to erroneous behavior.
- **Build and Use Model plus Verify and Validate, Deploy / Task and Output and Operate and Monitor:** Without explainability, or human understandable reasons for the AI outputs, it would be difficult for humans to interpret the result, and to take corrective actions. With explainability, people can assess better the "correctness" of the AI outputs taking into account other information not present during AI Model training.

Several standards related to AI risk management exists:

- The "ISO/IEC 23894:2023 – Information technology – Artificial intelligence – Guidance on risk management", published in 2023, provide guidance for organizations that develop, produce, deploy or use products, systems and services that utilize AI to manage AI related risks and to integrate risk management into the organization's processes.

- The "ISO/IEC 42001:2023 - Information technology—Artificial intelligence—Management system", published in 2023, provides requirements for setting up and continuously improving the Artificial Intelligence Management System for organizations providing or using AI-based products [82].
- The "ISO/IEC 38507:2022 - Information technology—Governance of IT—Governance implications of the use of artificial intelligence by organizations", published in 2022, this document provides guidance for governing the use of AI technology within an organization, specifically tailored for the organization's governing body [83].
- The NIST AI Risk Management Framework, published in 2023, was designed to enable organizations to increase the trustworthiness of AI systems, and foster responsible design, development, deployment and use of AI systems [84].

Focusing on the Cybersecurity risks of AI systems, Microsoft has released the AI Security Risk Assessment document, where they have suggested a rating scheme for severity, likelihood and impact, stressing the needed alignment with the specific industry and use case. The document also defines a set of control objectives for protecting AI systems against cyber-threats. Controls are any measure, whether procedural, managerial or technical, to mitigate or eliminate risks. Before delving into the controls, the organization must first inventory all the AI systems it is using or planning to use. The organization should assess the current state of AI within the organization, perform gap analysis, define recommendations from the results of the gap analysis, define the roadmap to implement these recommendations and have a progress monitoring process in place. Moreover, the AI systems should be scored based on their criticality for the organization, in order to prioritize protective measures implementation. Then, they must apply the adequate controls to fulfill the following objectives:

1. **Data Collection:** controls and policies for ensuring the integrity of data collected to be used by the AI system. These controls and policies protect the AI system against untrusted data sources, sensitive data misuse, insecure data storage, unauthorized data access and data integrity attacks.
2. **Data Processing:** controls and policies to secure the processing of data that will be used for training the AI model. These controls and policies protect the AI system against data processing pipeline manipulation (altering the intended processing of data) and data subsets reconstruction (recovery of parts of the dataset by an attacker).
3. **Model Training:** controls and policies for reviewing the AI model code. These controls and policies are intended for protecting the AI system from improper model design (which could lead to confidentiality, integrity or

availability breaches), adversarial conditions (e.g., where the AI system is exposed to adversarial attacks), and overfitting (which could lead to unintended behaviors that could be exploited by attackers).

4. **Model Deployment:** controls and policies related to the deployment of models, algorithms, and supporting infrastructure. These controls and policies are intended to protect the AI system against inadequate security testing of the model, and to protect the system from unsecured networks.
5. **System Monitoring:** Controls and policies for ongoing monitoring of AI systems and supporting infrastructure (e.g., securing log data and their infrastructure);
6. **Incident Management:** controls and policies related to securing log data and supporting storing infrastructure. These controls and policies ensure adequate definition of roles and responsibilities, AI systems incident reporting processes/technologies, and the definition of an incident response plan that should be tested regularly. These should guarantee a prompt response in case of AI system's incidents.
7. **Business Continuity Planning:** controls and policies to guarantee that the AI system can recover or can be remediated after an incident. These include the definition of Disaster Recovery Plan, Business Continuity Plan and continuous testing of those plans.

Regarding the data collection, data processing, data training and deployment environments, they could be all in-house for the organization, some parts could reside outside the organization, or all parts could reside outside premises. This would imply the adoption of cybersecurity standards, such as the ISO 27001/27002, CIS Cloud Security Controls, NIST Cybersecurity Framework for IoT (NISTIR 8259), OWASP IoT Security Guidelines, OWASP application security standard, to name a few. In the case of Medical Devices, the ISO 14971 standard must be considered if the AI system is deployed or somehow integrated in the medical device.

The complexity of considerations, standards and regulations, with an ever-changing landscape of the AI technology is posing enormous challenges to organizations. In the case of AI systems or Medical Device using AI systems, when regulation changes, the implications for the AI lifecycle and the whole functioning of an organization can be far-reaching. They can affect organizations' infrastructures (in-premise, cloud, or hybrid), systems integrated with AI (namely applications and sources of information), as well as providers' contracts and services.

Mapping and alignment of laws, regulations, standards, guidelines, and practices remains a challenge for organizations that aim at improving the implementation of compliance requirements and adopt best practices. As the AI landscape evolves, future AI risk management methods and frameworks should aim at being clear and intuitive, as well as adaptable as part of an organization's broader risk management strategy and processes. Also, they should be outcome-focused and non-prescriptive, by providing requirements and recommendations on outcomes and approaches, rather than prescribe one-size-fits-all requirements [85].

15.7 Outlook: Recommendations and Future Directions

Summarizing above, the integration of AI into medical devices presents unique challenges for ensuring cybersecurity, particularly when considering the regulatory landscape governed by the AI Act and the Medical Devices Regulation (MDR). Addressing these challenges requires strategic alignment of regulations, implementation of best practices, and the adoption of new policy recommendations to safeguard both patients and healthcare systems.

To ensure the cybersecurity of AI-enabled medical devices, it is essential to align the requirements of the AI Act and the MDR. One strategy to achieve this is through the harmonization of standards across both frameworks, with an emphasis on shared definitions of critical concepts such as cybersecurity risks, vulnerabilities, and risk management. One of the solutions could be *development of a unified standard* that addresses both the cybersecurity requirements in the MDR (Annex I) and the robustness and accuracy requirements in the AI Act (Article 15).

Another critical solution is fostering *collaborative guidance documents* between the Medical Device Coordination Group (MDCG) and the European AI regulators to avoid duplication and conflicting requirements. By providing clear guidelines that bridge both frameworks, manufacturers would have a streamlined process for ensuring AI-enabled medical devices comply with both sets of cybersecurity provisions. This would involve identifying overlapping conformity assessments and ensuring that these assessments address both AI functionality and cybersecurity risks.

Given the complexity of AI-driven systems, adopting best practices for cybersecurity in AI-enabled medical devices is essential. One of the solutions could be *the implementation of a secure development lifecycle (SDLC) for AI systems*, where cybersecurity is integrated from the design phase through to post-market surveillance. This approach ensures that manufacturers proactively address cybersecurity vulnerabilities throughout the product lifecycle, aligning with both MDR and AI Act requirements.

In addition, *applying standards such as ISO/IEC 27001 (Information Security Management) and ISO/IEC 62304 (Medical Device Software – Software Life Cycle Processes)* can provide a robust framework for managing cybersecurity risks. These standards should be adapted to address the unique challenges posed by AI, such as ensuring the accuracy and transparency of AI algorithms (AIA Article 10) while maintaining the integrity and reliability of data used in the device (MDR Annex I). *Risk assessment methodologies*, such as threat modelling and penetration testing, should also be embedded into the development of AI-driven medical devices, ensuring compliance with cybersecurity mandates under both the AI Act and MDR.

To improve regulatory coherence, several policy changes should be considered.

Firstly, *the revision of the MDCG Cybersecurity Guidance* (MDCG 2019-16) should be prioritized, incorporating new risks and challenges specific to AI-driven devices. The updated guidance could provide clear examples of cybersecurity requirements for high-risk AI systems as defined in the AI Act, ensuring that both AI-specific risks and traditional medical device cybersecurity are adequately addressed [86].

A second policy recommendation is *the development of a centralized regulatory body tasked with overseeing AI-enabled medical devices.* This body could facilitate coordination between AI regulators and medical device authorities, ensuring consistent enforcement of cybersecurity standards across both frameworks.

Additionally, *cross-border data-sharing policies should be clarified*, particularly as AI-enabled medical devices often rely on large datasets from different jurisdictions. *Enhancing international cooperation on data governance and cybersecurity standards* would ensure that AI systems are robust and secure across the EU.

As AI continues to evolve, future directions should be tailored to address emerging trends and technologies, ensuring that innovations are effectively integrated and regulated to meet evolving needs and challenges. Accordingly, several emerging trends will reshape the landscape of medical devices and their associated regulatory needs.

Edge AI—where AI computations are performed on-device rather than in centralized data centres—will become increasingly common in medical devices, particularly for real-time diagnostics and monitoring. This shift necessitates new approaches to cybersecurity, as data will no longer be transferred to a central server, thus reducing latency but increasing the risk of local vulnerabilities.

Another emerging trend is the growing use of federated learning in healthcare, which allows AI models to be trained across multiple decentralized devices without sharing sensitive patient data. While this addresses privacy concerns, it presents new cybersecurity challenges related to ensuring the integrity and security of the distributed data used in training models (European Commission, 2023). Regulatory frameworks will need to adapt to address these complexities, particularly around data integrity and model robustness in federated learning environments.

With the advent of these new technologies, regulatory needs will inevitably evolve. As AI systems become more autonomous and capable of decision-making in critical healthcare settings, the demand for explainability and transparency will increase. The AI Act already highlights the importance of these principles (Article 13), but future iterations of the MDR and AI Act should incorporate stricter requirements for auditability and post-market surveillance specific to autonomous AI systems in medical devices.

Moreover, as medical devices become more connected and integrated into broader Internet of Medical Things (IoMT) ecosystems, interoperability standards will become critical. Regulatory frameworks must address the cybersecurity implications of interconnected devices, ensuring that vulnerabilities in one system do not compromise the entire network. This shift will also necessitate real-time regulatory monitoring and adaptive compliance mechanisms, allowing for faster responses to emerging threats.

15.8 Conclusion

This chapter has delved into the intersection of the AIA and the MDR within the context of cybersecurity for AI-enabled medical devices. We outlined the shared objectives and differing approaches of these regulatory frameworks, demonstrating their mutual aim of ensuring safety and efficacy while highlighting their distinct focus areas. The MDR emphasizes device performance and patient safety, while the AI Act emphasizes algorithmic robustness, transparency, and fairness.

Strategies for aligning the two regulations were discussed, underscoring the need for regulatory harmonization to streamline compliance and reduce complexity for manufacturers. The chapter also presented best practices and standards for securing AI-enabled medical devices, such as implementing a secure development lifecycle (SDLC) and leveraging established cybersecurity frameworks like ISO/IEC standards. Furthermore, policy recommendations were provided, including updating the MDCG Cybersecurity Guidance and establishing a centralized regulatory body to oversee AI-driven medical devices.

For policymakers, the analysis suggests the importance of revising and harmonizing the AI Act and MDR to address the unique cybersecurity challenges posed by AI in medical devices. It is crucial that cybersecurity guidelines remain consistent and avoid regulatory overlap to support innovation while safeguarding patient safety. Additionally, policymakers must consider future-proofing regulations as AI technologies and medical devices continue to evolve.

Declaration of Competing Interest

Authors of the book chapter declare not to have any conflict of interest.

Data Availability

No data was used for the research described in this article.

Acknowledgement

This work was carried out as part of the CYLCOMED [Cyber securitY tooLbox for COnnected MEdical Devices] project, which has received funding from the European Union's (Horizon Europe) research and innovation programme under grant agreement No 101095542.

References

[1] World Economic Forum (WEF). 2024. "The Global Risks Report 2024". Global Risks Report 2024 |World Economic Forum |World Economic Forum (weforum.org)

[2] The White House. 2021. "Executive Order on Improving the Nation's Cybersecurity". https://www.whitehouse.gov/briefing-room/presidential-actions/2021/05/12/executive-order-on-improving-the-nations-cybersecurity/.

[3] Ursula von der Leyen. 2021. Speech "State of the Union 2021". September 15 2021, Strasbourg. State of the Union Address by President von der Leyen (europa.eu)

[4] The European Union Agency for Cybersecurity (ENISA). 2023a. "Health Threat Landscape". https://www.enisa.europa.eu/publications/health-threat-landscape.

[5] Federal Bureau of Investigation (FBI). 2023. "Internet Crime Report 2023". 2023_IC3Report.pdf

[6] Choi, D., Malvehy, M., et al. (2022). Artificial Intelligence in Medical Devices: Regulatory Overlap and Challenges in the EU. *European Journal of Medical Technology*, 5(4), 210–224.

[7] Malvehy, J., R. Ginsberg, L. Sampietro-Colom, J. Ficapal, M. Combalia, and P. Svedenhag. 2022. "New regulation of medical devices in the EU: impact in dermatology." Journal of the European Academy of Dermatology and Venereology 36, no. 3: 360–364. https://doi.org/10.1111/jdv.17830.

[8] Conor Stewart. (2024) "AI in healthcare - statistics & facts". Available at https://www.statista.com/topics/10011/ai-in-healthcare/#topicOverview.

[9] Yao, X., Zhang, Y., & Zheng, H. (2021). Deep learning in medical image analysis: A survey. *Neurocomputing*, 453, 1–14.

[10] Esteva, A., Kuprel, B., & Novoa, R. A. (2019). Dermatologist-level classification of skin cancer with deep neural networks. Nature, 542(7639), 115–118.

[11] Topol, E. (2019). Deep medicine: How artificial intelligence can make healthcare human again. Basic Books.

[12] Somashekhar, S. P., Mulgund, A., & Babu, S. (2018). Watson for Oncology and the future of clinical decision support in oncology. *Journal of Oncology Practice*, 14(12), 889–897.

[13] Liu, Y., Xu, Y., & Li, J. (2024). AI-driven integration of genomic and imaging data for improved cancer diagnosis and treatment planning. Nature Cancer, 7(1), 78–91. doi: 10.1038/s41571-024-00691-7.

[14] Banaee, H., Ahmed, M. U., & Loutfi, A. (2013). Data mining for wearable sensors in health monitoring systems: A review of the state-of-the-art. Journal of Biomedical Informatics, 46(5), 1–19.

[15] Miller, A., Mullen, A., & Thompson, A. (2020). Advances in pacemaker technology: The role of remote monitoring. Journal of Cardiac Failure, 26(12), 1100–1108.

[16] Battelino, T., Danne, T., & Philip, M. (2019). Clinical targets for continuous glucose monitoring. Diabetes Care, 42(6), 1150–1152.

[17] Beck, R. W., Riddlesworth, T., & Ruedy, K. J. (2017). Continuous glucose monitoring vs usual care in patients with type 2 diabetes receiving insulin: The DIAMOND randomized trial. JAMA, 317(4), 371–378.

[18] Gordon, P. B., Taourel, P., & Deslauriers, J. (2021). Artificial intelligence in ultrasound imaging: A review. Ultrasound in Medicine & Biology, 47(1), 112–122.

[19] Chen, J., Zhang, L., & Wang, X. (2023). Deep learning for automated detection and classification of diseases in chest X-rays. IEEE Transactions on Medical Imaging, 42(4), 1090–1102. doi: 10.1109/TMI.2023.3192378.

[20] Mittelstadt, B. D., Allo, P., & Taddeo, M. (2016). The ethics of algorithms: Mapping the debate. Big Data & Society, 3(2), 1–21.

[21] Bertolini, R., Morrison, K., & Krause, D. (2021). IoT security challenges and risks in healthcare: A systematic review. IEEE Access, 9, 155621–155635.

[22] Van Eeten, M. J., & Mueller, M. (2013). Where is the governance in Internet governance? New media & society, 15(5), 720–736.

[23] Dunn Cavelty, M. (2018). Cybersecurity in the European Union: Resilience and Adaptability in Governance Policy. European Security, 27(3), 338–355.

[24] Piggin, R. (2017). Motivations behind cyberattacks on healthcare systems. Cybersecurity Review, 9(2), 78–85.

[25] Humer, C., & Finkle, J. (2014). The black market for health data: An analysis of the illicit trade in electronic health records. Health Affairs, 33(12), 2102–2108.

[26] Stack, L. (2017). The black market value of healthcare data. Healthcare Data Security Journal, 11(1), 34–45.

[27] Javaid, M., Haleem, A., & Singh, R. P. (2023). Fraudulent activities and financial implications of healthcare data breaches. Journal of Healthcare Security, 15(2), 25–34.

[28] European Union Agency for Cybersecurity (ENISA). 2022. "NIS Investments 2022". https://www.enisa.europa.eu/publications/nis-investments-2022.

[29] IBM Security. 2023. "Cost of a Data Breach Report 2023". https://www.ibm.com/reports/data-breach.

[30] Silver, Julie K., David S. Binder, Nevena Zubcevik, and Ross D. Zafonte. 2016. "Healthcare hackathons provide educational and innovation opportunities: a case study and best practice recommendations." *Journal of medical systems*. DOI: 10.1007/s10916-016-0532-3.

[31] European Data Protection Board (EDBP). 2022. "Administrative fine imposed on psychotherapy centre Vastaamo for data protection violations. Administrative fine imposed on psychotherapy centre Vastaamo for data protection violations |European Data Protection Board (europa. eu)

[32] Porter, Sophie. "Cyberattack on Czech hospital forces tech shutdown during coronavirus outbreak". HealthCare IT News. March 19, 2020. Cyberattack on Czech hospital forces tech shutdown during coronavirus outbreak |Healthcare IT News.

[33] Howell, O'Neill Patrick. "Ransomware did not kill a German Hospital patient. 2020". MIT Technology Review. November 12, 2020. https://www.technologyreview.com/2020/11/12/1012015/ransomware-did-not-kill-a-german-hospital-patient/.

[34] Waegemann, C. (1996). The impact of data breaches on patient privacy and employment opportunities. Health Information Management Journal, 14(2), 77–88.

[35] Wirth, Axel. 2017. "Hardly ever a dull moment: the ongoing cyberthreats of 2017." Biomedical Instrumentation & Technology 51, no. 5 (2017): 431–433. DOI: 10.2345/0899-8205-51.5.431.

[36] Pattnaik, Nandita, et al. 2023. "It's more than just money: The real-world harms from ransomware attacks." *International Symposium on Human Aspects of Information Security and Assurance*. Cham: Springer Nature Switzerland. 3. https://doi.org/10.1007/978-3-031-38530-8_21.

[37] European Commission: Joint Research Centre, Reina, V. and Griesinger, C., Cyber security in the health and medicine sector – A study on available evidence of patient health consequences resulting from cyber incidents in healthcare settings, Publications Office of the European Union, 2024, https://data.europa.eu/doi/10.2760/693487.

[38] Levy-Loboda, Tamar, Eitam Sheetrit, Idit F. Liberty, Alon Haim, and Nir Nissim. 2022. "Personalized Insulin Dose Manipulation Attack and Its Detection Using Interval-Based Temporal Patterns and Machine Learning Algorithms." Journal of Biomedical Informatics. DOI: 10.1016/j.jbi.2022.104129.

[39] Allen, S. D., Gupta, A., & Wang, Y. (2019). The Risks of Cyberattacks on Medical Devices. Journal of Medical Devices, 13(2), 024501.

[40] Medtronic. "Security Bulletin". June 27, 2019 https://global.medtronic.com/xg-en/product-security/security-bulletins/minimed-508-paradigm.html.

[41] He, H., & Wu, D. (2018). Cybersecurity of Medical Devices: A Case Study of the Pacemaker and Implantable Cardioverter Defibrillator Vulnerabilities. *Journal of Biomedical Engineering*, 32(4), 123–135.

[42] The European Union Agency for Cybersecurity (ENISA). 2023. "Health Threat Landscape". https://www.enisa.europa.eu/publications/health-threat-landscape.

[43] European Union Agency for Cybersecurity (ENISA). 2022. "Threat Landscape for Ransomware Attacks 2022". https://www.enisa.europa.eu/publications/enisa-threat-landscape-for-ransomware-attacks.

[44] European Union Agency for Cybersecurity (ENISA). 2023. "ENISA Threat Landscape 2023". https://www.enisa.europa.eu/publications/enisa-threat-landscape-2023.

[45] Evans, Mark, Ying He, Leandros Maglaras, and Helge Janicke. 2018. "HEART-IS: A Novel Technique for Evaluating Human Error-related Information Security Incidents." *Computers & Security 80*, 74–89. https://doi.org/10.1016/j.cose.2018.09.002.

[46] National Institute of Standards and Technology (NIST). 2020. "Supporting the Growth and Sustainment of the Nation's Cybersecurity Workforce: Building the Foundation for a More Secure American Future". Supporting the Growth and Sustainment of the Nation's Cybersecurity Workforce | CISA.

[47] European Union Agency for Cybersecurity (ENISA). 2023c. "Foresight 2030 Threats". https://www.enisa.europa.eu/publications/foresight-2030-threats.

[48] ISC2. 2023. "Cybersecurity workforce study". Cybersecurity Workforce Study (isc2.org).

[49] Kotz, David, Carl A. Gunter, Santosh Kumar, and Jonathan P. Weiner. 2016. "Privacy and security in mobile health: a research agenda." *Computer* 49, no. 6: 22–30. DOI: 10.1109/MC.2016.185.

[50] Ray, Arnab. 2021. "Introduction to Medical Device Cybersecurity." *Cybersecurity for Connected Medical Devices*, (2021): 1–28. https://doi.org/10.1016/B978-0-12-818262-8.00004-8.

[51] Slabodkin, Greg. "Legacy medical devices, growing hacker threats create perfect storm of cybersecurity risks". MEDTECHDIVE. June 22, 2021. https:

//www.medtechdive.com/news/legacy-medical-devices-growing-hacker-threats-create-medtech-cyber-risks/602157/.

[52] Yaqoob, Tahreem, Haider Abbas, and Mohammed Atiquzzaman. 2019. "Security vulnerabilities, attacks, countermeasures, and regulations of networked medical devices—A review." *IEEE Communications Surveys & Tutorials* 21, no. 4: 3723–3768. DOI: 10.1109/COMST.2019.2914094.

[53] Ibidem [11].

[54] Ibidem [6].

[55] Mkwashi, A. and I. Brass (2022). "*The Future of Medical Device Regulation and Standards: Dealing with Critical Challenges for Connected, Intelligent Medical Devices*". London: PETRAS National Centre of Excellent in IoT Systems Cybersecurity. DOI: https://zenodo.org/doi/10.5281/zenodo.7054048

[56] Le, S., Brass, R., & Mkwashi, M. (2023). AI and Autonomous Medical Devices: Regulatory Gaps in MDR. *Healthcare Robotics & AI*, 6(2), 76–90.

[57] Biasin, E., Yaşar, B., and Kamenjašević, E. 2023. "New Cybersecurity Requirements for Medical Devices in the EU: The Forthcoming European Health Data Space, Data Act, and Artificial Intelligence Act ". *Law, Technology and Humans* 5 (2):43–58. https://doi.org/10.5204/lthj.3068.

[58] Biasin, E., Yaşar, B., and Kamenjašević, E. 2023. "New Cybersecurity Requirements for Medical Devices in the EU: The Forthcoming European Health Data Space, Data Act, and Artificial Intelligence Act ". *Law, Technology and Humans* 5 (2):43–58. https://doi.org/10.5204/lthj.3068.

[59] Biasin, E., E. Kamenjasevic, and R.K. Ludvigsen. 2023. "Cybersecurity of AI Medical Devices: Risks, Legislation, and Challenges." ArXiv. https://doi.org/10.48550/arXiv.2303.03140.

[60] Ibidem [7].

[61] Ibidem [43].

[62] Ibidem [7].

[63] Biasin, Elisabetta, and Erik Kamenjasevic. 2020. "Cybersecurity of medical devices: regulatory challenges in the EU." https://dx.doi.org/10.2139/ssrn.3855491.

[64] Ibidem [63].

[65] Ibidem [6].

[66] Ibidem [6].

[67] ISO 31000:2018, https://www.iso.org/iso-31000-risk-management.html.

[68] ISO 31000:2018, https://www.iso.org/iso-31000-risk-management.html.

[69] ISO 31000:2018, https://www.iso.org/iso-31000-risk-management.html.

[70] NIST AI Risk Management Framework.

[71] https://oecd.ai/en/ai-principles.

[72] Ibidem [72].

[73] Ibidem [72].
[74] Ibidem [72].
[75] Ibidem [72].
[76] OECD Framework for the Classification of AI Systems
[77] Ibidem [77].
[78] Ibidem [77].
[79] Ibidem [77].
[80] Ibidem [77].
[81] NIST AI Risk Management Framework.
[82] https://www.iso.org/standard/81230.html.
[83] https://www.iso.org/standard/56641.html.
[84] Ibidem [68].
[85] Ibidem [68].
[86] Ibidem [59].
[87] European Commission: Joint Research Centre, Soler Garrido, J., Fano Yela, D., Panigutti, C., Junklewitz, H. et al., Analysis of the preliminary AI standardisation work plan in support of the AI Act, Publications Office of the European Union, 2023.

Index

About the Editor

Konstantinos Loupos

In the capacity of editor for this publication, Mr. Konstantinos Loupos, whose remarkable expertise and substantial contributions to the fields of microelectronics, embedded systems, IoT/ICT technologies, and Cybersecurity have created a notable presence in the realm of technological innovation and research.

Mr. Loupos holds a distinguished academic record, encompassing an MBA from the Hellenic Open University (Greece), an M.Sc. in Microelectronics Systems Design with distinction from the University of Southampton (United Kingdom), and an M.Eng. in Electronic and Electrical Engineering from the University of Manchester (United Kingdom). His educational accomplishments serve as a testament to his commitment to academic excellence and his relentless pursuit of knowledge.

With a multifaceted career spanning in various domains, Mr. Loupos has accumulated extensive practical experience and knowledge in an array of critical areas. His research interests and activities encompass IoT/ICT systems, Cybersecurity, Sensors and Systems for Structural Health Monitoring (including tunnels, structures, bridges, and more), Robotics for Civil Infrastructure Inspection, Security Systems (comprising sensors and communications), Water Demand Management, and Wireless Sensor Networks. Additionally, his expertise extends to Application Specific Embedded Systems, further showcasing his versatility in the technological landscape.

Mr. Loupos's exceptional dedication to research is evident through his active participation in over 35 EC co-funded research projects, spanning from FP5 to H2020, Horizon Europe and beyond. His contributions have spanned diverse sectors, including transport, security, health, climate, cultural heritage, ICT, and nano-materials, highlighting his commitment to advancing knowledge and fostering innovation. Throughout his career, he has held significant roles, ranging from

Project Coordinator to Technical Manager and Leader of Development teams, all of which underscore his leadership and management capabilities.

Furthermore, Mr. Loupos's scholarly endeavors are reflected in his impressive portfolio of over 70 publications in conference proceedings, journals, and book chapters. His dedication to the academic community extends beyond publications, as he has actively served as an organizer, technical chair, and member of organizing committees for numerous scientific conferences, such as IoT Week, Global IoT Summit, International Conference on Availability, Reliability and Security, International Physical Internet Conference, Transport Research Arena, IoT World, IoT Solutions World Congress, IEEE World Forum on IoT, Globecomm, IoTi4, Mobisec and more.

In addition to his research and academic contributions, Mr. Loupos has played a crucial role as a formal evaluator (expert) of EC projects in various programs, including FP7, H2020, HEU, EUKERA/EUROSTARS, MCST, MARTERA, COST, ERANET, and MED. Simultaneously, he has undertaken the role of project reviewer (external technical expert) for ongoing Horizon 2020 and Horizon Europe projects, thereby contributing to the assessment and advancement of cutting-edge research initiatives.

Mr. Loupos's commitment to professional development is evident in his certifications as a Project Management Professional (PMP), Scrum Expert, and GDPR expert (Certified DPO). His active memberships in organizations such as the EUROPOL EC3 cyber security group, European Cybercrime Center, Secure Platform for Accredited Cybercrime Experts (SPACE), EUROPOL Data Protection Experts Network (EDEN), the Alliance for AI, IoT and Edge Continuum Innovation (AIOTI), and SPRINT Robotics further reflect his engagement in fostering collaboration and addressing contemporary challenges in the technological landscape.

Currently, Mr. Loupos serves as the R&D Director at INLECOM, where he holds positions on the board of directors and as the R&D strategy keeper and business development. His involvement in numerous research projects, both as a coordinator and technical manager, continues to shape and advance technological innovation in diverse domains.

Mr Loupos's experience deeply aligns with the core themes of this book, particularly in the realm of cybersecurity and the Internet of Things (IoT). Over the past decade, he has played pivotal roles in numerous projects that have shaped the landscape of IoT security, data connectivity, and platform design. His expertise encompasses a wide range of areas, including the development of robust cybersecurity systems, with a specific focus on identity and trust management within IoT ecosystems. This involves a deep understanding of cryptographic protocols, secure authentication mechanisms, and decentralized identity management solutions to ensure the confidentiality, integrity, and availability of sensitive data within IoT networks. He also has extensive experience in ensuring the secure lifecycle management of IoT devices, addressing vulnerabilities and threats throughout their operational lifespan. This includes secure device onboarding, firmware updates, vulnerability assessment, and incident response to mitigate potential risks and protect against cyberattacks. Moreover, his work has significantly contributed to establishing safe and trusted connectivity for IoT networks and devices, enabling secure data exchange and communication. This encompasses the development and implementation of secure communication protocols, data encryption techniques, and access control mechanisms to safeguard data transmission and prevent unauthorized access.

Projects like CHARIOT, ERATOSTHENES, INTERQ, CONNECTOR, PILOTING, among others, stand as testaments to his profound impact on advancing the field of IoT security and connectivity. These endeavors have not only deepened his understanding of the technical intricacies involved but also fostered a comprehensive perspective on the broader challenges and opportunities presented by the evolving IoT landscape. He has gained valuable insights into the diverse security requirements of different IoT applications, ranging from industrial automation and smart cities to healthcare and transportation. This broad perspective allows him to identify emerging trends, anticipate future challenges, and contribute to the development of innovative solutions that address the evolving security needs of the IoT ecosystem.

Contributing Authors

Luca Aceto
RINA, Palazzo R, Strada 7, Via Gran S. Bernardo, 20089 Rozzano MILANO – ITALY
luca.aceto@rina.org

Michail Bampatsikos
University of Piraeus, Piraeus, Greece
mbampatsikos@ssl-unipi.gr

Vaios Bolgouras
University of Piraeus. Piraeus, Greece

Goncalo Cadete
Instituto de Engenharia de Sistemas e Computadores Inovação (INOV)
goncalo.cadete@inov.pt

Roberto Cascella
European Cyber Security Organisation (ECSO), Bruxelles, 1000, Belgium
roberto.cascella@ecs-org.eu

Francesca Costantino
ENGINEERING Ingegneria Informatica S.p.A., Piazzale dell'Agricoltura, 24 – 00144 Rome, Italy
francesca.costantino@eng.it

Konstantinos Dafloukas
Inlecom Innovation, Tatoiou 11, Kifisia, Greece
Konstantinos.dafloukas@inlecomsystems.com

Rustem Dautov
SINTEF Digital, Forskningsveien 1, 0373 Oslo, Norway
rustem.dautov@sintef.no

Juan Manuel Vera Diaz
BDS R&D Spain, Atos IT Solutions and Services, Iberia, C/ Albarracin 25, Madrid Spain
juan.vera@atos.net

Tom Van Eyck
DistriNet, KU Leuven, Leuven, Belgium
tom.vaneyck@kuleuven.be

Aristeidis Farao
University of Piraeus, Piraeus, Greece

Apostolos Fournaris
Industrial Control Systems, Research Center ATHENA, Patras, Greece

Agustín Marín Frutos
University of Murcia, Department of Information and Communication Engineering, University of Murcia, 30100, Murcia, Spain
agustin.marinf@um.es

Sara Nieves Matheu Garcia
University of Murcia, Computer Science Faculty, 30100, Murcia, Spain
saranieves.matheu@um.es

Jesús García-Rodríguez
University of Murcia, Department of Information and Communication Engineering, University of Murcia, 30100 Murcia, Spain
jesus.garcia15@um.es

Juan Francisco Martínez Gil
University of Murcia, Department of Information and Communication Engineering, University of Murcia, 30100, Murcia, Spain
juanfrancisco.martinezg@um.es

Evangelos Haleplidis
Industrial Control Systems, Research Center ATHENA, Patras, Greece

Danny Hughes
DistriNet, KU Leuven, Leuven, Belgium
danny.hughes@kuleuven.be

Thodoris Ioannidis
University of Piraeus, Piraeus, Greece
th.ioannidis@ssl-unipi.gr

Wouter Joosen
DistriNet, KU Leuven, Leuven, Belgium
wouter.joosen@kuleuven.be

Sam Michiels
DistriNet, KU Leuven, Leuven, Belgium
sam.michiels@kuleuven.be

Dimitri Van Landuyt
DistriNet/LIRIS, KU Leuven, Leuven, Belgium
dimitri.vanlanduyt@kuleuven.be

Konstantinos Loupos
11 Tatoiou Street, 14561, Athens, Greece
Konstantinos.loupos@inlecomsystems.com

Rosella Omana Mancilla
ENGINEERING Ingegneria Informatica S.p.A., Piazzale dell'Agricoltura, 24 – 00144 Rome, Italy
rosellaomana.mancilla@eng.it

Evangelos K. Markakis
Electrical & Computer, Engineering Department, Hellenic Mediterranean University Estavromenos, Heraklion Crete, Greece
emarkakis@hmu.gr

Fotis Michalopoulos
Inlecom Innovation, Tatoiou 11, Kifisia, Greece
Fotis.michalopoulos@inlecomsystems.com

Dusko Milojevic
Centre for IT & IP Law (CiTiP), KU Leuven, Leuven, Belgium
dusko.milojevic@kuleuven.be

George Misiakoulis
Inlecom Innovation, Tatoiou 11, Kifisia, Greece

George.misiakoulis@inlecomsystems.com

Matteo Molé
European Cyber Security, Organisation (ECSO), Bruxelles, 1000, Belgium
matteo.mole@ecs-org.eu

Harris Niavis
Inlecom Innovation, Tatoiou 11, Kifisia, Greece
harris.niavis@inlecomsystems.com

Ekam Puri Nieto
University of Murcia, Department of Information and Communication Engineering, University of Murcia, 30100, Murcia, Spain
ekam.purin@um.es

Dimitra Papatsaroucha
Electrical & Computer Engineering Department, Hellenic Mediterranean University, Estavromenos, Heraklion Crete, Greece
dpapatsa@hmu.gr

Angel Palomares Perez

Georgios Petychakis
University of Piraeus, Piraeus, Greece

João Rodrigues
Instituto de Engenharia de Sistemas e Computadores Inovação (INOV)
joao.rodrigues@inov.pt

Stefano Sebastio
Collins Aerospace Ireland, Ltd, Cork, T23 XN53, Ireland
stefano.sebastio@collins.com

Antonio Skarmeta
University of Murcia, Department of Information and Communication Engineering, University of Murcia, 30100, Murcia, Spain
skarmeta@um.es

Hui Song
SINTEF Digital, Forskningsveien 1, 0373 Oslo, Norway
hui.song@sintef.no

Dimitrios Sygletos
Electrical & Computer Engineering Department, Hellenic Mediterranean University Estavromenos, Heraklion Crete, Greece
d.sygletos@pasiphae.eu

Shukun Tokas
SINTEF Digital, Forskningsveien 1, 0373 Oslo, Norway
shukun.tokas@sintef.no

Sokratis Vavilis
Inlecom Innovation, Tatoiou 11, Kifisia, Greece
Sokratis.vavilis@inlecomsystems.com

Stef Verreydt
DistriNet, KU Leuven, Leuven, Belgium
stef.verreydt@kuleuven.be

Laura Esbri Vidal

Christos Xenakis
University of Piraeus, Piraeus, Greece
xenakis@unipi.gr

Apostolis Zarras
University of Piraeus, Piraeus, Greece
zarras@ssl-unipi.gr

Cesar Caramazana Zarzosa
BDS R&D Spain, Atos IT Solutions and Services, Iberia, C/ Albarracin 25, Madrid Spain
cesar.caramazana@atos.net

Printed and bound by CPI Group (UK) Ltd, Croydon, CR0 4YY

15/09/2026

14962365-0004